Macmillan Foundations

A series of introductory texts across a wide range of subject areas to meet the needs of today's lecturers and students

Foundations texts provide complete yet concise coverage of core topics and skills based on detailed research of course requirements suitable for both independent study and class use – *the firm foundations for future study.*

Published

Biology
Chemistry
Economics
Physics
Politics

Forthcoming

History of English Literature
Mathematics for Science and Engineering
Modern British History
Modern European History
Nineteenth Century Britain
Psychology

Economics

CHRIS MULHEARN and
HOWARD R. VANE

MACMILLAN

First published 1999 by
MACMILLAN PRESS LTD
Houndmills, Basingstoke, Hampshire RG21 6XS
and London
Companies and representatives
throughout the world

ISBN 0–333–69183–0 paperback

A catalogue record for this book is available
from the British Library.

This book is printed on paper suitable for recycling and
made from fully managed and sustained forest sources.

10 9 8 7 6 5 4 3 2 1
08 07 06 05 04 03 02 01 00 99

Typeset by Footnote Graphics, Warminster, Wilts
Printed in Malaysia

Contents

Preface

TODAY foundation courses in economics are taught on a wide range of undergraduate degree programmes. First-year students reading for a single honours degree in economics are fortunate in that they can turn to a number of well-established and respected introductory textbooks covering the core material. Examples include: Begg, Fischer and Dornbusch (1997); Lipsey and Chrystal (1995); Parkin, Powell and Matthews (1997); and Sloman (1998). These books, however, tend to be less well received by students who are studying economics as part of broader degree programmes in areas such as Social Studies and Combined Studies. Students on such degree programmes are often intimidated by the sheer length of the specialist texts and a style or approach that relies heavily on diagrammatic presentation and frequently uses algebraic/mathematical notation.

The main aim of the present book is to meet the needs of non-specialist students taking an introductory course in economics by providing a rigorous yet concise coverage of the core material in a user-friendly and accessible fashion. The book should also prove useful to specialist students in highlighting the central issues addressed in some of the more voluminous texts currently on the market.

The book is organized as follows. At the start of each chapter a set of questions indicates the main issues to be addressed. As they are introduced, key terms and concepts are highlighted in the text and defined in the margin. Examples of actual economic problems and phenomena are presented in boxes so that the reader can verify the immediate relevance of the analysis under consideration and confirm his or her understanding of it. Frequent cross-references are also made to material covered in other chapters so that the reader can see important links between the different aspects of economics. Each chapter ends with a summary of the main issues discussed; a list of key terms; a set of self-test questions (where appropriate); questions for discussion; and, again where appropriate, suggestions for further reading and links to the Internet. Answers to the self-test questions, a glossary and a brief bibliography can be found at the end of the book.

The book is structured around two key themes. In its treatment of microeconomic material, there is an emphasis on the question of the appropriate role of the state in a modern economy. There is a tendency for specialized texts to dwell on the theoretically derived efficiency advantages of the market; this begs the question of why, in reality, there is such a weight and variety of state intervention. The book seeks to provide answers in respect of a range of microeconomic issues. The second theme interprets the macroeconomic issues as a series of problems that require elaboration as to their nature, their (competing) underlying explanations, and the range of policy options available for their resolution. The two themes are explicitly linked by their emphasis on the issue of public policy. In taking this approach we hope to demystify economics for non-specialist students and to aid their understanding of how economic analysis can be applied to 'real world' issues.

We should like to express our gratitude to a friend and colleague Steve Smith, who read and made a number of helpful and incisive comments on Chapters 1–8 and 10. We are also grateful for the helpful comments made by the anonymous reviewers used by Macmillan. However, above all, our thanks go to our families, who have been a constant source of support to us and to whom this book is dedicated.

CHRIS MULHEARN AND HOWARD VANE

Acknowledgements

Grateful acknowledgement is made to the following for permission to use copyright material:

The Boston Consulting Group for Box 7.2 from *Financial Times*, 10 February 1997.

Cambridge University Press for Table 8.3 from P. Gregg and S. Machin, 'Is the UK rise in inequality different?', in R. Barrell, *The UK Labour Market* (1994).

Financial Times Syndication Department for Box 1.5 from *Financial Times*, 16 April 1998; Box 1.6 from *Financial Times*, 5 July 1994; Box 2.2 from *Financial Times*, 19 November 1997; Box 2.4 from *Financial Times*, 15 February 1996; Box 5.1 from *Financial Times*, 21 December 1996; Box 6.2 from *Financial Times*, 16 January 1997; and Box 7.3 from *Financial Times*, 29 April 1997.

Guardian Syndication Department for Box 3.1 from *The Guardian*, 8 April 1996; Box 15.1 from *The Guardian*, 13 September 1996; and Box 17.2 from *The Guardian*, 10 September 1997.

HMSO for Box 7.1 from HM Treasury, *Employment Opportunity in a Changing Labour Market*, 27 November 1997; and Table 16.7 from UK Treasury.

The Independent Newspaper Publishing plc for Box 1.2 from *The Independent*, 14 November 1994; Box 2.1 from *The Independent*, 5 February 1997; and Box 6.1 from *The Independent*, 6 August 1996.

OECD for data for Table 1.2 from *OECD Health Data, 1960/1995* (1997); Figure 7.4 from *OECD Jobs Study* (1994); Tables 15.5 and 15.6 from *Main Developments in Trade* (1995); Table 17.2 from *OECD Economic Survey: Korea 1993/1994* (1994); Tables 9.2, 9.3, 11.1, 16.5 and 16.6 and Figure 11.9 from data in various issues of *OECD Economic Outlook*.

Office for National Statistics for Table 4.1 from *Business Monitor* PA1003; Tables 7.1, 8.5, 8.6 and 8.7 from *Economic Trends* (March 1997); Tables 8.1, 8.2 and 8.4 from *Economic Trends* (November 1987); Table 9.5 from *Economic Trends*; Table 7.2 and Figure 7.9 from *Labour Market Trends* (November 1997); and Table 16.3 from *UK Economic Accounts* (1994); all © Crown Copyright.

Oxford University Press for Box 17.1 and Table 17.3 from data in *Human Development Report 1997*, United Nations Development Programme.

Routledge for Table 6.1 from S. Martin and D. Parker, *The Impact of Privatization* (1997); and Table 17.1 from J.H. Dunning, *Explaining International Production* (1988).

The Scotsman Publications Limited for Box 6.4 from *The Scotsman*, 1 July 1997.

Tony Snape for Box 2.3 from *The European*, 30 May 1996.

Photographs and cartoons
Camera Press, p. 79; f8 Imaging, pp. 34, 44, 74, 103, 114, 271, 320, 333; Hulton Getty, pp.14, 18; PA News, pp. 168, 218; Private Eye, pp. 106, 115, 130, 141, 155, 188, 318, 321; Royal Mint, p. 224; Small Print, p. 243; Topham Picturepoint, pp. 9, 21, 81; University of Chicago News Office, p. 265.

Every effort has been made to trace all the copyright holders, but if any have been inadvertently overlooked the publishers will be pleased to make the necessary arrangement at the first opportunity.

CHAPTER 1

Economics and the Economy

Key issues

▶ What are the basic questions that every economy must face?

▶ What is resource scarcity, and what are its implications?

▶ Is the market or the government the best allocator of resources?

▶ What are microeconomics and macroeconomics, and how are they linked?

▶ What have been the central developments in the history of economic thought, and how relevant are they today?

Contents

1.1 Introduction

Most people can probably say what economics is about. It deals with issues such as inflation, unemployment, the profitability of firms, privatization, exchange rates, international trade, and so on. But lists of this kind do not really tell us what the essence of the subject is. Economics is concerned with how societies organize the production and consumption of **goods** (physical commodities such as cars, books, food, and housing) and **services** (such as those provided by banks, barbers, teachers, or railway companies). More precisely, it tries to explain and understand:

- what goods and services societies produce
- how they produce them
- for whom they are produced.

Consider the society or economy in which you live. What are its production and consumption priorities? Table 1.1 lists a range of familiar goods and services. Are they all produced in your economy? If so, how are they produced – by firms, or does the government assist or even take responsibility for the production of some of them? All of these goods and services are clearly available in the advanced 'Western' economies, but to whom are they available – everyone, or just those who are able to pay for them?

Table 1.1 categorizes our selected goods and services in terms of whether and in

Goods: Tangible products.

Services: Intangible products.

Table 1.1 Produced in the society in which you live?

Produced in some industrial countries	Produced in most industrial countries but in uneven quantities	Produced in industrial countries in declining quantities	Produced in all industrial countries in large quantities
Cars	Tourist services	Clothing	Education services
Professional football	Books, magazines	Sports goods	Health care
Wine	Contemporary music	Toys	Housing
CDs	Food		Fast food
	Beer		
	Feature films		

what relative quantities **resources** in the major economies are **allocated** to their production. (We define classes of economy more carefully in later chapters. For the purposes of this introductory example, the 'major' economies are taken to be to the long-established industrial economies such as those in western Europe and north America.) The following patterns can be discerned:

- Some goods and services are produced only in certain of the advanced countries: the car, for example. Cars are manufactured in countries such as the United States, Japan, Germany and the UK but not in (say) Ireland or Iceland. Similarly, in France and Italy there is heavy investment in professional football but none in Canada or Australia.

- For a second category of goods and services, the production question is a matter of degree. Over the last 20 or 30 years, as international travel has become easier, many industrial countries have become tourist destinations and now produce the kinds of services that foreign tourists want. However, for some countries, the commitment to tourism is particularly marked: France and Spain are obvious examples. Similarly, although many major film productions are American in origin, many other countries have their own but mostly more modest film industries.

- Clothing and footwear provide an instance of reduced production by most if not all the advanced countries. If you check your wardrobe, you will find that the labels on your clothes and shoes now mostly indicate origins in the Far East.

- Finally, there is a fourth category of good or service that virtually all industrialized countries continue to produce in large quantities: education and health services, for example.

We shall have more to say in this and other chapters (see Chapter 15, especially) about why patterns of country specialization in production arise, but for the moment let us proceed to the noted questions of how and for whom production takes place.

    The form taken by production – the 'how' question – can actually be discussed at two levels. We might be interested in the particular technicalities of production in different economies: does the organization of (say) car manufacture vary greatly between countries? Alternatively, as noted, we might ask to what extent governments involve themselves in production decisions. In recent years, in countries such as the UK and New Zealand, concerted attempts have been made to reduce the

Resource allocation: The commitment of a society's productive endowments, such as labour and machinery, to particular uses or patterns of use. Thus for a society to produce a particular good or service it must allocate resources to the appropriate industry.

influence of government over economic activity: through the privatization of state-owned firms, for example. Elsewhere experience has been divided: in the USA, to take the most obvious case, the economic impact of government has always been comparatively limited, whereas in the Scandinavian countries, for example, it is traditionally more pervasive.

The 'for whom' question is often closely linked to the latter form of the 'how' question. Where governments involve themselves in production decisions, they may, amongst other things, choose to provide quantities of goods and services to citizens that otherwise might not have been available, and to provide them without charge or at a subsidized rate. For example, in the Netherlands, the government sponsors a major 'social housing' programme. This means that a large proportion of the housing stock in the Netherlands is publicly owned; houses are built by the government according to the perceived general need, and rents are relatively cheap. As a result, few Dutch citizens are unable to find somewhere to live or find rents unaffordable. Here then, 'for whom' means for most people, if not everyone. In the UK, to take a contrasting case, although there is investment in public housing, much more of the housing stock is privately owned, and in the presence of private owner-ship the 'for whom' question turns not on need but on the ability to pay.

1.2 The market versus the state as an allocator of resources

We can see then that the key questions of what, how and for whom can be answered in very different ways. Using the example of health care in France and the USA, let us now explore the implications of alternative approaches to these questions in more detail.

France and the USA both produce and consume highly sophisticated health care services. In France the government or state assumes responsibility for most health care provision: it finances health care from money it obtains in taxes. At the same time, the French state makes health services freely available to *all* its citizens, irre-spective of their individual ability to pay for them. In fact, French citizens have already **collectively** paid – through taxation – for the health care services they receive. So, in France, the what, how and for whom questions are answered, for health care, **socially**. Society as a whole allocates the resources it needs to provide health care for everyone. In summary:

- **What is produced?** Health services deemed to be appropriate by the state and the medical profession.

- **How is production organized?** By the state and the medical profession using the proceeds of taxation.

- **For whom is production organized?** Health care services are freely available to all its citizens, irrespective of their ability to pay for them.

In the USA, health care provision is much more **market** based, and the role of the state is not nearly so well developed. This means that, although equally sophisticated health care is available in the USA, our three questions are answered rather differently there. As we shall see in Chapter 2, using the market to provide a good or service involves a greater reliance on *individual* economic agents: instead of

Collective or **social provision:** System in which the state taxes citizens and uses the money to make available goods or services it thinks they should have.

Market: A framework that brings buyers and sellers together.

◆ **Concept**

Consumer sovereignty

Consumer sovereignty implies that the consumption choices of individuals in competitive markets condition production patterns. Producers must follow the lead given by the purchasing decisions of consumers. If they produce goods and services that consumers do not want they will bankrupt themselves. Hence consumers exercise sovereignty over producers. The production of 'environmentally friendly' goods and services is an example of this kind of consumer power. The tuna fish producer who admitted to canning the occasional dolphin would not remain in business very long.

acting together collectively, people make their own economic choices and decisions. In the USA, the providers of health care – hospitals, doctors, clinics – are not financed by the state; their incomes are derived directly from the consumers of the services they offer. Similarly, those in need of health care are required to pay for it themselves directly – usually with the assistance of private medical insurance – instead of indirectly through taxation. An extensive market in private health insurance has developed in the USA because the cost of health care can sometimes be extremely high. For those who cannot afford private health care or health insurance, the state offers a basic publicly funded alternative, though, because it is not well resourced, this is generally recognized to be a vastly inferior system. In the USA then, the key economic questions of mainstream health care are essentially answered as follows:

- **What is produced?**   Health services that satisfy the demands of those who pay for them.
- **How is production organized?**   By the medical profession in response to perceived demand.
- **For whom is production organized?**   Health care services are available on the basis of ability to pay.

Given that there are at least these two ways of providing health care, how are we to decide which is best? For economists, this is a largely a **normative** question – in other words a matter of opinion and one they do not, as economists, claim to be able to answer. However, economists are able to provide answers to **positive** questions of fact upon which normative issues can be resolved. The predominantly market-based US health care system does, for example, have some innate advantages over the socialized French system, which economists recognize.

One of the most important of these concerns the notion of **consumer sovereignty**. This suggests that individual consumers have ultimate control over what markets produce. As each individual chooses to buy a good or service, he or she is affirming the existence and provision of the good or service. If consumers generally choose not to buy something that was formerly in demand then producers will withdraw it from the market. There is no point in trying to sell goods or services that people no longer want. Similarly, if consumers become avid purchasers of a good or service then producers will have an incentive to increase the amount they produce. The empowerment of individual consumers in this way is held to be a valuable pro-perty of the *free* market: that is, a market in which there is little or no state influence or intervention. The market basis of US health care thus elevates the influence of US health care purchasers over the kind of system that evolves. If US citizens choose to spend more or less money on cosmetic surgery, the services of psychiatrists or alternative medicines then, accordingly, more or fewer of these things will be produced. This is the free choice of individuals and the essence of consumer sovereignty.

In the socialized French system consumer preferences are less easily expressed. The French medical profession is rewarded not by its patients directly but by the state, and therefore it is the state that ultimately decides which kinds of service will be made available. Here there is not consumer but *producer* sovereignty. This is perceived by many economists to be inferior to consumer sovereignty. Why? In part, the answer is that these economists think that the best judges of people's needs are

Positive issues: Those that are factually based.

Normative issues: Those that are a matter of opinion.

individuals themselves. The free market then is simply a framework that allows people to exercise their own judgement about which goods and services they consume. If producer sovereignty intrudes into a market process, the free choices of individuals will be subverted by other priorities.

The market is also thought to be a superior method of motivating producers. If a doctor practising privately provides a consistently good service to patients, then he or she is likely to continue to be consulted by them and to be paid accordingly. Doctors providing a more indifferent service will lose both patients and the income derived from them. Thus in a private system it is better to be a good doctor than a bad one. However, in a socialized system patients have much less freedom to choose their doctor, and the medical profession as a whole is paid by the state. This breaks the crucial link between the performance of the doctor in the eyes of the patient and the reward that he or she receives. Hence in the absence of consumer sovereignty there is no simple means of discriminating between the pay of good and bad doctors, and there is less direct financial motivation to be a good doctor. Of course, the central point here is that the more good doctors there are, the better the quality of the medical services provided.

However, consumer sovereignty and producer motivation are not the only positive issues at stake here. Consider for example the implications for equity or fairness of the US system. We know that access to the best US health care is determined by the individual's ability to pay. Those who cannot afford private health care or health insurance are left with a relatively poorly resourced and inferior state system. Is this an acceptable situation? Is it fair? In France ability to pay is not a consideration, and everyone can obtain equal access to high-quality health care on the basis of need. This leads some economists to suggest that the largely public French system offers equity advantages over a market-based system.

The collective provision of health care can also be defended on the grounds that it produces *better health outcomes* for the society that it serves than any private system. In France health care is tailored to meet the anticipated health needs of French society as a whole. In the USA, the health system is skewed towards 'intensive' treatment for the paying proportion of American society. As Table 1.2 indicates, although the USA spends much more on health care per head of population than France does, it has proportionately fewer doctors and far fewer in-patient beds than France. The table also shows that infant mortality is higher in the USA, and life expectancy for both women and men is lower. To crystallize the difference

Table 1.2 Health in France and the USA compared

	Health expenditure per capita in $		Doctors per 10 000 of population		In-patient beds per 10 000 of population		Infant mortality % of live births		Life expectancy (years) at birth			
									Women		Men	
Year	1995	1985	1995	1985	1995	1985	1995	1985	1995	1985	1995	1985
France	1956	1088	29.4	22.9	8.9	10.5	0.58[a]	0.83	81.9	79.4	73.9	71.3
USA	3701	1733	26.3[a]	22.4	4.1	5.3	0.80[a]	1.06	79.2	78.2	72.5	71.1

Notes:
a. 1994
Source: OECD Health Data 1960/1995. © OECD 1997. Reproduced by permission of the OECD

Table 1.3 Relative advantages and disadvantages of different health care systems

Possible advantages of each system

Private	Public
• Consumers are sovereign	• Distribution of health care is equitable and based on need
• Producers are well motivated, thus raising service quality	• Health outcomes for society are relatively high

Possible disadvantages of each system

Private	Public
• The system is inequitable	• Motivation in the system may be low, and service quality may suffer as a result
• The system may produce relatively poor health outcomes for society as a whole	• The freedom of consumers may be constrained

between the two systems, one might argue that in France health service production is measured in terms of effective care for the population as a whole, whereas in the USA it is measured in terms of the incomes and profits earned on care directed towards the more affluent.

It is the role of economics to highlight positive advantages and disadvantages such as these (see Table 1.3 for a summary) in order to inform normative debate about which kind of health care system might be preferred. The ultimate choice, however, will be the outcome of a political process, not of economic analysis. Economics provides a review of the salient facts; it is for other disciplines, notably political science, to sift and judge between them.

1.3 Scarcity, choice and opportunity cost

So economics concerns itself with the production choices a society has to make: what goods and services . . . produced how . . . for whom? But we also need to know why these choices are so pressing. It is painfully obvious that many societies continue to struggle with the large-scale human tragedies of poverty, disease and malnutrition. The starkness of choice here needs little emphasis: people have basic needs for food, warmth and shelter, and will allocate what resources they have into producing these things first. But in affluent parts of the world the general levels of production and consumption are higher now than they have ever been. Food, warmth and shelter are largely taken for granted, as indeed is the availability of an at times seemingly boundless array of other goods and services. Is there really a problem here for economics to solve? We might of course point out that poverty and want are still present in many sections of the advanced societies, but even if they weren't economics would still be given purpose by the notion of **resource scarcity**.

In everyday usage scarcity is interpreted simply as a lack of ready availability. Diamonds might be considered scarce and therefore highly prized, but beer for example is not; you can get it relatively cheaply in quantities that you might the next morning live to regret. For economists, however, scarcity has a different emphasis: it

Concept

Resource scarcity

Resource scarcity implies that *all* a society's resources are scarce in relation to the limitless wants present in every society.

is always placed in the context of the potentially *infinite* demands upon a society's scarce resources. It is true that the advanced societies currently enjoy previously unparalleled standards of living, but that does not mean that there are no unmet needs or wants in these societies. As we have just seen, in a country as rich as the USA some people still lack comprehensive medical care, not everyone who wants one has a car, and many people would like to live in houses better than those they currently occupy. These are more than glib points: they suggest that a society's wants are in fact *limitless*. All resources must be considered scarce because of the vast range of competing uses to which they could be put.

In this context, while it would be possible to reform, say, the US health care system in order to facilitate high-quality service provision for all citizens, this could not be done without cost. Indeed, health care reform was high on the agenda of the first administration of President Clinton (1992–96). However, as Mr Clinton found, the changes necessary to produce a more comprehensive system demanded the allocation of many more resources to health care. Where would the money come from? This is the essence of the 'resource balancing act' that economics tries to understand and inform. The US government could have funded additional health spending in two broad ways: via higher taxes upon its citizens, or by taking money from other areas of government expenditure such as defence. In the end neither of these options proved politically acceptable, but using the tools of economic analysis it is possible to understand the positive implications of both of them as well as the implications of leaving things as they are.

Because, in an economic sense, resources are scarce, every society is faced with a potentially huge spectrum of choice. Committing resources to one set of production and consumption patterns necessarily means that others must be forgone. In economics the essence of resource choice is captured in the notion of **opportunity cost**. The opportunity cost of a particular resource commitment is the value of the best alternative use that must consequently be given up. But opportunity cost is more than a fancy way of saying societies can't do everything; it allows us to understand why economies make the particular production choices that they do.

Consider, for example, the issue of environmental pollution. In the advanced industrial countries of western Europe there is a relatively high standard of environmental protection, which is administered both by individual nation states and by the European Union. In contrast, protection standards in parts of Africa and South America are undoubtedly lower. Why? Is it simply a question of the degree of interest in and commitment to the environment, or are there other forces at work here?

An economic analysis would suggest the latter. A society's view of the balance between the imperative of industrial production and what is tolerable in terms of consequent environmental despoilation must be tempered by the level of economic development of the society in question. In, say, the relatively affluent German economy it might be possible to raise industrial output by relaxing the controls over the ways in which firms dispose of liquid waste. Instead of investing in expensive plant that treated such material, it could be pumped straight into rivers such as the Rhine and the Danube. Here the balance between what would be gained and lost by such action becomes critical. How highly are clean rivers valued as against a bit more output in an already rich society? The likely answer is that the opportunity cost of the increase in output is too great: clean rivers are more highly valued, and therefore there is an economic rationale for pollution control, and a particular production choice can be understood. Now, in much poorer countries the value attached to

Opportunity cost: The cost of an action measured in terms of the best forgone alternative action.

extra industrial output will undoubtedly be higher, and therefore the cost of some forms of environmental protection may be considered prohibitive in terms of the value of the output that must be sacrificed. If the extra output pays for necessary food or shelter, the priority it will be accorded is apparent. Here then the opportunity cost of environmental protection may be prohibitive, and the decision to pollute becomes an economically defensible one.

Although this example contrasts rich and poor countries as we approach the year 2000, exactly the same analysis could be used to compare the production priorities set by contemporary rich countries and those same countries in the nineteenth century. *Then*, industrial interests triumphed over the environment in the West too. This was because, then, the opportunity cost of lost output was higher than the value that society put on the environment.

The concept of opportunity cost also allows us to understand why some countries continue to specialize in the production of particular goods and services. Switzerland, for example, has a reputation for high quality clock- and watchmaking. Why? There are no climatic or natural resource attributes that make Switzerland an obvious place in which to manufacture clocks and watches. However, having – over time – developed skills in the production of these items, it is evidently an efficient use of resources to fully exploit such skills. This is because in economic terms the opportunity cost associated with reallocating some resources away from the production of watches and clocks into, say, the manufacture of cars – where the Swiss have no particular pedigree – would be too great. Certainly, the Swiss could make cars, but they would have to switch a disproportionate volume of resources away from something they are much better at in order to do so – thus sacrificing the output of many (too many: this is the critically high opportunity cost) watches and clocks. The case is made all the more compelling by the possibility of international trade. The Swiss can specialize in the production of watches and clocks and sell these on international markets in order to obtain the foreign currencies needed to buy cars and other goods and services produced more efficiently by other nations. The application of the concept of opportunity cost to international trade is discussed more fully in Chapter 15.

So economics is about understanding production choices in the context of resource scarcity and with an awareness of opportunity cost. Societies have limitless wants: which are to be satisfied and which neglected? Economics offers a range of arguments about these possible choices, which reflect the factual or positive implications of doing this or that, in this or that way. Now, if we return to our earlier health care example and, indeed, some of the others we used, it is apparent that one issue comes consistently to the fore: *whether the state should be involved in resolving the key economic questions that a society faces – what, how, for whom? – or whether the free market is the preferred mechanism for deciding these things.* Indeed, it might be argued that this is *the* issue for economics. Almost all societies aspire to have modern industries, comprehensive health care programmes, flourishing systems of education, good housing, efficient means of communication and transport, and so on; it then becomes a question of whether the state or the market, or indeed some combination of both, is the best means of providing them.

Given our earlier discussion of economics as a factually based discipline that can provide positive analyses of the spectrum of production choice, it appears that there really should not be a problem here. Let us take an aspiration that a society has set politically – say, an equitable health care system that provides a high standard of service for all citizens, the budget for which can grow at a 'modest' annual rate (the example does not require any greater degree of precision). Given such criteria, we might expect economic analysis to resolve that a state-run health care system is what is required. The equity criterion would certainly be met, as – probably – would the desire for good health outcomes. However, what of the issue of cost control? Some economists would point out that it is hard to control the costs of a system when its output – health care in this case – is effectively free at the point of use: that is, consumers can have as much as they want without having to pay for it directly. This is not to suggest that people will deliberately abuse a collective system – frivolously consuming medical services – but it does admit that, for instance, the decision to visit a doctor may be taken less carefully than if one was required to pay a consulting fee.

There is an additional point here. At one time it was thought that the costs of universal health care provision would fall over time as the general health of the population improved. However, as medical knowledge and technologies have advanced, the range of available treatments has increased, leading to an increase in the cost as well as the sophistication of modern health care. Positive claims such as these lead some economists to suggest that the cost control criterion cannot in the end be met by a collective system, and therefore that market influences need to be introduced. The presence of market influences would moderate the demand for health care as people are forced to pay for it directly. At the same time, however, other economists legitimately point out that the intrusion of market priorities, particularly ability to pay, undermines the principles of equity, and the quality of health care for some citizens is thereby diminished.

This example clearly raises the issue of *disagreement amongst economists*. A normative aspiration – good, equitably distributed health care with a reasonable measure of cost control – can engender different positive responses over the relative advantages of the state and the free market as mechanisms for the allocation of scarce resources. Note that disagreement does indeed rest on positive or factual claims: the theoretical and empirical work of some economists set against the work of others.

Now, not only is the question of the state versus the free market one of the central issues in *contemporary* economics, it is also the most prevalent theme in the *history* of economics. Let us illustrate the tenor of this debate historically. In what follows, we highlight a number of key milestones in the development of economic thought, and illustrate, with issue-based examples, their relevance to modern economics. After reading this section, you will be aware both of what economics is actually composed of *and* of how, as a discipline, it has been built up over time.

1.4 The historical development of economic thought and its contemporary relevance

Adam Smith

Adam Smith (1723–90) is widely recognized to be the founder of modern economics. He is also popularly held to be an advocate of free markets. Although this claim can be largely substantiated, Smith also recognized that, in certain areas, there was some legitimacy in particular forms of state intervention. Smith's most

Adam Smith, 1723–90

Box 1.1

Divisions of labour

How do individuals in modern societies provide for themselves? The usual answer is that they work: they perform some particular task in exchange for a wage. This in turn can be spent on housing, food, heat and light, entertainment and so on, which others produce. What people usually do *not* do is build their own house, grow their own food, generate their own electricity and dig a well for water. In other words, they are not *self-sufficient*.

The interdependence that people have in modern societies is in fact no more than an extended *division of labour*: the sharing out of work in all its different forms. Why do we do this? Why is interdependence in work preferable to independence? The answer in part is that a division of labour allows individuals to become greatly adept at their particular chosen tasks: in other words, such specialization raises the quality and quantity of work that people do. A teacher, for example, is good at his or her job because he or she has been

trained in this particular occupation and because of experience gained in it. So teachers, like those who undergo other kinds of training and acquire different skills, are *specialists*. There is a clear advantage in organizing work in this way: an individual who performs one task well, rather than many indifferently, is maximizing his or her *productivity* (the amount that one produces with given resources and in a given time). Now, as for individuals, so for society as a whole. Generally, the further the division of labour can be extended, the more productive a society becomes as an increasing number of economic agents refine their specialisms.

Importantly, specialization also permits the *mechanization* of tasks. As work is simplified, or its boundaries are more clearly defined, it becomes easier to replicate or complement with machines. Most of the enormous leaps in productivity that have occurred in the last two centuries have come about as a result of the introduction of various

forms of new technology to the workplace.

Finally, it is possible to conceive of *regional* and *international divisions of labour*. If we apply the same notion of specialization to localities or countries, it becomes possible to understand the economic basis of the apparent attachments of particular places to given kinds of work. Thus, for example, the aptly named champagne region of France is renowned as the centre for champagne production, while the Netherlands has an international reputation as a flower producer. In places like these, it would be foolish to underexploit painstakingly acquired skills in the vague pursuit of some greater degree of self-sufficiency. Far better to perform tasks at which you excel and use the fruits of these labours to pay for other goods and services that can be produced with a much greater degree of expertise elsewhere.

---

important book, *An Inquiry into the Nature and Causes of the Wealth of Nations*, was published in 1776. In this work, Smith identified a number of concepts that are still central to economic thought today. Of these, one of the most basic was the idea that free markets, when they function well, can simultaneously serve both the needs of the individual and wider social ends. Smith supposed that when individuals engage in transactions with one another – buying and selling goods and services – they do so because they perceive some personal advantage in the process. On the assumption that individualistic transactions do not adversely affect others who are not party to them, it follows that the greater the number of transactions, the greater the benefit to those that undertake them and hence to society as a whole (composed as it is of the same individuals). This is Smith's simple but compelling logic for the free market or **laissez-faire** as the framework that would allow such an enriching process to flourish.

Taking the argument a stage further, Smith suggested that individualistic market relationships had the added advantage of promoting a **division of labour** that both enhances the productive capacity of society and leads its members to adopt mutually supportive forms of economic behaviour. The concept of a division of labour can

Laissez-faire: Describes a situation in which there is little or no state interference in the market economy. Here all decisions are taken by individual producers (firms) and consumers.

work at several levels (see Box 1.1), but in each case the essential message is the same: develop some level of expertise in a particular trade, service or form of production and specialize in it. To the extent that others do the same, patterns of specialization begin to emerge. For individuals (as Box 1.1 demonstrates, the same analysis can be applied to regions and nations), this means that the relatively high level of output that their particular skill or trade enables them to produce can be sold in order to allow them to purchase some of the equally relatively high outputs that result from the specialisms of others. *The central point here is that the market actually fuses self-interest and wider social benefit.* As the individual becomes more productive, he or she is able to sell the output produced more cheaply. Those who do not match the highest levels of productivity and output quality will find their markets taken by their competitors. Self-interest clearly demands the closest attention to market conditions and, in particular, the interests of others as consumers (the reader will recognize the notion of consumer sovereignty here). In a free market, then, the better the individual serves the needs of others the better off he or she becomes. Smith summarized his argument in the following famous passage:

It is not from the benevolence of the butcher, the brewer, or the baker that we expect our dinner, but from their regard to their own interest.

At the same time, precisely because an individual specializes in the production of a particular good or service, he or she simultaneously frees others to develop their own niche in the division of labour. In this sense, the free market becomes a framework for the development of mutually supportive, even cooperative, economic relationships.

In a striking piece of conceptual imagery, Smith distilled the resource allocation properties of the free market into the notion of an **invisible hand**, which coordinates and oversees the complex of production and consumption decisions that take place daily in an economy. Imagine if you, the reader, had to organize the production side of, say, the food market for the economy in which you live for just one day some time in the near future. You have a huge workforce at your disposal, adequate volumes of basic foodstuffs, the factories to process these, the means to transport the finished products, and a retail network to sell them through. Is the task possible? Certainly it would pose enormous logistical problems: you would need something close to a meticulously detailed mega-plan to make certain that no one missed their dinner. A bureaucratic nightmare then. Yet in most societies this is done every single day, without fail, by the market, and it does not require any grand plan or expensive bureaucracy, just the enlightened self-interest of individual producers and consumers. Moreover, it is done not just for food but for many other goods and services too. This is where Smith's imagery helps us to grasp what is going on. It is as if there is some great agency or mechanism of coordination in place to ensure that the millions of consumption choices that occur daily in an economy are matched by millions of corresponding production decisions; but there isn't, beyond the invisible hand of a market animated by the self-interest of the individuals of which it is composed.

If, in this view, the free market is such a powerfully effective means of resolving the production and consumption choices that a society has to make – again, the 'what', 'how' and 'for whom' questions – is there *any* role here for the state? Smith thought that there was. In the first place, he recognized that an individualist system that rested upon the incentive of personal gain must have a system of justice that protected both economic liberty and property rights: people must be free to pursue their own economic ends and be able to enjoy the fruits thereof. This is a rationale for the state to act as a guarantor of law and order and to provide a system of national defence.

The general sentiment that Smith appears to be expressing here is that the competence of the state should be admitted where a precise task for it can be defined that

Concept

Invisible hand

The invisible hand is the metaphor that Adam Smith used to describe the sophisticated allocative powers of the free market. The market ensures that complex patterns of demand and supply for many goods and services are constantly kept in alignment. This happens not through the agency of some external bureaucracy but simply through the self-interested efforts of producers working to meet the expressed wants of consumers.

cannot be performed by the market. It would be difficult to imagine how a market-based system of law and order could work in an advanced society: a framework of justice must necessarily operate at the collective level. Using the same kind of reasoning, Smith identified another form of state activity, this time in the economy proper, which was legitimized by market incompetence. Free markets require the presence of individuals: individual producers or firms and individual consumers. However, what if the nature of a good or service renders it unsuitable for individualist production or consumption? In such cases Smith supposed that was a rationale for state provision. He specifically identified certain forms of physical infrastructure – roads, bridges, canals and harbours, for example – that would be too expensive for individuals or even groups of individuals to construct, but from which society as a whole would clearly benefit. In Smith's view then, because the market could not make such necessary things available, the state should. Modern economics labels these **public goods** (for a more detailed discussion see Chapter 6, Section 6.3). Note, however, that some forms of infrastructure in modern societies *are* now subject to market influences. For example, in south-west England a private firm has recently built and now operates a private motorway bridge over the River Severn. Given that he thought that if the market could do something well then it should, would Adam Smith have approved of such a development?

This really is a significant question in our attempt to gain an understanding of the central thrust of Smith's work. In our view, Smith would have had serious doubts about the privately run Severn Bridge crossing. Why? The private owner sells right of passage across the bridge to individual motorists prepared to pay a given toll. There is no coercion here, and motorists are free to use another (longer) route across the river if they do not wish to incur the toll. However, although this appears to be a simple and therefore intrinsically attractive market arrangement, Smith would have pointed to an additional complication. Because it conveys **monopoly power** to its operators, the privately run bridge actually distorts the way the market operates. Monopoly power exists where the access to a market by rival producers is restricted. In the absence of meaningful competition, the owners of the Severn Bridge can set higher tolls than would be possible if there were other crossings nearby. In turn, the higher tolls discourage the use of the bridge by some motorists. The end result is that fewer crossings are made than would be the case in a more competitive environment. Here then, the free market appears to work in the interests of the monopolist and to the detriment of the interests of consumers, some of whom pay higher tolls while others absent themselves from the market altogether. The presence of monopoly power therefore raises doubts as to the ability of the free market to allocate resources effectively: the regrettable outcome in this case being too few bridge crossings consequent upon an uncompetitive toll. Issues of monopoly and monopoly power are discussed in more detail in Chapters 5 and 6. Again then, the acid test for Smith is not simply can the market be used to deliver a good or service but does the market work well in doing so? In the Severn Bridge case, the answer appears to be no, and there is scope for the state to intervene – either providing the crossing itself, or regulating the tolls that the private operator sets.

In concluding this section, it is worth reflecting upon why Smith appears so attached to the properly functioning free market. Like all innovative economists, Smith did not work in a vacuum; he sought answers to the real practical problems of the time in which he lived. As noted, the *Wealth of Nations* (the shortened title) was published in 1776: in other words at the start of the industrial revolution in Britain –

Monopoly power: Arises where potential competitors can be excluded from a market. Most obviously this occurs where there is a sole supplier with such power.

generally held to date from 1750. This is more than a coincidence. Smith was actually a champion of the new **entrepreneurial** industrial capitalism, and he was concerned to promote conditions that would see it flourish. Unfortunately, among the legacies of the pre-capitalist era were a complex of anti- (competitive) market institutional and social norms, of which monopoly power was one of the most important. Because it protected particular interests from the competitive process and restricted the freedom of entrepreneurs to innovate and take risks in markets, monopoly power was, in Smith's view, a drag on wider economic progress. One of the purposes of the *Wealth of Nations* was then to provide a set of arguments against the vested interests of the old economic and social order so that a new period of prosperity based on *laissez-faire* might be ushered in.

Entrepreneur: The risk-taking individual producer who perceives a demand in the market and organizes resources to meet that demand in the anticipation of profit. The entrepreneur was thought to be a pivotal figure in the free market.

Smith's relevance today

What then of the contemporary relevance of Smith's work: are his ideas still a useful guide to the conduct of economic affairs? If they are, we should expect to see modern arguments that are critical of state interference in markets, and which recommend the promotion of open and competitive market processes. The general policy framework of the Conservative governments in the UK during the 1980s and 1990s provides an example of this kind of approach. Box 1.2 describes the policy of compulsory competitive tendering (CCT) and its intended effects upon computing services in local government in England and Wales. Local authorities traditionally run their own computing operations but the Conservatives thought that the private sector could do the job more cheaply. Accordingly, they introduced legislation that requires local authorities to put a range of activities – including computer services – out to tender. If private firms can demonstrate that they can provide more cost-effective services then they must be contracted to do the work instead of the local authority itself. The critical point here is the expectation that competition will reduce costs. Private firms (and local authority computer services departments) must compete against one another to offer a cheaper and better service. The existing

---

Box 1.2

Adam Smith and compulsory competitive tendering

By Stephen Pritchard

Computing staff in local government could be forgiven for feeling undervalued ... for the past two years they have been living with the prospect of competing with the private sector for their own jobs.

The first batch of authorities, the London boroughs and the metropolitan districts, are expected to come under the compulsory competitive tendering (CCT) regime for information technology next year, with contracts to be in place by October 1996. By 1999 all but the smallest councils will be required to advertise their IT functions. Existing staff will be allowed to tender for the work, but there is no guarantee of success.

Critics argue that exposure to competition is long overdue. The Audit Commission, which monitors spending by councils in England and Wales, reported in May that £50 million a year could be saved on authorities' central computing services, which include tasks such as revenue collection and payrolls. In the longer term this could rise to £130 million out of a total of £290 million if all councils performed at the level of the most efficient the commission surveyed. In some cases, auditors found councils paying twice as much as their neighbours for comparable services.

Source: The Independent 14 November 1994

system, in the Smithian view, is uncompetitive. It permits many functions of local government to be conducted under what are effectively monopoly conditions: certainly, computing and other services are provided but there is no effective economic sanction on the provider should the services be poor or too costly. The argument is that only competition can guarantee such an effective sanction; in the presence of competition, a poor or expensive service provider can be replaced whereas, before CCT, the sole in-house local authority provider could not.

Classical economics

David Ricardo, 1772–1823

The Smithian notion that the free market is a powerful and effective mechanism for the allocation of scarce resources was subsequently taken up in the nineteenth century by the classical school of economists. The work of those in the classical school such as David Ricardo (1772–1823) and Jean Baptiste Say (1767–1832) served to consolidate and extend the foundations laid down by Smith to the extent that a *classical view* of the general operation of the capitalist economy became discernible. As we explain in more detail in Box 1.3, modern economics is conventionally divided into two complementary parts: **microeconomics** and **macroeconomics** (or micro and macro for short):

- Microeconomics deals with issues at the level of the *individual*: the individual consumer, producer, market or industry, worker and so on.

- Macroeconomics, on the other hand, considers the workings of the economy as a *whole*: inflation, the overall levels of employment and unemployment, the rate at which the economy grows, and how it fits into the international economic environment, are all macro concerns.

In terms of our discussion of the development of economic thought so far, an emphasis on micro issues has been evident: Adam Smith's work was primarily an analysis of individualism. Although the classical school fully absorbed and began to develop this emphasis, the micro foundations of classicism – and indeed the micro themes of the *Wealth of Nations* itself – had a number of important *macroeconomic implications* (even though macroeconomics did not emerge as a coherent entity in

---

Box 1.3

Microeconomics and macroeconomics

Microeconomics focuses upon disaggregate and individualistic economic issues. Macroeconomics, on the other hand looks at the behaviour of the economy as a whole.

The concerns of microeconomics include individual consumer and producer behaviour. It looks, for example, at factors that influence people's purchasing and firms' production decisions. Microeconomics also considers the behaviour of economic agents in particular markets, such as the labour market. Wage determination is therefore an example of a micro issue. Which factors influence the level of a worker's wage? Why do wages between different occupations vary? Would a government-set minimum wage affect the numbers of people employed in particular industries? These are all questions that micro-analyses are able to address.

Macroeconomics studies the behaviour and performance of the economy as a whole. It is chiefly concerned with the four major aggregates: economic growth, unemployment, inflation, and the balance of payments. Macroeconomics seeks both to understand the factors that determine these aggregates and to inform the government policies that are used to try to influence them.

itself until the 1930s). The most striking of these proceeded from Smith's notions of the division of labour and the invisible hand. Taken together, it is evident that these concepts provided the beginnings of a theoretical basis for believing that the allocation of resources across the free markets of which much of the early capitalist economy was composed was highly efficient. The division of labour facilitated a relatively high degree of specialization in work that, together with the introduction of machinery, produced consequent improvements in output levels and output quality. Complementing this, the invisible hand offered a supremely effective means of signalling the forms and quantities of output that consumers demanded. *Now, because resources were allocated effectively at the micro level, at least some macro-economic questions could start to be answered.* There would, for example, be both a basis for growth in the economy as a whole, as more goods and services were produced, and related improvements in economy-wide employment, as more workers were required to participate in the burgeoning production process. Of course, the further the division of labour was extended and the greater its technological sophistication, the better prospects on both these counts would become.

The work of Ricardo and Say served in part to elaborate upon some of the macroeconomic implications just outlined. Let us briefly consider each of these important members of the classical school in turn. Amongst other important contributions to economic thought, Ricardo advanced a pivotal analysis of the labour market, which suggested that *laissez-faire* conditions would tend to promote a **'natural' wage** rate for labour and – as a consequence – full employment. If wages increased beyond this level the inference was that fewer workers would be employed. Consequently, Ricardo specifically counselled against state interference in the setting of wage levels. We consider this argument and its contemporary relevance in more detail in Chapter 7.

Say's great contribution was the concept that subsequently became known as **Say's law**. This states that *supply creates its own demand*. In essence Say's law means that the production of goods and services must necessarily generate incomes (in the form of wages and profits, for example, earned, respectively, by labour and firms) that are equivalent to the value of, and will be spent purchasing, the same goods and services. The central implication of Say's law is that there can never be *general* overproduction in an economy in the sense that too many goods and services are produced in relation to the level of demand for them. This means that it is possible to sustain any output level that an economy is able to achieve; economy-wide there is no danger that goods and services will remain unsold with the consequent possibility that producers would be forced to cut output and reduce the numbers of people they employ.

Now, putting Ricardo's work on the labour market together with Say's law produces a powerful argument about the state of the *macro* economy under *laissez-faire micro* conditions. The 'natural' tendency of the labour market is to generate full employment, so all workers in a free economy are occupied in the production of goods and services. The question now arises: what happens to this considerable volume of output? The simple answer is that it is all sold – the operation of Say's law guarantees that there is sufficient income and demand in the economy to let this happen. In summary, we have a fully employed workforce producing an output for which there is a self-generating demand. Thus upon the micro foundations of *laissez-faire* is founded the highly desirable macro or economy-wide outcome of a sustained high output of goods and services *and* full employment.

Concept

'Natural' wage

Ricardo's theory of the 'natural' wage supposed that under competitive labour market conditions all workers would find jobs. There would in other words be full employment. If the state or workers themselves (via trade union activity) increased wages beyond their natural level then some workers would become unemployed.

Say's law: States that supply creates its own demand. It rests on the assumption that the incomes earned from the supply of goods in an economy will be spent purchasing this supply of goods.

As Box 1.3 makes clear, there are two other major macroeconomic concerns beyond the levels of output and employment in the economy: inflation, and the balance of payments. What interpretation did the classical school put on these issues? Without straying too far into territory to be covered in more detail in later chapters, we note at this point that the general position was for classical economics to reassert the central message gleaned from Adam Smith. This, of course, was that *free markets* are most often capable of meeting desired economic ends. In the context of inflation, the implication was that any (preferably minimal) state activity in the economy had to be funded in a financially prudent manner. This reflected a belief that inflation was caused by an expansion of the amount of money in an economy in relation to a relatively fixed volume of goods and services. Very simply, more money would be 'chasing' a given output, leading to increases in the general price level. Because the most likely source of monetary expansion was the state, the classical view was that its activities should be self-financing. Thus any expenditures made by the state had to be both modest and fully covered by taxation or borrowing; in other words, the state budget had to balance so as not to fuel inflation.

In the view of Ricardo, in particular, a country's trading relations with the rest of the world would also be best served by minimizing state interference. *Free trade* between nations would permit the extension of Smith's division of labour – with all its productive advantages – across international boundaries. Therefore for the state to restrict or distort this process for balance of payments or other reasons would be the greatest folly. Why should the gains that Smith identified from free national markets be refused from free international markets? This issue is more fully discussed in Chapter 15.

In summary then, the classical view of the economic system had a primarily *microeconomic* focus. This supposed that the best way of answering the basic economic questions – what is produced, how is it produced, and for whom? – usually involved the use of free markets because, wherever these worked well, they offered a superior method of resource allocation compared with any alternative. Moreover, the micro foundations of classical analysis had uniformly positive *macroeconomic* implications. Although the evolution of modern macroeconomics only began in the 1930s, the classical school consistently indicated the positive economy-wide benefits of their market-based prescriptions: *laissez-faire* could deliver an unrivalled combination of micro and macro benefits.

Ricardo's relevance today

As noted, Ricardo was an advocate of open competition in international as well as domestic markets. Indeed, he is best remembered today as a champion of free international trade. In 1995 a new international agency for the promotion of free trade – The World Trade Organization (WTO) – was created. Box 1.4, taken from the WTO's Internet site, explains why both it and the majority of the world's nations that are its members are in favour of free or open trade. Think about the concept of comparative advantage, which the box introduces. This is explained fully in Chapter 15, Section 15.2, but for the moment you should be able to see the very close connection between it and the notion of the division of labour, which we have already discussed in some detail. Comparative advantage encourages a country to concentrate on what it does best. The division of labour suggests precisely the same thing, whether for an individual, a region, or a nation. Thus in his advocacy of free trade

Box 1.4

Ricardo and the WTO: the case for free trade

The economic case for an open trading system based upon multilaterally agreed rules is simple enough and rests largely on commercial common sense. But it is also supported by evidence: the experience of world trade and economic growth since the Second World War. Tariffs [import taxes] on industrial products have fallen steeply and will average less than 4 per cent in industrial countries by 1999. During the first decades after the war, world economic growth averaged about 5 per cent per year, a high rate that was partly the result of lower trade barriers. World trade grew even faster, averaging about 8 per cent during the period.

The data show a definite statistical link between freer trade and economic growth. Economic theory points to strong reasons for the link. All countries have assets – human, industrial, natural, financial – which they can employ to produce goods and services for their domestic markets or to compete overseas. Economics tells us that we can benefit when these goods and services are traded. Simply put, the principle of 'comparative advantage' says that countries prosper first by taking advantage of their assets in order to concentrate on what they produce best, and then by trading these products for products that other countries produce best.

Firms do that quite naturally on the domestic market. But what about the international market? Most firms recognize that the bigger the market the greater their potential – they can expand until they are at their most efficient size, and they can have access to large numbers of customers.

In other words, liberal trade policies – policies that allow the unrestricted flow of goods and services – multiply the rewards that result from producing the best products, with the best design, at the best price.

Source: World Trade Organization (1998)

almost 200 years ago Ricardo remains at the cutting edge of key aspects of modern economic theory and policy.[1]

The Keynesian revolution

Even the most ardent nineteenth century critics of capitalism could not fail to be impressed with its unparalleled capacity to orchestrate the production of huge quantities of goods and services in a bewildering variety of new and different forms. Consider Karl Marx and Friedrich Engels in *The Communist Manifesto*, first published in 1848:

The bourgeoisie, in its reign of barely one hundred years, has created more massive and more colossal productive power than have all previous generations put together. Subjugation of Nature's forces to man, machinery, application of chemistry to industry and agriculture, steam navigation, railways, electric telegraphs, canalization of rivers, whole populations conjured out of the ground – what earlier century had even a presentiment that such productive forces slumbered in the lap of social labour?

Beyond the acknowledgement of capitalism's 'colossal productive power', notice that Marx and Engels locate the source of this power in social labour. Marx is sometimes categorized as a member of the classical school, and his assertion here that the motive force of capitalism is its organization of labour – in other words, its highly developed and technologically sophisticated division of labour – shows why.

The certainties and confidence of the classical school thus rested, above all, upon the actual productive performance of the growing capitalist economies of the nineteenth and early twentieth centuries. Now, the renowned Canadian economist John Kenneth Galbraith has argued that new economic ideas are invariably the result of the emergence of specific economic problems. When economies run smoothly and in line with economic thinking there seems little point in questioning the existing framework of understanding. However, when problems emerge and economic

[1] This does not mean that free trade is beyond criticism. Chapter 15, Section 15.3, presents some alternative viewpoints to the Ricardian orthodoxy.

progress falters, questions must eventually be asked: what has gone wrong and, equally important, what can be done about it? From the time of Adam Smith's analysis of the early industrial revolution in the 1770s until the late 1920s there was little reason to question the classical view of the world: capitalism quite literally delivered the goods. Certainly, economies grew at different rates, and on occasion there were pauses in the growth process. Overall, however, the decisively expansionary path of the system was firmly established. But then, from 1929, with the onset of an unprecedented *worldwide economic slump*, the validity of the classical system of economic thought was thrown into doubt along with the integrity of the capitalist system itself.

The catastrophic fall in the level of economic activity at the time of what has since become known as the Great Depression defied the framework of understanding of classical economics. Smith had identified the productive potential of the division of labour under *laissez-faire*, Ricardo and others had argued that the system would provide for full employment, and Say's law had shown that the output produced would always find a market: essentially, there could be *no possibility* of permanent depression. This discontinuity between economic theory and real economic conditions provided the basis for the emergence of a new economic orthodoxy based on the work of the Cambridge economist John Maynard Keynes (1883–1946).

John Maynard Keynes, 1883–1946

THE COLLECTED WRITINGS OF
JOHN MAYNARD KEYNES

VOLUME VII

THE GENERAL THEORY
OF EMPLOYMENT
INTEREST AND MONEY

MACMILLAN
ST. MARTIN'S PRESS
FOR THE
ROYAL ECONOMIC SOCIETY

In *The General Theory of Employment, Interest and Money* (1936), Keynes produced the first *macroeconomic* analysis of the operation of the capitalist market system. As his work is covered in more detail in later chapters (see Chapter 11, on unemployment, especially), it is sufficient for our purposes here to note that Keynes challenged both the classical view that economies could not settle into depression – in fact he thought this *more* likely than not – and the classical certainty that government intervention in the economy at the aggregate level was unnecessary and even dangerous. The Keynesian revolution was therefore founded on two basic premises:

- that economies could slip spontaneously into depression from which early recovery was highly unlikely (unthinkable for the classicists)
- and that government policy, orchestrated at the macro level, would be required to either engineer recovery or offset an anticipated depression (again, unthinkable for the classical school).

Essentially, Keynes's prescription for the depressed economy was something that became known as **aggregate demand management**. This entailed the government's actively increasing the level of demand for goods and services in the economy as a whole, the intention being to encourage new economic activity in the ailing private sector. Keynes recommended that demand should be increased using fiscal policy (the manipulation of government spending or taxation). *Expansionary* fiscal policy could entail extra government spending in the economy, on things such as new roads or hospitals and/or lower taxes, so that individuals themselves with more income to spend would raise their demand for goods and services.

Aggregate demand management: Involves government-induced changes in the total demand for goods and services in an economy.

These basic ideas quickly assumed the proportions of a new orthodoxy to the extent that after 1945 they closely informed the emergent macroeconomic policies of most major Western economies. At the same time the economic prospects for the capitalist world generally appeared to be wholly transformed. The first two decades after the end of the Second World War became known as the period of the **postwar boom**. For most economies, the boom was characterized by unprecedented rates of economic growth, low inflation, and full employment.

While Keynes provided a new – macro – way of thinking about the economy and a rationale for *macroeconomic intervention*, his work also carried with it the seeds of *far wider* changes in the general view of the validity of the *laissez-faire* system as a whole. The Keynesian legacy in the postwar period (Keynes died in 1946) paved the way for varied and far-reaching forms of interventionist state policy at both the micro and macro levels, which would have had far less intellectual justification if the classical view of the world had prevailed. In the UK the emergence of the welfare state (sometimes called, significantly, the Keynesian welfare state) encapsulated the widely perceived new competence of the state to answer, for many goods and services, the basic what, how and for whom questions. Thus the state became heavily and even overwhelmingly involved in the markets for housing, health care and education. Moreover, beyond welfare provision, the UK state began to develop new forms of industrial and labour market policies, directing resource allocation in ways that would once have been the sole prerogative of market forces. In other parts of Europe there were parallel extensions of state responsibility after 1945. In Germany, for example, the *soziale Marktwirtschaft* or 'socially responsible market economy' sought to blend the productive advantages of a market system with a number of state-endorsed institutional features that raised both Germany's competitiveness and the fairness of its economic system. Thus the German system of industrial relations extended democratic rights to workers, giving them a measure of influence and control over the firms in which they worked. It is argued that this arrangement provided for more harmonious and therefore more effective industrial relations, especially in comparison with the adversarial 'us and them' systems typical elsewhere. Similarly, in postwar France the state developed and used a battery of controls over prices, incomes, credit and international trade, together with direct forms of intervention in the labour market and manipulation of the exchange rate. One purpose of such intervention was to directly raise the rate of growth of the French economy: a distinctly Keynesian approach.

Developments such as these and similar changes in many other advanced countries have given rise to the notion of the **mixed economy**: that is, one that contains some combination of private (or market) and public (or state) resource allocation. The mixed economy can be distinguished from two other forms of economic system which either enthusiastically embrace the **free market** and largely exclude the state, or tend to reject the market in favour of large-scale state intervention or **central planning**. The principles of the free market are most evident in some of the fast-growing so-called 'tiger' economies of the Far East such as Hong Kong and Taiwan. As noted, the USA too has consistently followed a freer market development path than the western European mixed economy model. Central planning, in contrast, has until recently been most fervently practised in the countries of eastern Europe and the former Soviet Union as well as in the Far East – in China and Vietnam, for example.

A notable feature of the very recent history of many centrally planned economies is of course their conversion to free (more accurately freer) market principles. This is interesting for at least two reasons. First, it parallels noted shifts in some mixed economies towards a greater reliance on markets rather than on the state as an allocator of resources. Second, the general resurgence of the market was under-

Postwar boom (1945–1970): Denotes a period of relatively fast growth, low inflation, and full employment, enjoyed by most Western economies.

Mixed economy: One that combines market and state forms of resource allocation.

Free market economy: One in which resource allocation is predominantly market based.

Centrally planned economy: One in which resource allocation is predominantly organized by the state.

pinned by yet another revolution in economics. The once dominant Keynesian framework that displaced classicism eventually itself came under severe pressure from a reinvigorated classicist-inspired school of economic thought.

The contemporary relevance of Keynes

Before we examine this second revolution in economic thought, it is useful to reflect on the *continuing relevance* of central aspects of Keynesianism. At the time of writing there is great concern about the economic prospects of the Asian economies, the largest of which, Japan, appears to be on the threshold of recession. This has caused alarm most obviously for the Japanese government but also amongst the leaders of the other major economies, who fear that Japan's sluggish performance may cause a downturn in world economic prospects. The question now arises: what, if anything is to be done to prompt economic recovery in Japan? Box 1.5 reports on a meeting of the G7 leading industrial countries that considered the response of the Japanese government to the problem. As the box makes clear, Japan has attempted to revive growth prospects by introducing a 'fiscal stimulus package', although the G7 appears worried that this might be of insufficient weight. If anything, the G7 would prefer more decisive tax cuts and bigger increases in government spending. This kind of approach – an explicit attempt at aggregate demand management – is clearly Keynesian in origin.

Box 1.5

G7 steps up pressure on Japan to stimulate its ailing economy
By Robert Chote in Washington

The Group of Seven leading industrial countries yesterday stepped up the pressure on Japan to revive its ailing economy amid scepticism about the effectiveness of its latest fiscal stimulus package, announced last week. The G7 fears that if Japan fails to reflate its economy with permanent tax cuts and spending increases, it could prompt further instability in Asia and a steeper slowdown in world economic growth.

Officials said that, with the impact of the package still uncertain, the best finance ministers could hope for at their meeting in Washington was evidence of greater political will from the Japanese authorities.

The weakness of the Japanese economy was illustrated by data yesterday which showed that year-on-year Tokyo department store sales plunged in March by more than 20 per cent.

Gordon Brown, the UK Chancellor, described Japan's latest stimulus package as 'a step in the right direction', a cautious assessment shared by other ministers. The International Monetary Fund believes it should be sufficient to restore positive growth in the second half of this year.

Source: *Financial Times* 16 April 1998

The re-emergence of market perspectives

So what explains the emergence of a major critique of Keynesianism, amounting some would argue to a second revolution in economics? The link between the predictions of economic theory and what actually happens in practice is again relevant here. The success of Keynesianism was predicated on its ability to understand the great economic event of its time: the Great Depression, and the consequences this had for unemployment. Keynes held up a policy framework for the eradication of slump, and the subsequent postwar boom appeared to validate both his analysis and the kind of macroeconomic policy that proceeded from it. Yet in the late 1960s and the 1970s the boom fizzled out, and many economies once again had to begin to grapple with the difficulties of slower growth and rising unemployment. Except that this time there was an additional and arguably more dangerous problem: inflation. Now, the Keynesian analysis of slump and what to do about it was well established, but the Keynesian framework paid relatively little heed to inflation and, in particular, it could not explain the simultaneous appearance of *stag*nation and in*flation* (so-called 'stagflation'). Herein then lay a weakness in the Keynesian framework: like the classical school after 1929, it appeared unable to comprehend events in the real economy or say what should be done about them.

This weakness was in effect seized upon by new groups of economists who were concerned to reassert the classical tradition in both micro and macro terms. To some extent, the central core of the classical tradition – that free markets are the best way of organizing the use of scarce resources – had never gone away. The well-known market economist, the American Milton Friedman (b. 1912), had been consistently and vociferously advancing this view during the 1950s and 1960s in the face of the most widespread adoption of Keynesianism in both academic and government circles. If Keynesianism could neither fully explain the appearance of relatively high and rising rates of inflation from the end of the 1960s, nor produce policies that might effectively reduce it, Friedman – resurrecting and extending the classical *monetarist* tradition in economics – claimed that his ideas could. Again, the detail of Friedman's work is covered later in this book (see Chapter 12, on inflation, especially), but one or two general points can be made here.

Milton Friedman, b. 1912

Whereas Keynes supposed that certain forms of state intervention at the macro level – notably aggregate demand management – could prevent depression and provide for consistently low levels of unemployment, Friedman argued that the large state expenditures that Keynesian policy necessarily involved were potentially harmful. In his view, when the state incurred budget deficits (spending more than it raised in taxes), which it financed by rapid expansion of the money supply, it simply fuelled inflation. Moreover, Friedman thought that the effect of Keynesian policy on unemployment had been much overrated. Unemployment might fall in the presence of Keynesian policy but only in the short run; to bring unemployment down permanently, another approach was required.

Friedman's preference was for a much more market-oriented policy framework, operating at both macro and micro levels. In *macro* terms, he advocated a modest and neutral role for the state in expenditure terms. This meant both reducing the scale of state expenditure and balancing what expenditure there was with appropriate levels of taxation. This would prevent the state introducing inflationary pressure into the economy. At the *micro* level, lower levels of state expenditure would necessarily extend the role of the market in resource allocation. In line with the classical tradition, Friedman supposed that this was generally the most effective way to organize the production of goods and services. However, he also reinforced the classical view of the operation of the labour market in particular. In Friedman's view, the permanent reduction of unemployment could only result from appropriate behaviour on the part of economic agents in the labour market. The influence of the competitive process and the directives of consumer sovereignty would underpin appropriate decisions by firms or employers, but what of the other side of the labour market: labour itself? Here Friedman argued that if market forces were allowed free reign then high and stable levels of employment would result. If, however, groups of workers were successful in exercising monopoly power through trade union activity, for example, then higher wages for some would necessarily mean unemployment for others. Thus *laissez-faire* in the labour market is, in this view, the most effective way to combat unemployment.

In summary then, the broad school of thought that Friedman re-established has, at its core, the following propositions:

- At the macro level the state should restrain its public expenditure inclinations for fear of inflationary consequences.

- At the micro level there is a reciprocally confirming affirmation of the power of free markets to effectively answer the basic economic questions of what is to be produced, how is it to be produced, and for whom. Moreover, in the context of the labour market, *laissez-faire* is a uniquely potent means of securing permanently low levels of unemployment.

The real-world application of modern market perspectives

The approach that Friedman recommends has been adopted with varying degrees of commitment by a number of countries. Box 1.6 provides an illustration of the application of market-based policies in New Zealand. In the 1980s New Zealand

---

Box 1.6

Bit more pain for future gain: New Zealand's economic reforms are starting to bear fruit

By Terry Hall and Nikki Tait

When Jim Bolger, New Zealand's prime minister, meets Paul Keating, his Australian counterpart, this week, they are likely to discuss closer economic ties between the two countries. But Mr Bolger might be tempted to offer his neighbour a few tips about how to turn a highly protected welfare state into a deregulated market economy.

Last week, Mr Bill Birch, New Zealand's finance minister, presented a budget which showed a NZ$527m fiscal surplus for the 12 months to the end of June, the first by New Zealand for almost 20 years. The figure surpassed the government's forecast a year ago, and its predictions now suggest rising surpluses for the next three years. The first use for them, said Mr Birch, was the repayment of foreign debt, which accounts for about 38 per cent of total net public debt.

Contrast that with Australia. There, as in New Zealand, recovery has come more quickly than expected, and the economy is growing at a similar rate – close to 5 per cent a year. So, like New Zealand, Australia has had the benefit of higher than expected tax receipts, giving the government fiscal leeway.

But in his May budget, Mr Ralph Willis, Australian treasurer, announced a A$11.7bn deficit for 1994–95 (2.5 per cent of gross domestic product), after A$2.4bn of asset sales. Much of the 'growth dividend' would be used to fund a jobs programme, costing A$6.5bn over four years. It will be the late 1990s, according to official estimates, before Australia moves into surplus. The comparison is only relevant because the two countries started from similar positions a decade ago. Both had economies which were protected behind high tariff walls; both labour markets were regulated and depended on centralized awards; and industrial sectors such as telecommunications were dominated by public sector monopolies.

The greater speed of New Zealand's reform process has already won international praise. But there is no secret about the way in which the budget surplus has been achieved – and no hiding the price. During the past 10 years, unemployment has soared as former government activities were privatized in the interests of efficiency, and the new profit-minded owners pared away unnecessary services. New Zealand's jobless rate peaked at more than 11 per cent in early 1992, and currently stands at about 9 per cent. Union power has been broken with the Employment Contracts Act, and wage levels have fallen in real terms over the past decade. Schools and hospitals have been reformed, welfare spending, including unemployment benefits, has been slashed as the government has sought to lower its costs.

All this has led to substantial savings in government spending. Now that recovery is under way, a virtuous circle is also taking effect, augmenting the gains. The improving economy is leading to a sharp increase in tax receipts as people rejoin the workforce. Lower wage bills are boosting company profits, with the result that these are rising, again lifting tax receipts.

Source: *Financial Times*, 5 July 1994

embarked on a programme of micro and macro reform. As the box indicates, at the micro level, the government privatized – that is, returned to the market – many activities for which it had assumed responsibility. At the macro level, it sought to assert much stronger controls over public spending, with resulting improvements in its budgetary position. The box suggests that the reforms, although costly in unemployment terms, have left New Zealand's economy in a healthy position, with growth now re-established and unemployment falling.

Reflections on the history of economics

It should be clear from the preceding discussion that the usefulness of the free market is the foremost issue in the history of economic thought. We might also add that the general consensus at any one time is strongly conditioned by the ability of the prevailing school of thought to explain contemporary economic events and produce a policy framework that can positively influence them. Indeed, to the extent that the macroeconomic progress of many economies over the 1980s and 1990s has been distinctly uneven – with concerns over various combinations of faltering growth, inflation, and stubbornly high unemployment – it is possible to argue that no one school of thought is currently able to claim the high ground of economic orthodoxy. Thus, for example, as discussion in Chapter 11 makes clear, the problem of relatively high unemployment in Europe may be best solved by some combination of policies from different schools of thought.

At the micro level too there are some significant signs of **eclecticism**. In 1992 the countries of the EU combined their economies into a single market (see Chapter 2, Section 2.5). The main purpose of this move was to try to raise the levels of economic activity and growth in Europe by following the Smithian logic of an extended division of labour. The *laissez-faire* credentials of the European single market are clear. However, at the same time, the EU introduced a number of additional *interventionist*

Eclectic approach: One that combines themes and policies from different schools of thought.

Period	Key figure	Dominant school	Contribution	Prompted by
Late 18th C. 19th C.	**Smith Ricardo and Say** →	Classicism →	Theory of the effectiveness of competitive markets; identification of limited role of the state in the economy.	→ Support for new industrial capitalism
1936–1970s	**Keynes** →	Keynesianism →	Theory of depression in the macroeconomy. Identification of the role of the state in preventing depressions.	→ The Great Depression (1929–33) and mass unemployment
1970s–1980s	**Friedman** →	Monetarism →	Monetary explanation of inflation. Much reduced scope for state intervention especially at the macro level.	→ The resurgence of inflation from the late 1960s
1990s	**Eclecticism** →	None →	A general acceptance of the importance of monetary control and an acknowledgement that, at times, governments need to manage aggregate demand to reduce unemployment.	→ Success in the control of inflation and persistence of unemployment problems

Fig. 1.1 A timeline of key contributions to economic thought.

measures that it hoped would offset some anticipated detrimental effects of the single market. For example, the EU doubled the funds it allocates to assist poorer regions in Europe because it expected that, at least for a time, some of these might be 'outcompeted' by the traditionally more affluent regions, thus causing higher unemployment in the poorer regions. Again then we appear to have some combination of faith in the allocative abilities of free markets and simultaneous doubts that their effects are universally benign. For a timeline summary of the key contributions to economic thought discussed in this chapter, see Fig. 1.1.

◼ Summary

◆ Economics is concerned with three basic questions: what goods and services a society produces, how these are produced, and for whom they are produced. It recognizes that these questions can be answered in many different ways, but also that a key issue is whether the answers are left to the free market or whether the state involves itself in resource allocation.

◆ The free market facilitates the extension of the division of labour. Because this permits economic agents to specialize in activities to which they are best suited, it offers the possibility of raising the quantity and quality of goods and services that a society produces.

◆ All resources are scarce in the context of the infinite demands that can be placed upon them. Society is therefore faced with a myriad of choices concerning how the resources it has should be used. The concept of opportunity cost allows us to begin to understand the choices that particular societies make at given times.

◆ Economics is concerned with positive issues of fact, rather than normative issues of opinion. However, there is still scope for disagreement between economists who produce different analyses – equally robust in theoretical and empirical terms – of the same question.

◆ The history of economic thought is at root a history of the explanation of economic events or processes. The orthodoxies established successively by Adam Smith, Keynes and Friedman were each founded on an understanding of the (then) contemporary performances of economies and how, if at all, these could be improved.

◆ The key issue that divides Smith and Friedman on the one hand from Keynes on the other is a difference over the ability of the free market to adequately orchestrate the production of goods and services.

◆ Currently, economics lacks an established orthodoxy. There are many economic issues that appear amenable to eclectic resolution.

◼ Key terms

◆ Resource allocation
◆ Scarcity and choice
◆ Opportunity cost
◆ *Laissez-faire*
◆ State intervention

◆ Division of labour
◆ Mixed economy
◆ Classical school
◆ Keynesianism
◆ Classical resurgence
◆ Eclecticism

Self-test questions

True (t) or false (f)

1. The discovery of North Sea oil meant that, for the UK, oil was no longer a scarce resource.

2. Economists disagree over normative issues.

3. The rate of inflation is a microeconomic issue.

4. Say's law states that supply creates its own demand.

5. The classical school broadly favoured *laissez-faire*.

6. Keynes's work was motivated by the appearance of high rates of inflation.

7. Stagflation describes the coincidence of high unemployment and high inflation.

8. Stagflation was a problem of the 1930s.

9. Friedman's work centres on a strong positive relationship between the rate of growth of the money supply and the rate of inflation.

10. Economic orthodoxy is now increasingly eclectic.

Complete the following sentences by inserting the missing word(s)

1. ____ questions are factually based.

2. The idea that buyers determine the nature of what is produced is known as ____.

3. It is the fact that ____ are limitless that makes resources scarce.

4. The ____ of an action is the cost measured in terms of the best forgone alternative action.

5. A situation in which there is little or no interference in the economy is referred to as ____.

6. Smith likened the allocative powers of the market mechanism to an ____.

7. Specialization in the organization of work is known as the ____ of ____.

8. The risk-taking producer is called an ____.

9. The period of fast growth, low unemployment and low inflation enjoyed by most Western economies between 1945 and 1970 is referred to as the ____.

10. *Laissez-faire* and the ____ economy are at polar extremes from each other.

Questions for discussion

◆ What is economics?
◆ How can the notion of opportunity cost help us to understand the production choices that a society makes?
◆ What were the central tenets of the classical school?

◆ (A harder version of the same question) Explain the macroeconomic implications of classical microeconomic analysis.

◆ Economic thought evolves when new economic problems present themselves. Discuss this statement in relation to emergence of the Keynesian orthodoxy.

◼ Further reading

Galbraith, J.K. *A History of Economics* (London: Hamish Hamilton, 1987). Clarity, wit and elegance are the hallmarks of Galbraith's writing. In our view this is one of the best overviews of economic thought there is.

Jowsey, E. *100 Essay Plans for Economics* (Oxford: Oxford University Press, 1998). Offers a comprehensive summary of micro and macro issues and is also a very useful revision guide.

Artis, M.J. (ed.) *The UK Economy* (14th ed.) (Oxford: Oxford University Press, 1996). Provides a thorough overview of UK economic performance and policy.

For those with interests in *other* economies, a good starting point is the OECD *Economic Surveys* series. This offers regularly published updates on economic policy and performance in a large number of countries, including less developed economies and those in transition from central planning.

Ormerod, P. *The Death of Economics* (London: Faber and Faber, 1994). Provides a jaundiced view of the state of modern economics.

◼ Using the Internet to study economics

The Internet provides a wealth of sources for anyone studying economics. At the end of each chapter, where appropriate, we suggest links to Internet sites that will help you to follow up on what you have learned. However, because in our experience a lot of time can be spent searching through the contents of sites (and as site addresses are prone to change) we do not think it worthwhile providing lengthy lists for you to work through. Instead, we highlight selected Internet sites that we think students new to economics will find especially useful. We provide a brief description of the contents of each recommended site, together with the relevant address. In any particular instance, should you find that the address we have given fails to provide a link, you should be able to locate the relevant site using a search engine. Alternatively, you may access an 'economics links' page we maintain at Liverpool John Moores University. This can be found via the Macmillan site at: **http://www.macmillan-press.co.uk**.

◼ Internet links

To complement the introductory chapter you have just read you might try the following:

The Economist offers a free digest of articles on contemporary economic issues, written in an accessible style. The Economist can be found at: **http://www.economist.com/** The OECD also offers issue-based articles free of charge, together with useful data covering many economic issues and countries. The OECD is at: **http://www. oecd. org/**.

The Market

CHAPTER 2

Key issues

▶ Which factors determine the demand for a good or service?

▶ Which factors determine the supply of a good or service?

▶ How do demand and supply interact?

▶ How can market theory be applied to the real world?

Contents

2.1 Introduction

Chapter 1 presented the central issue in the development of economic thought as the usefulness, or otherwise, of free markets. Some schools of thought hold closely to the view that *laissez-faire* provides a generally superior means of deciding how an economy's scarce resources should be allocated. Other schools are much less convinced that the free market 'gets it right' most of the time. In this chapter we offer a more detailed analysis of how the market is actually supposed to work. This is important for two reasons.

First, it allows us to fully elaborate the simple elegance of the market mechanism. In Chapter 1, following the work of the classical school, we noted the productive potential of the extended division of labour that the free market makes possible. We are now in a position to see exactly how the market can, in theory, ably coordinate the millions of production and consumption decisions that take place every day in the modern economy.

Second, having established the nature of the case for the free market, we shall, in later chapters (principally Chapters 5 and 6) review the generally recognized possibilities of **market failure**. Market failure gives rise to a number of important forms of state intervention in modern economies.

This chapter is concerned with markets for goods and services: so-called **goods markets**. These are composed of two sets of economic agents: consumers who demand goods and services, and producers who supply them. In order to understand how goods markets work, we thus need to give some thought to the respective aspirations and motivations of producers and consumers in the market process.

Market failure: Arises where the market either fails to provide certain goods, or fails to provide them at their optimal or most desirable level.

Goods markets: Markets in which goods and services can be bought and sold.

2.2 Consumers and demand

For a particular good or service, which factors influence the precise **quantity demanded** by consumers over a given time period? The obvious factor is price. If we assume that all other influences upon demand remain unchanged (the so-called **ceteris paribus** assumption), then higher prices will usually be associated with a lower quantity demanded. Similarly, lower prices will usually be associated with a greater quantity demanded. We can illustrate the *inverse* nature of the relationship between price and quantity demanded graphically.

In Fig. 2.1 the price of a good is depicted on the vertical axis, while the quantity demanded is depicted on the horizontal axis. At price P_1, the amount Q_1 is demanded. However, if the price increases to P_2, then the quantity demanded falls, or contracts, to Q_2. Conversely, if there is a reduction in price from P_1 to P_3, then the quantity demanded rises, or extends, to Q_3. If several such links between price and quantity demanded are established, it becomes possible to discern a *demand curve*, D_1, which shows *ceteris paribus* the *entire* relationship between price and quantity demanded for the particular good in question. It should be clear that the relationship is indeed an inverse one. In other words, higher prices are associated with **contractions** in the quantity demanded, and lower prices prompt **extensions** in the quantity demanded. The convention in economics is to refer to *movements* along a single demand curve as either contractions (where the quantity demanded is falling) or extensions (where it is rising).

So the particular price of a good determines, over a given time period, the precise quantity demanded: 50 aircraft, 2 million cars, 50 million newspapers, and so on. But beyond price there are other factors that have some bearing upon the **demand** for a good, again over a given time period. Here, demand refers not to a particular quantity and a particular price but to *all* possible prices and quantities demanded. Consider, for example, the influence on demand of a change in the incomes of consumers. If incomes rise then *ceteris paribus* we would anticipate that the demand for a **normal good** would increase whatever its particular price. Conversely, a fall in consumer incomes would prompt a decrease in the demand for a normal good.

It is possible to illustrate the effects of a change in income on demand graphically.

Quantity demanded: The amount of a good or service that consumers wish to purchase at a particular price, *ceteris paribus*.

Ceteris paribus: A commonly used assumption in economics. It means 'other things remaining the same'. Its purpose is to allow us to examine the influence of one factor at a time on something – in this case, price on quantity demanded – that we are trying to explain or understand.

Contractions, extensions: Movements along a demand curve that result from a change in the price of the good are referred to as contractions or extensions in the quantity demanded.

Demand: The quantity of a good or service that consumers wish to purchase at each conceivable price, *ceteris paribus*.

Normal good: One for which demand increases when income increases.

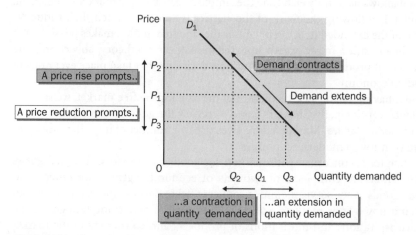

Fig. 2.1 The effect of a change in price on the quantity demanded of a particular good or service.

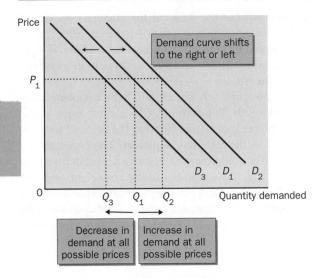

Fig. 2.2 The effect of a change in income on the demand for a normal good or service.

In Fig. 2.2 the demand curve D_1 represents the range of possible relationships between the price of a normal good and the quantity demanded at an initial level of consumers' income. For example, at price P_1 the quantity demanded is Q_1. Now, what happens if the incomes of consumers rise? The higher levels of income prompt consumers to increase their demand for the good. Note that this is the case *regardless of the level of the assumed price*: if it was higher or lower than our arbitrary selection, P_1, the outcome would be the same. The increase in demand that results from the higher level of consumer income is captured graphically by a rightward shift of the demand curve from D_1 to D_2. At each and every possible price demand will increase. For example, at a price of P_1 quantity demanded increases to Q_2. Conversely, because it prompts a decrease in demand, a fall in consumers' income is associated with a leftward shift of the demand curve. In the diagram this is captured in the movement from D_1 to D_3. At price P_1 the quantity demanded is Q_3. To distinguish them from the extensions and contractions in the quantity demanded caused by a change in the price of a particular good, changes in demand, which are associated with **shifts** in the demand curve, are conventionally referred to as **increases** or **decreases** in demand.

In addition to changes in consumers' incomes, there are a range of other factors that also prompt shifts in the demand curve for a particular good or service and consequent increases or decreases in demand. Amongst the most important of these are the prices of other goods and services, and the preferences or tastes of consumers.

The prices of other goods and services

Some goods and services have **substitutes** – for example, viewing a film at home on a rented video might be thought of as substitute for a visit to the cinema to see the same film. Home videos might not be perfect substitutes for the cinema – many people prefer the cinema 'experience', and new releases are shown exclusively in cinemas first – but they are certainly close substitutes. So, considering the demand for cinema seats, what would we expect to happen if the rental charges for videos

Increases or decreases in demand: Refer to shifts of the demand curve.

Substitute: A good that can replace another good.

Complement: A good that is used with another good.

increase? The answer is that *ceteris paribus* the demand for cinema seats should increase. In other words, following the logic of Fig. 2.2, the demand curve for cinema seats would shift to the right as demand by consumers increases. Similarly, if video rental charges fall, we would expect to see the demand for cinema seats decrease and the demand curve for them shift to the left.

On the other hand, some other goods and services are said to be **complementary**, in the sense that they are consumed jointly. For example, CDs are not much use on their own; you need to have a CD player too. So, considering the demand for CDs, what would be the outcome of a fall in the price of CD players? The expectation is that *ceteris paribus* the demand for CDs would increase as more people demand CD players and CDs too. In terms of Fig. 2.2, this would be reflected in a rightward shift of the demand curve (for CDs). Alternatively, a rise in the price of CD players would *ceteris paribus* lead to a fall in the demand for them and an associated decrease in the demand for CDs. In Fig. 2.2 this would be depicted by a leftward shift in the demand curve.

The preferences or tastes of consumers

At different times consumers take different views as to the attractiveness of particular goods and services. In virtually every city in Europe over the last 20 years there has been an explosion in 'fast food': a relatively narrow product line of burgers, shakes, coffee and doughnuts, mostly served through the same restaurant chains. People clearly like fast food, so more and more of it is produced. There may of course come a time when it wanes in popularity. If and when this happens the resources given over to its production will be reallocated to different uses. This is one example of the possible effects on demand (and resource allocation) of changes in consumer preferences, but other interesting cases are not hard to find. For instance, over the last 10 or 15 years consumers have become much more aware of the environmental implications of some of their consumption decisions. This has prompted increases in the demand for goods and services that are, or are perceived to be, 'environmentally friendly' (demand curve shifts to the right). Political issues can also influence demand. During the years of apartheid in South Africa an effective consumer boycott of South African goods was enacted in other countries by people concerned to register their opposition to an odious regime (demand curve shifts to the left). Finally, in the UK in the 1990s beef producers have experienced a decrease in the demand for their output because of the BSE-related health worries of domestic consumers (demand curve shifts left).

A summary of the main factors influencing demand is given in Table 2.1.

Table 2.1 Factors that influence the demand for a particular good: a summary

Factor	Effect
• Price	Price changes cause movements along a demand curve. Price decreases are associated with extensions in the particular quantity demanded. Price increases are associated with contractions in the particular quantity demanded.
• Income • Tastes and preferences • Prices of other goods	A change in any one of these factors will cause a shift in the demand curve itself, with increases or decreases in demand at every possible price.

2.3 Producers and supply

The second economic actor or agent in the market is the producer. The role of the producer is to supply goods and services to the marketplace. So what influences producers' decisions in respect of the **quantity supplied** of a particular good or service? The question of price is again relevant here. The proposition is that the higher the price of a particular good, the greater the incentive for producers to supply it. What is the reasoning behind this statement? We know from Chapter 1 that the motive force of capitalism is self-interest. For producers this translates as profit. We shall see in later discussion that the standard assumption made is that producers seek to maximize the profits they earn, and they do this by producing as many profitable commodities as they can. The profit on an individual good is simply the price it fetches less the cost of its production. Now, it follows that if the price of a good increases, then *ceteris paribus* more of it will become profitable to produce. Thus a higher price for a particular good will prompt producers to raise the quantity supplied.

The relationship between the price of a good in a market and the quantity supplied over a given time period can be illustrated graphically. In Fig. 2.3, as for our discussion of demand, price is depicted on the vertical axis. The horizontal axis depicts the quantity supplied. At price P_1 producers are motivated to supply Q_1 of the good or service in question. If price increases to P_2 then the quantity supplied extends to Q_2. Conversely, if price falls from P_1 to P_3 then the quantity supplied contracts from Q_1 to Q_3. If we examine a range of such links between price and quantity supplied, it becomes possible to distinguish a *supply curve* (S_1), which shows the entire relationship between price and the quantity supplied. It can be seen that the relationship is *positive* in nature: that is, price and quantity supplied move in the same direction. Increases in price prompt **extensions** in the quantity supplied; decreases in price prompt **contractions** in the quantity supplied (as for demand, the convention is that *movements* along a given supply curve are referred to as extensions or contractions).

Quantity supplied: The amount that producers wish to sell at a particular price, *ceteris paribus*.

Contractions, extensions: Movements along a supply curve that result from a change in the price of a good are referred to as contractions or extensions in the quantity supplied.

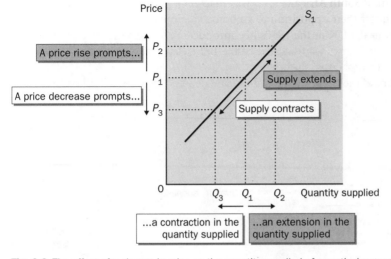

Fig. 2.3 The effect of a change in price on the quantity supplied of a particular good or service.

So the particular price of a good determines, over a given time period, the precise quantity supplied: 5 ships, 2 million burgers, 5 million canned drinks and so on. But, as for demand, there are other factors beyond price that have some bearing upon the **supply** of a good, again over a given time period. Here, supply refers not to a particular quantity and a particular price but to *all* possible prices and quantities supplied. We have already noted that producers are interested in the profit yielded by their output, and that this is a function of both price and the cost of production. It follows that lower production costs will occasion increases in supply. If, for example, the producers of baked beans find that the costs of **factor inputs** such as tin, beans, sugar or tomatoes fall, then *ceteris paribus* they will be motivated to supply more tins of baked beans at each and every possible price. This is because the higher ranges of output that were formerly unprofitable are less costly and now yield a profit. The nature of the link between the cost of production and supply can be illustrated graphically.

In Fig. 2.4 the supply curve S_1 represents a set of possible relationships between price and quantity supplied with a given set of production costs. Operating with this supply curve, it can be seen that at, say, price P_1, producers are motivated to supply Q_1. The effect of a fall in production costs is to shift the supply curve to the right from S_1 to S_2. Operating with the new supply curve, S_2, and the given price P_1, it can be seen that producers would wish to supply an increased output Q_2 to the market. Note that this would be the case regardless of the (given) price of the good. In other words, at each and every possible price supply would increase. Conversely, an increase in production costs would reduce the number of profitable tins of beans that could be produced at any given price; so if costs rise, producers will be motivated to decrease supply. In Fig. 2.4, higher production costs have the effect of shifting the supply curve to the left (from S_1 to S_3). With S_3 operating, at a price P_1 producers are motivated to supply Q_3 to the market. Note that the terms **increase** and **decrease** in supply refer to changes arising from *shifts* of supply curves, as opposed to extensions and contractions in the quantity supplied, which arise, as noted, from price-related movements along given supply curves.

Changes in production costs that shift the supply curve for a good or service can

Supply: The quantity of a good or service that producers wish to sell at each conceivable price, *ceteris paribus*.

Factor inputs: Any goods and services used in the process of production.

Increases or decreases in supply: Refer to shifts of the supply curve.

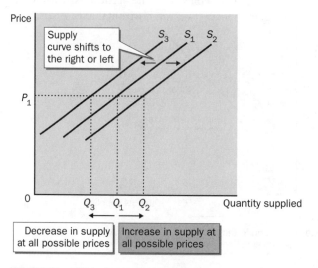

Fig. 2.4 The effect of a change in production costs on the supply of a particular good or service.

also result from a change in technology. In terms of Fig. 2.4, an improvement in technology that reduces production costs will shift the supply curve to the right. This is because, at each possible price, more units of output become profitable, thus prompting increases in supply. For example, car production was revolutionized by Henry Ford's introduction of the mechanized assembly line in the early years of this century. Ford didn't invent the car, but his new method of production vastly reduced the cost of producing cars, first in the USA and subsequently worldwide, leading to a vast increase in supply (the supply curve shifted to the right).

A summary of the main factors influencing supply is given in Table 2.2.

Table 2.2 Factors that influence the supply of a particular good: a summary

Factor	Effect
• Price	Price changes cause movements along a supply curve. Higher prices are associated with extensions in the particular quantity supplied. Lower prices are associated with contractions in the particular quantity supplied.
• Input costs • Technology	A change in either of these factors will cause a shift in the supply curve itself, with increases or decreases in supply at every possible price.

2.4 The market: bringing demand and supply together

The equilibrium price and market equilibrium

Having reviewed the two sides of the market in isolation, we are now in a position to see how they interact: it is this interplay between consumers and producers – or demand and supply – that produces market conditions satisfactory to both. The necessary analysis is easiest to conduct graphically. Fig. 2.5 represents the market for a particular good or service. Price is again depicted on the vertical axis, while the quantities demanded and supplied are depicted on the horizontal axis. At price P_1

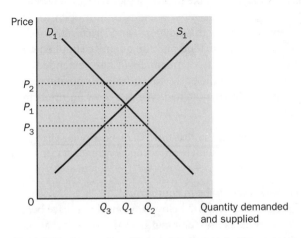

Fig. 2.5 The interaction of demand and supply in the market for a particular good.

The car boot sale: a market of the 1990s

notice that the quantity demanded, Q_1, as given by the demand curve D_1, *exactly matches* the quantity supplied (also Q_1), as given by the supply curve S_1. Thus at price P_1 the market is said to **clear** in the sense that, in any given time period, all goods supplied are actually sold. This situation appears to have some intrinsic merit as there are no gluts or shortages in the market: no consumers are left with demand unsatisfied, and no producers are left with stocks they cannot sell.

The price P_1 can also be shown to be an **equilibrium price**. In economics, the term 'equilibrium' is used to describe a state of balance from which there is *no tendency to change*. How then does P_1 prompt an equilibrium? Consider the prices P_2 and P_3, also shown in Fig. 2.5. At P_2, the quantity supplied, Q_2, exceeds the quantity demanded, Q_3, and there is said to be **excess supply** in the market. Now, because they are saddled with unsold stocks, this situation leaves some producers dissatisfied (those consumers in the market at price P_2 are able to buy all they desire, so we judge them content). In order to change things, the most obvious option open to producers is to reduce the price they charge. As this happens, and price starts to fall below P_2, the quantity demanded begins to extend and the quantity supplied contracts. Eventually, as price falls to P_1, quantity demanded will have extended and quantity supplied will have contracted sufficiently to entirely eliminate excess supply, leaving demand and supply perfectly matched. We can draw an important general implication from this analysis:

Any price above P_1 will be a disequilibrium price so that there is a tendency for change to occur. Excess supply will encourage producers to initiate price reductions until demand and supply are harmonized.

When this happens, the market itself is said to be in equilibrium.

So much for prices above P_1, but what of those below it? Consider a price below P_1: P_3, for example. At price P_3 there is **excess demand** over the supply that producers choose to make available. Now, although producers are content with this

Clear: A market is said to clear when all goods or services supplied in it are sold.

Equilibrium price: The price at which the quantity demanded equals the quantity supplied.

Excess supply: Occurs when the quantity supplied exceeds the quantity demanded at some given price.

Excess demand: Occurs when the quantity demanded exceeds the quantity supplied at some given price.

situation (as they sell all they wish to offer to the market), the same cannot be said of consumers. At P_3, consumers wish to buy Q_2 of the good or service in question but only Q_3 is available: the demand of some consumers is left unsatisfied. Now, as their output is rapidly and avidly swallowed up by consumers, producers will be aware that there is excess demand in the market. This results in the price being 'bid up'. Notice that, as price rises above P_3, the quantity demanded begins to contract and the quantity supplied extends. However, it is only when price reaches P_1 that the excess demand in the market is entirely eliminated. Again, we can draw an important general implication from this analysis:

Any price below P_1 will be a disequilibrium price. Excess demand will encourage producers to initiate price increases until demand and supply are harmonized.

Moreover, it is now evident that P_1 is in fact a unique equilibrium price in the market depicted in Fig. 2.5. All other possible prices are associated with either excess supply or excess demand conditions, which prompt spontaneous movements back towards *the* equilibrium price.

Changes in the equilibrium price and market equilibrium

Let us now think about how the plans of consumers and producers are harmonized following changes in market circumstances. We shall do this using examples of the interaction of demand and supply in three 'real world' markets: those for canned tuna fish, for coffee, and for the metal palladium. Although the outcomes in each case are different, these examples demonstrate that markets do have the ability to respond to change, and can readily produce new equilibrium positions.

The UK market for canned tuna fish grew from 1.3 million cases annually in the early 1980s to 9 million cases by the mid-1990s (a case contains 48 of the familiar 200 g cans). The market continues to increase by about 10 per cent per year (Source: *The Grocer*, 12 April 1997). There is little doubt that this expansion is demand led. Research by the industry shows that consumers see tuna as a low-cost, high-protein food and an attractive alternative to meat. Diagrammatically, the increase in demand can be represented by a rightward shift of the demand curve in Fig. 2.6,

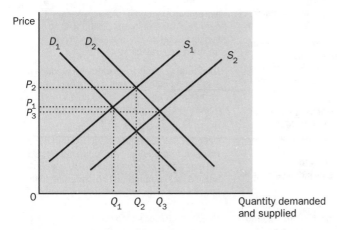

Fig. 2.6 A stylized representation of recent developments in the UK market for canned tuna fish.

from D_1 to D_2. The outcome *ceteris paribus* would be an increase in the equilibrium price from P_1 to P_2 and a new equilibrium quantity Q_2 bought and sold. However, demand changes are not the end of the matter. Over the past 15 years, most major tuna producers have invested heavily in new, modernized plant and equipment. Recall that technological improvements in a market have the effect of shifting the supply curve to the right (from S_1 to S_2). When we incorporate this feature into Fig. 2.6, the end result is given by the intersection of D_2 and S_2: an equilibrium price of P_3 and an equilibrium quantity of Q_3. This is broadly consistent with what has happened in the tuna market: a marked increase in the equilibrium quantity demanded and supplied, with relatively little movement in price.

Recent developments in the world coffee market appear rather less benign. These are described in Box 2.1. In reading the box you should be able to discern five factors that have served to disrupt the market. Four of these are on the supply side, and all serve to *reduce* supply. They are:

- bad weather in Central and South America
- strikes by coffee bean farmers in Columbia (the world's second largest coffee exporter)
- higher input costs for Columbian coffee farmers as the cocaine trade competes for labour
- insect problems.

Box 2.1

There's not a lot of coffee in Brazil this year: prices will rise as farmers are ground down

By Phil Davison

Brace yourself for a surge in the price of coffee. And you can blame it on Columbian cocaine producers, a plague of insects, Brazilian showers or financial speculators.

Experts predict your coffee break is about to cost you considerably more within the next few days as supermarkets stick higher price tags on coffee beans, both ground and instant. They are distinctly less clear about the reason.

What we do know is that the price that the big roasting corporations pay to producers has rocketed 40 per cent since December and is about to be reflected on your supermarket shelves ...

Why? Take your pick. One factor is certainly bad weather during the recent harvesting season in Central and South America – particularly the world's top two producers, Brazil and Columbia. It is likely to cut their exports and further reduce dwindling stocks in the consumer nations.

Then there are reports of a pending strike by Columbia's coffee farmers. They are angered by the fact that the world price rise has not been passed onto them by their National Coffee Federation ...

On his farm ... Columbian coffee grower Fabio Zuluaga notes another problem. 'An experienced coffee bean picker earns around twice the minimum wage during the November–December picking season,' he said. 'But the traditional pickers can now earn five times that much by picking cocoa leaves for the narco-traffickers.'

Like other Columbian growers, Mr Zuluaga has also been battling a plague of insects known as broca, barely visible to the human eye but deadly to the coffee bean ...

But the International Coffee Organization's Director, Celsius Lodder admitted that there was some confusion. 'The fundamentals are not explaining price variations 100 per cent,' he said ... He appeared to be referring to the speculation in the coffee futures market.

Source: The Independent 5 February 1997

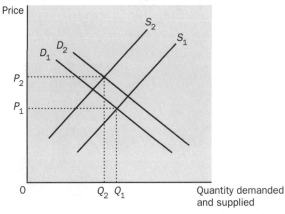

Fig. 2.7 An approximation of changes in demand and supply conditions in the world coffee market in 1997.

On the demand side, speculation in coffee (buying it in the anticipation that prices will rise) is also blamed for unwelcome price movements. The effects of these developments are summarized in Fig. 2.7. The supply influences produce a leftward shift of the supply curve (from S_1 to S_2), while rising speculative demand shifts the demand curve to the right (from D_1 to D_2). The end result is the 'surge' in the price of coffee anticipated in Box 2.1 (from P_1 to P_2). Incidentally, note that although our summary of influences on supply (see Table 2.2) mentions only technology and input costs, these can also be taken as proxies for some of the 'coffee specific' supply factors mentioned here. Thus the effects of bad weather and the broca pest are the equivalent of temporary adverse movements in technology: in their presence, a given assemblage of coffee-growing equipment and infrastructure yields a lower output than would otherwise be the case.

Finally, we come to the market in palladium. As Box 2.2 explains, palladium is used to make components for portable electronic goods such as mobile phones. The demand for these goods and therefore for palladium itself continues to grow

Box 2.2

Electronics industry warns of palladium shortage

Warning was given yesterday of a severe shortage of palladium, a metal essential for some components of portable electronic equipment such as mobile telephones and laptop computers, as well as for catalytic converters that remove pollutants from car exhausts.

'Palladium use continues to grow very strongly but production lags well behind. Soon after 2000 we could be in a very difficult situation unless industrial users take heed now,' said Mike Steel, research director at Johnson Matthey, the world's biggest platinum and palladium marketing group.

He said consumers had been relying on

Russia's palladium stocks to fill a substantial gap between demand and supply. JM believes these stocks will run out soon after the end of the century.

Mr Steel said there had been a preview of potential trouble earlier this year when Russia, which exports 70 per cent of the world's palladium, stopped exporting the metal for six months. This helped to drive the price to its highest level for eighteen years ... Although it has fallen back since Russian exports restarted, the price remains roughly double its level at this time last year.

Source: Financial Times 19 November 1997

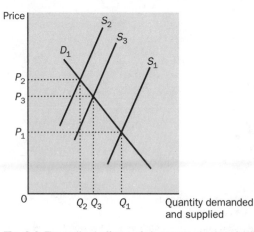

Fig. 2.8 The stylized effects of short-term changes in the supply of palladium.

strongly. Unfortunately, however, supply has been constrained by the unreliability of the world's major palladium producer, Russia. Indeed, Russian exports of palladium have actually been wholly suspended for a time. Such supply difficulties have seen palladium prices driven to record highs. In Fig. 2.8, the severe reduction in supply is represented by the decisive leftward shift of the supply curve from S_1 to S_2, prompting an increase in price from P_1 to P_2. As Box 2.2 reports, although Russian exports have since resumed, prices remain relatively high. In effect, the supply curve has begun to shift to the right again but only slowly (say to S_3, with price P_3).

2.5 Applying market analysis: the example of economic integration in the European Union

If markets can work as our theoretical arguments have so far suggested – prompting equilibria in the face of various forms of change and disruption – we might expect to see them promoted and supported in many 'real world' situations. Using policies adopted by the European Union (EU) towards the organization of markets as an example, let us now see if this is the case. In fact our findings will demonstrate that the EU appears to be somewhat ambiguous in its attitudes towards the free market. On the one hand, it has introduced the so-called single market programme, which seeks to use the market mechanism in a positive way, harnessing it to coordinate the production and consumption of many goods and services across Europe. On the other hand, however, in the market for agricultural goods in particular, the EU prefers intervention to *laissez-faire*. In what follows, we use the principles of demand and supply to explain such ambiguity.

The EU is currently composed of 15 member states. These are:

- Austria
- Belgium
- Denmark
- Finland
- France

- Germany
- Greece
- Ireland
- Italy
- Luxembourg

- Netherlands
- Portugal
- Spain
- Sweden
- UK

A central aim of the EU is to enhance the economic prospects of its member states. This is to be achieved by binding their separate national territories together to form a *single market* in Europe. The result will be the creation of a unified economic space that, it is anticipated, will enjoy the kind of cohesiveness currently evident inside the separate national economies. Consumption and production decisions, decisions about where to live and work, decisions about where to invest – *all* will begin to be taken more and more at the European level.

The single market was born out of a concern that, over the 1970s and early 1980s, the existing form of the so-called European 'common market' was unable to help its members sufficiently to match the economic performances and potential of other advanced nations: the USA and Japan in particular. The source of the problem was thought to be the increasingly *fragmented* nature of the European economy. The European 'common market' was an economic space that provided for the free movement of goods and services between member nations. Since its creation in 1957 as part of the Treaty of Rome, citizens in member states all over Europe could buy and sell freely to one another, without the hindrance of any barriers to trade such as tariffs (see Chapter 15, Section 15.5). Commercial freedom of this form should in theory have brought substantial benefits. German citizens would not have to buy goods and services from mostly German firms, they could buy just as easily from French firms if these offered better or cheaper products. Similarly (say) Italian and Dutch firms would be able to sell wherever their products merited a demand. In this way, a more open European market would allow European consumers to buy from European firms that offered them the best value. Moreover, because the best firms would tend to be rewarded with more custom, they would thrive at the expense of their inferior rivals. The long-term effect of the 'common market' would therefore be the encouragement and promotion of the best producers: Europe would become a more productive and competitive place.

How then did the concern over the fragmentation of the European economy arise? The problem was that in some important respects Europe appeared by the late 1970s and early 1980s to be *retreating* back into its national economic components. For example, it was felt that the free movement of goods and services was increasingly hampered by various kinds of what we might term 'administrative' trade barrier, such as those concerned with national standards for certain classes of good. In addition, it was evident that despite their apparent commitment to European integration, national governments themselves tended to purchase along very nationalistic lines. Thus the British government usually bought from British firms, the French government from French firms, and so on. In this context the single market, introduced in 1992, is an attempt to *refresh the integration project*. Its intention is to sweep away all forms of trade barrier in the markets for goods and services, and in addition to allow the free movement of labour and capital in Europe. By opening up economic opportunity in this way, it is hoped that the single market will re-establish the EU's competitive edge *vis-à-vis* the USA and Japan.

Box 2.3 offers a brief discussion of one particular European market where the benefits of the single market programme are apparent, at least in theory. This is the market in financial services, such as banking and insurance. As the box makes clear, when national barriers in financial service provision disappear, consumers will certainly gain: a greater choice of services will become available at lower prices. The most efficient producers offering the best services will also gain: they will be rewarded with more custom. The only losers are likely to be the weaker producers,

Box 2.3

Towards a single market in financial services in Europe?

By Tony Snape

Pity the poor European consumer. The practical benefits of the single market continue to elude them. Chargeless banking, generous life assurances, cut-price mortgage rates and cheap car insurance ... look set to remain the province of domestic institutions for a long time to come.

You could blame the European Commission; it is blamed, after all, for everything else that goes wrong with the single market. The Commission launched a new green paper last week – *Financial Services: Meeting Consumers' Expectations* – which went off like a deflated balloon. But if the Commission had

its way, by now the Belgians would already be saving 30000 Belgian francs (£650) a year by buying comprehensive cover in Britain for their Peugeot 205s. Britons, in turn, would be throwing money at Spanish savings banks offering over 9 per cent interest a year. And Germans would be seeking French life assurance policies ...

... So pity the poor consumer. The choice in financial services is not [yet] there for the asking.

Source: *The European* 30 May 1996

who are currently able to stay in business only because their customers find it difficult to access markets in other parts of the EU.

We can express the anticipated gains from a European financial services market using our knowledge of demand and supply. In diagrammatic terms, the movement towards a single market in financial services in Europe would resemble the case depicted in Fig. 2.9. Here, because the market becomes composed only of more efficient producers (the weaker ones having lost custom and left the market), the supply curve shifts to the right from S_1 to S_2. *Ceteris paribus*, this is associated with an increase in the quantity of financial services demanded and supplied (from Q_1 to Q_2) and a fall in price (from P_1 to P_2). Note that the origin of the movement in the supply curve is consistent with our earlier analysis. The fact that the market is served by only the most efficient producers means that the cost base of producers on average has fallen. This is the equivalent of a reduction in input costs – which, as we know from our theoretical discussion, shifts the supply curve to the right. In essence,

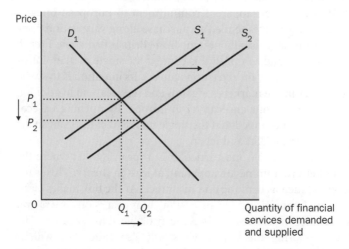

Fig. 2.9 The effect of the creation of a European market in financial services.

the single market programme is about promoting changes such as this in as many markets in Europe as possible. However, as our next case illustrates, in some markets there is relatively little room for manoeuvre.

The European car industry provides a somewhat contrasting example of the potential of the single market to effect major changes in the organization of production and consumption in the EU. As Box 2.4 makes clear, the central problem currently facing Europe's car makers is essentially that of excess supply. In Section 2.4 and Fig. 2.5 we argued that the usual reaction to excess supply in a market is for producers to lower prices until a market-clearing equilibrium is attained. There is some evidence (from the box) that this is happening in the European car market. However, there appear to be limits to the extent to which car makers are prepared to lower prices, because of the tightness of profit margins. A second possibility is for car makers to decrease supply. Box 2.4 suggests that this too is something that they have been trying: for example, by introducing short-term working and partial factory shut-downs.

Fig. 2.10 provides a demand and supply illustration of both options. Let us suppose that the market would be in equilibrium at price P_e and quantity Q_e, with demand curve D_1 and supply curve S_1. At price P_2, however, there is excess supply equal to FB. This is the disequilibrium position, which has been the focus for change.

Box 2.4

Engine of demand splutters: mergers and joint ventures should top European carmakers' agendas as they face overcapacity and declining profits

It has been an inauspicious start to the year for Europe's carmakers ... Excess production capacity and the poor outlook for car sales has reinforced the belief that Europe's car industry requires *structural changes to balance supply and demand*. Manufacturers have already taken limited steps to reduce costs by collaborating with each other. But the improbability of a long-term upturn in the market means that much more drastic steps – including big mergers – are again on the agenda.

'The essential problem is that long-run demand is not matched to long-run supply and Europe's carmakers have been too sluggish to react to the new realities in the market,' says Professor Garel Rhys, a specialist in motor industry economics at Cardiff Business School.

In spite of Western Europe's economic recovery after the recession, demand for new cars has been stalled ... Lower demand and the need, in many cases, for expensive special offers to sell cars have been reflected in poor profitability. 'Europe's car market has become saturated. Demand is now on a replacement-only basis, and even that is fragile,' says Mr Graham Morris, of Volkswagen's Audi subsidiary.

Excess capacity is the main problem. Europe's carmakers have been loathe to rationalize for fear of labour unrest, and governments have exerted pressure to minimize politically sensitive redundancies.

Many European carmakers have opted for short-term working and partial shutdowns to counter excess supply. But their efforts have been undermined by new capacity at other car companies. Toyota, Honda and Nissan, the three Japanese car companies which have set up in the UK, want to expand capacity to 650 000 vehicles a year by 1999 from 500 000 today.

The obvious answer to overcapacity, slack demand and tougher competition is rationalization and mergers. But Europe's carmakers have moved mountains to keep their independence ... The industry's economic importance – it can contribute almost a sixth of a country's gross domestic product – means any merger is bound to have a big macroeconomic impact. So not only private shareholders, but also trade unions and governments, are reluctant to make concessions when jobs and earnings are at stake.

In the absence of mergers, manufacturers have focused on reducing their production costs to compete with lower-priced rivals. 'Lean production' techniques, involving a plethora of measures to streamline organization on the shopfloor, have become ubiquitous.

Other tactics to achieve savings have included simplifying model ranges around a simple number of basic 'platforms' for vehicles and wresting price cuts from suppliers.

... While such attempts to lower manufacturers' costs are understandable, motor industry analysts doubt [these] will be enough to overcome the long-term problems of excess capacity and insufficient demand.

Source: *Financial Times* 15 February 1996 (emphases added)

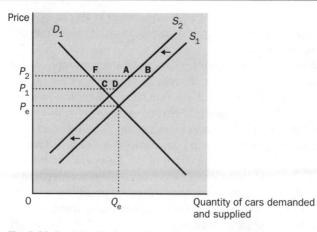

Fig. 2.10 Dealing with the problem of excess supply in the European car market.

Short-term working and partial factory shut downs, decreasing supply from S_1 to S_2, have reduced excess supply from FB to FA. As, in addition, prices have been bid down – in this illustration from P_2 to P_1 – excess supply has been squeezed still further: from FA to CD. The difficulty, however, is that – to date – these measures have been insufficient to deal *fully* with the problem of excess supply in the market. The longer-term solution suggested in the box is for the weaker firms to leave the industry or be taken over by the stronger ones, thus effecting a more sizeable re-duction in supply in the long term (shifting S_2 further to the left and squeezing the remaining excess supply CD out completely), leaving the European car market very much closer to, or even at, equilibrium. The main reason why this is not happening, or is happening only slowly, is that as the box indicates, Europe's car makers, backed by national governments and powerful trade unions, are reluctant to concede their independence. In the European car industry, then, the single market appears less likely to have the sort of impact anticipated in financial services.

While carmaking and financial service provision offer examples of industries where, in its single market programme, the EU seeks to reap the benefits of *laissez-faire*, in other areas *intervention* in markets is the preferred option. As noted, heavily state-managed agricultural production in Europe is the most obvious and – with associated claims of 'butter mountains' and 'wine lakes' – notorious case. We can again use supply and demand here to follow what is going on.

Agriculture in the EU is regulated by the Common Agricultural Policy (CAP). The CAP is actually a determined attempt to *prevent* the operation of market forces in European agriculture. This of course must mean that a free market in agriculture would produce outcomes that the EU does not want. In effect, the CAP works to pre-serve the kind of localized production that, for the most part, the EU would like to sweep away in its single market programme. If the CAP were abolished, a free market in European agriculture would tend to drive less efficient farmers out of business and, in the search for **economies of scale**, encourage the creation of much larger farms. These would be necessary to compete with low-cost food producers outside Europe who, given free market conditions, would be able to export greater volumes of output to meet European demand. So why does the EU wish to preserve relatively small-scale, fragmented and less efficient localized production? The simple answer is that it wants to protect the jobs and incomes of its farmers. Let us see how this is achieved.

Economies of scale: Arise when a larger output is produced without a proportionately equal increase in the costs of production. In agriculture this might involve, for example, the more intensive use of existing machinery as a farm extends its cultivated acreage. More output results but no new machines are required to help produce it, so unit costs fall.

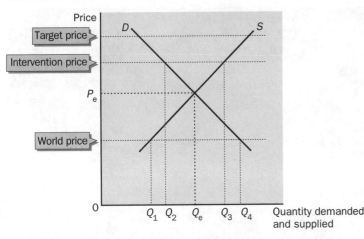

Fig. 2.11 Market intervention: the case of the Common Agricultural Policy.

Fig. 2.11 depicts the EU market for a particular agricultural commodity, say cereals. The supply and demand curves therefore represent the dispositions of EU producers and consumers respectively. Assuming there is no possibility of trade between the EU and the rest of the world, the equilibrium in this market is given by price P_e and quantity Q_e. Now, let us also assume that cereals can be produced more cheaply in the rest of the world (which, as it happens, *is* actually the case). This means of course that the prevailing world price for cereals is lower than P_e. Thus if free trade between the EU and the rest of the world were possible, European consumers could buy their cereals at the lower world price. In this case, the quantity demanded would be Q_4 but European producers would offer only Q_1. At the world price, therefore, cereal imports into the EU would amount to $Q_4 - Q_1$. In a completely free market for cereals, then, the relatively low world price would appear to benefit European consumers, who would pay less and collectively consume more. However, the EU's cereal output would fall and so, presumably, would the number of EU farmers in the now 'world articulated' cereals market.

This means that, for the CAP to fulfil its noted objective – the retention of the jobs and incomes of EU farmers – it must insulate or protect EU agricultural markets from those of the rest of the world. This is done by setting a target price for each agricultural commodity to be protected (not all are). Target prices are decided on the basis of farm production costs in the EU, with a 'mark-up' to allow for profit. Clearly, in Fig. 2.11, there is a big difference between the world price for cereals and the EU's target price, which means that EU consumers must be prevented from obtaining cereals at the lower world price (because they would not then buy EU cereals). This is done by the imposition of a tariff on cereal imports into the EU. A tariff is a tax on traded goods, and in this case it has the effect of raising the price of the EU's cereal imports close to the level of the target price. (If importers have to pay a tax on cereals they ship to the EU, the assumption is that they will pass the costs of the tax onto EU consumers in the form of higher prices.)

In addition to the target price, the EU also sets an intervention price for the agricultural commodities that it wishes to protect. This is a minimum price that the EU guarantees its farmers for the output they produce. In Fig. 2.11, note that at both the intervention price and the higher target price there is excess supply in the EU cereal

Overproduction in agriculture: part of the EU's grain mountain

market. As we have seen, disequilibrium prices of this sort are unstable. The accumulating unsold stocks they are left with should prompt farmers to sell at lower prices until the equilibrium price P_e is attained. To prevent this happening – and to prevent EU farmers from leaving the market – the EU itself purchases whatever excess supply arises at the intervention price. In Fig. 2.11 this amounts to $Q_3 - Q_2$. Purchases of this kind are the source of the infamous food 'mountains', for which the EU is often criticized. Because there is no demand for these agricultural surpluses, they are simply stored indefinitely at the EU's expense.

In summary, the effect of the CAP is to raise the prices of agricultural commodities in the EU. This encourages more farmers to remain in business than would be the case in a free market, fully integrated with the rest of the world. The positive outcome of the policy is therefore a higher number of farmers supported by subsidized incomes. The less attractive implications of the policy include the higher prices that EU consumers have to pay for agricultural produce, the sheer cost of the policy (alone it consumes over half of the EU's total budget), and its distortion of world trade (as, for example, the rest of the world has its capacity to export to the EU restricted).

Concluding remarks

On the basis of the examples reviewed in this section, the EU appears to have a rather inconsistent view as to the usefulness of the market mechanism. For industry in general, it anticipates that the articulation of market processes at the widest level will serve to enhance Europe's competitiveness in the world economy. However, for agriculture, the same market processes are judged to be harmful. Why the difference? The answer lies in the conditions of industry and agriculture in the EU relative to their conditions in the rest of the world. European industry already enjoys a level of overall competitiveness that is equivalent or very close to the world's best, and it is currently integrated into international markets in the same general way that, for example, US and Japanese industries are. Thus progress for European industry might well be predicated on the market-based improvement of an existing highly creditable performance. The relative performance of the agricultural sector in the EU when compared with the rest of the world is, however, generally inferior. The integration of European agriculture into the world market in agriculture is therefore difficult for the EU to accept because it would expose the uncompetitiveness of European farmers, and many of them would be driven out of business. The reason why this has not been allowed to happen has much to do with the political and lobbying strength of agricultural interests in the EU: witness for example the familiar spectacle of European capital cities clogged by the tractors or sheep of demonstrating farmers. The agricultural community is an able defender of the CAP, while those who have most to gain from its removal – EU consumers who would benefit from lower food prices – are largely without a collective voice.

Summary

◆ In theory, the free market provides a framework that allows producers and consumers to interact to their mutual satisfaction, without the need for any form of government intervention.

◆ For any given set of supply and demand schedules or curves, there is one equilibrium position where price, the quantity demanded, and the quantity supplied are in balance. All other prices indicate positions of disequilibrium in the market where producers and consumers are motivated to change their behaviour.

◆ The articulation of markets at wider levels raises the possibility of greater choice in production and consumption decisions.

◆ The EU's single market programme is an example of the wide-ranging application of market analysis to the real economic problem of slower growth in Europe over the 1970s and early 1980s.

◆ Nonetheless, where it feels it is justified and in response to strong producer lobbies, the EU continues to intervene heavily in certain agricultural markets.

Key terms

◆ Demand
◆ Supply
◆ The free market
◆ Equilibrium
◆ Excess supply
◆ Excess demand
◆ Disequilibrium
◆ The single market programme

◆ Common Agricultural Policy

◆ Market intervention

▮ Self-test questions

True (t) or false (f)

1. A change in the price of a good causes extensions or contractions in the quantity demanded.

2. Demand and supply in a market are always equal.

3. A change in the price of a good causes a shift in its demand curve.

4. Excess demand and excess supply can coexist in a market.

5. Changes in consumer incomes influence supply.

6. If the price of sugar falls, *ceteris paribus*, more sweets will be produced.

7. There is a positive relationship between the price of a good and its supply.

8. Excess supply will usually prompt increases in price.

9. 'Butter mountains' in Europe are a product of the market mechanism.

10. The Common Agricultural Policy raises the prices of many agricultural products in Europe.

Complete the following sentences by inserting the missing word(s)

1. The amount of a good or service that consumers wish to purchase at a particular price is called ____.

2. A movement along a demand or supply curve is referred to as an ____ or a ____.

3. A good used in conjunction with another good is called a ____.

4. When there is no tendency to change in a market, the market is said to be in ____.

5. When all goods are sold the market is said to ____.

6. The Common Agricultural Policy is an example of ____ in a market.

7. Butter and margarine are ____ for one another.

8. A price that fails to equate the quantities demanded and supplied in a market is said to be a ____ price.

▮ Questions for discussion

◆ What are the principal determinants of the demand for a particular commodity?

◆ What are the principal determinants of the supply of a particular commodity?

◆ Explain the process by which disequilibrium prices in a market give way to one unique equilibrium price.

◆ For a particular good, what will happen to the equilibrium price and quantity bought and sold following:

(i) an improvement in technology;

(ii) a change in tastes away from the good;

(iii)   an increase in the cost of producing it;

(iv)   an increase in consumers' incomes?

◆ Using an analysis of markets, explain the basis of the single market programme in Europe.

◆ How can governments offset movements toward equilibrium in markets?

◼ Further reading

If you have access to CD-ROM newspaper search facilities, you will be able to research conditions in many markets yourself. Try entering the keywords 'demand' and 'supply' together with the particular good you have in mind: 'apples', 'tea', 'wheat' or whatever. This is usually sufficient to locate material on recent developments in the markets for such goods. You will then be in a position to try to sketch out your own 'real world' market diagrams.

Levacic, R. 'Markets as coordinating devices' in R. Maidment and G. Thompson (eds) *Managing the United Kingdom* (London: Sage Publications, 1993). Offers a brief overview of the basis of the operation of markets.

Eatwell, J., M. Milgate and P. Newman (eds) *The Invisible Hand – The New Palgrave* (Basingstoke: Macmillan, 1987). Contains a number of short essays on Smith's metaphor for the operation of markets.

McDonald, F. and S. Dearden (eds) *European Economic Integration* (3rd ed.) (London: Longman, 1998). Provides a good summary of the economics of the European single market.

Seabrook, J. *The Myth of the Market* (Bideford: Green Books, 1990). Chapter 1 offers a brief and interesting polemic against the market.

◼ Internet links

More information about the European single market and other EU initiatives is available from the European Union Web site at: **http://europa.eu.int/index-en.htm**

CHAPTER 3

Markets and Economic Efficiency

Key issues

▶ Can markets produce levels of output that society as a whole judges appropriate?

▶ How can we add to our knowledge of how markets work?

▶ What factors determine how consumers and producers respond to price changes?

3.1 Introduction

In Chapters 1 and 2 we built up a picture of how markets can be used to answer the basic economic questions of what to produce, how to produce, and for whom to produce. In Chapter 1 we introduced the ideas of Adam Smith on the division of labour. Smith supposed that markets allowed individuals the freedom to develop and make the best use of their skills. Recall that this was good not just for the individual but for everyone. An extended division of labour allows all members of society to engage in a mutually supportive constellation of production and consumption activities. In Chapter 2 we saw that markets can also serve to harmonize the interests of individuals in their guises as producers and consumers. Left to freely adjust, markets reach equilibrium positions at which supply and demand are perfectly matched. However, we also noted that the state may choose to intervene in markets where the outcomes that result are not to its liking or are in some other way undesirable. We elaborate upon the reasons for state intervention in markets in Chapters 5 and 6, but for the moment we continue with our discussion of the operation of the free market.

In the present chapter we shall show that markets do not simply bring supply and demand together; they can do so in a way that optimizes the level of output of each good and service. In other words, the level of output of each good and service that free markets bring forth may be exactly the level desired by society as a whole. So the free market in western European economies for, say, televisions, provides for an output that we can demonstrate to be **socially efficient**. This is more than simply saying that there are no gluts or shortages of televisions; it suggests that, in some calcula-

Socially efficient output: One that society as a whole deems to be most desirable.

tion, we can judge that a market-derived level of television production is the *most* beneficial that society could have.

Having detailed this notion of free market social efficiency, we then move on in this chapter to consider two further market-based concepts: consumer and producer surplus, and elasticity. These add new layers to our knowledge of how markets work.

3.2 The market and socially efficient production

Demand and marginal utility

In Chapter 2, Sections 2.2 and 2.3, we discussed the shapes of demand and supply curves for a particular good or service. *Ceteris paribus*, demand was assumed to be inversely related to price: as price rises quantity demanded contracts, and *vice versa* (Fig. 2.1). By contrast, supply was assumed to be positively related to price: increases in price prompt extensions in the quantity supplied, and *vice versa* (Fig. 2.3). Now, while these assumptions are eminently reasonable, and indeed are fundamental to the whole canon of economics, a little reflection suggests that in their present form they are also *partial*, and therefore require some further elaboration.

We shall begin by reconsidering the relationship between demand and price. While reaffirming the noted inverse relationship here, let us look behind price as a determinant of the demand for a good or service, to include also the *satisfaction* that the consumer gets from the good or service: it is surely undeniable that this has some bearing on demand. How then might one adequately conceptualize and measure satisfaction? One approach to this problem involves the notion of **utility**. Utility and satisfaction are synonyms: both refer to the subjective pleasure that consumers derive from the goods and services they purchase. Now, because utility is subjective, it is in fact impossible to measure: we cannot know the precise degrees of satisfaction that different people get from a good or service because the scales of measurement they 'use' are internally generated. However, all is not lost; we can make one initial and general statement about the utility of consumers. This proposes that, as an individual's consumption of a particular good or service increases, so the extra or **marginal utility** he or she gets from it declines.

A simple example will serve to illustrate. It's a hot day in the park and you've been walking for half an hour. Fancy an ice cream? Of course you do. When you've had one you're very content: you derived a lot of utility from it. Fancy another? Well ... ok, yes, I will thanks. This is quite nice too but not quite as good as the first. It's the same kind of ice cream but you're feeling a bit full by the end of it. So, what has happened? You've had two ice creams, you enjoyed them both, and therefore your total utility went up on both occasions. However, the first ice cream was more enjoyable than the second, which means that the marginal or extra utility of the second was not as high as that from the first: marginal utility declines as consumption of the good increases. Now, fancy a third ice cream? Er, not really, but go on if you're buying. You manage to stuff this one down but, to be honest, it's a bit of an effort. Your total utility has again increased but only by a relatively small amount, and clearly the marginal utility of this third ice cream is also relatively small: marginal utility has declined still further. You decline the offer of a fourth: making yourself ill would mean a fall in total utility and negative marginal utility.

Utility: The satisfaction that a consumer receives from the consumption of a good or service.

Marginal utility: The extra utility that a consumer derives from each additional unit of a particular good or service he or she consumes.

The concept of declining marginal utility can be illustrated graphically. In Fig. 3.1, the marginal utility of ice cream consumption is depicted on the vertical axis, while the quantity consumed is depicted on the horizontal axis. MU is a marginal utility curve. The first ice cream at Q_1 yields MU_1 marginal utility. When consumption increases to Q_2, marginal utility falls to MU_2. Note, however, that total utility has increased. This is the vertical sum of MU_1 and MU_2. If consumption increases to Q_3, then marginal utility falls to MU_3. Finally, if Q_4 is consumed, the marginal utility of this fourth ice cream is less than zero, MU_4. In fact, at Q_4, marginal utility *and* total utility fall (total utility at $Q_4 = MU_1 + MU_2 + MU_3 + MU_4$).

So the general position is that, as consumption of a particular good or service increases, the marginal utility or extra satisfaction derived from successive units declines: this is known as **diminishing marginal utility**. But to what use can we put this finding? Consider again the demand curve introduced in Fig. 2.1. It depicts an inverse relationship between price and quantity demanded, whereas the marginal utility curve in Fig. 3.1 depicts a similar inverse relationship between marginal utility and quantity consumed. It follows that, *if* we can express marginal utility in terms of money, the two curves are congruent.

In our ice cream eating example, what valuation might be placed on each individual unit consumed? The first ice cream, Q_1, we know gives most utility, and therefore will be valued the highest by our consumer. The second ice cream, Q_2, gives less utility than the first and will be deemed less valuable as a consequence. Similarly, the third ice cream, Q_3, is less valuable than the second. Now, assume our consumer pays a price for each ice cream that is commensurate with the utility derived from it. This is shown in Fig. 3.2. Here, marginal utility (in money terms) and price are equated for each unit consumed, and accordingly the marginal utility and demand curves are shown as congruent curves (that is, they coincide exactly when superimposed on one another). Note that although, for ease of presentation, we have set this discussion at the level of the individual consumer, the same analysis can be applied to *all* consumers in a particular market. Their utility experiences, because they are subjective, will be different, but they will all unfold according to the same principle of marginal decline.

The congruence of the marginal utility and demand curves is important for two reasons. First, it demonstrates that the basic nature of demand reflects both the price

Diminishing marginal utility: The decline in marginal utility that occurs as more and more of a good or service is consumed.

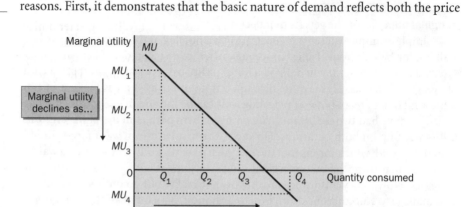

Fig. 3.1 Declining marginal utility.

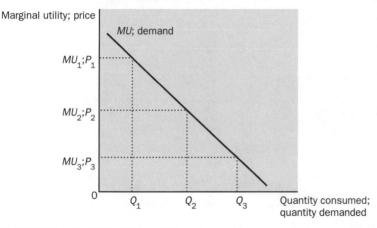

Fig. 3.2 The individual's marginal utility and demand curve.

of a good or service and the utility subjectively derived from it. Thus it provides for a more satisfactory conceptualization of demand. Second, it helps us to understand how the market can produce socially efficient outputs of goods and services. However, before we illustrate this point we need first to take another look at supply.

Supply and marginal cost

In Chapter 2, Section 2.3, we noted that higher prices encourage producers to increase the quantities supplied of a particular good or service. *Ceteris paribus*, higher prices make additional units of the good profitable, and hence to supply them becomes worthwhile. However, we now need to consider what happens to the *cost of production* as more units are produced. In fact, if firms try to raise production over a relatively short space of time, they come up against the well-known problem of **diminishing returns**. The concept of diminishing returns has clear implications for production costs.

We can illustrate this by reference to the example of ice cream production. In a very hot month (when demand is strong) the owner of a fleet of ice cream vans may think that increasing production is a good idea. This would involve a greater outlay on the ice cream itself, and higher petrol and maintenance costs for ice cream vans (more intensive use means more breakdowns). It would also involve greater staffing costs if drivers were paid overtime for working late on warm evenings. The general point is that the new *extra* units of output cost more than the *existing* units of output to produce. Moreover, as output successively increases, the greater the cost of each extra unit. Now, the cost of an extra unit of production is known as **marginal cost**. What we are arguing, therefore, is that as output is increased the marginal cost of output also increases.

This point is illustrated graphically in Fig. 3.3. The marginal cost curve MC is positively sloped such that, for example, the lower output, Q_1, carries a relatively low marginal cost MC_1, while the higher output, Q_2, carries a relatively higher marginal cost MC_2. Following our treatment of marginal utility and demand, the prescient reader will have anticipated that, because both costs and prices are expressed in money terms, we can determine that, in a perfectly competitive market (see Chapter 5, Section 5.3) the marginal cost and supply curves are in fact identical. In Fig. 3.4,

Law of diminishing returns: States that if more of a variable-factor input is employed, holding the quantity of other inputs constant, the marginal product of the variable factor input will eventually decrease.

Marginal cost: The change in total cost resulting from increasing production by one unit.

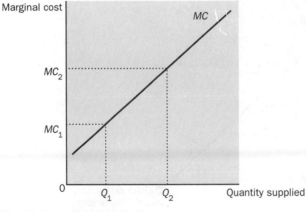

Fig. 3.3 Increasing marginal cost.

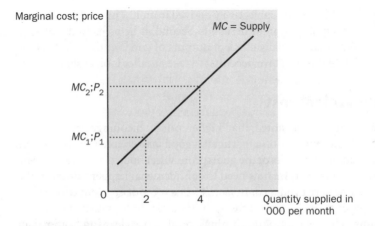

Fig. 3.4 The producer's marginal cost and supply curve.

operating with a single marginal cost/supply curve, price P_1 and marginal cost MC_1 encourage the production of 2000 ice creams per month. However, if price rises to P_2, then this enables the producer to absorb the higher marginal cost MC_2 and encourages the production of 4000 ice creams per month. The higher output level is therefore justified only if the warm weather permits the producer to set the higher price. Note that for ease of presentation, although we have again set the discussion at the level of the individual (in this case the individual producer), the same analysis can be applied to all producers in a particular market: all will experience the same phenomenon of rising marginal cost, and will therefore increase output only when higher prices allow them to. This analysis makes our conceptualization of supply a little more sophisticated than that presented in Chapter 2, as it now explicitly references both price and cost, rather than just price alone.

Having deepened our knowledge of the basis of demand and supply using the notion of marginality, we are now in a position to demonstrate how the market may be able to produce a socially efficient output of any particular good or service. As noted in Section 3.1, this implies more than the matching of demand with supply; it suggests that society considers a market-derived output to be the most desirable in terms of the *satisfaction* it obtains from the output and in acknowledgement of its *social cost*.

Marginal social cost and marginal social benefit

In Fig. 3.5, two schedules are depicted: **marginal social cost** (*MSC*) and **marginal social benefit** (*MSB*). Following our earlier analysis, these are congruent with the supply and demand curves for the particular good in question. *MSC* is the cost to society of producing an additional unit of output. In the analysis that immediately follows, we can justifiably deem it to be a representation of society's view of marginal cost on the grounds that (i) individual suppliers will be motivated to minimize the costs they incur and (ii) these costs are assumed to be borne only by producers, with no other costs being incurred by other members of society. In Chapter 6 we relax the latter assumption to examine the damaging effects of so-called negative externalities or third-party effects on markets. The *MSB* curve is the combination of all the individual marginal utility curves in the market. It represents *society's* view of the marginal benefit of additional output consumed because it summarizes the subjective perceptions of a good's marginal utility for all those consumers who choose to enter the market in question.

Now consider the four outputs marked in Fig. 3.5. For ease of analysis, let us interpret these as representing four single units of output. Of these only one, Q_3 (or 3 units), represents a market equilibrium. Here the supply and demand curves intersect, and therefore both consumers and producers in the market are content and there is no motivation for changes in price (P_3) or output. Using the congruent *MSC* and *MSB* curves, we can also show that Q_3 is a *socially efficient* output. Consider the other three output positions represented in Fig. 3.5. What is the social view of the unit Q_1: should this unit be produced? The decision rests upon society's view of the benefit derived from this unit, set against its cost. The *MSB* of Q_1 is represented by the price that consumers are prepared to pay for it: that is, P_5. So society values this unit as the equivalent of price P_5. The marginal social cost of Q_1 is P_1: lower than society's valuation of it. This unit, therefore, *should* be produced because its value to society is greater than its cost. The net social benefit of Q_1 is $P_5 - P_1$, measured in Fig. 3.5 by the distance AB. Following the same line of argument, it should be clear that

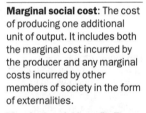

Marginal social cost: The cost of producing one additional unit of output. It includes both the marginal cost incurred by the producer and any marginal costs incurred by other members of society in the form of externalities.

Marginal social benefit: The money value of the benefit from one additional unit of consumption.

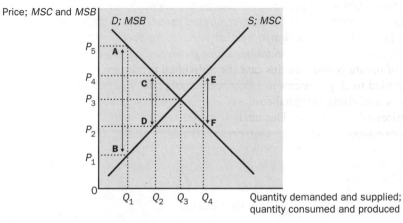

Fig. 3.5 Equating marginal social cost and marginal social benefit: a socially efficient output.

the production of the second unit, Q_2, is also socially justified. The *MSB* of Q_2 is P_4: higher than its *MSC* of P_2. The net social benefit associated with Q_2 is measured by the distance CD: this unit too merits production. The unit of output Q_4 is, however, a rather different proposition. The marginal social cost of Q_4 exceeds its marginal social benefit and therefore there is a net social cost associated with this unit indicated by the distance EF. The social judgement is therefore that *this unit should not be produced*. Note that any additional units of output beyond Q_4 would carry progressively larger net social costs, and their production would also be socially undesirable.

We are now in a position to reconsider the market equilibrium output Q_3. Here *MSC* equals *MSB*, and so there is neither net cost or benefit associated with the production of this unit. Should it be produced? The answer is yes. To understand why, imagine that the quantity axis in Fig. 3.5 represents not 4 discrete units of production but 400. If Q_2 represents 200 units, we can see that units 201, 202, 203 etc. all carry net benefit, and therefore their production is socially justified. In fact, each successive unit up to the 300th (Q_3) carries some net benefit, although it is declining as production increases. After the 300th unit, however, each extra unit carries an increasing net *dis*benefit. Thus none of these extra units are socially desirable; they should not be produced. This means that the 300th unit marks the 'boundary' between socially desirable and socially undesirable production for the good in question. The socially efficient output therefore must be at Q_3 where the *MSB* and *MSC* curves intersect and the production of net 'benefit yielding' units is maximized. This analysis demonstrates that the market can produce both an equilibrium output as a result of the interaction of supply and demand *and* one that is judged to be efficient in terms of the criteria of social benefit and cost.

Producer surplus: The difference between the price at which a producer would have been willing to supply a good and the price the producer actually receives.

3.3 Producer surplus

Let us now examine **producer surplus**, a concept best explained diagrammatically. In Fig. 3.6 we show the supply curve of a single producer. Following our earlier analysis

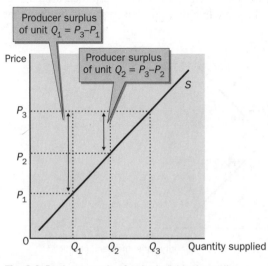

Fig. 3.6 Producer surplus for the individual supplier.

of price and rising marginal cost, we know that this slopes upwards from left to right. We have marked three price and supply points on the curve. Let us assume that P_3 is the equilibrium market price faced by our supplier. At this price, he or she is motivated to supply Q_3 units of the good or service in question. Now, assuming these are three individual units, consider the supplier's view of each unit in turn. For the first unit Q_1, the supplier receives the prevailing market price P_3. However, in the case of this particular unit alone, he or she would be prepared to accept only P_1 – as motivation is reflected in the supply curve. For this unit, then, the producer obtains a surplus of $P_3 - P_1$ over and above the price necessary to induce its supply. In the case of the second unit Q_2, the price received by the producer is again the market price P_3 but the price required to induce Q_2's supply is P_2. The producer surplus on Q_2 is therefore $P_3 - P_2$. Finally, for Q_3, the market price and the price the producer requires to make this unit available are identical at P_3 and therefore there is *no* producer surplus on this unit.

Fig. 3.7 illustrates producer surplus for an entire market, rather than for a single supplier. Here, at the prevailing market price P_1, producers are motivated to supply Q_1 units. Total producer surplus is given by the combined surpluses earned on each particular unit sold in the market. In Fig. 3.7, this is indicated by the area of the triangle ABC. It is also useful at this point to note that the rectangle ABDE, as it is formed by the product of the price of each unit and the quantity sold, simultaneously represents the total expenditure of consumers and the total revenue earned by producers in the market. Finally, it follows that the quadrilateral CBDE indicates the volume of revenue that producers require to induce them to supply Q_1 units of the good or service in question.

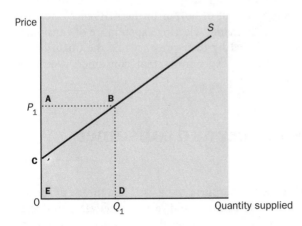

Fig. 3.7 Producer surplus in the market.

3.4 Consumer surplus

We now turn to the related concept of **consumer surplus**. Fig. 3.8 depicts the demand curve for an individual consumer. Let us assume that P_3 is the prevailing market price such that he or she demands Q_3 (individual) units. Now consider, in turn, each unit demanded, starting with Q_1. Here, although the consumer is required to pay the market price P_3, he or she is actually willing to pay the higher

Consumer surplus: The difference between what a consumer would have been willing to pay and what the consumer actually pays.

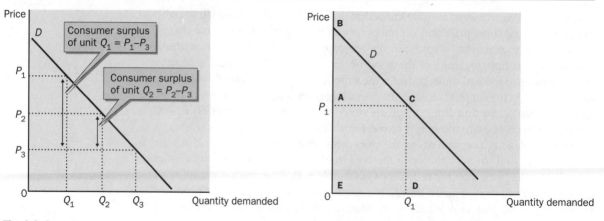

Fig. 3.8 Consumer surplus for the individual.   **Fig. 3.9** Consumer surplus in the market.

price P_1. The difference between the price paid and the price the consumer is willing to pay $(P_1 - P_3)$ is the consumer surplus associated with the unit in question. For Q_2 the price paid is P_3, but the consumer would be content to pay P_2; here, then, consumer surplus is $P_2 - P_3$. Finally, because the price paid for the last unit, Q_3, is the same as the price that the consumer is willing to pay for it, there is no consumer surplus associated with this unit.

Fig. 3.9 illustrates consumer surplus at the level of the market rather than of the individual. Here, at price P_1 and quantity demanded Q_1, the total amount of consumer surplus in the market is given by the triangle ABC. This is the sum of the consumer surplus associated with each unit of output in the market. Notice that the rectangle ACDE represents the total market-clearing expenditure of consumers (the number of goods bought multiplied by their price), while the quadrilateral BCDE represents the higher amount of expenditure that consumers would be willing to undertake to obtain Q_1.

3.5   Applying producer and consumer surplus

The concepts of producer and consumer surplus can be used as a means of further developing our understanding of the sometimes fluid relations between producers and consumers in a market. Consider for example the differences between the operation of the market for packets of plain biscuits and the second-hand car market. For the sake of argument, we may reasonably assume that the prices of packets of plain biscuits are generally uniform, despite differences in branding. It seems to make sense, therefore, to think of *the* equilibrium market price for packets of plain biscuits. In the second-hand car market there is, by comparison, much less certainty over prices. In part, this reflects variation in the quality of the goods on offer. Over and above make and model, the price of each second-hand car will be influenced by such factors as age, condition, mileage, the presence or absence of a service history, and so on. However, even after taking these things into account, the price paid for a second-hand car will still usually be the result of a *bargaining process* between buyer and seller. If you're in the market for a car and you see one you fancy for, say, £2750, you might think it reasonable to offer £2250. Eventually a price of £2500 is agreed. What has happened here? You, the consumer, have in fact made implicit use of the concept of producer surplus. You suspected that the seller would accept a lower price than advertised, and you were right. Conversely, if the seller pitched his or her original price fairly high, it might have been in the expectation that the buyer could be persuaded to pay more: an attempt, in other words, to annex some of your consumer surplus. In the market for plain biscuits, bargaining like this does not occur. Individual consumers buy at the prevailing market price or they don't buy at all: there are no offers and counter-offers for a packet of plain biscuits, and there are no real designs on the surplus of the other side of the market. The differences between the two markets reflect their particular institutional settings and traditions. The small second-hand car dealer can treat customers differently because each customer will be unaware of the exact prices paid by others. In contrast, in the biscuit market consumers are aware of, and expect to pay, the ruling market price.

While the second-hand car market provides a ready and notorious example of how producers and consumers can try to annex each others' surpluses, the same thing happens in many other markets, though perhaps in less obvious ways. Consider, for example, the opportunities afforded to producers by **market segmentation**. If producers can divide up their market into different parts and, crucially, prevent consumers from moving between them, then it becomes possible to charge different prices to different sets of consumers for the same product. This allows producers to tap elements of consumer surplus in the market. Rail fares, for example, usually vary between peak and off-peak periods. In this case, the market is segmented by *time*. Higher fares during peak hours take advantage of people's need to get to and from work and their willingness to pay more to fulfil this need than would be the case if they were simply taking an occasional trip during the middle of the day.

Fig. 3.10 illustrates how market segmentation can be used by producers to siphon off some element of consumer surplus. At price P_1, the demand (for rail journeys) would be Q_1. Here, consumer surplus is represented by the triangle CEF. Now, let us

Market segmentation: Involves the division of a market by the producer into a number of discrete parts between which consumers cannot easily move.

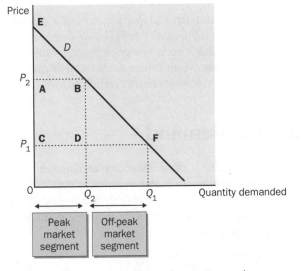

Fig. 3.10 Market segmentation and consumer surplus.

assume that Q_2 rail journeys are made during peak hours and that, for these hours, the market will bear the higher price P_2 (as indicated by the demand curve). In effect we have two separate markets for the same service: a peak market in which price P_2 yields a demand for Q_2 journeys, and an off-peak market in which price P_1 yields a demand for $Q_1 - Q_2$ journeys. Notice that the outcome of the exercise has been extremely beneficial to the producer. Of the area of consumer surplus CEF, a portion ABCD now accrues to the producer instead of the consumer. Of course, we have to assume here that the higher peak price is tolerated by consumers, and does not for example induce them to resort to alternative forms of transport, such as the private car, for peak period journeys. Incidentally, referring again briefly to our earlier example, you might notice that the seller of second-hand cars, striking a series of individual deals with his or her customers, is in effect segmenting the market to the finest possible level.

3.6 Elasticity in the market

The concept of elasticity is the final element to be introduced into our analysis of the operation of markets. What is elasticity? In Chapter 2, Sections 2.2 and 2.3, we reviewed the respective sets of factors that determine the demand for and supply of a particular good or service. For example, following the usual *ceteris paribus* assumption, higher prices reduce the quantity demanded and lower prices push it up (the analytical terms we used were contractions and extensions of the quantity demanded), but what about the *strength of response*? When, for example, the price of a good increases by say 5 per cent, by how much does the quantity demanded contract – about the same, more, much more, or less? This is clearly a significant question, both for economists who want to understand how markets work, and particularly for those who have to make their living in them. If a firm is considering a price change for a product it makes, it will want to know the likely effect of the change. Will a price reduction allow it to sell a lot more units of output, or only a few more, and what will be the effect upon the overall level of revenue? The concept of elasticity allows us to answer such questions.

We conceptualize the response of supply and demand to other economic changes as the *elasticity* of supply or demand. When the quantity supplied or demanded is relatively unresponsive to a particular stimulus – such as a price change – they are said to be *inelastic*. When they are more responsive and change substantially they are said to be *elastic*. We define and extend these categories more carefully below.

3.7 Price elasticity of demand

Price elasticity of demand:
The proportionate (or percentage) change in the quantity demanded of a good divided by the proportionate (or percentage) change in its price that brought it about.

The most commonly used form of elasticity is **price elasticity of demand**. This measures the responsiveness of the quantity demanded of a particular good or service to changes in its price. More formally, the price elasticity of demand of a good or service, P_{ed}, is measured by the proportionate change in its quantity demanded divided by the proportionate change in price that brings this about:

$$P_{ed} = \frac{\text{Proportionate change in quantity demanded}}{\text{Proportionate change in price}} \qquad (3.1)$$

Price elasticity of demand can be illustrated diagrammatically. In Fig. 3.11 we show a hypothetical market for new cars. Two among many possible prices are considered, together with the respective quantities demanded at each price. Now, we wish to use the concept of elasticity in this market, which means, following the equation above, that we have to find proportionate changes in quantity demanded and price. But there is a snag here. The proportionate change in price will depend upon whether we are considering a price *increase* (from £12 000 to £15 000 per car) or a *decrease* (from £15 000 to £12 000). When price increases, the proportionate change is one quarter, or 25 per cent (an increase of £3000 over the original price of £12 000). But if price falls from £15 000 to £12 000, then the proportionate change is one fifth, or 20 per cent (a decrease of £3000 on the original price of £15 000). In order to overcome this problem and arrive at the same number for a proportionate price change in either direction, we express the change in price as a proportion or percentage of the average

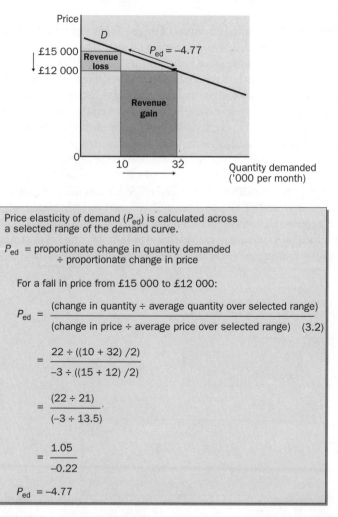

Price elasticity of demand (P_{ed}) is calculated across a selected range of the demand curve.

P_{ed} = proportionate change in quantity demanded
          ÷ proportionate change in price

For a fall in price from £15 000 to £12 000:

$$P_{ed} = \frac{\text{(change in quantity} \div \text{average quantity over selected range)}}{\text{(change in price} \div \text{average price over selected range)}} \quad (3.2)$$

$$= \frac{22 \div ((10 + 32)/2)}{-3 \div ((15 + 12)/2)}$$

$$= \frac{(22 \div 21)}{(-3 \div 13.5)}$$

$$= \frac{1.05}{-0.22}$$

$$P_{ed} = -4.77$$

Fig. 3.11 Price elasticity of demand in the market for new cars. (Note that, although our calculation is for a decrease in price, the same figure of 4.77 would result for a price increase. This is because we have expressed the change in price and quantity as a proportion of their average values over the selected range.)

Price elastic: Describes a situation in which the proportionate change in quantity demanded is greater than the proportionate change in price; elasticity is greater than 1.

Price inelastic: Describes a situation in which the proportionate change in quantity demanded is less than the proportionate change in price; elasticity is less than 1.

price over the range in which we are interested. In this case, the average price is £13 500 ((£12 000 + £15 000)/2). We follow the same procedure when calculating proportionate changes in quantity demanded.

We now have a slightly more sophisticated means of calculating price elasticity of demand. In Fig. 3.11, following equation (3.1), we arrive at a value for price elasticity of demand in our example of –4.77 (correct to two decimal places). But what does this number tell us? In fact, it indicates that, for the range in question, demand is **price elastic**: in other words, the price change (in either direction) will produce a *more than proportionate response* in the quantity demanded. Notice also that, as price is cut, there is an increase in the net revenue earned on the sale of cars. This increase is derived from the combination of the area of revenue loss (£3000 × 10 000 cars = £30 million per month) and the area of revenue gain (£12 000 × 22 000 cars = £264 million per month), and amounts to £234 million per month. Of course, for a price increase from £12 000 to £15 000 there would be a net revenue loss of £234 million per month.

Fig. 3.12 presents two further worked examples of price elasticity of demand. In the first case, as price falls from £10 to £9, demand can again be seen to be price elastic. The gain in net revenue associated with the price reduction is also clearly evident in this case. However, when price falls from £3 to £2 price elasticity of demand is calculated at –0.43. This is a case of **inelastic demand**, in that the price change induces a *less than proportionate response* in the quantity demanded. Notice here that the price reduction is clearly associated with a net loss in revenue (the areas of revenue loss and gain for this price reduction are marked L and G respectively). We have now uncovered the two *main* classes of elasticity. When the quantity demanded responds more than proportionately to a price change it is said to be elastic, and will carry a value greater than 1. On the other hand, when the quantity demanded responds less than proportionately to a price change it is said to be inelastic, and will carry a value less than 1. Although, given the inverse relationship between price and quantity demanded, the values of price elasticity of demand are negative, the convention is to omit the minus sign to avoid any possible confusion. We shall follow this custom from now on.

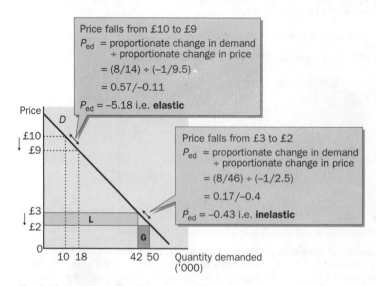

Fig. 3.12 Variation in elasticity along a demand curve.

Beyond the two main cases of price elastic and inelastic demand, the prescient reader may have anticipated other possibilities. The quantity demanded may respond *proportionately* to a change in price. Here $P_{ed} = 1$. This is known as **unit elasticity**. An example of unit elasticity is presented in Fig. 3.13(a). Notice, incidentally, that here the loss and gain in revenue resulting from changes in the price and quantity demanded are identical. Of course, it may be that quantity demanded is completely *unresponsive* to changes in price. In such cases demand is said to be **perfectly inelastic**. Or there may be a *perfect* response, inasmuch as the quantity demanded is infinitely large at one unique price and zero at all other possible prices. Here demand is said to be **perfectly elastic**. Fig. 3.13(b) and (c) depict examples of these two cases. Notice that for the vertical perfectly inelastic demand curve, regardless of whatever price is set over the range of the curve, the quantity demanded remains static at Q_1. Here P_{ed} = zero, consistent with the complete unresponsiveness of quantity demanded to a change in price. In the case of the perfectly elastic curve, at price P_1 there is an infinitely elastic demand for the good or service but at all other prices quantity demanded evaporates completely. Here $P_{ed} = \infty$ (infinity), consistent with an infinitely large response of quantity demanded to the change in price.

In summary, then, price elasticity of demand can range in value from zero (perfectly unresponsive) to infinity (perfectly responsive) as follows:

- *Perfectly inelastic demand*: Quantity demanded fails to respond to price changes ($P_{ed} = 0$).
- *Inelastic demand*: The response of quantity demanded is proportionately smaller than the price change; ($P_{ed} < 1$).
- *Unit elastic demand*: The response of quantity demanded is proportionately equal to the price change ($P_{ed} = 1$).
- *Elastic demand*: The response of quantity demanded is proportionately greater than the price change ($P_{ed} > 1$).
- *Perfectly elastic demand*: The response of quantity demanded to the price change is infinitely large ($P_{ed} = \infty$).

Unit elasticity: Situation where the proportionate change in quantity demanded is equal to the proportionate change in price; elasticity is 1.

Perfect inelasticity: Arises where the quantity demanded does *not* respond to a change in price; elasticity is 0.

Perfect elasticity: Situation in which the response of quantity demanded to a price change is infinitely large; elasticity is ∞.

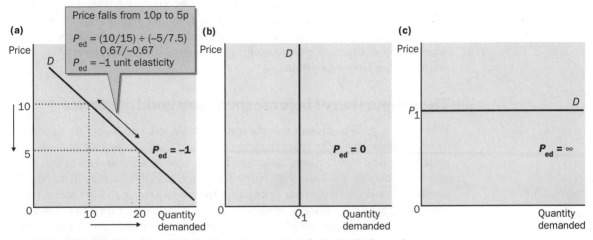

Fig. 3.13 (a) Unit elasticity, (b) perfectly inelastic demand, (c) perfectly elastic demand.

3.8 Determinants of price elasticity of demand

The most important determinants of price elasticity of demand are the availability of substitutes; the proportion of income spent on a good or service; and time.

The availability of substitutes

Goods and services that have close *substitutes* tend to have relatively price elastic demand structures; those with only distant substitutes tend to be more price inelastic. There are for example many brands of chocolate bar sold in Europe, and most tend to be similarly priced. Manufacturers are generally unwilling to raise their prices for fear that custom will leak to their competitors' products. This is an implicit acknowlegement that the demand for any particular chocolate bar is price elastic and is so precisely because consumers enjoy a wide range of choice. Incidentally, where a market is characterized by a high degree of choice-driven price elasticity, producers have a great incentive to develop brand loyalties. Brand loyalty establishes the superiority of a particular good or service over its rival products in the mind of the consumer, and serves to reduce its price elasticity: people may be willing to pay a little more for it because of its perceived qualities. In the chocolate industry the Mars bar has such a reputation.

Oil is an often quoted example of a good with *few close substitutes* (at least in the short run) and, as a consequence, an inelastic demand structure. In 1973–74 and 1979, a group of the world's leading oil producers – the OPEC nations, in what became known as 'oil shocks' – effectively quadrupled and then doubled the world price of oil. The industrialized non-oil-producing nations had little immediate choice except to meet the inflated oil prices as their economies were highly oil-dependent. This of course led to significantly increased flows of revenue from oil-importing countries to the oil producers.

The price inelastic demand qualities of cigarettes and alcohol are equally known, not least by those governments that choose to tax these commodities in order to raise revenue. Such taxes are passed by producers on to their customers in the form of higher prices. The working assumption here, of course, is that the higher prices, because they brush up against inelastic demand, do not significantly reduce consumption. Governments could not tax (demand elastic) chocolate bars with the same degree of impunity: people would snack instead on the dozens of alternatives available from any sweet counter.

The proportion of income spent on a good or service

When only a small portion of income is spent on a good, purchasers are thought to be relatively indifferent to price changes in terms of their demand for it: demand in such case will be more inelastic. Consider for example the little packets of sauce sold in fish and chip shops. These cost only a few pence. Will the quantity demanded be significantly reduced if say their price jumps from say 4p to 5p: a 22 per cent increase (on the average price principle introduced earlier)? The suggestion is that it will not: when the pubs shut and people are buying their chips or whatever, a penny extra won't lever many of them away from their usual order. Demand here then is *price inelastic.* However, what might be the demand reaction to an equivalent proportionate rise in the price of, say, a washing machine? Washing machines cost several hundred pounds, which is a much more significant slice of the average person's income. The same order of price increase here might involve the outlay of an extra £100 or so. This, it is suggested, would be more likely to significantly affect the quantity demanded: the response in other words would be more *elastic* in nature because the good in question takes up a greater proportion of the consumer's income.

Time

Demand patterns often do not respond instantaneously to price changes. Take, for example, the demand for national newspapers. Newspapers have substitutes readily available in the form of rival titles and rival news media. This suggests that the demand for particular newspaper titles should be price elastic, and this indeed is the case. However, demand is not *instantaneously* elastic. If the price of one title rises, those who customarily buy it may not at first notice because they have the paper delivered and pay for it weekly or because they're not particularly alert in the shop first thing in the morning. They continue to buy it for these reasons and also perhaps because it reflects their views, they like a particular commentator whose byline it carries, and so on. However, some readers will notice the price rise – certainly after a day or two, or when they next pay their paper bill – and they may then begin to sample rival titles. This *gradual* change means that price elasticity of demand is likely to be more inelastic immediately after a price rise than later on. Once consumers have had time to register the price change in their minds they *then* begin to seek out close substitutes for the good or service in question. This is the case even for commodities that are generally recognized to be price inelastic in character, such as oil. The oil price rises referred to earlier did not immediately send consumers off in search of alternatives because these did not readily exist. It did, however, prompt oil-importing countries to begin to introduce economizing measures that *over time* reduced the amount of oil they needed to import – most obviously people began to drive cars that offered better fuel consumption. Oil is still a price inelastic commodity, it is just *less* price inelastic after the price increases of 1973–74 and 1979 and the passage of time.

3.9 Applying price elasticity of demand

An awareness of price elasticity of demand is clearly essential if we are to understand consumer responses to the pricing structures set in particular markets. We are already aware that producers cannot afford to misread market conditions. If, for example, price is set above its equilibrium level, the market will fail to clear: there will be excess supply. However, the extent of excess supply will increase as price elasticity of demand increases.

As an illustration of this possibility, Box 3.1 reviews the rather unimaginative pricing structures set by the English Football Association for the FA Cup semi-finals in 1996. These are compared with the much more nuanced pricing arrangements of the Royal Opera House. What the material in the box demonstrates is that the FA assumed that the demand for semi-final tickets was much more price *inelastic* than was actually the case. For both games some of the tickets for the most highly priced

Box 3.1

The Football Association and Opera House share a worthy goal

Recent events ... in football showed a total failure to appreciate basic supply and demand principles ...

The Football Association came under fire for somehow failing to sell out one of the highlights of the soccer calendar, the semi-final between two of Britain's most passionately followed and on-form clubs. The game between Liverpool and Aston Villa should have been played in front of a capacity crowd. It was held at Old Trafford, the home ground of Manchester United and a modern, high class stadium. It was within easy travelling distance of both visiting teams' fans.

Granted, it was on Sky television, but any good football supporter will tell you that watching the match on TV is not as good as being there. So why was the ground only 80 per cent full? Liverpool returned 6000 of their 23 500 tickets unsold and Aston Villa returned 4400 of their 23 004. The FA imposed a pricing structure at Old Trafford which took the average weighted price to £31.68. Almost all of the Old Trafford returns were tickets priced at the top level of £38.

But at Villa Park, the venue of the other semi-final played on the same day and televised live by the BBC, Chelsea sold all of their 18 500 allocation while Manchester United sold all but 700 of their 19 000. The 700 outstanding were all priced at £38.

The key difference seemed to be that the smarter Old Trafford ground had 86 per cent of its seats priced at £38 or £30, while Villa Park mustered 67 per cent of the better appointed [seats]. The market almost cleared at Villa Park but by the accident of its seating status rather than by the design of the FA.

The FA got it wrong in both cases. It assumed that demand was less [price] elastic than it proved to be and so the market did not clear.

Perhaps the FA could have learned a lesson from the Royal Opera House, an organization which has become used to the allegation of unjustifiable prices. On closer inspection the allegations seem a little harsh. The Opera House has a pricing system with 131 levels. The range depends on the performance. Thus, for Wagner's *The Ring*, which corporate affairs director Keith Cooper

compared with an FA Cup semi-final as opposed to a Domingo concert which would be the final itself, the average price was £76 with the range starting at under £50 (800 of the 2000 tickets) and rising to £140 (for 124 of the total). Result: full house. But for a recent performance of three modern ballets, the average ticket price was £17.80 with a range of £2 to £34, and 800 of the seats available priced at £13.50 or less. Result: also full house. The comparison, like most, is flawed because the Royal Opera House's supply curve goes vertical at 2000 tickets whereas Old Trafford's has to reach almost 25 times that before no more seats are available. There are other factors to consider, such as popular appeal and income. Is opera's popularity as widespread as football's, and do most football fans enjoy the same earnings as opera devotees?

The logical step, economically speaking, would be for football and opera organizers to test the elasticity of demand until they discovered the price equilibrium.

Source: The Guardian 8 April 1996.
© *The Guardian* 1996.

seats were unsold, and at the ground with more seats in this category the attendance was only 80 per cent of capacity. Demand, in other words, was too elastic to permit the market to clear in the face of high ticket prices (and, most significantly, prices much higher than fans were accustomed to paying for the season's league games). So what caused the FA to misread the elasticity conditions? In each football season there are only two FA Cup semi-finals. This might suggest that the availability of close substitutes is minimal. However, as Box 3.1 indicates, both games were screened live on television, which is certainly one form of substitute. In addition, other rarely available high-quality (and highly priced) football matches were to follow close on the semi-finals: most obviously the final itself but also the 31 international matches of the Euro 96 championship, which were to be played in England. Taking these factors into account, the pricing structure for the semi-finals almost certainly needed to be closer to that set for normal league games. This would have ensured the norm for FA Cup semi-finals of capacity attendances. In the case of the Royal Opera House, the *much greater* variability of the pricing structure is intended to reflect the uneven level of demand anticipated for different kinds of performance. This is an explicit recognition that elasticity conditions must be respected if markets are to clear. Assuming that capacity attendances are desired at semi-finals, the FA would do well to take heed.

3.10 Other forms of elasticity

Income elasticity of demand

In Chapter 2, Section 2.2, we considered a range of factors other than price that influenced the demand for a good or service. These factors too can be placed in an elasticity framework. We suggested for example that demand can vary positively with consumers' income: higher incomes *ceteris paribus* prompted the demand curve for a normal good to shift to the right, while lower incomes caused it to shift to the left (Fig. 2.2). The question now arises: how responsive is the quantity demanded of a good to a change in income? We can resolve this issue using the concept of **income elasticity of demand**.

Income elasticity of demand, Y_{ed}, measures the responsiveness of the quantity of a good demanded to changes in income. It is calculated using an approach similar to that which allowed us to calculate price elasticity of demand. The equation for income elasticity of demand is

$$Y_{ed} = \frac{\text{Proportionate change in quantity demanded}}{\text{Proportionate change in income}} \tag{3.3}$$

Generally, we would expect Y_{ed} to be positive. In other words, higher incomes would be associated with an increase in demand, and *vice versa*. However, this is not always the case; in some circumstances higher incomes can prompt a decrease in the demand for particular goods and services. In such cases Y_{ed} will be negative. For example, rising incomes in Britain over the last 30 years have substantially altered the way people spend their holiday time. As many more people can afford to travel abroad for longer periods, the demand for holidays in traditional seaside towns has declined. Where Y_{ed} is negative, the relevant goods and services are said to be **inferior**. In contrast, as noted in Chapter 2, *normal* goods are those for which demand increases as income increases.

We can identify two sets of normal good. The first is that for which Y_{ed} is *inelastic* (<1 i.e. less than 1). An obvious example here is the demand for basic foods. In Europe, where incomes are already relatively high, the demand for basic foods is unlikely to increase much even when incomes rise still further. Consumers are more likely to spend their extra incomes on 'luxury' goods such as cars and foreign holidays. Of course, there may be changes in the *way* people consume food as incomes rise – they will be more likely to eat out, for example – but the actual level of basic food consumption will increase relatively slowly.

The second kind of normal good possesses an *elastic* Y_{ed} (>1 i.e. greater than 1). Here, when incomes rise, there is a proportionately greater increase in demand. Examples of income-elastic goods would typically include the kinds of luxury items mentioned above. In the richer societies, most basic needs – such as those for food and housing – are already amply met, and so further increases in income tend to be directed towards cars, foreign holidays and so on.

Applying income elasticity of demand

The concept of income elasticity of demand can usefully contribute to, amongst other things, an understanding of the patterns of specialization and development that have emerged in the international economy over the last 30 years. Before this

Income elasticity of demand: The proportionate change in the quantity of a good demanded divided by the proportionate change in consumers' incomes.

Inferior good: One for which demand decreases when income increases.

period there was a clear and long-established *international division of labour* within which, broadly speaking, the industrial countries produced manufactured goods while most other less developed countries (LDCs) specialized in the production of agricultural output and raw materials. However, during the 1960s and 1970s a number of LDCs successfully reallocated productive resources away from old dependences on agriculture and raw materials and switched them instead into manufacturing. Foremost amongst these so-called *newly industrializing countries* (NICs) are South Korea, Hong Kong, Singapore and Taiwan. Now the point here is that the economic success of the NICs is underpinned by their awareness of the pattern of world income elasticity of demand. Despite regrettably wide differences in economic growth between its different regions, the world itself is as a whole a richer place than it has ever been hitherto. This implies that, especially in its most advanced European, North American and Far Eastern economies, most basic needs are met. Any growth in incomes in these places is then inevitably translated into higher demand for *income-elastic luxuries*, many of which are manufactured: cars, TVs, video players, cameras, hi-fi equipment, fridge-freezers, sports equipment, clothes, children's toys and so on. This of course means that the decision to switch resources into the production of this class of goods was extremely wise: the demand for them will continue to increase at a faster rate than the growth in world income. Meanwhile, the many countries that continue to rely on exports of agricultural goods and raw materials find the more sedate (income inelastic) demand for them constrains wider national prospects for faster economic growth and development (see Chapter 17, Section 17.10).

Price elasticity of supply

As the reader will expect from our discussion in this section so far, **price elasticity of supply**, P_{es}, measures the responsiveness of quantity supplied to changes in price. It is given by the following equation:

Price elasticity of supply: The proportionate change in quantity supplied of a good divided by the proportionate change in price that brought it about.

$$P_{es} = \frac{\text{Proportionate change in quantity supplied}}{\text{Proportionate change in price}} \qquad (3.4)$$

Fig. 3.14 provides two worked examples of price elasticity of supply. These follow precisely the same general principles as those introduced in Fig. 3.11 for the calcula-

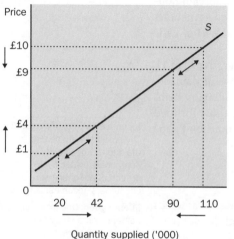

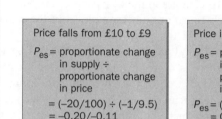

Price falls from £10 to £9

P_{es} = proportionate change
    in supply ÷
    proportionate change
    in price

    = (–20/100) ÷ (–1/9.5)
    = –0.20/–0.11
P_{es} = 1.82 i.e. **elastic**

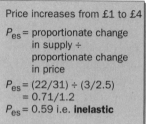

Price increases from £1 to £4

P_{es} = proportionate change
    in supply ÷
    proportionate change
    in price

P_{es} = (22/31) ÷ (3/2.5)
    = 0.71/1.2
P_{es} = 0.59 i.e. **inelastic**

Fig. 3.14 Price elasticity of supply.

tion of price elasticity of demand. It can be seen from Fig. 3.14 that price elasticity of supply can vary along a single supply curve. In this case we observe both an instance of price-inelastic supply, where the proportionate response of quantity supplied is less than the proportionate change in price that brings it about, and an elastic response, where the proportionate change in quantity supplied is greater than the proportionate change in price. Instances of unit elastic, perfectly inelastic and perfectly elastic supply are also possible. These are depicted in Fig. 3.15. Notice that, as in Fig. 3.15(a), any supply curve that passes through the origin will have unit elastic supply characteristics. In Fig. 3.15(b), a situation of perfectly inelastic supply indicates that the quantity supplied will not respond regardless of the scale or direction of any price change. Finally, in Fig. 3.15(c), where supply is perfectly elastic, all prices other than P_1 induce an infinitely large fall in the quantity supplied.

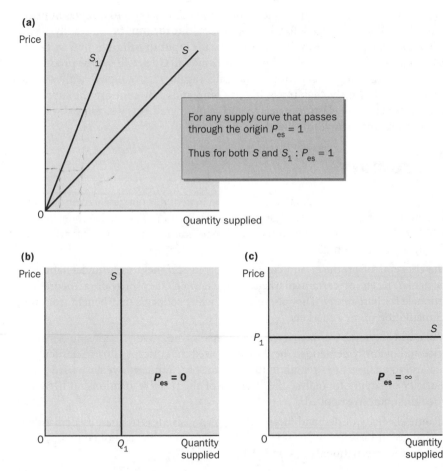

Fig. 3.15 (a) Unit elasticity, (b) perfectly inelastic supply, (c) perfectly elastic supply.

Determinants of price elasticity of supply

There are two principal determinants of elasticity of supply: time, and the elasticity of supply of factor inputs.

Concept

Factor inputs

Economists generally recognize four factor inputs – or factors of production – some or all of which are required in order to supply a good or service. These are: land, labour, capital, and entrepreneurial – or business – skill.

Time

We noted earlier that the demand for many goods and services does not respond instantaneously to changes in price; a similar constraint operates on supply. In some markets, such as that for newspapers, output may be increased (or decreased) relatively quickly in response to a new market price. It is simply a matter of extending the print run; all the requisite machinery and raw materials will already be in place. In other markets, however, the task is more difficult. A given season's total supply of seats at football matches is fixed. The only way to increase the quantity of seats supplied is to extend football grounds or build new ones: a process that can take several years. Incidentally, this makes apparent the economic basis of ticket touting at popular games: a strong demand meets an inelastic supply.

The elasticity of supply of factor inputs

The responsiveness of the supply of a particular good or service to changes in price will also depend on the degree to which additional **factor inputs** are readily available. To take an extreme example, the prime factor input to paintings by Van Gogh is the labour of the artist himself. No more work by Van Gogh will ever be produced, and therefore its supply is perfectly inelastic (again this, coupled with strong demand, accounts for the high prices his art commands). By contrast, the supply of lolly ices is much more elastic because the principle ingredients – sugar and water – are not constrained to anything like the same extent.

Summary

◆ Using the concepts of marginal social cost and benefit it is possible to demonstrate that the level of output produced in a free market is a socially efficient one: that is, one that is desired not only by those consumers and producers in the market but also by society as a whole.

◆ The concepts of producer and consumer surplus can help us to understand the particular facets of certain markets. For example, they provide a theoretical rationale for bargaining. They also illustrate why producers may benefit from the segmentation of their markets.

◆ While in Chapter 2 we uncovered the inverse or negative relationship between price and quantity demanded, here we have used the concept of price elasticity of demand to analyse the strength of the relationship. Similarly, we have used price elasticity of supply to analyse the strength of the positive relationship between price and quantity supplied.

◆ Income elasticity of demand measures the responsiveness of quantity demanded to changes in incomes. It may be used to understand the basis of contemporary shifts in the international division of labour.

Key terms

◆ Marginal utility
◆ Total utility
◆ Marginal cost

◆ Marginal social cost
◆ Marginal social benefit
◆ Socially efficient output
◆ Producer surplus
◆ Consumer surplus
◆ Price elasticity of demand
◆ Income elasticity of demand
◆ Price elasticity of supply

Self-test questions

True (t) or false (f)

1. The marginal utility derived from a good increases as the quantity consumed increases.

2. The total utility derived from a good will usually increase as the quantity consumed increases.

3. The producer surplus associated with *individual* units of output declines as the quantity supplied extends.

4. The consumer surplus associated with *individual* units of output demanded increases as quantity demanded extends.

5. Price elasticity of demand measures the responsiveness of price to changes in demand.

6. When price elasticity of demand is less than 1, price reductions are associated with net losses in revenue for producers.

7. When demand is perfectly price inelastic the quantity demanded does not change regardless of what happens to price.

8. Demand becomes more price elastic over time.

9. Supply becomes more price inelastic over time.

10. The supply of rare fossils is perfectly inelastic.

Complete the following sentences by inserting the missing word(s)

1. Utility measures the personal ____ that an individual derives from the consumption of a good or service.

2. Socially efficient quantities demanded and supplied in a market equate marginal social benefit and ____.

3. Units beyond the equilibrium quantity in a market carry an increasing net ____ from society's point of view.

4. Producers may be able to annex consumers' surplus by market ____.

5. Price elasticity of demand measures the ____ of the quantity demanded to a change in ____.

6. When price elasticity of demand is 1, it is said to be ____.

7. Goods with few ____ are more likely to be price inelastic in character.

8. Cars are likely to be in price inelastic demand because they absorb a greater proportion of consumers' ____ .

9. If the income elasticity of demand for a good is negative then the good is said to be ____.

10. For any supply curve that passes through the origin, price elasticity of supply equals ____.

Questions for discussion

- If consumer satisfaction is subjective how can economists begin to understand and analyse it?
- How does the free market produce a socially efficient output of a particular good or service?
- How might a knowledge of consumer surplus help us to understand the pricing policies of cinemas, which typically have different pricing structures for students, OAPs and children, and which may vary their adult charges according to the time of day?
- Use the concept of price elasticity of demand to explain why governments are able to continually raise the tax they levy on cigarettes. Why is a tax not levied on boxes of matches?

Further reading

Le Grand, J., J. Propper and R. Robinson *The Economics of Social Problems* (3rd ed.) (Basingstoke: Macmillan, 1992). Offers a good theoretical overview of the operation of the market and then applies this in a number of specific social issue contexts.

Dunnett, A. *Understanding the Market* (2nd ed.) (Harlow: Longman, 1992). This book provides an accessible general introduction to microeconomics with real world applications.

Barr, N. and D. Whynes *Current Issues in the Economics of Welfare* (Basingstoke: Macmillan, 1993). Another useful look at markets and their operation in applied contexts.

The Producer

Key issues

▶ What is the role of the firm in the modern economy?

▶ Why do *firms* necessarily have to fulfil this role?

▶ What different kinds of firm exist in the modern economy?

▶ What is entrepreneurship, and what is its significance?

▶ What difficulties are there for the firm in managing its affairs?

Contents

4.1 Introduction

The first three chapters of this book have been primarily concerned with the operation of markets. Markets permit individual producers to pursue their own economic ends by serving the consumption needs of others. At the same time, they encourage and facilitate what is at the heart of the dynamic of capitalism: the development of an extended division of labour. Up to this point, however, we have neither considered in any *detail* how market processes actually influence producers nor, indeed, reflected upon the institution of the *firm*, the most common organizational form that capitalist production assumes. In this chapter and Chapter 5 we fill in these gaps. The present chapter provides an overview of the contribution that firms make to answering the basic economic questions of what to produce, how and for whom. Chapter 5 offers a common framework for analysing the different kinds of **market structure** in which firms are located. It also considers the extent to which firms actually match up to the ideals that conventional economics supposes that they follow. There are for example serious doubts about whether consumer sovereignty can prevail in the presence of firms with **monopoly power**. Monopoly power, the argument runs, permits the firm – rather than consumers – to direct the general course of production. It is in Chapter 5, then, that we begin to encounter some of the *shortcomings* of the market system.

Market structure: Characterizes a market according to the degree of competition in it. Monopoly is an example of a market structure in which there is an absence of competition.

Monopoly power: Exists where a firm has the ability to exclude competing firms from the market. But competition is the process that empowers consumers: each firm in a competitive market seeks to offer a better deal to consumers than its rivals. Monopoly power removes this incentive and may leave the firm less responsive to consumer interests.

4.2 What do firms do?

Firms are organizations that buy or hire factors of production in order to produce goods or services that can be sold for profit. As defined in Chapter 3, economic theory recognizes four factors of production. These are:

- land
- labour
- capital
- entrepreneurship.

The supposition is that a firm will require some combination of all four factors in order to produce goods or services. Let us reflect briefly on the nature of each factor.

Land embodies all natural resources. Thus it includes not only the physical space in which production occurs but also all the unprocessed materials present in the environment. For economists, houses and factories are built on land; animals, minerals and vegetables can be reared, extracted and grown on it; even fish swim in it.

Labour is the time and effort of people hired by firms to perform specialist production tasks and to increase the scale of production of the individual firm.

Capital consists of all those production goods that are used to produce other goods and services. Thus machines, tools and factories are all forms of capital: their value lies not in immediate consumption but in what can be made with them.

Finally, entrepreneurship – the ability to read the market, anticipate the demands of consumers and manage land, labour and capital to meet these demands – is *the* pivotal factor of capitalist production. If a firm is lacking in entrepreneurship, it risks destruction simply because it will fail to correctly judge the market. Most obviously, it may produce goods and services for which there proves to be little or no demand. By contrast, the entrepreneurial firm must by definition be profitable and therefore successful: it is effectively producing things that consumers demand. Note also that the Smithian conceptualizations of the *invisible hand* and the *extended division of labour* are captured in the notion of entrepreneurship. Entrepreneurial skill enables firms, in their thousands, to dovetail production into incredibly complex patterns of demand; it also encourages them to continually refine what they produce and how they produce it so that they can better meet demand in the future. Because of its centrality to the market process, we elaborate upon the role of the entrepreneur within the firm in a later section.

The particular factor mix – how much land, labour and capital – used by a firm will of course reflect the nature of the production process that the firm is engaged in. Economists recognize that certain forms of production favour particular **factor intensities**. For example, the manufacture of chemicals is a capital-intensive process in that the typical firm employs relatively more capital than labour or land. On the other hand, the manufacture of footwear and clothing is a labour-intensive activity, and most forms of agriculture are land intensive.

Finally in this section we should note the payments that firms make for the factors of production they employ. The returns paid to each factor are as follows:

- Land earns *rent*.
- Labour is paid a *wage*.

Factor intensity: Refers to the emphasis in production towards the use of one particular factor of production above others.

- Capital earns *interest*.
- Entrepreneurship is rewarded with *profit*.

We elaborate upon the earnings of land, labour and capital in Chapter 7; for the moment we concentrate upon profit. As noted, a firm's entrepreneurial ability is rewarded in the form of profit. If, by organizing land, labour and capital, the firm produces goods that consumers are willing and able to buy at a price that exceeds the cost of production, then the difference between price and cost is retained by the firm as profit. The conventional assumption is that firms attempt to *maximize profits*. Now this might appear to place the firm and the consumer slightly at odds, given that higher profits could simply result from firms pushing up the prices they charge. However, such a view neglects the significance of the competitive environment in which firms, in theory at least, operate. Because firms must compete with one another for customers, no single firm can risk speculative price increases, for fear that its rivals will not follow suit and will maroon it in an uncompetitive position. At the same time, the competitive environment places a *cost control* imperative on firms. No firm can absolve itself of the need to produce as efficiently as possible for fear of the competitive disadvantage that it would incur in the presence of more cost-conscious rivals.

The competitive environment thus makes profit maximization advantageous both for the firm *and* for the consumer. That profit maximization benefits the firm is self-evident (though see our discussion of the principal–agent problem in Section 4.6). Consumer interests are served by the familiar Smithian principle of the indivisibility of (the firm's) self-interest and wider social interest: the firm's profits rest upon its ability to satisfy consumers. Neglect of the consumer in the presence of rival firms is, axiomatically, a threat to profitability and to the survival of the firm.

4.3 Why are firms necessary?

We begin here with an obvious question: what is the purpose of firms? Why do markets not simply consist of large collections of individual (sole) producers and consumers? By way of an answer, consider the following example. If a person wishes to obtain a new house, one option open to him or her is to organize the details of its construction single-handedly. Land would need to be purchased and an architect commissioned to design the house. The requisite materials and tools would also have to be obtained, and a bricklayer, joiner, plumber, roofer and so on hired. Overall, the project might take, say, six months to complete, and it would probably require a good deal of management attention from our potential house owner; conceivably, he or she might have to work full-time in a managerial capacity. This kind of approach involves building the house through the *use of the market*: the consumer hires the skills and experience of individual producers and puts them to work on designated tasks. Now in the UK some houses might be built in this way, but most are not. This is because most buyers of new houses find it more convenient and cheaper to rely on specialist building *firms* instead. In our example, the individual must devote six months of his or her time to construction management. The opportunity cost of this work would include the loss of income from employment that must be given up while building is going on. Moreover, the individual would have to have confidence in his or her ability to effectively manage and coordinate the project. Because few people find it possible to easily open up a six-month window in their working lives, and because few are likely to have the requisite building management skills, the favoured option for the many is to turn to an established building firm.

But opportunity cost and the questionable managerial abilities of consumers are not the only factors that militate against market-coordinated production and therefore give rise to the existence of firms. Firms also offer a range of additional advantages as organizers of production which consumers would not otherwise benefit from. The most important of these are as follows.

Savings on transaction costs

A building firm that constructs several thousand houses a year will contract for consistently large volumes of building materials; it will not order individual loads of sand, cement, brick and timber for each house. To repeat order small loads in this way would clearly be less efficient: it would cost more in time and in paperwork. Similarly, the workers the firm employs will not be issued new contracts as they move from house to house, and the tools and equipment they use will not be re-hired each time a house is finished: *one* set of contracts or transactions would cover a year's work or more for the firm. Now, if the houses *were* built by their eventual owners through the market, as described above, the number of transactions taking place could be multiplied several thousandfold. Therefore, in terms of transaction costs, firms appear to offer a much more efficient means of organizing production than a market without firms.

The capacity of firms to extend the division of labour

If production was predominantly organized by individuals through the market process then some or all of the signal leaps in productivity that have occurred over the last 250 years might never have been realized. Perhaps the most famous of these was

The modern-day 'robotized' car production line

the utilization by Henry Ford in the early 1900s of 'flow-line' car assembly. This process involved the fragmentation of carmaking into very simple tasks, which could be repeated easily and quickly. The flow-line enabled the cars themselves to move at a given pace while the stationary workers repeated their allotted tasks on each unit. Ford demonstrated that cars could be made in their millions in this way at a *much lower cost per car than had ever been achieved before*. Subsequently, this method of production – sometimes known, after its originator, as *Fordism* – spread beyond carmaking to many other branches of industry, and provided the basis for a general and marked improvement in productivity in the advanced economies. The point here is of course that the flow-line principle, resting on an extended division of labour, could not have been put into practice outside the firm. To produce efficiently, Ford's output needed to be at least in the *hundreds of thousands* per annum. Car production (and, by implication, most forms of industrial production) on any meaningful scale is clearly most efficiently done by firms.

The motor industry also provides an example of the way in which firms can extend the *external* as well as their own internal division of labour. Although most of the world's cars are now produced by a fairly limited number of large **transnationals**, these firms usually rely on supplies of auto parts from other specialist producers. Car radios, tyres, windscreen wipers, upholstery and electrical components as well as other items are 'bought in' by carmakers. This arrangement allows the car firms to concentrate on the central tasks of design and body, engine and transmission production, as well as final assembly, while the specialist suppliers refine their own particular product contributions. Again, such a complex and highly integrated production system would be unlikely to emerge in the absence of the institution of the firm.

The potential of firms to innovate

Where do new products come from? How can we account for the vast array of goods and services that modern societies make available? The answer in each case is *innovation*. Innovation can of course be driven by solitary genius. For example, the vulcanizing process that makes rubber malleable and therefore usable in so many ways in heat or cold was discovered after a long and lonely struggle by one individual: Charles Goodyear. Innovation may also result from military imperatives. It is well known that the design and manufacture of aircraft was revolutionized as a result of pressures that emerged during the First and Second World Wars. Of course, research and development into new products and processes is also sponsored by firms: the manuscript of this book was prepared using the remarkable Word 6 word processing software produced by the American Microsoft Corporation.

Innovation then has a variety of sources. Most importantly, however, in capitalist economies, it is usually firms that *apply* advances in technology to the marketplace, regardless of how these arise in the first place. Indeed, for many branches of production, it is difficult now to imagine how it could be otherwise. While an individual consumer might be capable of hiring the factors of production that he or she needs to build a house or repair a car, following the same process to obtain computer software or a television set would be immensely difficult. Indeed, it would be virtually impossible for a complex society to organize production as a whole in this way. Of course, though our reference here is to private sector firms, there are areas in capitalist economies where public sector institutions such as nationalized industries, hospitals

Transnational: A firm that owns and controls assets (usually production facilities) in more than one country.

and universities bear some burden of both production and innovation. However, it still appears reasonable to conclude that the firm is the uniquely important source of *marketable* innovation – the introduction of new goods and services to markets where individuals pay directly for what they consume. Note also that this still leaves the firm subservient to the market, and therefore preserves the central principle of consumer sovereignty. An innovation that fails to bring forth sufficient demand is itself destined for oblivion, regardless of any other considerations. Some readers may recall the ill-fated single-passenger vehicle, the *C5*, which met a quick and ignominious end when it was launched in the UK in the 1980s.

4.4 Different kinds of firm

In this section we describe the main kinds of firm that exist in the modern economy. Although the examples and data we use are primarily UK specific, the general patterns they reveal are applicable to other advanced capitalist economies, such as those in North America and in other parts of western Europe.

Firms are legally distinguished by their forms of *ownership*. There are three main categories of ownership:

- sole proprietorship
- partnership
- companies.

Sole proprietorship

A firm owned by one individual is a sole proprietorship. The firm's owner receives all the profits it makes, but these are taxed as income, in the same way as wages and salaries. The owner is also responsible for any debts or losses that the firm may incur; in fact, he or she has **unlimited liability** for such losses. This means that the entire personal wealth of the owner – savings, a house, a car or any other asset – is at risk if losses are sufficiently large. Sole proprietorships are typically small, and are most common in the service sector, in areas of work such as retailing, and property and business services (especially plumbing, electrical work and so on).

Partnership

A partnership divides ownership of the firm between two or more individuals. This is clearly a more complicated arrangement than the sole proprietorship, as the management of the firm and the disbursement of its profits must be the subject of agreement between the partners. However, partnerships also allow more individuals to participate in the firm, perhaps bringing in more money and a wider range of business expertise. As for the sole proprietorship, the profits of a partnership are taxed as the income of its owners. Partners are also subject to joint unlimited liability. This means that the personal wealth of all partners is at risk if the firm runs into financial difficulty. In the UK, partnerships predominate in retailing, agriculture, and property and business services (typically in firms of accountants and solicitors).

Companies

Companies are owned by their shareholders. The more shares that are held, the greater the proportion of ownership that the holder enjoys. Shares in private limited

---

Unlimited liability: Places the entire personal wealth of the owner of a firm at risk in respect of losses the firm may incur.

companies can be bought and sold only when there is mutual agreement to do so amongst existing shareholders. By contrast, shares in publicly quoted limited companies may be bought and sold openly by anyone on the stock exchange. Shareholders also enjoy the important advantage of limited liability. This means that, unlike sole proprietors and partners, their financial exposure is limited to the value of the company itself. In the event of poor trading and a decision to wind up the company, any debts that cannot be covered by selling stocks of goods, plant and machinery etc. will remain unmet. Creditors of the company are not entitled to any claim on the personal wealth of shareholders. In the UK, the government levies corporation tax (currently at 33 per cent) on the profits earned by companies. After the payment of corporation tax, profits are disbursed amongst shareholders as dividends on each share held. For shareholders these dividends are then subject to a second income tax. One evident disadvantage of shareholding therefore is that profits may be subject to two taxes compared with the single tax on income from profits that sole proprietors and partners pay.

Table 4.1 summarizes the distribution of the three main types of firm according to their respective annual turnovers. From the table it can be seen that sole proprietorship is most numerous in the UK, with almost 600 000 firms. However, it is also evident that most of these are relatively small. 71 per cent have a turnover of less than £100 000 per annum. Partnerships are the least numerous type of firm but have a greater proportion of larger firms compared with sole proprietorships. Finally, it is amongst the slightly more than half-million companies and public corporations that the largest firms are to be found: 19 per cent (104 770 firms) in this category have turnovers in excess of £1 million as compared to only 4 per cent (17 165 firms) in the other two categories taken together.

Table 4.1 UK private sector firms by type and turnover, 1996

Turnover in £'000	Sole proprietorships		Partnerships		Companies and public corporations	
	Number	%	Number	%	Number	%
1–49	236 750	40	78 950	20	90 295	17
50–99	182 695	31	97 400	25	84 150	16
100–249	128 560	21	125 695	32	105 635	20
250–499	33 915	6	52 045	13	75 097	14
500–999	11 320	2	22 170	6	62 680	12
1000+	4 930	1	12 235	3	–	–
1000–1999	–	–	–	–	43 065	8
2000–4999	–	–	–	–	32 625	6
5000–9999	–	–	–	–	13 050	2
10 000+	–	–	–	–	16 030	3
Totals	588 170	100	388 130	100	522 620	100

Source: Business Monitor PA1003, Office for National Statistics, © Crown Copyright 1998

The relative advantages and disadvantages of different forms of ownership

In sifting through the three main forms that a firm might assume, the decisive factors of choice are:

- the taxation of the firm's profits
- the extent of liability of the firm's owners for any losses that might arise
- how easily capital can be raised
- the way the firm is to be managed.

Let us consider each of these factors in turn.

The taxation of the firm's profits

As noted, the profits of sole proprietorships and partnerships are taxed – once only – as the personal income of the firm's owners. Company profits, in contrast, are subject to tax twice: corporation tax is levied initially, and subsequently any dividends paid to shareholders are liable to income tax. Moreover, in the UK, as income tax commences at a lower rate than corporation tax, sole proprietorships and partnerships that make only modest profits will pay proportionately less in tax than companies.

Liability

Though tax arrangements might appear to favour sole proprietorships and partnerships over companies, the issue of liability works in the opposite direction. While shareholders risk nothing more than the stake that they own in a company, sole proprietors and partners lay open their entire personal wealth should their firms collapse. While this might appear a major burden under which to conduct business, it must also be remembered that most sole proprietorships and partnerships are relatively small, and their financial exposure is therefore limited (see Table 4.1). Moreover, as these firms are usually under the immediate supervision and control of their owners, any risk-taking will presumably not be done in a cavalier or reckless manner.

Raising capital

New and existing businesses need money for investment to help them grow. For sole proprietorships and partnerships, additional capital may come from the owners themselves, from their families and friends, or from the bank. Generally, however, *large* injections of capital will not be available from these sources. This helps to explain why sole proprietorships and partnerships tend to be small. Companies, by contrast, find it easier to secure substantial amounts of new money. One way in which they can do this is by selling shares. These are attractive to individuals and investment institutions because, if the company performs well, the shares will yield a stream of dividends, and because the value of the shares may rise as demand for them increases. Note that limited liability underpins the attractiveness of shareholding as the purchaser shoulders a risk only equivalent to his or her investment. Indeed, this explains the origin of the principle of limited liability: it was devised as a means to help firms secure larger amounts of capital at minimal risk to investors.

The management of the firm

For sole proprietorships and partnerships, management and ownership of the firm are usually fused into one. In tandem with the generally smaller scale of operations, this makes for relatively simple management and decision-making. In the case of companies, however, both the typically, larger scale of the firm and its diversified form of ownership may make for more complex and unwieldy management structures. Some economists, notably J.K. Galbraith, claim that this is a major source of weakness in advanced capitalism. We begin to introduce his views on this subject in Section 4.6.

As Table 4.1 makes clear, in the UK, all three types of firm are well represented. *This suggests that no one type has an overwhelming advantage over the others.* Indeed, there is emerging evidence that different forms of ownership can be made to complement one another. For example, consider the growth in franchising in Western economies in recent years. Franchising involves a firm's selling or leasing the right to produce and/or sell its brand of goods to a third party. In the UK, it has been estimated that 10 per cent of retailing is franchise based. Perhaps the world's most famous franchising operation is McDonald's: eighty-five per cent of McDonald's restaurants are actually run by franchisees. The attraction of franchising is that it can combine the resources, experience and expertise of a large company with the commitment of the franchisee. The franchisee can take the same kind of risks as (say) a sole proprietor but does so in the knowledge that he or she is treading on proven ground. At the same time, the franchiser is assured that each individual franchisee has a direct personal stake in the development of the business and is therefore highly committed to it.

4.5 Firms and entrepreneurship: an Austrian view

Earlier in this chapter we defined entrepreneurship as the capacity to organize the remaining factors of production: land, labour and capital. We also argued that it is the pivotal factor in capitalist production in that it is uniquely able to discern the demands of consumers. This latter claim is derived from the *Austrian School* of economic thought, and merits further elaboration here. Austrian economics emerged in Vienna in the 1870s in the works of Carl Menger (1840–1921), Ludwig von Mises (1881–1973), and Friedrich von Hayek (1899–1992). As a result of Nazism, the school's leading proponents moved abroad, especially to the USA. The major contemporary figure in Austrian economics is Israel Kirzner (b. 1930), who has written extensively on entrepreneurship.

Friedrich von Hayek, 1899–1992

For pre-Austrian economists, including Adam Smith, the *organizational role* of the entrepreneur was of primary interest: he or she assembled the necessary factors of production in the appropriate form and received the appropriate reward – profit – for so doing. With its emphasis on the attainment of market equilibrium (as detailed in Chapters 2 and 3), mainstream economic thought has tended to reinforce this view that the entrepreneurial task is not possessed of any particular dynamism. The market process balances supply and demand – all entrepreneurs have to do is produce the appropriate quantities of goods and services at the appropriate price while controlling their costs. Rather like an engine that has been set running, each firm can simply 'tick over' with the entrepreneur supplying the fuel and the occasional tune-up as required.

In the Austrian view, this kind conceptualization of entrepreneurship is *far too passive*. For Austrians, entrepreneurs – whether individual producers or firms – anticipate and help to shape the market; they do not meekly follow it. To illustrate, think about the two different car markets in the former East and West German economies. In East Germany, the car industry and car market were both state run. Demand for the single model produced – the Trabant – generally tended to run ahead of supply. East German carmakers were not dissatisfied with this arrangement; whatever output they produced was sold. Most importantly there was no competition from the West: Western models could not be imported, not that many people in East Germany could have afforded them anyway. The result of this state of affairs was a notable degree of industrial complacency and lethargy: the Trabant, made partly from cardboard, changed hardly at all over 30 years. In the West German car market, however, things proceeded on an altogether different basis. West German carmakers were (indeed, still are) private firms operating in a highly open and competitive environment. They must compete both with each other and with overseas firms for the domestic and foreign markets. This means that they cannot simply parcel up factors of production and churn out a given model range indefinitely: they must continually strive to outperform their rivals, both on price and in terms of the quality of product. In a word, these firms must be *entrepreneurial*. The outcome is that names such as Mercedes and BMW have become bywords for quality and excellence, while Trabants, shorn of state protection following German reunification, are no longer made.

While this example gives us a flavour of what Austrians mean by entrepreneurship, it doesn't quite capture their interpretation completely. Entrepreneurial firms must certainly observe the imperatives of consumer sovereignty and follow the patterns of demand that consumers lay down. But, crucially from the Austrian perspective, they also help to *anticipate* demand. The key here is the ability of the entrepreneurial firm to *innovate*. For example, the impressive range of new computerized electronic goods that have emerged over the last two decades – personal computers, video and CD equipment, advanced communications technologies and so on – are all available because of the entrepreneurial skill of firms. Note again that this does not mean that all or even many firms have to *invent* new goods; their contribution is to *find market applications* for technologies as they emerge. Indeed, innovation does not necessarily have to embody sophisticated new technologies at all. For example, in the UK at present there is a phenomenal interest in cooking. All the major TV channels show cooking programmes, and there are numerous promotional spin-offs in 'book of the series' publications, specialized kitchen equipment, and even cooking holidays. The entrepreneurial skill here was to *anticipate* the level of popular demand for this kind of activity and to *persuade and even educate* people that cooking is something most of us can enjoy doing. Of course, however strong the persuasion, the consumer remains the final arbiter. If demand is not forthcoming, the product or products will inevitably fail.

Now, the Austrian version of entrepreneurship has some interesting implications for the notion of *market equilibrium*. Recall the definition of equilibrium we offered in Chapter 2: a position from which there is no tendency to change. At an equilibrium price, the quantities of a good demanded and supplied are perfectly matched.

Accordingly, because both consumers and producers are satisfied with existing conditions, there is no pressure from either group that might result in changes in the quantities demanded or supplied. Yet entrepreneurs, in the Austrian view, are clearly *never* satisfied with the existing state of affairs in a given market. Prompted by the pressure of a competitive environment and the prospect of profit, they are *continually* seeking to engineer changes in the market, to introduce modified or wholly new goods and services to make consumers aware of wants and needs they did not know they had. In this sense, equilibrium is always just out of reach and inevitably so. A market in equilibrium would be one in which entrepreneurship was dead: an impossibility under capitalism but a state of affairs that Austrians would recognize in (say) the East German car industry. In the Austrian view, then, markets are dynamic and uncertain arenas in which entrepreneurs innovate and compete under the ultimate sanction of the consumer; entrepreneurship is in effect the *motive* force of capitalism.

4.6 Firms and the principal–agent problem

In our discussion so far, we have taken it as read that firms are *single-minded* organizations in that their primary goal is profit maximization. The underlying assumption is that firms cannot do other than compete with one another for the patronage of the consumer, profit being the indicator of success. Yet there is a potential difficulty here. What if firms have an agenda that is not wholly centred on profit? If this is the case, a potentially serious problem arises. Those firms that neglect the profit motive clearly risk bankruptcy at the hands of rivals who do not. For such firms, the urgent task is to ensure that the profit motive is restored and retained as *the* priority. The possibility that profits may not be at the top of a firm's agenda can be explained by reference to a concept known as the *principal–agent problem*.

The basic premise of the principal–agent problem is that the firms may not always behave in ways anticipated by economic theory. This is because firms are often not simple organizations: their structures are riven by relationships between different economic groups, which can effectively pull the individual firm in different directions. For example, consider the potential gulf between what is desired by the *owners* of a firm and the objectives of *those simply hired* to run it. In this case, the firm's owners are the *principals*. They employ others – managers – as *agents* to operate the firm on their behalf. Now, the principals' interest is in profit – this is their ultimate motivation for investing in the firm in the first place. But what motivates the manager-agents? It may be, as for example the economist John Kenneth Galbraith has argued, that the managers, particularly of large firms, are interested not in profit maximization but in maximizing the size of the firm itself. The bigger the firm, Galbraith argues, the greater the power, influence and remuneration of its managers. This is their preferred objective, to be pursued if necessary at the expense of profits. The result, assuming that the ambitions of principal and agent are both partly met, is that the firm is indeed pulled in two different directions simultaneously.

John Kenneth Galbraith, b. 1908

Another instance of the principal–agent problem concerns the relationship between the managers of a firm and its workers. Here the managers assume the guise of principals and the workers are their agents, charged with certain job functions. But what if the worker-agents do not perform their allotted tasks as well as they might? Here again, the firm's effectiveness will be compromised by the establishment of two incompatible agendas: the managers' (principals') and the workers' (agents').

The solution to the principal–agent problem in both of these cases is the same: the principals must take steps to bind the objectives of the agents to their own. This can be done, depending on context, in a variety of ways. For example, the motivation of managers as agents may be achieved by conferring part ownership of the firm on them. In effect, this would mean that managers become both principals *and* agents in the firm. The awarding of shares or share options – the right to buy shares, often on favourable terms – is usually rationalized on this basis. Of course, the distribution of shares to workers may also serve to bind them to *their* principals.

In recent years a more common strategy to overcome the principal-agent problem in respect of workers as agents has involved the reorganization of work itself. In manufacturing industry especially, the introduction of computerized technology has allowed managers to define more autonomous and challenging roles for production workers. The objective here is to push more responsibility for the organization of work and for the quality and quantity of what is produced onto the worker-agents; in other words, to make them behave more like (self) managers or principals. Once again, the solution to the principal-agent problem is an attempt to fuse the agent to the principal.

◼ Summary

◆ Firms are a key institution in capitalism. They use factors of production to produce goods and services that can be sold for profit. Economic theory assumes that firms attempt to maximize profits.

◆ Profit maximization, while self-evidently beneficial for the firm, is also held to serve the interests of consumers. Firms operate in a competitive environment, and must produce goods and services that consumers demand at an appropriate price. Thus the most successful and most profitable firms are those best able to satisfy the consumer.

◆ Firms exist because they offer a number of advantages as organizers of production that individuals operating through the market cannot attain. Thus firms provide savings on transaction costs; they facilitate the extension of the division of labour; and they are accomplished innovators.

◆ There are three main categories of firm, as defined by ownership: sole proprietorships, partnerships, and limited companies. Sole proprietorships and partnerships are generally smaller, simpler to manage and taxed less than limited companies, but they find it harder to raise capital, and their owners have unlimited liability for losses. Companies tend to be larger, more difficult to manage, and are subject to heavier taxes. However, they can raise capital more easily as their shareholders' risk is limited to the size of their immediate investment. All three categories are well represented in most advanced capitalist economies, suggesting a fairly even balance of advantage and disadvantage between them.

◆ In the view of Austrian economists, the central attribute of the firm is its entrepreneurial skill. Motivated by profit, entrepreneurial firms operating in a competitive environment are at the dynamic and innovative heart of capitalism.

This conceptualization of the firm leaves the consumer as the ultimate arbiter of the course of capitalist production, but it sits rather uneasily with the notion of equilibrium as defined by mainstream economic theory. For Austrians, equilibrium is always just out of reach as entrepreneurs consistently reshape what they produce and how they produce it in the search for more profit.

◆ The principal–agent problem is an acknowledgement that, in the real world, firms may not always approximate the seamless profit-maximizing entities of economic theory.

Key terms

◆ Firms
◆ Entrepreneurship
◆ Factors of production
◆ Profit maximization
◆ Limited and unlimited liability
◆ Austrian approach to entrepreneurship
◆ Principal–agent problem

Questions for discussion

◆ What is the prime function of the firm and how is it motivated?
◆ What advantages do firms, as opposed to individuals, offer as organizers of production?
◆ What are the relative merits of the three main types of firm?
◆ What perspective do Austrian economists have on entrepreneurship?
◆ What is the principal–agent problem and what implications does it have for the firm?

Further reading

Putterman, L. and R.S. Kroszner (eds) *The Economic Nature of the Firm* (London: Cambridge University Press, 1996). Offers a combination of classic papers and modern interpretations on the nature of the firm.

Kirzner, I. *The Meaning of Market Process* (London: Routledge, 1992). A collection of writings on Austrian economics by one of its leading exponents.

Internet links

The Department of Trade and Industry offers a website designed as a resource for business and industry. The site contains details of programmes intended to improve the competitiveness of British firms, and can be found at: **http://www.dti.gov.uk/**

CHAPTER 5

Market Structures

Contents

Key issues

▶ What are the major market structures in the modern economy?

▶ What implications do different market structures have for competition?

▶ Is monopoly always regrettable from an economic viewpoint?

▶ Do competitive or uncompetitive market structures dominate in the real world?

5.1 Introduction

In the previous chapter we discussed the role of the firm in the capitalist production process, and considered some specific advantages offered by firms as organizers of production. In the present chapter we introduce the different *market structures* in which firms operate, and reflect on the implications of each of these structures for the firm, for the consumer, and for wider society. As we shall see, despite the outlined claims of mainstream economic theory in favour of firms as effective organizers of production, real-world market structures place clear limits on their ability to efficiently allocate scarce resources. Firms, it appears, may not always 'get it right' as far as the consumer and wider society are concerned.

5.2 Market structures

A market structure is a means of characterizing a market by reference to the *level of competition* that prevails between firms in it. Think about the intensity of competition between firms in the markets for the following goods and services:

- haircuts
- groceries
- new cars
- train travel.

Competition actually varies quite considerably in intensity and form across these markets. Let us briefly consider each in turn.

Haircuts

Barber shops and hairdressing salons are numerous, and they offer a fairly uniform service. True, customers may elect to patronize one establishment regularly, but if it closes, there are many others to choose from. Because they are plentiful, barber shops are in fairly intense competition. This may manifest itself in several ways: for example, in the form of investment in furniture and fittings to improve the appearance of the shop. Most obviously, however, barber shops have to be competitive in terms of the price they charge. In any given city or district there will be a 'going rate' for a haircut, which few barbers will exceed by more than a modest amount. To do so would entail the risk of losing customers to rivals. Note that the main connection we have established here is between, on the one hand, the *large number* of firms competing in the market and, on the other, the wide range of *consumer choice* and consequent need for firms to remain price competitive.

Groceries

What about the market for groceries? Here too there appears to be extensive consumer choice and fairly strong competition, based on the relatively large number of retail outlets in most towns and cities. However, in some countries, such as the UK and France, grocery retailing is increasingly the preserve of a smaller number of very large supermarket chains: the likes of Tesco, Asda and Sainsbury's in the UK and L'Eclerc and Mammouth in France. The growing presence of such chains has not eliminated smaller 'corner shop' grocery retailers, but their numbers have certainly declined over the last 20 years or so. What then can we say about the level of competition in grocery retailing? Is it becoming less intense than formerly because of the declining numbers of firms in the market? We can certainly say that competition is changing in *form*. In the UK at least, while the major grocery retailers assert their commitment to price competitiveness, most also offer 'loyalty cards' and other similar inducements to entice regular patronage, novelties that traditional grocers tended not to indulge in. Here it appears that price competition has been partly superseded by *non-price* competition. In this case then it is possible to link *falling* numbers of firms with an increase in non-price competition.

New cars

Cars are produced on a *world* scale by a small number of very large firms: Ford, BMW, Toyota, Renault and so on. Clearly, these firms are in competition with one another, but because there are only about a dozen of them in total the ways in which they compete may be different and less intense than if there were 1000 or 2000 carmakers. So how does competition between carmakers manifest itself? Unlike groceries, cars are highly differentiated products with a host of particular design features and optional 'extras'. Typically, because they are few in number and because they make highly 'branded' products, carmakers tend to compete *less* on price and more on the intrinsic merits of the product. BMW do not suggest that their cars are cheaper than Toyota's or Renault's. Their advertising asserts that BMWs are *better* cars. Here then there is relatively little price competition but more *persuasion* of consumers through the medium of advertising. Again the prevalence of non-price competition appears to be based in part on the restricted number of firms in the industry, and it is again possible to identify a causal link between constrained consumer choice and limited price competition.

Train travel

Finally, the example of train travel. Usually, suppliers of train travel have no immediate competitors in the shape of rival train firms. Of course, train firms *are* in competition in the wider travel market: alternative forms of transport are offered by coach firms, airlines and private motoring. However, it is the absence of *immediate* rivals that gives train operators relative freedom from the imperatives of price competition. Train operators advertise standards of service and comfort rather than fare comparisons with other transport providers. Where they *do* advertise fares, the intention is usually to tap into consumer surplus by the process of market segmentation discussed in Chapter 3, Section 3.5. Thus, in a market where there are very few firms (here arguably only one), price competition is at its lowest relative intensity, and non-price competition – with less immediate potential competitors – appears to dominate.

Now, to what use can we put this discussion of different market types? Economic theory also recognizes four major market structures. These are differentiated by the intensity of price and non-price competition. Now, as we shall see, although the examples we have just given are *not* literal illustrations of each theoretical market structure, there are some parallels between them. The four major market structures identified by theory are as follows.

- **Perfect competition:** This is a benchmark or 'ideal type' with which other market structures may be compared. It is characterized by an infinitely intense level of price competition, to the extent that all firms in the market are forced to charge the same price. The number of firms in a perfectly competitive market is large, and, as suggested by our examples, this has an important bearing on the form and intensity of competition that prevails.

- **Imperfect competition:** Here, although the number of firms is still high, the relative intensity of price competition is somewhat moderated by the presence of slightly differentiated products. Differentiated products enable firms to charge different prices to those of their competitors. Firms that elect to charge higher prices may do so in the knowledge that consumer preferences for their particular product will to some extent safeguard the level of demand.

- **Oligopoly:** An oligopolistic market is dominated by a small number of firms, each large in relation to the market. Oligopolistic firms tend not to engage in intensive price competition, concentrating instead on non-price competition.

- **Monopoly:** A pure monopoly exists where there is one firm in a market selling a good or service for which there are no close substitutes. Here, as might be anticipated, competition in both price and non-price forms is relatively weak.

For ease of analysis, we shall confine detailed discussion of market structures in this chapter to a contrast between perfect competition and monopoly. Although we also consider imperfect competition and oligopoly, the essential critique of firms that we wish to elaborate here can made by reference simply to the most and least competitive market structures.

5.3 Perfect competition

A perfectly competitive market is defined by a series of definitive assumptions, a brief glance at which will convince the reader that this is indeed an 'ideal type', rather than an attempt to depict any real-world market structure. The assumptions run as follows.

- A perfectly competitive market is composed of a large number of independent profit-maximizing firms, each of which is small in relation to the market. As such, none is in a position to influence market conditions. There are also many consumers, each small in relation to the market.
- Any firm may leave the market if it chooses to do so, and other firms are free to enter it.
- Factors of production enjoy perfect mobility. This means that land, labour, capital and enterprise can move with ease between uses.
- There is perfect knowledge in the market. All firms and consumers are constantly aware of all prevailing economic conditions.
- Firms in the perfectly competitive market produce a homogeneous product: that is, one with no identifiable brand. This assumption means that loyalties to firms cannot be developed.

These assumptions are not reproduced in their entirety in any typical market. While the first two might be observable in the real world, the possibility of the simultaneous existence of perfect mobility and perfect knowledge is clearly remote. The final assumption is, moreover, probably the antithesis of concrete business practice. Virtually every firm tries to persuade the consumer that its product or service is in some way superior to that of its competitors. Consider the following anecdotal example. While engaged in some research a few years ago, the authors interviewed a director of a major UK biscuit and confectionery firm. In his industry, the director claimed, the ambition of every firm was to invent the equivalent of the Mars bar, such was the brand loyalty and unique level of demand enjoyed by this product.

The perfectly competitive firm as a price taker

While perfect competition does not exist, it is useful as a means of assessing the performance of actual market structures. What then are the implications of the restrictive assumptions that we have just outlined? The most important of these is that firms in a perfectly competitive market are *price takers*. In other words, all perfectly competitive firms must observe the single equilibrium price set by the market. Any one firm that imposed a higher price for its output would quickly cease to trade because it would immediately lose all demand. This is because consumers in the market would immediately be aware (given the assumption of perfect knowledge) that they could buy exactly the same (homogeneous) product elsewhere at a lower price. Nor would it be in the interest of any one firm to try to raise demand for its output by charging a price below the ruling market price given that it can sell all it wants at the ruling market price. Also, as we shall later demonstrate, in the long run perfectly competitive firms have strictly defined profit margins. To lower price below the prevailing market price would necessarily entail losses: hence no firm will do this.

Perfect competition: A market structure characterized, most notably, by a situation in which all firms in the industry are price-takers, and there is freedom of entry into and exit from the industry.

The revenue curves of the perfectly competitive firm

Average revenue: Total revenue divided by the number of units sold; it also equals price.

Total revenue: The amount of money that a firm receives from the sales of its output; equals the price of output multiplied by the number of units sold.

Marginal revenue: The amount of money that a firm receives from an additional unit of output.

Fig. 5.1 illustrates how price taking in a perfectly competitive market works. In Fig. 5.1(a) the market is in equilibrium with quantity demanded and supplied, balanced at Q_1. The equilibrium price is P_1. Fig. 5.1(b) illustrates conditions in a representative firm in the market. When analysing firms, the convention is to measure output on the horizontal axis and revenue and/or costs on the vertical axis. Notice that the firm's demand curve (D) is *perfectly elastic*. This is because, by assumption, every firm must take the prevailing equilibrium market price P_1 as given. Demand for the firm is then perfectly responsive to a change in price. We should also note here that the firm's demand curve is the equivalent of its **average revenue** curve. Average revenue simply indicates the amount that a firm receives per unit of output sold. If a firm produces and sells 100 units of output a day at a price of £10, it will receive a **total revenue** of £1000 (100 × £10). Its average revenue per unit is £10 (£1000 ÷ 100). Clearly, because the perfectly competitive firm is a price taker, its average revenue per unit of output will not change, regardless of how much it actually produces: each unit must be sold at price P_1, and therefore P_1 is always the average revenue per unit of output. Finally, the average revenue curve for a firm in perfect competition is also its **marginal revenue** curve. Recall from Chapter 3 that, in economics, the term 'marginal' simply means *extra*. A marginal revenue curve, therefore, indicates the *extra revenue* associated with each additional unit of output produced. In Fig. 5.1(b), because the firm always charges P_1, the marginal revenue of each additional unit of output must also be P_1. For example, if a perfectly competitive firm increases its production and sales from 100 units a day to 101 units, its total revenue will increase from £1000 (100 × £10) to £1010 (101 × £10). In consequence, the extra revenue gained from producing an additional unit of output is also £10 (£1010 − £1000). For a perfectly competitive firm, average revenue equals marginal revenue.

As the representative firm in Fig. 5.1(b) faces a perfectly elastic demand (average revenue) curve it can in theory sell as much output as it wants at price P_1. So how much should it produce? Remember that we are assuming that the firm's objective is to *maximize profits*. In order to do this the firm will need to know about the *revenue* and *costs* associated with each particular level of output: the difference between them determines whether the firm makes a profit (or loss). Up to now we have an awareness only of revenue; what about costs?

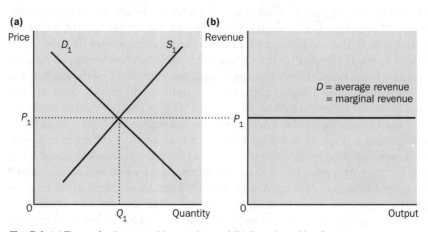

Fig. 5.1 (a) The perfectly competitive market and (b) the price-taking firm.

The cost curves of the firm

Fig. 5.2 depicts the average cost curve and marginal cost curve faced by the representative firm in a perfectly competitive market. *In fact, as we shall see, these curves are the same shape for firms in all market structures.* Let us think about how such cost curves are derived. The **average cost** of a particular output is its total cost divided by the number of units produced. In the short run a firm's average cost will fall over an initial range of output before beginning to rise again. This means that the average cost curve is *U shaped*, as in Fig. 5.2. Average cost falls at first because, as the firm begins to produce, although its **total costs** will rise, **fixed costs** are shared over (that is, divided by) an increasingly large output.

Imagine a firm that has been set up to manufacture beds. It has factory space and the appropriate machinery in place. Let us assume that these fixed factors have cost £1 000 000. Note that this sum has to be found regardless of whether any beds are produced or not: it is, in other words, a fixed cost of production. Fixed factors are so called because their composition cannot be altered in the short run: building and equipping a factory is not a simple process. Our firm may in the future decide it needs a new and bigger plant but this is clearly a long-term issue. Economists assume that fixed factors are alterable only in the long term; in the short term they are fixed.

Now the firm is about to make its first beds. To do so it must employ labour and raw materials in proportion to the number of beds it wishes to produce. Labour and raw materials here are *variable* factors, which incur **variable costs** of production: unlike fixed factors, the volume of variable factors employed can be increased or decreased relatively quickly and easily. Thus variable factors and costs are those that are alterable in the *short term*. To make an initial 10 beds let us assume our firm has to obtain labour and raw materials costing £1000. The firm's total costs are now £1 001 000 (i.e. the sum of the fixed and variable costs), and its average cost for the output of 10 beds will therefore be £100 100 (£1 001 000 ÷ 10). How would its costs change if the firm decided to make 100 beds? In this case it would pay £10 000 for raw materials and labour, taking its total costs to £1 010 000. But what then happens to average cost? In fact average cost per bed produced falls to £10 100 (£1 010 000 ÷ 100). The reader should be able to see that small increases in total cost are far outweighed in the arithmetic by the rising output total.

We now understand why average cost falls over its initial range, but why does it

Average cost: The total cost of producing any given output divided by the number of units produced; can be divided into average fixed and average variable costs.

Total cost: The sum of the costs of all inputs used in producing a firm's output; can be divided into fixed and variable costs.

Fixed costs: Costs that do not change with the output level; also referred to as overhead and unavoidable costs.

Variable costs: Costs that vary with the output level; also referred to as direct and avoidable costs.

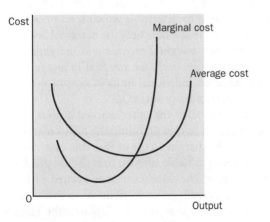

Fig. 5.2 Cost curves for the firm in a perfectly competitive market.

Marginal cost: The change in total cost resulting from increasing production by one unit.

eventually begin to rise despite further increases in the output total? The answer lies in the law of diminishing returns, first introduced in Chapter 3, Section 3.2. Diminishing returns imply that after a certain point, as more variable factors are added to a given set of fixed factors, the marginal and average costs of production begin to increase. In the bed factory let us assume that all equipment is fully utilized over a 'normal' 40 hour working week, and that this results in an output of 200 beds per week. Could more beds be produced? Clearly they could, but in the short term by increasing the working time of the factory and paying overtime to workers for their extra effort. In the long term, of course, the firm might build a new factory but that for the moment is another issue. Now, the central point here is that any additional beds above the 200 would cost *more* to produce than those made during normal working time – simply because of the overtime pay of labour. On average then, the cost of bed production increases. This explains why the U-shaped average cost curve in Fig. 5.2 begins to rise after a certain level of output has been reached.

What of the J-shaped **marginal cost** curve in Fig. 5.2? How is this derived? It should be clear from our example that there is a close link between average and marginal cost. It is the rising marginal cost of beds that pulls up their average cost. Note also that the marginal cost curve cuts average cost at its lowest point. This happens for the following reason. When marginal cost is less than average cost, average cost must be falling. Any extra cost that is less than the average must drag the average down. However, when marginal cost and average cost are equal, the average cost curve will be at the bottom of its U (that is, at its minimum point), neither decreasing nor increasing. Thereafter, as marginal cost rises in the face of diminishing returns, it pulls the average cost curve up.

The following additional simple example may help to conceptualize the relationship between marginal and average values. Suppose you are in a tutorial class where the average age is 20 years. Someone, who is younger than average, arrives late to join the class. What happens to the average age of the marginally enlarged class? Clearly the average age will fall. Alternatively, if the late arrival is older than average, then the average age of the class will rise. Only where the extra (marginal) person has exactly the same age as the average will the average age of the class remain unchanged.

The profit-maximizing output decision

We are now clear as to the composition of the perfectly competitive firm's revenue and cost schedules, but how can these be used to determine which level of output will produce maximum profit? In fact we need to use here only the marginal revenue and marginal cost curves. *The point at which marginal revenue and marginal cost intersect indicates the output position of maximum profit for any firm in any form of market structure.* Thus in Fig. 5.3, of the seven individual units of output that are illustrated, the unique output that yields maximum profit is Q_6.

To see why, let us consider the circumstances of the other marked output positions. At Q_1, for example, the individual unit of output Q_1 brings the firm a marginal revenue equivalent to its price (P_1), but the marginal cost of just this one unit is below P_1, at point B. The unit Q_1 is therefore profitable, and the firm should produce it. What of the next unit, Q_2? Is this profitable? The extra revenue associated with Q_2 is again price P_1, and its marginal cost has actually fallen to point A, so this unit is even more profitable than Q_1 and should also be produced. Similarly, the reader should be able to confirm that units Q_3, Q_4 and Q_5 with a marginal revenue of P_1 and

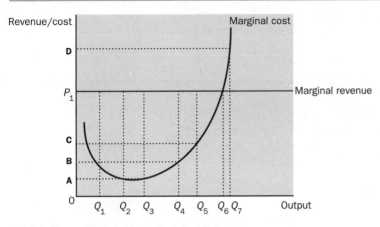

Fig. 5.3 The profit-maximizing output decision.

respective marginal costs at A, B and C are also profitable and therefore merit production. What then of unit Q_6? This unit again yields extra revenue of P_1, but the marginal cost of producing this unit is also the equivalent of P_1. The firm therefore breaks even on unit Q_6. Finally, there is Q_7. Here, extra revenue P_1 is outweighed by the greater marginal cost at point D. This unit is unprofitable, and the firm should not produce it, nor any further units after Q_7 as marginal cost continues to rise sharply. It appears then that Q_6, where marginal cost (MC) and marginal revenue (MR) indeed intersect ($MC = MR$), marks a boundary between profitable and unprofitable units of output: it is in other words the point at which profit is maximized: all units that yield profit are produced and none that would carry a loss.

One further point of clarification in respect of Fig. 5.3 should be made here. The $MC = MR$ rule applies only when the marginal cost curve is *rising*: that is, where the marginal cost curve cuts the marginal revenue curve from below. Although we have not shown the MC curve in its entirety, it actually cuts MR twice – the first time at a low level of output when it is falling.

Finally, it is important for the reader to verify that if the market price that the individual firm has to take as given were to rise or fall, it would induce an extension or contraction of output. In other words, the marginal cost curve for the individual, perfectly competitive firm is its supply curve, and the summation of the marginal cost curves of all firms that make up the industry will produce the market supply curve.

The short-run position of the perfectly competitive firm

In Fig. 5.4 we consider the short-run position of the perfectly competitive firm. The firm's output decision reflects its assumed desire to maximize profits, and accordingly it produces at Q_1 where $MC = MR$. Reference to the vertical axis reveals that the *average cost* of this level of output is at point A, while the *average revenue* associated with it is at P_1. *Total cost* is indicated by the rectangle $0ABQ_1$ (average cost multiplied by the number of units produced), while the rectangle $0P_1CQ_1$ indicates total revenue (average revenue times the number of units produced). Thus the shaded area AP_1CB – total revenue less total cost – represents the (maximum) profit earned at Q_1. For reasons that we shall explain shortly, this level of profit is also known as **supernormal profit**.

Supernormal profits: Profits that exceed the minimum amount a firm must earn to induce it to remain in the industry.

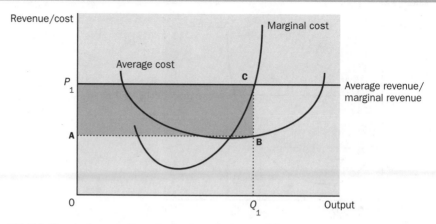

Fig. 5.4 The short-run position of a firm in perfect competition.

As noted, this is a short-run position for the firm. Earlier we defined the short run as that period in which *only* variable factors of production, such as labour, could be altered. In the long run all factors are variable, which also means that, should they wish to, firms can enter or leave the market. The question is: why would they choose to do so? The answer, of course, is the existence of supernormal profit. Given our assumption of perfect knowledge, others will be aware of the level of profit in the market: they can enter it, by securing the requisite factors of production. As new entrants come into the market, conditions change and the short run gives way to the long run.

The long-run position of the perfectly competitive firm

Some of the details of the movement from the short to the long run are sketched out in Fig. 5.5. In Fig. 5.5(a) we see the effect of the new entrants on the market. The supply curve shifts to the right from S_1 to S_2. This results in a fall in the market-clearing equilibrium price from P_1 to P_2 and an increase in the equilibrium quantity demanded and supplied from Q_1 to Q_2. For the representative firm, the implications

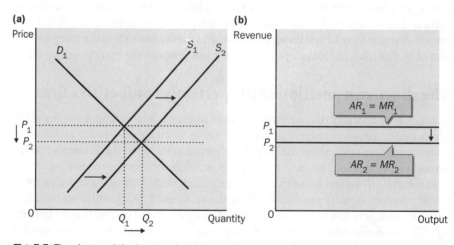

Fig. 5.5 The short and the long run in (a) the perfectly competitive market and (b) the price-taking firm.

of this change in market conditions are clear. As a *price taker* the firm must observe the new equilibrium market price. Accordingly, in Fig. 5.5(b), its demand curve (which, remember, is also its average revenue and marginal revenue curve) shifts downwards from AR_1, MR_1 to AR_2, MR_2.

Normal profit: The minimum amount of profit a firm must earn to induce it to remain in the industry.

The remaining question is, of course, what effect does this have on the supernormal profit that the firm was earning in the short run? In Fig. 5.6 the representative firm's AR/MR schedule has fallen in line with Fig. 5.5(b). The firm still seeks maximum profit, and therefore output is fixed at Q_{PC}, where $MC = MR$. Here, however, we can see that the rectangles of total revenue and total cost are one and the same: $0P_2AQ_{PC}$. This means that the firm is now covering its costs but is no longer earning supernormal profit. In fact, economists refer to this as a position where **normal profit** is being earned. Normal profit is the return required to keep the firm in the market, and includes requisite payments to all factors of production. In the long run then the perfectly competitive firm earns only normal profit, but this is sufficient to keep it in business. Notice also that should too many firms enter the market, to the extent that each firm's AR/MR schedule falls below the average cost curve, all firms will incur losses. This will provide an incentive for firms to leave the market until normal profit positions are achieved for those that remain.

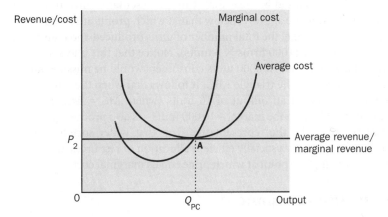

Fig. 5.6 The long-run position of a firm in perfect competition.

The perfectly competitive firm and allocative efficiency

In Chapter 3 we saw how the free market is in theory capable of facilitating a socially efficient allocation of resources. Recall that this implied that the market produces exactly the levels of output of particular goods and services that society as a whole desires. The market therefore makes the best possible use of scarce resources: it is an efficient and effective allocator of those resources. We can usefully replicate this analysis using the model of the perfectly competitive firm developed here.

In Fig. 5.7(a) we depict the MSB and MSC curves in a perfectly competitive market. Recall from Chapter 3 (Section 3.2) that the intersection of these curves indicates the socially desirable output for the good or service in question. In this case the socially desired output is 10 000 units. In Fig. 5.7(b) we depict the long-run equilibrium of a representative firm in this market. The firm produces at that output which equates MC with MR: namely, 10 units (as our firm is representative, we

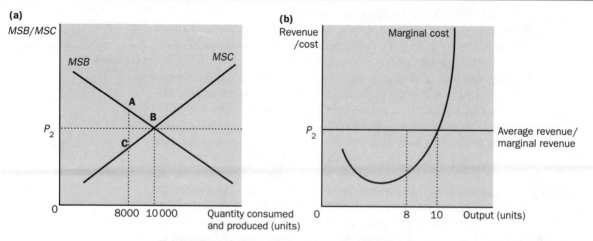

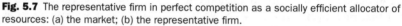

Fig. 5.7 The representative firm in perfect competition as a socially efficient allocator of resources: (a) the market; (b) the representative firm.

assume that the other firms also produce 10 units each, giving the total market supply of 10 000 units). It should be clear that if the representative firm produced only 8 units its output would be at a level below that at which profits are maximized. Assuming all firms did the same, the total number of units produced and consumed in the market would be 8000 (1000 firms × 8 units). Notice that this is less than the socially desirable market output. At 8000 units consumers would be missing out on an area of net benefit equal to the triangle ABC. It follows that when the representative firm maximizes profits at an output of 10 units (where $MC = MR$) and the socially desirable output level in the market – 10 000 units – is also produced, there is an allocation of resources by the representative firm that wider society prefers. Finally, note that, when there is a socially efficient allocation of resources, the representative firm is producing at a point at which price equals marginal cost.

Perfect competition: a summary

The perfectly competitive market produces some highly desirable outcomes. In the long run it provides sufficient incentive in the form of normal profit to retain firms in the market. At the same time, the output that firms produce can be seen to be set at a socially efficient level. In this case, then, we must apparently conclude that the free market is an effective means of allocating scarce resources. Yet perfect competition is only a *model*; its assumptions are not validated, in their entirety, in any real markets. Its usefulness therefore lies in the establishment of standards against which to judge market reality. We must ask in particular: does the firm's allocative preference match that of society as a whole? Let us now explore this issue by considering the least competitive market structure: monopoly.

5.4 Monopoly

The word 'monopoly' conjures up images of gigantic firms that dominate markets and consumers. For economists, this is not an appropriate way to conceptualize monopoly. Monopoly is defined by *market exclusion*. Whenever a firm can prevent others from entering the market, it is in a position to exploit *monopoly power* in that market. This means that the scale of the firm has no necessary bearing on whether or not it is a monopoly; what counts is its ability to keep potential rivals out.

Exclusion can happen in a variety of ways. Buffet cars on trains possess monopoly power because, for the duration of a journey, passengers have no other place to go for refreshment. Motorway service stations have monopoly power because they are the most readily available source of fuel for those driving long distances. In cases such as these, monopoly power arises because of a lack of close substitutes. The train passenger could make some sandwiches and a flask of coffee before leaving for the station; and the driver could leave the motorway to find cheaper petrol. But these options involve delays, or work the consumer would rather not do: thus he or she patronizes the supplier with monopoly power.

The question now arises: what does the monopolist *do* with monopoly power? One possibility is that because, by definition, monopoly power involves some *absence of competition*, the monopolist is able to charge higher prices than would otherwise be the case. Hence one would normally expect to pay more for food and drink on trains and for motorway service station fuel.

Before examining the economic implications of monopoly in detail, let us complete our review of the forms it can take.

- **Pure monopoly**: A pure monopoly exists where there is a sole supplier of a good or service in a market for which there are no close substitutes. The qualification concerning substitutes is an important one. There is for example only one tunnel under the English Channel. However, Eurotunnel, its operator, does not have a pure monopoly on cross-Channel travel because of the presence of a number of rival ferry operators. By contrast, the postal service in the UK *does* enjoy the status of a pure monopoly as the state forbids any other operator to carry mail for less than £1 per item. This means that all mainstream letter business is reserved for the Royal Mail. Note, however, that recently emerging close substitutes threaten even this monopoly: fax and email are the most obvious examples.

- **Legal monopoly**: In the UK, a monopoly is defined in law as a market share of 25 per cent or more. Monopolies and potential monopolies are liable to investigation by a government body, the Monopolies and Mergers Commission (MMC). The MMC seeks to establish whether or not particular monopolies operate against the public interest, in particular by limiting competition. Its recommendations are forwarded to a government minister, who decides whether or not to act on them (see Section 5.5 below).

- **Natural monopoly**: Some industries, because of their technical characteristics, tend to be most efficiently organized under the mandate of a single firm. The most common examples of natural monopoly are the electricity, water, gas and telecommunications industries. Clearly, it would be wasteful if an economy had several rival firms in, say, the supply of gas. Each firm would have its own separate infrastructural supply network, running pipelines to customers or potential customers – a pointless duplication when one would suffice. In the UK, until the 1980s, in order to protect consumers from the abuse of monopoly power, these industries were publicly owned. Now they are all in private ownership but subject to forms of public regulation and accountability. We examine the issues surrounding privatization in Chapter 6, Section 6.7.

Pure monopoly: A market structure in which there is a sole supplier of a good or service that has no close substitutes and for which there are barriers to entry into the industry.

Legal monopoly: As defined in the UK, arises when a firm enjoys a market share of 25 per cent or more.

Natural monopoly: Arises when a single firm is the most efficient structure for the production of a particular good or service.

Sources of monopoly power

We have seen that the existence of monopoly power requires exclusivity in a market for goods or services with no close substitutes. As in the case of the Royal Mail, such exclusivity can be granted by the state. There are a number of other instances of state-sanctioned monopoly. For example, monopolies may be created where this encourages artistic or technological innovation. Thus musicians and authors are granted copyrights on their work, and new inventions are similarly protected by patents. The assumption here is that without the right to exclusively exploit their work for a period, innovators would not have the incentive to commit scarce resources to the processes of research and development. This implies that, though monopoly might be associated with certain problems, it is acceptable for (say) the duration of a patent because of the wider long-term benefits it brings.

5.5 The economic implications of monopoly

The monopolist's cost and revenue curves

On the familiar assumption of profit maximization, we begin here by reviewing the cost and revenue curves of the monopolist in order that the profit-maximizing output might be determined. Note that, as for perfect competition and all other market structures, the profit-maximizing output for monopoly is where the marginal cost and marginal revenue curves intersect.

We have already explained that the average cost (AC) and marginal cost (MC) curves of firms do not change across market structures. This means that the U-shaped AC curve and the J-shaped MC curve depicted in Fig. 5.2 are again relevant here. We do, however, need to think about the monopolist's revenue curves. We saw that, in perfect competition, the firm is a price taker: it must take the ruling market price as given. For the monopolist, no such restriction applies. In the case of pure monopoly, the firm *is* the industry. The monopolist faces a demand curve that slopes downwards from left to right, as in Fig. 5.8. The demand curve is also the monopo-

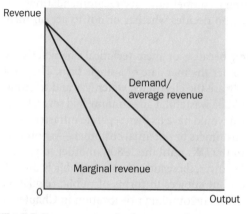

Fig. 5.8 Revenue curves for the monopolist.

list's average revenue curve, as it indicates the revenue received per unit of output (and this must be the selling price).

What of the monopolist's marginal revenue curve? Now, any linear marginal curve slopes twice as steeply in the same direction as the average curve from which it is derived. Fig. 5.8 also depicts the MR curve for the monopolist. Again, a simple numerical example will help to illustrate why the marginal revenue curve lies below the average revenue curve for a monopolist. Suppose a monopolist is producing and selling 100 units of output at a price of £10 per unit, generating a total revenue of £1000 (100 × £10) and an average revenue of £10 (£1000 ÷ 100). As the demand (average revenue) curve that the monopolist faces is downward sloping, in order to sell an extra (marginal) unit the price on all units must fall. For example, suppose sales of 101 units force the price of all units sold down to £9.95. In consequence – unlike the case of a firm in perfect competition – for the monopolist, marginal revenue of £4.95 (new total revenue 101 × £9.95 = £1004.95 *less* original total revenue of £1000) is less than average revenue (£9.95).

The monopolist's output decision

In order to maximize profits, the monopolist will produce at an output that equates MC and MR. In Fig. 5.9 this is at Q_M. At Q_M the monopolist will set price at P_1, which will also be the average revenue associated with this output. The average cost is at point A. We are now in a position to determine the level of supernormal profit earned by the monopolist. The total revenue associated with Q_M is the price of this output times the output itself. Thus total revenue is represented by the rectangle $0Q_MCP_1$. Total cost is given by the rectangle $0Q_MBA$. Taking total cost from total revenue leaves the shaded area $ABCP_1$, which represents profit. Significantly, because monopoly is defined by barriers to entry, this position (and the supernormal profits that go with it) is a *permanent* one. Unlike the case of the perfectly competitive market, here there will be no new entrants, and therefore supernormal profits will not be competed away by other firms.

Monopoly and allocative efficiency

In perfect competition we saw that the output generated by each firm both maximized profits and was socially efficient. In monopoly, profit maximization and

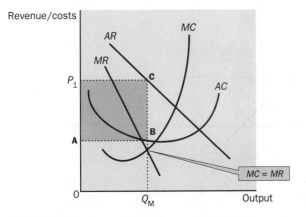

Fig. 5.9 The long-run position of the monopolist.

socially efficient resource allocation can be *incompatible*. Recall that the criterion for a socially efficient level of output is that price and marginal cost should be equal. The price of a good is taken to represent society's marginal valuation of it, while its marginal cost approximates society's view of the costs of its production. Thus where price is above marginal cost, the output concerned is deemed to be socially desirable, but when marginal cost exceeds price that unit of output should not be produced. It follows that the output at which price and marginal cost are equal is *the* socially efficient one as it marks the boundary between socially desirable and socially undesirable output.

In Fig. 5.10 we can see that the output for profit maximization, which the monopolist will select, is Q_M (where $MC = MR$). However, a socially efficient allocation of resources demands that output be set at a higher level: Q_2 (where price $= MC$). This means that the economic implication of monopoly is that it misallocates resources: the social preference would be for more resources to be committed to the industry and a greater output produced (Q_2) at a lower price (P_2).

We must stress here that the problem with monopoly is that, compared with the perfectly competitive market structure, it misallocates resources. If a monopolist took over a perfectly competitive industry, it might be expected to restrict output and raise prices, but this is not necessarily so. Take, for example, the case of an industry that is a natural monopoly but which is organized along perfectly competitive lines. Recall that the single supplier is the most effective form of organization for a natural monopoly. In perfect competition, with output divided between a large number of small firms, costs are unnecessarily high as each firm maintains its own (say) infrastructure of gas pipelines. With the emergence of the monopolist only one set of pipelines is retained, and the cost basis of the industry falls sharply. This possibility is illustrated in Fig. 5.11. In a perfectly competitive industry, equilibrium occurs where supply (the summation of individual firm's marginal cost curves, MC_1) equals demand (AR). A perfectly competitive output Q and price P are established where $P = MC_1$. If the industry is monopolized, with the monopolist facing the same cost and demand conditions as previously prevailed when the industry was perfectly competitive, then output would fall to Q_1 and price would increase to P_1. If, however, costs were reduced following monopolization, say from MC_1 to MC_2, then it is possible for the price to fall below, and output increase above, that which would prevail under a perfectly competitive industry, i.e. P_2 compared with P and Q_2 com-

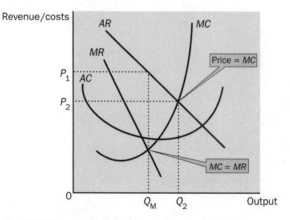

Fig. 5.10 The monopolist as a misallocator of resources.

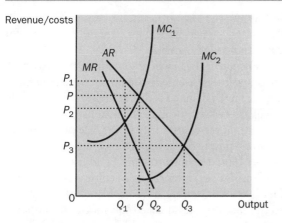

Fig. 5.11 From perfect competition to natural monopoly: lower prices and greater output but a misallocation of resources.

pared with Q. This of course means that the economic effect of monopoly is not, as is sometimes claimed, always to lower output and increase price. Monopoly does, however, *consistently misallocate resources*. Notice in Fig. 5.11 that a socially efficient allocation of resources for the monopolized industry would require an output of Q_3 (where price $= MC_2$) and price set at P_3.

Reflections on monopoly

Although allocative inefficiency is a major problem of monopoly, it is not the only one. By definition, monopoly involves some restriction of competition. This has wider significance because competition is the ultimate guarantor of consumer sovereignty. In a competitive market, no one producer will be able to set excessively high prices or offer substandard goods or services, because others will always be prepared to better meet the perceived demands of consumers. Now, as the whole canon of conventional economic theory rests on the certainty that free markets are indeed created and conditioned by the demands of consumers, the impairment of consumer sovereignty raises some serious questions concerning the validity of economic theory itself. So, just how serious are these questions?

For many economists, there is actually little cause for alarm here. Even where there is an absence of competition and monopoly exists, wider interests usually, at some level, prevail. Consider the following two examples.

First, the outcome of the pricing policies of the oil **cartel**, the Organization of Petroleum Exporting Countries (OPEC) in 1973–74 and 1979. OPEC, which controls most of the oil consumed by the advanced Western economies, is without doubt a very strong monopoly. For industrialized societies, oil is an important fuel with no readily available substitute. Knowledge of this fact permitted OPEC to reap the rewards of a fourfold increase in the price of oil in 1973–74, followed by a further twofold increase in 1979. The initial response in the oil-importing nations was stoicism: the oil was vital and nothing could replace it, so the higher prices simply had to be met. OPEC's monopoly seemed then to have placed it in an extremely powerful position, and further price increases might have been expected. However, although OPEC was not threatened by any serious competition, its ability to control events in the market was sharply curtailed in the first half of the 1980s, and the price

Cartel: A group of firms or producers that agree to act as if they were a single firm or producer, for example with regard to pricing and output decisions.

of oil actually fell over this period. Why? The answer lies in the response of the oil-importing nations to the price rises: they scaled back their demand for oil as, for instance, people began to run cars with smaller engines.

This example reveals the *limits to monopoly*. Even where something close to a pure monopoly exists, the monopolist is not free to set any price he or she likes without suffering the consequences. The basic law of demand – that at higher prices less will be demanded (and *vice versa*) – will assert itself through the actions of consumers. Yet even if consumers are the ultimate source of authority in the face of monopoly, this does not mean that monopoly can simply be ignored as an economic issue. In the OPEC case, the oil price increases caused major problems of adjustment for the oil-importing nations. Many countries experienced difficulties in adapting to the relative price of oil. Indeed, the continuing debt problems of some less-developed countries can be directly traced to the so called 'oil shock'. Monopolies may cause significant disruption to markets for a time, which would be less likely to occur in more competitive environments. Thus the oil shock could not have happened had the members of OPEC been in competition rather than collusion.

Second, what of the noted encouragement of monopolies by the state? How does this policy – implemented through the granting of patents and copyrights – square with the notion that monopolists dominate markets and act contrary to social preferences on resource allocation? The suggestion here is not that governments favour the creation of monopolies, rather that they recognize monopoly as an important potential source of *innovation* in the economy. Innovation is a challenging process. It may require years of effort and heavy investment to develop a new marketable product or piece of technology. There would be little point in a firm spending decades and large sums of money in, say, coming up with a cure for the common cold if, as soon as it was put on the market, rival manufacturers simply copied it and sold it themselves. However, an incentive to undertake the necessary research and development would be created if the firm was granted a patent on its invention for a period of time. This argument was first advanced by Joseph Schumpeter (1883–1950). Schumpeter also suggested that the greater size of the typical monopolist would enable it to finance research and development on a scale beyond most smaller competitive firms. In this view then, while monopoly might indeed restrict output, raise prices and misallocate resources, these are not the only criteria by which it should be judged. Monopoly may also be an important source of innovation in the modern economy.

Government control of monopoly

We now turn to the question of whether or not monopoly should be controlled or regulated by the state. If monopolies can disrupt markets, if they can set high prices secure in the knowledge that competitors are absent, or indeed if they are able to offer poor-quality goods or services because the consumer has little other choice available, should the state – recognizing a case of **market failure** – step in and do something to rectify matters? In practice, most governments in Western economies do, though as we shall see in Chapter 6 some economists of the *liberal school* think that state intervention to control monopoly may actually create bigger problems than monopoly itself.

As noted, in the UK issues of monopoly are investigated by the Monopolies and Mergers Commission (MMC). This agency decides whether or not a monopoly (or potential monopoly in the case of a proposed merger between firms) is likely to be

Market failure: Arises where the market fails either to provide certain goods, or fails to provide them at their optimal or most desirable level.

The regulation of monopoly: a case study
MMC demands guarantees from coach operator

The National Express Group [Britain's largest coach operator] was yesterday ordered to give guarantees on coach fares and timetables to win Monopolies and Mergers Commission approval for its 10-year franchise to run Midland Main Line rail services.

But Mr Ian Lang, President of the Board of Trade, stopped short of ordering the company to divest itself of any coach services or of allowing rival operators to be given access to the company's timetables or network of ticket agents. This was the solution preferred by the Office of Fair Trading.

National Express ... was the first company to fall foul of the competition authorities because of its expansion into

rail. It said it was 'on the whole pleased with the outcome of the investigation'. Mr Lang said the acquisition of the franchise would reduce the choice available to the leisure traveller between Sheffield, Chesterfield, Derby, Nottingham and Leicester, and London. Rail and coach services accounted for 97 per cent of public transport journeys between these destinations, with 90 per cent of coach passengers travelling for leisure purposes.

National Express will be expected not to increase coach fares above the retail price index, to maintain the current availability of coach tickets, to maintain capacity on its coaches and to keep the quality of the service at least as high as elsewhere on

its network. It has until March 20 to give these undertakings.

'The commission believed that, if National Express were required to divest itself of the coach services concerned, there was a serious risk of service levels being reduced, particularly if alternative operators did not have access to the benefits of National Express's network such as inclusion in its timetable and use of its agents for sales of tickets,' said Mr Lang. Even if National Express was required to provide these facilities for rivals, 'this would create an artificial arrangement within which effective competition could not be expected to flourish.'

Source: *Financial Times* 21 December 1996

---

against the public interest. A government minister, the President of the Board of Trade, at his or her discretion, then acts upon the MMC recommendation. A second government agency, the Office of Fair Trading, has the job of initially recommending to the President of the Board of Trade that particular monopolies or mergers should be investigated by the MMC. This rather convoluted process is designed to prevent the MMC's becoming 'judge and jury' in a case. Box 5.1 summarizes a recent instance of monopoly regulation.

What this example makes clear is the potential for monopolists such as National Express to both increase prices and reduce output in precisely the way that economic theory predicts that they may do. Notice that the government's response is to require that the firm give guarantees as to future pricing policy and the level of service it will offer to its existing coach passengers. Only then will it be allowed to acquire the rail franchise it seeks. As the passage indicates, an option considered and rejected by the government was to insist that National Express surrender some of its coach services to rivals. This of course would have involved limiting the extent of the monopoly. The preferred choice has been to allow the monopoly but to limit its commercial freedom.

5.6 Imperfect competition and oligopoly

Imperfect competition and oligopoly are the two intermediate market structures that lie between the extremes of perfect competition and monopoly. Both exhibit a greater degree of competition than monopoly. Like monopolies, imperfectly competitive firms and oligopolies are *price makers*. They are, in other words, able to set prices independently of their competitors. Recall that price-taking firms in perfect competition must all take the market price as given (see Section 5.3).

Imperfect competition

Imperfectly competitive firms are price makers because they sell *differentiated prod-ucts*. Differentiated products are similar to each other, but they do possess some distinguishing features. City centre pubs and bars, for example, might be thought to be in imperfect competition. There are plenty of them, and they mostly sell the same beers, wines and spirits. The market is also relatively easy to enter and leave. The distinguishing features here might be the ambiance of any particular establishment, or the quality of its beer.

As price makers, imperfectly competitive firms face a normal downward-sloping demand/average revenue curve, such as that depicted in Fig. 5.8. They also have a marginal revenue curve of the same general form as the *MR* curve in the figure. Moreover, we know that the average and marginal cost curves of all firms are similar to those in Fig. 5.2. Putting all this information together, and assuming profit maximization, we arrive at a supernormal profit position for the imperfectly competitive firm that is identical to that of the long-run position of the monopolist (as depicted in Fig. 5.9). However, for the imperfectly competitive firm, this is a *short-run* position only. An imperfectly competitive market allows firms freedom of entry and exit. Thus, because supernormal profits attract new entrants, the demand/*AR* curves of all firms in the market shift to the left as the level of demand is 'shared out' between more firms. This means that imperfectly competitive firms will in the long run earn only normal profits. New firms continue to enter the market until all supernormal profit is eroded. The long-run position of the representative imperfectly competitive firm is depicted in Fig. 5.12. As always, the profit-maximizing output, at Q_1, is determined by the *MC* = *MR* rule. That only normal profits are earned here is evident because total revenue and total cost are equal (both are represented by the rectangle $0P_1AQ_1$). Notice also that, unlike the firm in a perfectly competitive industry, the firm is not producing at the lowest point of its average cost curve.

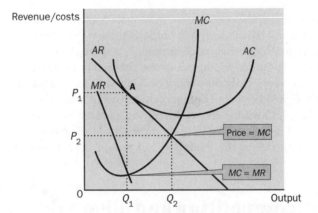

Fig. 5.12 The long-run position of the imperfectly competitive firm.

Oligopoly

Oligopoly is typified by the presence of a small number of firms, each large in relation to the market. Market entry here is more difficult than in imperfect competition, and so profits earned by oligopolists tend to be less easily 'competed away'. The obstacles to entry into an oligopolistic market may be significant but they are not, as in the case of monopoly, insurmountable. Consider the following three examples.

Oligopoly can be protected by *industrial scale.* As discussed in Chapter 4, the car industry is composed of firms that produce very large volumes of output as a means of keeping down the average cost of each car. This has the incidental effect of dissuading new entrants to the industry. To compete effectively in the 'mass production' car market, it is necessary to mass produce at the outset. This means that any potential entrant has to risk a huge volume of capital to break into the industry. For many potential rivals, such risks are prohibitive.

A second means of preserving oligopoly involves the development of an *extensive product range.* If a market can be segmented by subtle variations on a single product, then this can be a highly effective deterrent to entry. The most infamous example of this source of oligopoly is the soap powder industry. In the UK, two firms – Lever Brothers and Procter and Gamble – produce between them an extensive range of soap powders. Any third market entrant, manufacturing and selling one new powder, would not gain a third of the market but only a small proportion of it.

Finally, *brand loyalties* offer firms the possibility of creating exclusive market space for their goods and services. We noted the example of the Mars bar earlier in this chapter. It might be argued that firms such as Coca Cola and the fast food chain, McDonald's have achieved a place in global popular consciousness that accords their output an even greater degree of brand loyalty. Branding this successfully decisively establishes the oligopolistic position of these firms.

Same kind of product, different packaging

A noted feature of the oligopolistic market is the degree of *price stability* that it is sometimes thought to exhibit. Although oligopolists in the same market are clearly in competition with each other, this can be restricted to non-price forms. For example, in petrol retailing, competition has traditionally been of the 'free gift' or 'bonus points' variety, where customers are given drinking glasses, mugs and other assorted items according to the volume of petrol they buy. For a long time petrol prices did not vary greatly between different garages, and price rises – when they occurred – tended to happen everywhere simultaneously. However, in the UK in recent years the petrol market has become much more price competitive, chiefly as a result of the entry into the market of the large supermarkets such as Tesco and Sainsbury's, and their practice of selling cheaper petrol than the established garage chains.

Fig. 5.13 illustrates a possible reason for price stability under oligopoly. Notice that the oligopolist's *AR* or demand curve is assumed to be 'kinked'. This is because the oligopolistic firm thinks that any increase in price above P_1 will be ignored by its rivals, and that they will accordingly gain market share rapidly at its expense. However, the firm also supposes that, should it cut price below P_1, all its rivals will follow suit. In these circumstances, its market share will be unchanged. The net result of these deliberations is that the firm will tend not to indulge in price competition, and, because they follow the same reasoning, nor will its rivals. Fig. 5.13 demonstrates a second reason for price stability amongst oligopolists. The kink in the demand curve produces a discontinuity in the firm's marginal revenue curve. This means that the same profit-maximizing output Q_1 (where $MC = MR$) will apply irrespective of shifts in the marginal cost curve between MC_1 and MC_2. Thus the oligopolist can absorb some limited shifts in cost without a change in output or price.

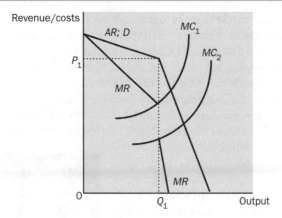

Fig. 5.13 Price stability under oligopoly.

5.7 Market structures: an institutionalist view

Having reviewed the four major market structures, an obvious question now arises as to the relative importance of each in the real economy. Although perfect competition has been presented as an ideal, its near neighbour – imperfect competition – appears to possess some important attributes that might be thought to recommend it over both oligopoly and monopoly. In particular, the imperfectly competitive market retains a high degree of openness and intensity of competition, and imperfectly competitive firms have few powers of market exclusion. The key to their survival must therefore be their ability to remain competitive, one against the other, in the way that they satisfy consumer demands. It follows that, if an economy is characterized by the presence of many imperfect markets, the pre-eminence of consumer sovereignty is still firmly established. Such an economy will be close to, if not quite at, the Smithian ideal. So what do modern advanced economies actually look like? Do they approximate imperfect competition or do they tend to be dominated by oligopoly and monopoly?

Of the various schools of economic analysis, *institutionalism* has the most decisive perspective on such questions, particularly in the writings of John Kenneth Galbraith. Galbraith's work has concentrated on the US economy but its generalities are applicable to the other advanced capitalist nations in Europe and the Far East. Galbraith's primary claim is that in many respects the advanced economies are in fact increasingly dominated by relatively small numbers of extremely large and therefore powerful firms. Power here means the ability to manipulate and control one's own environment. Thus, Galbraith argues, the largest firms are able to organize the markets in which they are situated to the exclusion of other interests, such as those of smaller firms and – especially – the consumer.

This situation is a relatively new one. The capitalism that Smith, Ricardo and Marx studied in the eighteenth and nineteenth centuries was not of this form; it was typified by the kind of imperfectly competitive markets characterized above. Then, the tenet of consumer sovereignty did generally apply. But in the interim, and especially since 1945, the key *institutions* of capitalism – including the firm – have undergone profound change. This postwar period has witnessed not only the emergence of giant firms but also the development of 'big' government and very large trade unions. Galbraith argues that the reshaping of these key institutions of capitalism has important implications for the way the system actually works and, moreover, in *whose interests* it works. Here we concentrate on his analysis of firms.

The emergence of significant numbers of large firms across a variety of industries in the advanced capitalist economies since 1945 is, in the institutionalist view, the result of rapid *technological development* over this period. We noted in Chapter 4 (Section 4.3) that Henry Ford's adoption of the flow-line method of car assembly, while making cars cheaper and easier to produce, required the overall scale of production to be much higher than it had ever been before. As elements of 'Fordism' were taken up by other industries, they too increased their scales of production. In industries unsuited to the flow-line, other forms of technological change with associated high investment costs also tended to make the efficient scale of production higher such that, again, the size of firms tended to increase.

So how far has this process gone? In Galbraith's view, approximately *half* of private sector production in the USA now rests in the hands of large firms that are either monopolies or oligopolies. The other half can be attributed to firms that broadly conform to the rules of imperfect competition. In this latter segment, then, the principle of consumer sovereignty still applies: in attempting to maximize profits, firms must prioritize the interests of consumers, and the course of production is strongly conditioned by consumer demand. Galbraith calls the uncompetitive part of the economy the *planning system* and the competitive part the *market system*. The term 'planning' is appropriate because firms in this sector are able to plan and direct the development of their own markets. This is clearly a very strong assertion and, moreover, one that flies in the face of the orthodoxy of consumer sovereignty: how is it justified?

As noted, the institutionalist approach suggests a link between the *size* and the *power* of a firm. Now there can be no doubt that the leading firms in the advanced economies are indeed extremely large. For example, the total annual sales of the US carmaker General Motors have in recent years been consistently greater than the national income of Belgium, and the total sales of Ford similarly exceed the national income of Austria. But how *precisely* does scale translate into power? The Galbraithian claim is that the largest firms enjoy a measure of influence over consumers, costs and prices that escapes smaller firms. Let us think about each of these 'spheres of influence' in a little more detail.

Consumers, to take the first case, are clearly receptive to advertising, otherwise firms – large and small – would not bother to do it. The largest and best-resourced firms will be able to afford the heaviest advertising: this is also clear. But what does advertising do? In the conventional view, it allows the individual firm to provide information about its product in the hope of persuading people of its particular merit. Ford promotes the Mondeo in the hope that car buyers will prefer it to a Rover or a Renault. For Galbraith, however, the picture is complicated when one considers the combined and cumulative effect of advertising by the car industry as a whole. This amounts to continuous persuasion not that this car or that car is better but that private motoring is desirable *per se*. While this might indeed be the case, private motoring is only one way of getting from place to place. An obvious alternative would be to use buses, an environmentally friendlier option in these congested times. But are bus services promoted as extravagantly as new cars? Of course the

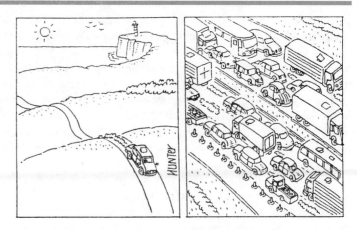

Car advertising: the reality behind the image

SPOT THE CAR ADVERT

answer is 'no', because bus firms are generally smaller and not so well off as car-makers. The combined effect of car advertising is then to affirm a psychological desire for private motoring above other forms of transport when in fact the material need is only for mobility.

Now, although virtually all firms can and do advertise, the superior resources of the planning sector mean that only its members are likely to be able to generate persuasion on a scale sufficient for general product affirmation, such as that achieved by the giant car firms. None of this means that consumers become mere dupes of the planning system, but it does suggest that firms in the planning system can fix the interests and generate the allegiance of consumers in ways denied to the smaller firms in the market system.

The scale of firms in the planning system also permits them to exert unusually strong influence over *costs and prices*. A good example of this is the power that the major UK supermarkets have over the producers of food and other goods that they sell. Because the largest supermarkets now account for the vast proportion of retail sales their suppliers are forced into a subordinate business relationship for want of alternative outlets for the goods they produce. Turning now to prices, we have already characterized imperfectly competitive firms, oligopolies and monopolies as price makers, but there is an important difference between the first of these and the other two in the extent to which the prices they set have significance in the wider market. The ability of the imperfectly competitive firm to establish a unique price is conditioned by the degree of product differentiation that it can achieve in a crowded and fairly competitive market. Even when substantial product differentiation permits relatively high prices to be set compared with the market 'norm', these have no general market relevance: consumers can elect to buy the product in question or choose a readily available and cheaper alternative. In markets dominated by oligopoly and monopoly the situation is rather different. Here, because most production is (at best) shared amongst a small number of large firms, whatever prices are set *are* significant for the market as a whole because consumer choice is relatively limited. This is most apparent in the case of pure monopoly, but it is also a familiar trait in oligopoly where, as noted, there tends to be a degree of price stability amongst firms, with competition − such as it is − restricted to non-price forms.

Once again, then, firms in the planning system enjoy a measure of market control far beyond that available to their counterparts in the market system.

The implications of this analysis are profound. Galbraith refers to the notion of consumer sovereignty as the *accepted sequence*, meaning that the chain of command in a market economy flows from the consumer to the producer. As we have seen, Galbraith's work contends that, in the market system at least, the accepted sequence works largely as anticipated, and the firm is subordinate to the consumer. However, given the conditions outlined above, in the planning system there is a dramatic reversal of influence. Here the firm has the power to shape and control the market and to impose its priorities and preferences on the consumer: in Galbraith's phrase there is then a *revised sequence* as consumer sovereignty is replaced by *producer* sovereignty. While conventional economics does not wholly ignore the concept of power – market exclusion is clearly a form of power – in the institutionalist view it fails to recognize the extent of the power of the planning sector and its negative implications for the trumpeted ideals of competitive capitalism.

Summary

◆ Economic theory recognizes four market structures: perfect competition, imperfect competition, oligopoly, and monopoly. Perfect competition provides an idealized view of how markets should work given the highest possible level of competition between their constituent firms. Its principal attributes are absolute consumer sovereignty and the socially efficient allocation of resources. Although the assumptions of perfect competition are not all met in the real economy, it provides a useful benchmark against which the relative merits of actual market structures may be assessed.

◆ In contrast to perfect competition, pure monopoly is characterized by an absence of competition. This inevitably entails a misallocation of resources. However, it is not the case that monopolies always restrict output and raise prices to the detriment of the consumer. In the case of natural monopoly, a single supplier may raise output and lower prices to levels that could not be achieved in a competitive environment. Nor need monopolies be especially large. Monopoly power is defined by barriers to entry, not size. Finally, monopolies necessarily impinge upon the sovereignty of the consumer.

◆ Firms in the two remaining market structures are, like monopolies, price makers. Arguably, oligopoly is characterized by lower levels of competition and weak consumer sovereignty, while imperfect competition, because it retains competitiveness, necessarily prioritizes consumer interests.

◆ Finally, the work of Galbraith contends that large parts of modern capitalist economies tend towards oligopolistic and monopoly organization. This poses serious questions as to the ultimate *raison d'être* of the contemporary capitalist system: whose interests does it primarily serve, those of the consumer or the producer?

Key terms

◆ Market structure
◆ Perfect competition

◆ Imperfect competition

◆ Oligopoly

◆ Monopoly

◆ Price taker

◆ Price maker

◆ Profit maximization

◆ Socially efficient resource allocation

◆ Resource misallocation

◆ Institutionalism

◆ Planning system

◆ Market system

◆ Accepted sequence

◆ Revised sequence

Self-test questions

True (t) or false (f)

1. Perfectly competitive firms are price takers.

2. Firms in perfect competition can earn supernormal profits in the short run only.

3. Firms maximize profits by selling goods at the highest possible price.

4. Allocative efficiency for society as a whole is where firms produce an output that equates price and marginal cost.

5. When an industry is monopolized the outcome is always a higher price and reduced output.

6. In the long run monopolists can earn supernormal profits.

7. Imperfectly competitive firms are price takers.

8. Imperfectly competitive firms enjoy powers of market exclusion.

9. Oligopolists enjoy powers of market exclusion.

10. For institutionalists, capitalism is an increasingly uncompetitive system.

Complete the following sentences by inserting the missing word(s)

1. The demand or average revenue curve of a firm in perfect competition is ____.

2. Perfectly competitive firms produce ____ goods and services.

3. Supernormal profits are profits that ____ the minimum amount a firm must earn to induce it to remain in the industry.

4. Normal profit is the ____ amount a firm must earn to induce it to remain in the industry.

5. Monopoly is sustained by ____.

6. For any firm, the maximum profit output is where ____.

7. Imperfectly competitive firms, oligopolists and monopolists are all price ____.

8. Price stability under oligopoly has been explained by the ____ demand curve faced by the oligopolist.

9. Galbraith calls the less competitive part of the private sector in the modern economy the ___.

10. Where consumer sovereignty is subverted by less competitive firms, there exists a ___.

Questions for discussion

◆ Why should the profit-maximizing firm always produce at that output which equates marginal cost with marginal revenue?

◆ To what extent might the following exert monopoly power: a regional newspaper such as the *Liverpool Echo* or the *London Evening Standard*; Everton Football Club?

◆ Do monopolies tend always to raise price and lower output?

◆ What is the significance of Galbraith's notion of the 'revised sequence'?

Further reading

George, K.D., C. Joll and E.L. Lynk *Industrial Organization* (4th ed.) (London: Routledge, 1991). A comprehensive examination of the economics of the firm.

Atkinson, B., F. Livesey and B. Milward *Applied Economics* (Basingstoke: Macmillan, 1988). Chapters 1–5 provide an overview of the firm in applied UK and European contexts.

Shepherd, W.G. *The Economics of Industrial Organization* (Englewood Cliffs, NJ: Prentice-Hall, 1990). Contains a complementary mix of theory and well-presented industry case studies.

Dunning, J.H. *Multinational Enterprises and the Global Economy* (Harlow: Addison-Wesley, 1993). A major survey of the scope, form and implications of the activities of multinational firms. This book is also recommended as further reading for Chapter 17.

Galbraith, J.K. *Economics and the Public Purpose* (Harmondsworth: Penguin, 1973). Offers a summary of Galbraith's views, including those on the structure and influence of large firms.

Internet links

The Monopolies and Mergers Commission (MMC) investigates and reports on matters relating to monoplies, mergers and anti-competitive practices. Its website contains MMC reports from 1950 to date. The site can be found at: **http://www.open.gov. uk/mmc/mmchome.htm**
The Office of Fair Trading (OFT) is charged with protecting consumers and enforcing UK competition policy. Its Web site – with excellent further Internet links – is at: **http://www.oft.gov.uk/**

Market Failure Versus Government Failure

Key issues

▶ Do markets sometimes fail to produce desirable outcomes in coordinating the demand for and supply of some goods and services?

▶ If markets do 'fail', can the state intervene to correct the problem?

▶ Can the state itself similarly fail when it intervenes in markets?

▶ What kinds of policy are informed by the debate over market and state failure?

6.1 Introduction

Chapters 1-4 of this book elaborated the perspective that the free and competitive market is an effective means of resolving the basic economic questions surrounding the use and allocation of scarce resources. However, in Chapter 5 we saw that once the implicit assumption that free markets are necessarily competitive is relaxed, established certainties as to the inherent strengths of *laissez-faire* begin to melt away. In *real* markets, the existence of monopoly and oligopoly directly undermines consumer sovereignty, and may be inimical to general consumer interests.

In the present chapter we extend this critique of the free market by introducing the notion of **market failure**. Conventional economic theory recognizes three main forms of market failure:

- monopoly
- public goods
- externalities.

We saw in Chapter 5, Sections 5.4–5.5, that the existence of monopoly, because it is perceived to distort the proper functioning of the market, may give rise to various forms of state intervention. For example, the government may take steps to limit the commercial freedom of monopolists (see Chapter 5, Box 5.1, for a case study), or it may choose to assume the ownership of a monopoly by nationalizing it. Now, because they too are forms of market failure, the existence of public goods and

Market failure: Arises where the market either fails to promote certain goods, or fails to provide them at their optimal or most desirable level.

externalities provides an *additional rationale for state intervention*; this chapter explains why.

Yet some *liberal* economists claim that market failure is a relatively rare occurrence, and that the problems associated with its particular forms can be overstated. The liberal school also raises the issue of *state or government failure*. Its argument is simply that, in intervening to 'solve' a particular case of market failure, the government itself often gets things wrong, and the economic problem becomes worse rather than better. This suggests that market failure, such as it is, should be tolerated because in many instances it is preferable to state failure. The present chapter also considers these views.

In the UK especially, but also in many other economies, the belief that the market – regardless of certain shortcomings – is the best means by which to allocate scarce resources has informed the policy of *privatization*. Privatization involves the surrender of some aspects of state influence over economic activity and the consequent reassertion of market priorities. We use an overview of the privatization process in the UK as a means to further illustrate the market failure/state failure debate, which is the core theme of this chapter.

6.2 Market failure

What does market failure mean? A successfully functioning free market is based on the tenets first identified by Adam Smith in *The Wealth of Nations* (1776). These have undergone remarkably little modification in the intervening 200 years. As we know from previous chapters, Smith supposed that free markets were composed of many independent producers and consumers. This makes markets *competitive* and *individualistic*. Producers compete against one another to try to secure the business of each individual consumer. When a transaction takes place, it assumes the form of a discrete contract between the producer and the consumer in which a clearly identifiable volume of goods or services changes hands. These are not trite observations. They closely define the necessary elements without which the market would not work as anticipated: it would indeed then exhibit signs of failure.

We have already seen that competition is an important source of dynamism in the market. Without it, the incentive for producers to be entrepreneurial and innovative is reduced; they can churn out the same old goods and services and earn a profit, unconcerned that their lethargy will be exposed by the dynamism of rivals simply because there are no current rivals. If it becomes established, such stagnation certainly merits the charge of market failure, and its most obvious source is monopoly.

Similarly, free markets must be *individualistic* in the sense that the goods and services bought and sold pass privately from producer to consumer. It would not be possible for a market to exist in cases where the nature of particular goods and services prevented individuals from exclusively owning or consuming them. As we shall see, such **public goods** do exist, and the market fails because it is unable to coordinate their production and consumption.

Finally, Smith's notion of the successfully functioning market rests on its discretion. When individual producers and consumers participate in market transactions, they do so willingly and voluntarily because they expect to gain from such transactions. Smith supposed that as the millions of individual economic agents present in

Public good: One that once produced can be consumed by everyone.

society worked away, undertaking more and more transactions, the overall volume of gain would increase. The general effect would therefore be a more productive and contented society. There is, however, a crucial and implicit assumption here that each and every transaction affects *only* those who directly participate in it. But what if there are, as it were, 'innocent bystanders' at the edge of a transaction who are in some way harmed or advantaged by it? When such *external effects* (externalities for short) arise, the free market, with its working assumption of discrete individualism, fails to recognize them.

These then are the senses in which free markets can fail: where the underlying *necessary* assumptions of competition, individualism and discretion – which are at the heart of the Smithian framework – break down. We have already (in Chapter 5) reviewed aspects of market failure that can be attributed to monopoly. Although we return to this issue in our discussion of privatization, for the present we concentrate on the remaining two forms of market failure: *public goods* and *externalities*.

6.3 Public goods

Many kinds of goods and services are consumed privately and exclusively. If I drink a pint of beer no one else can drink the same pint. If you visit the cinema to watch a film I cannot sit in the same seat as you at the same screening. In each case, the good and service are comprehensively and exclusively 'used up'. In fact, as we shall see, these **private good** characteristics are essential if the market is to be employed as the framework for their delivery.

However, some goods and services do not have such private attributes. Take, for example, street lighting. If I take a walk at night I consume street lighting but my consumption does not diminish the supply available to anyone else: thus street lighting is said to be *non-rival* in consumption. At the same time, once street lighting is provided it is difficult to imagine how individuals could be prevented from consuming it if they wished to: they would simply have to step outside on a dark evening. Street lighting is therefore also *non-excludable*. These two public good characteristics make it very difficult to see how a street lighting service could be made available via the market mechanism.

The central obstacle is what is known as the **free rider problem**. If a private firm elects to supply street lighting, who will buy it? Every potential consumer would know that if just *one* person agrees to pay for the service everyone else can consume it for free: its supply will not be eroded with consumption (it is non-rival), nor can the provider or the paying consumer prevent free consumption by others (it is non-excludable). Thus the public characteristics of the service mean that no one has an incentive to buy it; everyone is content to be a free rider. Hence there is no private demand and – as a consequence – no private supply. Now, because public goods are not available through the market, if they are judged to be intrinsically desirable we have an economic rationale for their provision in some way by government. Effectively, the government forces society to pay collectively through taxation for something it will not pay for privately. Of course, in democratic societies governments have an electoral mandate for such action.

Other examples of public goods include national defence, the justice system, and roads. Let us consider this list a little more closely in the context of the noted public good characteristics of non-rivalness in consumption and non-excludability.

Private good (or service): One that is wholly consumed by an individual.

National defence, to take the first case, effectively 'blankets' any society for which it is provided. Whether they like it or not all UK residents are equally safeguarded by the UK's defence system. Even those who are pacifists or members of the Campaign for Nuclear Disarmament 'consume' the services of the armed forces, and they do so just as intensively as any general or admiral. National defence is therefore a *pure* public good because it exhibits *perfect* non-rivalness and non-excludability.

Similarly, the justice system is administered on behalf of all citizens equally. Every individual is protected from criminal activity by the police and the courts. However, notice here that it is possible for the private sector to become independently involved in some aspects of this service. Private security firms, for example, offer protection to individuals, shops and businesses in exactly the same way as, say, cleaning firms offer their services. This means that part of the security element of the justice system – effectively the 'criminal dissuasion' work of the police – has limited non-rivalness and non-excludability. In this respect then the police service may be thought to lie somewhere between a pure public good and a private good. Overall, however, its responsibilities for the administration of justice and the maintenance of public order elevate its essential public good characteristics.

Roads are a rather different matter. Non-rivalness applies here only up to a point. On a road where traffic is flowing freely, additional vehicles may join without undue hindrance to other road users. However, on a motorway such as the M25, which orbits London, there are notorious congestion problems, which means by definition that consumption has become rival. As more and more vehicles join the M25, traffic flow slows down, ultimately to a stop. It is also possible to exclude traffic from roads. Large parts of the French motorway network are tolled; only those who pay are able to use it. So neither non-rivalness or excludability applies with any degree of completeness here.

Yet conventionally roads are still classed as public goods, although their form is less pure than both national defence and the justice system. The main reasons for their 'public good status' are the practical and political difficulties that would be associated with systematic exclusion and wholly private provision. Thus, while tolling systems might be appropriate for motorways, they could hardly be installed on most or even many roads. Moreover, given the cultural significance of private motoring in Western societies – typically embodied in notions of the 'freedom of the open road' – systematic exclusion would hardly be likely to command a popular mandate. The implication here is that for the most part governments must indeed assume responsibility for road provision. However, it is also clear that some roads could be (and indeed are) supplied and operated by the market.

6.4 **Externalities**

The third form of market failure arises because many ostensibly market-based and private transactions between individuals affect other third parties or 'innocent bystanders'. The result may be a good or a bad one but in either case the market is unable to comprehend what is happening. Generally, the market produces too many transactions that have **negative externalities** and too few that have **positive externalities**. As for public goods, the appearance of externalities provides a rationale for state intervention in the market. It is the state's purpose here to reduce negative externalities and promote positive ones.

Externalities or third-party effects: Costs incurred or benefits received by other members of society not taken into account by producers and consumers.

Negative externalities

Environmental pollution is a notorious form of negative externality. If a firm uses a river as a sink into which it releases waste products this clearly impacts upon those who use and value the river. Ornithologists, anglers and those who simply like to take a riverside walk will all be adversely affected by the firm's decision to pollute. Now the firm's interests clearly lie in producing an output as efficiently as possible, so from its own standpoint polluting the river is sensible if cleaner methods of waste disposal are more expensive. Similarly, for those who consume the firm's products the decision to pollute is also preferred as they will wish to pay lower product prices rather than higher ones. The key point here is that both the firm and the consumer are acting rationally in the *individualistic world of the market*. Their focus is entirely upon the cost of the private transaction to which they are party; the interests of river users simply do not register economically.

Now this is clearly a problem, because a clean river *does* have value to those who use it or who might use it in the future. If the firm could be made to recognize this it would presumably take steps to dispose of its waste in an environmentally friendly, if more expensive, manner. This would mean that the firm appreciated both the private and wider social costs of its activities. In such circumstances the firm's output would become dearer – higher prices reflecting higher production costs – but only because the pollution externality had been *internalized*. So how can the firm be made to take account of the externalities it generates? This is where the state comes in. If river pollution carried a financial penalty of sufficient weight, then all potential polluters would have an incentive to find clean methods of waste disposal even where these carried higher costs – better to meet the higher cost than the even higher fine. In the UK, river pollution is discouraged in precisely this way. Box 6.1 provides an example.

Air pollution: a negative externality

Box 6.1

Record fine for polluting river

By Nicholas Schoon

Britain's second largest water company was yesterday fined a record £175 000 for poisoning a river and killing thousands of fish. It was the largest pollution fine a water company has ever received. Severn Trent Water Authority admitted leaking ferric sulphate – used to treat drinking water – into one of the best stretches of salmon river in Wales, killing all but 2 per cent of the stock.

It was the company's 34th conviction since privatization seven years ago, Cardiff Crown Court heard. Judge John Prosser told company executives that the leak was due to a combination of design defects, gross mismanagement and inferior maintenance. 'To be convicted so many times shows that the management of the company is very slack indeed,' he said.

Prosecutor Mark Bailey, acting for the government's new Environment Agency, said the pollution from Severn Trent's Elan Valley water treatment works at Rhayader, Powys, flowed down the small river Elan and into the Wye, where it

killed 33 000 young salmon in June last year. 'The sheer number of fish killed is higher than (in) any other incident,' he said. The chemical had turned the river acid, causing large quantities of aluminium to be released from sediments. This metal is highly toxic to fish.

The company, which pleaded guilty to polluting the river, was also ordered to pay costs and compensation of almost £44 000, including £8500 towards restocking with fish.

Severn Trent's barrister, Benjamin

Nichols, told the court that the chemicals leaked through a hairline crack in a pipe, which was repaired as soon as it was spotted.

After the verdict, Peter Gough, of the Environment Agency, said it showed that 'thorough investigations into incidents such as this pay off. Companies must realize the seriousness of their actions.' Severn Trent said it was distressed by the size of the fine but had no plans to appeal.

Source: The Independent 6 August 1996

There are of course other forms of negative externality and consequently other forms of preventive state intervention. Building and construction for example is subject to development control and planning legislation. For instance, if you own a house with a garden, the local authority will not permit you to build a second house in the garden, because your private decision involving your own property would negatively impact upon your neighbours. Box 6.2 offers a second example of the externality issues associated with a more substantial construction project. Here, the government has approved an application by Manchester Airport to build a new run-way but on the understanding that the airport authorities will take substantial steps to protect the environment. The chief concerns mentioned in the box are the distur-bances (that is, the externalities) caused by night flights and noise. Notice, however, that protesters have also raised concerns over woodland that, the government accepts, will be destroyed by the development. This particular externality (the lost wood-land) is therefore deemed to be tolerable given the substantial economic benefits associated with the new runway.

Positive externalities

A positive externality arises when private transaction produces *unintended benefits* for economic agents who are not party to it. Because the market does not recognize anything beyond the immediacies of the transaction itself, it is unable to appreciate

Box 6.2

Second runway approved for Manchester Airport

Manchester Airport won government approval yesterday to build a second runway but faces bitter opposition from environmentalists who pledged to continue their fight against the £172m project.

Business leaders in the north-west welcomed the runway as a substantial boost to the regional economy. The airport's expansion is forecast to create about 7000 jobs on site and more than 43 000 in the region as passenger numbers double to 30m over the next decade.

The airport won planning permission after a nine-month public inquiry in 1995 which focused on the scheme's environmental impact. Construction of the 3050 m runway – the first to be built

in the UK for 20 years – will begin in the spring and is due to be completed in three years.

Mr Graham Stringer, chairman of Manchester Airport, said: 'The second runway is the biggest postwar economic boost to the region. It will create 50 000 new jobs – the equivalent employment potential of 10 Nissan car plants.' However, environmentalists promised to seek a judicial review of the government's decision. They warned that the construction would be fought along similar lines to the campaign against the Newbury bypass, the scene of clashes between security guards and protesters.

Mr Chris Maile, of the Green Party in the north-west, said the airport would draw

campaigners from anti-road protests . . . He added: 'This will destroy three woods and part of the Cheshire countryside which is as scenic as anything in Kent . . .'

The airport argues that the impact of the runway has been overstated. It has agreed to more than 100 measures to protect the environment, including no night flights from the second runway and noise limits.

Sir George Young, Transport Secretary, praised the environmental measures as he announced planning approval. He said the second runway would also help to relieve the capacity constraints at airports in the south-east . . .

Source: Financial Times 16 January 1997

its true (higher) value. For society as a whole, private transactions that generate positive externalities are clearly a good thing. However, the problem is that, because they are *only* private transactions, they occur entirely at the discretion of individuals. Now, as some individuals may choose not to undertake the transactions in question, some wider social benefit will inevitably be lost: in other words, the market under-provides transactions that carry positive externalities. Again, this creates a rationale for the state to intervene in the market to ensure that the extra transactions do take place so that their associated external benefits can be realized.

An example is in order here. Before 1958 many people in the world faced the threat of contracting smallpox: a fatal disease. In 1977 the disease disappeared entirely: now no one will ever die of smallpox again. The worldwide eradication of smallpox was achieved by a vaccination programme sponsored by the World Health Organization (WHO). This is a supranational health promotion body, which is funded by most of the world's governments.

Smallpox eradication is in fact a majestic example of the externality principle. Vaccination for smallpox, or indeed any other contractable disease, could be left to the market. Individuals would then subjectively balance the costs and benefits of vaccination. The costs would include the price, the discomfort of consumption (own up – who's scared of needles?), and of course the risk of catching the disease. The benefit to the individual would be personal immunity from infection. Given such costs, *some* individuals would choose not to be vaccinated, or – more to the point in less developed parts of the world especially – would not be able to afford vaccination. They would not therefore gain the benefit of personal immunity. But there is also a wider benefit here, which the individual (and hence the market) fails to take into account. This is that everyone who is vaccinated achieves both a personal safeguard against disease and the status of a *non-carrier*: that is, someone from whom disease cannot be caught. The point of course is that non-carriers benefit everyone; they reduce the risk of disease being passed on. In this sense, the private vaccination decision has clear potential social benefits, and the more people who are vaccinated the better – from *society's* point of view. Here then is the rationale for state intervention of the form undertaken by the WHO. If the state provides free vaccination, the level of consumption may rise to the point at which the risk of contracting disease is very small or even, as in the case of smallpox, eliminated entirely.

6.5 Externalities and the welfare state

While the examples of the externality principle we have outlined so far are important, they do not extend to some of the more substantial forms of government intervention in modern economies. In western Europe most governments are heavily involved in the markets for health, education and housing. Hospitals, clinics, schools, universities and large numbers of houses and flats are all provided by governments using money obtained from taxes levied on private citizens. But why does the state involve itself in these markets for 'welfare' goods and services? Would it not be better to tax less and leave people to provide for themselves? Why, in short, do we need a welfare state?

A little history will help here. Let us briefly reflect upon the emergence of the state provision of housing and health in the UK to try to uncover the motivations for government involvement in each case. Though our examples are selective we suggest that they can be applied to other national and local contexts. We begin by considering the first instance of public housing provision in Liverpool in 1869. One of the first of its kind, this was an initiative by Liverpool Corporation, a local authority. The decision to build public housing reflected the appalling consequences of failure in Liverpool's private housing market. At the time, some 70 000 of the city's residents were living in 2532 back-to-back 'court' buildings, which had been officially condemned as unfit for human habitation. Each court had only one tap and 'trough closet' (toilet). The sanitary and health implications could hardly have been more serious with, according to Liverpool's Medical Officer of Health, 'whole districts as plagued as the cholera-smitten cities of India'. Even though supply and demand in Liverpool's housing market might have been in equilibrium, the situation clearly required drastic remedy. Accordingly, the Corporation began to demolish the courts, replacing them with public tenement buildings. The outcome was a *halving* of the death rate amongst the inhabitants of Liverpool's worst districts.

Here then, state intervention was motivated by the human cost of market failure, but we should also be aware that there was an underlying externality issue also present at the time. That 70 000 people lived in appalling conditions was clearly a problem for them, but it was also a problem *for the city as a whole*. The epidemics attendant upon insanitary overcrowding in Liverpool – typhus (1865), cholera (1866), relapsing fever (1870), and smallpox (1870–71) – were a threat to every citizen. Given that the market was incapable of confronting such externalities, the state had to. This of course is not to say that in Liverpool today, or indeed in any other town or city, were the state to relinquish its role as a housing provider, exactly the same problems would return. But there is an argument that *other* externalities would manifest themselves: the links between rising homelessness, poverty and social disaffection are clear enough, and they would certainly impinge upon wider society.

What of the origins of the National Health Service in the UK: how relevant is the externality principle in this case? The National Health Service (NHS) was founded in 1948. Its architect was Aneurin Bevan, a minister of health in the first Labour administration of the postwar period. In creating the NHS, Bevan's aim was to replace the existing private market in medical care with one that was publicly funded and largely free at the point of use: people would no longer have to pay directly for the treatment they received. Bevan advanced two main arguments to justify his creation of the new institution. The first was that in a modern industrial society the health of its most important economic resource – people themselves – could not be left to the vagaries of the market, with its first-order insistence on the ability to pay. In other words, Bevan supposed that the price of tolerating a market system would be waste of scarce human resources (through unnecessary ill health) by society as a whole. Again, this is a rationale for state intervention based on the externality principle: it is to society's benefit that all its members are healthy enough to be productive. Bevan's second argument also had an externality dimension, though this was more than tinged with the equity consideration (see Chapter 1) that there should be equality of access to health care. Quite simply, he supposed that the National Health Service would make for a society more 'at ease with itself' because its members would know that their families and fellow citizens would never be denied health care that they needed. This view is outlined in Bevan's own words in Box 6.3.

Box 6.3

Aneurin Bevan's equity argument for the National Health Service

'No society can legitimately call itself civilized if a sick person is denied medical aid because of a lack of means. Society becomes more wholesome, more serene, and spiritually healthier, if it knows that its citizens have at the back of their consciousness the knowledge that not only themselves, but all their fellows, have access, when ill, to the best that medical skill can provide.'

Source: Foot, M. *Aneurin Bevan 1945–1960* (London: Paladin, 1975).

The contention here then is that both housing and health care carry external benefits that the market does not recognize because of its individualistic focus. The same is true of education. If society ensures that all its members have good access to high-quality education, the result will clearly be a better educated, more skilled and more productive workforce: something that benefits every member of society and not just those who would otherwise have been denied educational opportunity. By implication, if any of these important welfare services were left to the market they would tend to be underprovided to the detriment both of those excluded from their consumption and of everyone else as the economic potential of society is reduced. In this way the externality principle can be used in part to justify the welfare state, which in essence is the embodiment of the mixed economy introduced in Chapter 1. Recall that this allows for some combination of market-determined and state-determined resource allocation. As noted, the mixed economy approach is dominant in the advanced economies of western Europe. It rests on the implicit assumption that where free markets work well they should be left alone, but when they exhibit signs of failure some corrective form of state intervention is usually required.

6.6   The liberal view: market failure and state failure

The mixed economy is not, however, the preference of every group of economists. The *liberal school*, for example, contends that economies that adhere as closely as possible to free market principles are inherently superior to those that permit the state to substantially encroach on questions of resource allocation. This view rests on three propositions:

- that the state too 'fails'
- that state failures may be worse than those of free markets
- that the failures of the free market are, in any case, invariably overstated.

Let us examine each of these propositions in turn.

State failure

The notion of state failure has one central theme: that the presence of the state in resource allocation ruptures the vital *individualist* connection between consumer and producer. Markets we know are organized on *voluntarist* principles. Every consumer who enters a market does so because he or she wants to: because there is a good or service in that market for which he or she is willing to pay. Liberals argue that voluntarism is extremely important. It is in fact the *only* way we can be sure that markets are delivering goods and services that people actually want. When the state involves itself in a market – such as housing or health care – it may for example tax individuals in order to provide them with the housing or health care *it* thinks that they should have. In the liberal view, the individual's perceptions of his or her own needs are replaced with bureaucratic interpretations of those same needs. This, the liberals claim, is an insurmountable problem. The state seems to be asking 'Who knows best what you should spend your money on?', and replying 'We do.'

There are three particular aspects of state failure that flow from this analysis. First, it seems quite obvious that the state's interpretation of the needs of the individual can be mistaken. Indeed, how can a bureaucracy assess with any accuracy the highly nuanced desires in an entire society? The liberals argue that only the market can do this because – through Smith's invisible hand – it does actually respond to each and every individual's expressed demand. But is the corollary true: does the state actually provide things that people do *not* want? Consider the following example. In the field of housing, it is not unreasonable to point to the 1960s and 1970s government preoccupation with the construction of tower blocks as the solution to a perceived housing problem. Now widely viewed as a mistake, tower blocks are no longer built, and many have been demolished because people simply do not want to live in them. Tower blocks are, literally, a monumental example of state failure.

The second aspect of the liberal interpretation of state failure is *coercion*. The market, we know, is voluntarist in nature: economic agents engage in market transactions because they want to. For liberals this means that markets underscore both economic and personal freedom. However, as the state involves itself in various ways in the provision of goods and services, it necessarily impinges upon the freedom of individuals to dispose of their own resources in ways that they themselves choose.

Individuals find themselves taxed by the state so that it can service what the leading liberal Hayek has called 'abstractions' such as 'the good of the community'. Yet although taxpayers may vehemently resent what is done with their money (recall our earlier example of taxes levied on members of the Campaign for Nuclear Disarmament helping to finance nuclear weaponry, regardless of their evident disapproval), they have no choice in the matter. Those who evade taxation are liable to be fined or even imprisoned. In the liberal view this is coercion pure and simple, and it betokens a wider constraint on economic and personal freedom in proportion to the amount of state intervention in what would otherwise be free markets.

The third and last particular aspect of state failure is that state intervention in part of a market can have the effect of subverting the efficient operation of the whole of that market. For example, as noted, local authorities in the UK have been active in the provision of public housing for more than 100 years. The liberal claim is that this has had a devastating effect upon the general functioning of the UK housing market. The problem here is one of **crowding out**. There are three generally recognized types of housing tenure: owner occupied, privately rented, and rented from the state. However, for a long time the housing market in the UK has been dominated by owner occupation and state-rented accommodation, with only a relatively small private rented sector. How has this situation come about? Partly, the answer lies in the determination of the state that there should be more collective housing provision. As more public housing has been built and let at relatively low rents subsidized by the taxpayer, the effect has been to reduce the level of demand for private rented accommodation; consequently less private rented accommodation has been supplied. Moreover, at the same time the state has also seen fit to give tax relief to owner-occupiers on their mortgage interest payments. This has had the effect of simultaneously raising the demand for owner-occupied property. The private rented sector has been caught in the middle of these two broadening avenues of intervention and (hence the phrase) crowded out. This state-inspired distortion of the housing market has also had consequences for the effective functioning of other parts of the UK economy. For example, the liberals claim that unemployment could be reduced if the unemployed were more easily able to move around in search of work. At present this is difficult because the most flexible element of the housing market – the private rented sector – is too small.

Concept

Crowding out

Strictly, crowding out refers to the reduction in private expenditure that results following an increase in government expenditure. Here we are using the concept in a more general way to describe the relative suppression of private sector activity by an expansion in related state sector activity.

State failure versus market failure

Liberalism accepts aspects of the conventional economic argument that markets can fail: monopoly, public goods and externalities are all valid concepts that may legitimize state intervention. However, we are also aware of the liberal notion of state failure. This creates an interesting dilemma: if a market is not able to function effectively, should we use this as justification for state intervention, with its attendant risk of state failure, or should we simply tolerate market failure itself? Effectively, what we have here is a competition between two inferior options. The preferred situation is a properly functioning free market; thereafter it becomes a choice between state intervention and possible failure and the failing market – which is worse? The liberal position is that each case should be judged on its merits. This may be contrasted with the conventional view, which, liberals infer, seems to proceed on the intrinsic assumption that when the state intervenes to 'correct' a market failure, it is usually effective in doing so.

Market failure in the liberal view

Liberal economists do not deny that markets can fail. They concede that, because of their innate indivisibility, pure public goods such as national defence and the greater part of the public road network must be provided by the state; markets that operate on an *individualist* basis cannot deliver goods and services that must be consumed *collectively*. However, beyond this, the liberal view is that market failure can be over-stated. Consider for example the externality issue. Here the liberal school argues that, while certain externalities clearly demand government intervention, many others are merely conveniences, which permit the state to involve itself in markets that would be better served by *laissez-faire*.

The leading liberal Milton Friedman has for example argued that while the provision of city parks is an appropriate 'externality justified' activity for government, the maintenance of national parks is not. Urban public parks are an unlikely private sector interest. They certainly provide benefits to many city dwellers. Some will use them directly; others might simply walk past or live nearby and enjoy the view. The problem for the potential operator of the private city park is that he or she will not be paid for benefits accruing to the latter group. Even direct users may not be prepared to pay if their intention is simply to take a brief stroll past some greenery on their way to another destination. So although most citizens will gain from a city park, it is unlikely to be profitable. This, Friedman concedes, means that the state may usefully provide such amenities in order that their external benefits may be realized. He thinks, however, that national parks are different. Generally, people do not walk past them or live overlooking them. Nor do they use them as pleasant short-cuts. Thus users of national parks are usually purposeful visitors who could be charged – via an entrance fee – for the benefits they derive from such use. For Friedman, this is the decisive point. As individuals can be made to pay for the benefits of consumption, if there is a demand for a national park the market will have an incentive to provide it and there is no need for state involvement at all. If, however, there is insufficient demand then why should the state tax individuals to provide them with something they do not wish to have? Here then the externality justification for state intervention has been stretched too far. Friedman argues that this has happened in a range of markets to erroneously justify *inter alia* public housing, price support in agriculture (see discussion of the EU's common agricultural policy in Chapter 2, Section 2.5), and legislation imposing minimum wage levels (see Chapter 7, Section 7.5).

Liberalism: a summary

Conventional economics supposes that the main areas of market failure readily justify state intervention. The state should control or regulate monopoly, arrange for the provision of public goods, and attempt to control negative externalities while simultaneously promoting positive ones. The liberal position is that this interpretation of state competences is too simple. Liberals dispute the presence of many externalities that are used to justify intervention in the real economy. They also harbour doubts about the ability of the state to correct actual instances of market failure. For liberals, the state too can fail, and its failures may be more serious than those of the market. Ultimately, then, state intervention should always be both a matter of careful judgement and, because of its potentially adverse consequences, one of last resort. In the liberal view, the restriction of state activity gives the freest reign to the superior allocative mechanism of the market.

6.7 Privatization

Privatization entails the surrender of some aspect of state influence over economic activity and the consequent reassertion of market priorities. There are many · contemporary examples.

Over the last 20 years in countries such as the UK and New Zealand governments have adopted policies intended to return most nationalized industries to the private sector. Table 6.1 lists the major UK privatizations that have occurred since 1979. In the formerly planned economies of eastern Europe and the Far East, where

Table 6.1 Major privatizations in the UK

Organization	Year of sale	Industry
British Petroleum	1979	Oil
National Enterprise Board Investments	1980	Various
British Aerospace	1981	Aerospace
Cable & Wireless	1981	Telecoms
Amersham International	1982	Scientific goods
National Freight Corporation	1982	Road transport
Britoil	1982	Oil
British Rail Hotels	1983	Hotels
Associated British Ports	1983	Ports
British Leyland	1984	Cars
British Telecom	1984	Telecoms
Enterprise Oil	1984	Oil
Sealink	1984	Sea transport
British shipbuilders and naval dockyards	1985	Shipbuilding
National Bus Company	1986	Transport
British Gas	1986	Gas
Rolls-Royce	1987	Aero-engines
British Airports Authority	1987	Airports
British Airways	1987	Airlines
Royal Ordnance Factories	1987	Armaments
British Steel	1988	Steel
Water	1989	Water
Electricity distribution	1990	Electricity
Electricity generation	1991	Electricity
Trust ports	1992	Ports
Coal industry	1995	Coal
Railways	1995–7	Railways
Nuclear energy	1996	Electricity

Source: *Martin*, S. and D. Parker *The Impact of Privatization* (London: Routledge, 1997)

economic activity was under very extensive state control until 1989, an even more decisive privatization programme of this sort is currently under way.

Privatization can also assume more subtle forms. In the UK's National Health Service (NHS), for example, the government has introduced a system of GP fund-holding. This allows family doctors a much greater degree of choice than hitherto in the referral of patients to hospitals and clinics. Effectively, doctors can choose which hospital they think will provide the best service. Although the system is still wholly in the public domain, the change is intended to instil a degree of *consumer sovereignty* into the NHS. Hospitals can no longer simply provide surgical and other procedures that GPs then have to consume on behalf of their patients; they must now compete against one another in order to attract the 'custom' of GPs. Here, then, privatization involves the incorporation of market principles by the public sector.

In the UK, many of the services provided by local government have been made subject to a process of compulsory competitive tendering (CCT). This requires local authorities to allow bids from private firms for work that was formerly done by the authorities themselves. If a private firm can do the job more cheaply than the local authority then it gets the contract for a given period. As a result of CCT, services such as refuse collection, street cleaning and the provision of school meals in many towns and cities are now undertaken by private firms. Again, as the state still finances and has ultimate responsibility for such services, this falls short of local 'denationaliza-tion' but, again, it does admit private sector influences into what had been a wholly public domain.

The rationale for privatization

Why privatize? The answer to this question lies in the purported advantages of the free market, which were sketched out in Chapters 1–4 of this book. The market empowers the consumer; it promotes the division of labour; and it sparks the entrepreneurial zeal of the profit-motivated producer. The case for privatization is that it extends these features into new areas of economic activity and at the same time necessarily compresses the boundaries of undesirable state-determined resource allocation.

But on what *necessary* basis are forms of state-determined resource allocation rejected? The proponents of privatization argue that historically, when the state assumes responsibility for industrial activity in particular, chronic poor perform-ance and decay is the inevitable result. Nationalized industries, it is argued, tend to suffer from general deficiencies, which arise as a result of the insulation of the (state) producer from the 'realities' of the market. Private firms, on the other hand, *must* respond to consumer demands; they must introduce new technologies and new working practices in order to remain competitive; they cannot pay workers more than their competitive position allows; they cannot tolerate indolent or incompetent management. The suggestion is that these and other strictures do not apply with anything like the same force in industries that are nationalized. In the public sector, the state is always able to excuse poor commercial practice because the ultimate mar-ket sanction of bankruptcy is removed.

While state ownership might protect industry at one level, it can also dangerously frustrate its development at another. Nationalized industries such as the former British Telecom, privatized in 1984, had their ability to raise investment capital strictly controlled. This is because governments wish to constrain the rate of growth of public expenditure. At the same time the capacity of nationalized industries to enter foreign markets is limited: in the British Telecom case it was clearly not politically acceptable for the British government (in its British Telecom guise) to start to compete with, say, Deutsche Telecom for its domestic market. Now, in an extremely dynamic internationalizing industry such as telecommunications, the ability to innovate and achieve economies of scale is crucially important. Therefore it was argued that, if it was to become a 'leading edge' telecommunications provider, British Telecom had to be freed from the constraints imposed by nationalization: it needed to raise adequate amounts of investment capital and gain access to bigger markets. Privatization enabled both of these imperatives to be realized.

So far we have concentrated on the *microeconomic* benefits of privatization: the stimulus it gives to firms as they are forced to compete in the market, and the opportunities for better resourced growth it also provides for them. However, privatization has also been defended on macroeconomic grounds. Since 1979, the privatization programme in the UK has yielded over £60 bn. As this sum is regarded as negative government spending, its effect has been to substantially reduce government borrowing – sometimes thought to be a desirable outcome for *macroeconomic* management reasons.

The case against privatization

The central weakness of the privatization view is that a change of ownership in itself confers no obvious benefits. Where the privatized firm is a monopoly, the normal rules of competitive practice remain suspended. Because it lacks competitors, a private

---

Box 6.4

£10 may be cut from gas bills

Scottish gas bills will fall sharply this winter after moves by the industry watchdog, Ofgas, to open the household market in Scotland to competition from November.

It is estimated that new entrants into the market may be able to cut £10 a month off winter bills in Scotland, and around £80 a year off the average yearly bill of £330 north of the border.

Ofgas announced the move as part of a programme to open the whole of the UK market to free competition by next June.

Clare Spottiswoode, director general of Ofgas, said this would bring the benefits of competition to 20 million customers across Britain, following trials in southern England.

She said: 'This will be the world's biggest competitive domestic gas market. People in (trial areas) have been able to reduce their bills by 20 per cent

by switching supplier. This sort of saving will soon be available to everyone.' Around 18 per cent of the 2 million customers covered by the two trial areas have so far chosen to switch suppliers.

Margaret McKinlay, the recently appointed director of Scottish Gas, said she welcomed the start of competition, even though Scottish Gas would initially be barred from cutting its own prices to compete. She said: 'Initially we will only be able to compete on service and reliability and I will make it my business to see we deliver on what our customers want so they are less likely to shift away purely on price.' At least half a dozen companies, including Scottish Power, are expected to try to persuade customers to switch from Scottish Gas, the current monopoly supplier to 1.2 million homes north of the border.

Northern Electric, the English regional electricity company, said it planned to

compete in the Scottish Gas market. Its own home market will also be opened up at the same time as Scotland.

Scottish Power has already poached around 70 000 customers from British Gas in England after an aggressive campaign in the area covered by its Southern Water subsidiary. It offered new customers a £30 signing on fee and cuts of around 20 per cent off bills, and it has said it expects to take at least 12 per cent of the Scottish Market.

The consultation document published yesterday by Ofgas proposes that, after Scotland, competition will roll southwards starting with the north-west of England next February, with the rest of England opened up in four more stages in the months between March and June. The final go-ahead for the proposals is expected in August.

Source: The Scotsman 1 July 1997

monopoly is just as insulated from the 'realities' of the market as the nationalized industry; indeed, given the freedom to exploit its exclusive position more assidu-ously, a private monopoly might be considered to pose more problems than a public one. This means that the acid test for the success of privatization must be the extent to which it *promotes competition*.

In the UK the privatization process has been attended by the creation of a number of regulatory 'watchdogs', such as the Office of Telecommunications (Oftel) for the telecommunications industry and the Office of Gas Supply (Ofgas) for the gas industry. The purpose of these bodies has been to prevent the newly privatized monopolies from exploiting their monopoly positions, and to oversee the intro-duction of more competitive environments in each industry. Yet progress on the latter front has been slow. For example, although British Gas was privatized in 1986 a competitive market in industrial gas supplies emerged only in 1992, and supplies to households remained exclusive to British Gas until 1998. However, wherever com-petition *has* been introduced, it is significant that prices to consumers have fallen (see Box 6.4). This has led disinterested researchers to suggest that UK government privatization policy would have been improved had it put the promotion of com-petition above the simple transfer of ownership from the public to the private sector. Adam Smith would surely have agreed.

Summary

◆ The existence of clear forms of market failure provides a rationale for state inter-vention in free markets. Indeed, the notion of market failure underpins the mod-ern form of the mixed economy and, in particular, its welfare state component.

◆ Not all economists share this orthodox view. One branch of dissent comes from the liberal school. Liberals raise doubts about the real extent of market failure, and introduce the issue of state failure. We saw in Chapter 5 that the institutionalist school raises a different set of questions about monopoly in particular. In the institutionalist view, orthodox approaches understate both the extent and dangers of concentrations of monopoly power in modern economies.

◆ Finally, this chapter briefly reviewed the policy of privatization. Ostensibly, pri-vatization appears to sympathize with a *laissez-faire* perspective. However, the important conclusion is that the extent of competition in a market matters more than the distribution of ownership between the public and private sectors.

Key terms

◆ Market failure
◆ Monopoly
◆ Public goods
◆ Free rider problem
◆ Negative externalities
◆ Positive externalities
◆ Welfare state

◆ Mixed economy
◆ State failure
◆ Freedom
◆ Crowding out
◆ Privatization
◆ Ownership
◆ Competition

▊ Questions for discussion

◆ Explain the significance of the 'free rider' problem.

◆ In most economies, taxis are licensed by the state for externality reasons. What externalities might unlicensed taxis generate?

◆ What is state failure? Give some examples.

◆ What are the implications of state failure for orthodox economics?

◆ Why is the privatization of a nationalized industry, such as the railway network, no guarantee in itself of improved economic performance?

▊ Further reading

Alt, J.E and K.A. Chrystal *Political Economics* (Brighton: Wheatsheaf Books, 1983). Provides an excellent overview of the debate in economics over the role of the state.

Waller, P.J. *Democracy and Sectarianism: A Political and Social History of Liverpool 1868–1939* (Liverpool: Liverpool University Press, 1981). The source for the material in this chapter on the history of public housing in Liverpool.

Friedman, M. *Capitalism and Freedom* (Chicago: University of Chicago Press, 1962). Provides a brief and very readable exposition of the liberal view of market failure and market competence.

Hayek, F.A. *The Road to Serfdom* (London: Routledge, 1944). Slightly more difficult but perhaps the most eloquently written liberal polemic.

Jackson, P.M. and C.M. Price (eds.) *Privatization and Regulation* (Harlow: Longman, 1994). Offers a useful overview of privatization issues in the UK and the wider international context.

Foot, M. *Aneurin Bevan 1945–1960* (London: Paladin, 1975). The standard biography of Aneurin Bevan.

▊ Internet links

The Office of Gas Supply (Ofgas), created to regulate the privatized monopoly British Gas, promote competition in the gas industry and protect the interests of gas consumers. Ofgas can be found at: **http://www.ofgas.gov.uk/**

The *Adam Smith Institute* is an independent body that promotes market-based reform, following a broadly liberal ethos. Its Web site is at: **http://www.cyberpoint.co.uk/asi/**

The *Institute for Public Policy Research* does the same kind of job as the *Adam Smith Institute* but from a left-leaning perspective. It was created specifically as an alternative to free-market think-tanks. Its Web site is at: **http://www.ippr.org.uk/**

Factor Markets

Contents

Factor market: A market for a factor of production.

Key issues

▶ Do factor markets work in the same way as markets for goods and services?

▶ In the labour market, which factors determine demand and supply?

▶ How is skill in the labour market rewarded?

▶ Does minimum wage legislation destroy jobs?

7.1 Introduction

In previous chapters much of our discussion tended to concentrate on markets in goods and services. In the present chapter we extend some of the concepts we have already introduced to the analysis of **factor markets**. Recall that there are four factors of production, the services of which are combined by firms in order to produce an output. They are:

- labour
- capital (factories, machines and so on)
- land (all natural resources used in production)
- entrepreneurial skill.

Factor markets are clearly of interest in themselves. It is important, for example, to understand the operation of the labour market. If the labour market fails to clear, unemployment may result. In such circumstances we need to consider what, if anything, can be done about it (see Chapter 11). An analysis of factor markets also allows us to understand how the income that a society generates is distributed amongst the groups that comprise it. In other words, such analysis will tell us why particular social groups – workers, entrepreneurs, the owners of capital and land – earn what they do. However, as we considered entrepreneurship in conjunction with the theory of the firm in Chapters 4 and 5, we shall concentrate here on the markets for capital, land and, especially, labour. We begin with an analysis of the labour market.

7.2 The labour market

Essentially, factor markets and goods markets work in the same way. The principles underlying the interaction of demand and supply are as applicable to labour markets as they are to the markets for office furniture, cinema tickets, or any other good or service. A useful way to start to look at the labour market would therefore be to examine it as a *perfectly functioning abstraction*. We began our analysis of market structures and firms in precisely the same way, with a model of perfect competition. The purpose behind this kind of approach is to allow us to see how a market might work under 'ideal' conditions, and to contrast this with the much greater – and more problematic – complexity of the real world.

One of the by now familiar tenets of conventional economics is that free markets clear. In other words, markets are possessed of forces that push them towards situations in which the quantities demanded and supplied are perfectly matched. At such points in every market, because there is no tendency for further change to take place, each prevailing price is by definition an equilibrium price. Given certain assumptions, we can reproduce exactly the same kind of analysis in the context of the labour market. Thus, if we assume

- that work is not qualitatively different between occupations
- that labour is (like a good in perfect competition) homogeneous
- that there exist perfect mobility and perfect knowledge in the labour market
- and finally that there exist large numbers of independent buyers (firms) and sellers (individual men and women)

then *the* labour market in an economy – our assumptions mean that there would be only one – can be represented as in Fig. 7.1. Here, the wage rate – the *factor price* that firms must pay to hire the services of labour – is depicted on the vertical axis while the quantity of labour demanded and supplied is depicted on the horizontal axis. The market is in equilibrium at wage rate W_e, with the quantity demanded and supplied at Q_e. From our discussion in Chapter 2 the reader should be able to verify that at all possible wage rates below W_e there will exist an excess demand for labour.

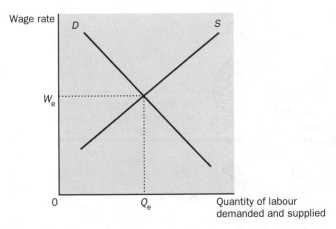

Fig. 7.1 The interaction of demand and supply in the labour market.

This will be eroded as firms begin to offer higher wage rates in an attempt to overcome labour shortages. Higher wages encourage more workers to enter the market, and supply extends. However, at the same time higher wages also cause the demand for labour to contract. Eventually a point will be reached where the quantities demanded and supplied are equal: this will be at wage rate W_e. Conversely, at all possible wage rates above W_e, there will be an excess supply of labour. In other words some workers who are willing to work at the prevailing wage rate will not be able to do so because the requisite demand is not there. Recognizing such conditions, firms will begin to offer lower wages, secure in the knowledge that they will still be able to recruit all the labour they need. Wages will continue to fall until W_e is again reached and the quantities demanded and supplied are equal. We consider the influences on the positions of the demand and supply curves for labour in later sections.

For the moment, consider the familiar implicit message that this analysis delivers. The suggestion is that if markets are left alone and are competitive then they will tend to clear. In the case of the labour market, this means that labour is in neither excess demand nor excess supply. 'Competitiveness' in the labour market entails both the capacity for individual workers to freely enter and leave the market and flexibility in wage rates. As we shall see, some economists claim that many problems in labour markets can be overcome if they are characterized by openness, and if wages are sufficiently flexible (see Chapter 11, Section 11.2).

Let us now examine the effects of relaxing some of our highly restrictive assumptions. To begin with the first assumption, there are plainly significant differences in the quality of work between occupations. For example, miners and people who work on oil rigs are exposed to more unpleasant and dangerous working environments than teachers, librarians and others in what we might term the 'indoor professions'. This means that if all jobs were rewarded with the same generally determined equilibrium wage, many miners, oil rig workers and others would choose to take up less arduous and less hazardous jobs instead. So, because occupations vary greatly in quality, wage rates must differ to compensate those who undertake the less pleasant tasks. The level of compensation is conditioned by something called the *principle of net advantages*. This requires that the pecuniary (money) and non-pecuniary advantages

Highly paid so-called 'fat cats' in the privatized utilities in the UK are a popular target for cartoonists

"We're talking British Telecom numbers"

of different jobs should, when taken together, tend to be equal. When the principle of net advantages applies, workers will not be collectively repelled from the least attractive jobs. The implication of this first concession to the real world is that we have not one uniform labour market but a series of labour markets across which differences in occupational quality are perceived and in which different wage rates are paid.

Yet some very pleasant jobs are extremely well paid. This suggests that differences in the quality of work should not be our only concession to reality. In professional football, for example, the most successful players are amply rewarded for doing what many people would joyfully do for nothing. Unfortunately, however, Everton are not going to sign you (probably) or us (definitely) for the simple reason that in the real world our second assumption doesn't apply. Labour is not homogeneous. To be a professional footballer requires a natural talent that most people do not possess. This means that the supply of top-class footballers is extremely limited, and, as we know, when restrictions on supply are coupled with strong demand, higher market prices result.

For the purposes of comparison, let us also consider the ability requirements of a second occupation: a bus driver. Here the 'natural talent' element of the job is relatively modest: many if not most people of working age could be trained to drive a bus competently. Even if labour is not homogeneous it would seem that the potential supply of drivers is very large. Now, when plentiful supply is coupled with relatively low demand, lower market prices result. However, there is an additional issue here. Most bus operators tend to recruit trainee drivers not from the general labour force but only from the male half of it. Why? Although women are clearly not physically incapable of this kind of work, it appears that reciprocally confirming *social and institutional barriers* prevent them from participating in it to any significant extent. Driving a bus is socially regarded as 'men's work'. Accordingly, bus operators have a tradition of recruiting and training men. There are many such examples of 'gendered' work, and most similarly incline against employment opportunities for women. Our point is that these further separate or **segment** the labour market into discrete elements. Indeed, the greater the degree of natural, social and institutional heterogeneity of labour, the greater the degree of labour market segmentation. Of course, social and institutional heterogeneity in the labour market is *socially constructed* and includes all forms of discrimination, whether on the basis of ethnic origin, religious belief, disability, sexual orientation or gender; it has no independent objective existence.

Our third initial simplifying assumption was that there is perfect mobility of labour and perfect knowledge in the market. We have just discounted one element of the first part of this assumption: that labour is able to move freely between occupations. But in addition to natural talent and the kinds of social and institutional barriers to work mentioned above, many jobs require specialist qualifications. For example, to obtain a licence to drive a hackney cab in London it is first necessary to 'do the knowledge'. This entails learning, usually over a period of years and in great detail, the layout of London's major roads and principal destinations. Similarly, people are not permitted to fly aircraft, pilot ships, or practise medicine, law or accountancy without the appropriate training.

It is also important to recognize the existence of *geographical* barriers to mobility in the labour market. An excess demand for labour and excess supply can coexist in different parts of an economy simply because unemployed workers cannot (perhaps

Labour market segmentation: Arises when labour faces barriers to entry to a particular labour market.

because of a lack of affordable housing) or do not want to move to where the jobs are. The degree of labour mobility in the European single market is an interesting case in point. All citizens of the European Union (EU) are now free to live and work in any EU country, but how many actually choose to search for work abroad is a very open question (for a discussion of the single market see Chapter 2, Section 2.5). The implication here is that labour markets can also be geographically segmented as individuals restrict their search for work to familiar localities. Finally, the segmentation of markets may be compounded by *poor information flows*. Our initial simplifying assumption was perfect knowledge, but workers cannot compete for jobs that they do not know exist.

The final assumption in our specification of a perfectly competitive labour market was the presence of many independent workers (the suppliers of labour) and firms (the institutions that demand it). But in the UK, for example, roughly 40 per cent of workers belong to trade unions, whose aim is to provide a **collective** presence in labour markets for their members. Insofar as trade unions are successful in **bargaining** higher wage rates than the market would bear in more competitive circumstances (say above W_e in Fig. 7.1), the effect of their action is to reduce the numbers employed while securing more favourable returns for those who remain in work. Of course, collectivity can be attractive to firms too. It is not uncommon for employers' organizations to negotiate with trade unions on behalf of their member firms. For example, in the UK engineering industry the Engineering Employers' Federation undertakes such a task. However, perhaps the most marked form of labour market distortion comes under the guise of the closed shop. Here, in order to secure or continue in employment, workers are required to join a designated trade union. This arrangement is thought to be attractive to both unions and firms because, according to Paterson and Simpson (1993) – see guide to further reading at the end of this chapter – it provides for 'stability and order' in the workplace. Its economic effect is of course to constrain labour supply by throwing up yet another barrier to independent activity and freedom of movement in the labour market.

Real-world labour markets are then far removed from our idealized model. What we appear to have is a complex set of labour markets with a range of uneven barriers between them. The barriers include natural talent or skill, training, qualifications, age, gender (and other forms of discrimination), distance, information, and trade union membership. Now, recall our definition of monopoly power from Chapter 5, Section 5.4. Monopoly power can arise wherever there are barriers to entry in a market. This means that in reality many labour markets are characterized by the presence of monopoly power. Of course, in those cases where there are the most stringent and daunting barriers to entry, labour will enjoy the highest levels of monopoly power, and may find its rewards magnified accordingly. But what does all this mean for our opening remarks about the governance of the labour market by the familiar laws of demand and supply? Are the propositions concerning excess demand and supply, and notions of the equilibrium market-clearing wage depicted in Fig. 7.1, now irrelevant? Fortunately, they are not. What we must recognize, however, is the changed context in which they operate. Within each segmented labour market, *particular* demand and supply conditions will determine the *particular* equilibrium wage rate for that market. In the next two sections of this chapter we consider the determinants of labour demand and supply in more detail. This analysis then allows us to conclude our discussion of labour as a factor of production by reviewing the operation of some real-world labour markets.

Collective bargaining: Involves negotiations between a trade union and one or more employer over pay or workplace conditions.

7.3 The demand for labour

The firm's demand for labour – and, indeed, for any factor of production – is a **derived demand**. This means that firms do not hire labour for itself but for the services it can perform in the production process. Labour is demanded because it helps to produce goods and services, which can then be sold, yielding the firm revenue: the source of profit. Let us now examine how it is possible to derive the individual firm's demand curve for labour.

Recall that a firm maximizes profit by producing an output at which the marginal or extra cost (*MC*) associated with the last unit produced equals the marginal or extra revenue (*MR*) derived from the last unit sold (the *MC* = *MR* rule). Let us apply this principle to the individual firm's demand for labour. We begin with an analysis of the firm's short-run demand for labour. In the short run, we assume that the quantity of some factors of production are fixed (capital, for example) while others can be varied. Thus a firm can increase output relatively easily by hiring more labour, but it takes time to buy and install new machinery. On the basis of this assumption, labour is often referred to as a variable factor of production in the short run, while capital is a fixed factor, again in the short run. In the long run all factors of production are variable.

The firm's demand for labour in the short run

In the short run, the question of how much labour the individual firm demands turns on the contribution that each extra worker makes to profit. In other words, for every extra worker, the firm asks itself: is this person adding more to revenue than he or she is costing to employ? If the answer is yes, then the person is employed; if no, then he or she is not. The contribution an extra worker makes to the firm's profit depends on three things:

1. how much additional output he or she produces
2. the price the extra output sells at
3. his or her wage.

The first of these – the additional output he or she produces – is called the **marginal physical product** (*MPP*). Now, recall from Chapter 3, Section 3.2, that the law of diminishing returns states that, as additional units of a variable factor are used by a firm in the context of a given volume of fixed factors, the marginal product of the variable factor will eventually begin to fall. Here the implication of the law of diminishing returns is that, as extra workers are employed, *MPP* falls. The second point is the price at which the extra worker's additional output is sold. If we assume the firm to be perfectly competitive, this price will be given: the perfectly competitive firm can sell as much as it likes at the prevailing market price. Putting (1) and (2) above together, we can now say that the extra revenue associated with each additional worker hired by a perfectly competitive firm will be given by his or her *MPP* multiplied by the market price of the product in question. This extra revenue is called the **marginal revenue product** of labour (*MRP*).

Fig. 7.2 depicts the individual perfectly competitive firm's marginal revenue product schedule, *MRP*. At a market wage *W*, for example, its demand for labour

Derived demand: A derived demand for a factor of production arises because of the demand for the output that the factor helps to produce. The factor in itself does not generate demand.

Marginal physical product: The change in total output resulting from a unit change in the variable factor.

Marginal revenue product: The change in a firm's total revenue resulting from the sale of output produced by one more unit of the variable factor.

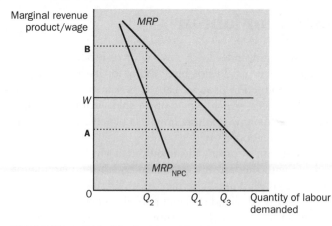

Fig. 7.2 The individual firm's demand for labour.

will be set at Q_1. At this point the contribution made by the last worker to the firm's revenue is identical to his or her wage, W. This means that earlier workers over the range of the schedule MRP will be contributing more to revenue than cost. For example, for the worker at Q_2 the cost/wage is still the market rate W but the MRP is 0B. The 'profit' on this worker is therefore 0B − 0W. On the other hand, for workers beyond the point Q_1, MRP is below the market wage rate. It is clearly not in the firm's interest to extend employment beyond Q_1 because workers in this range add more to cost than revenue. For example, at Q_3 the wage W exceeds the MRP by 0W − 0A. The MRP schedule is the individual firm's demand curve for labour. A fall in the wage rate will *ceteris paribus* engineer an extension in the quantity of labour demanded, while an increase in the wage rate will be associated with a contraction in the quantity of labour demanded by the firm.

For a perfectly competitive firm, when the market price increases, the marginal revenue product of labour also increases. Simply, the goods produced by each worker bring in more revenue. This causes the MRP schedule to shift to the right, and leads to an increase in the firm's demand for labour. In Fig. 7.3 the MRP schedule shifts from MRP_1 to MRP_2. At a market wage W, for example, the quantity of labour demanded would increase from Q_1 to Q_2. Conversely a reduction in the market price of the perfectly competitive firm's output will cause the MRP schedule to shift left (from MRP_1 to MRP_3 in Fig. 7.3), resulting in a decrease in its demand for labour. At a market wage W, the quantity of labour demanded would fall from Q_1 to Q_3.

What happens to the individual firm's demand for labour when we relax our assumption that it is perfectly competitive? The essential difference concerns our point (2) above: the selling price of the firm's output. A *non*-perfectly competitive firm faces a downward-sloping demand curve. Unlike the perfectly competitive firm, it cannot sell as much as it likes at a given market price. For the non-perfectly competitive firm, higher output means a lower selling price. The implication here is that the additional output produced by an extra worker will reduce the price of all the firm's output and thus steepen the slope of its MRP curve as the MRPs of all employed workers fall. In Fig. 7.2 the non-perfectly competitive firm's MRP curve is labelled MRP_{NPC}. At the market wage W, the quantity of labour demanded by the non-perfectly competitive firm will be Q_2. Note that, assuming that the non-perfectly competitive firm and the perfectly competitive firm have the same technology, this is

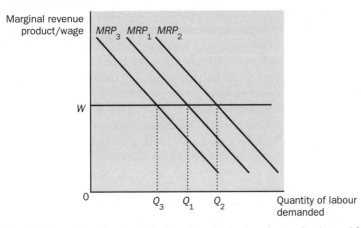

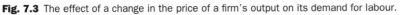

Fig. 7.3 The effect of a change in the price of a firm's output on its demand for labour.

less than the quantity of labour demanded by the perfectly competitive firm at the same wage rate.

The firm's demand for labour in the long run

As noted, the difference between the short and the long run is that in the long run all factors of production become variable. This means that it is possible for the firm to increase (say) the amount of capital it employs. Two kinds of effect upon labour demand can then occur. First, if the price of capital relative to labour changes then the firm will alter its demand for labour. If capital falls in price, relative to the price of labour, then *ceteris paribus* the firm will elect to introduce more mechanized production methods at the expense of labour, and *vice versa*. Second, changes in production technologies may also cause the demand for labour to change. For example, an improvement in technology that results in an increase in the marginal physical product of labour will lead to an increase in the demand for labour.

7.4 The supply of labour

The supply of labour in an economy

The total supply of labour in an economy is strongly conditioned by changes in population. For example, according to the Organization for Economic Cooperation and Development (OECD), over the 1980s five-sixths of the increase in the labour force in its member countries was attributable to population growth. However, the population of working age in the OECD area is now growing much more slowly (half of 1 per cent per year in the early 1990s) than it did in the 1970s (more than 1 per cent per year), and the OECD suggests that the expected continuation of this trend will lead to an increase in the proportion of older workers in the labour force. Labour supply is also influenced by international migration. Increased migration into western Europe has been particularly marked since the liberalization of the formerly planned economies of eastern Europe, which began in 1989. Moreover, greater freedom of movement in the East has been mirrored by the abolition of border and passport controls between mainland EU countries following the Schengen Agreement, an aspect of the EU's single market programme.

Inside the general constraint of population growth, institutional and social factors will also influence the supply of labour in an economy. For example, an increase in the school-leaving age or a lowering of the retirement age will compress the population of working age. Similarly, longer holidays and a shorter working week will also reduce labour supply. While these factors have traditionally been decided at the national level, it is interesting to note that for EU member countries they are now increasingly determined collectively through the EU itself. The length of the working week is a case in point. Under the Social Chapter of the Maastricht Treaty (1991) it was agreed that the length of the working week in most EU countries should be restricted to a maximum of 48 hours.

While what we might term the 'boundaries' of the working population are conditioned by the socially acceptable and institutionally determined ages of entry and exit, the duration of the working week, and holiday entitlement, these factors do not wholly determine actual labour supply. To be of working age is one thing; to be **economically active** in the labour market is another. The economically active are those people of working age who are either in some kind of paid employment or who are seeking it. Table 7.1 describes economic activity for women and men in Great Britain (the UK excluding Northern Ireland) in 1986 and 1996. Notice from the table that the economic activity rate for women over this period has increased from

Economically active individuals: Those people of working age who are either in work or actively seeking it. People of working age not in employment and not seeking it are deemed to be economically inactive.

Table 7.1 Economic activity in Great Britain: women and men of working age (16-59/64) 1986 and 1996; spring of each year (not seasonally adjusted)

	1986 ('000)	1996 ('000)	% change 1986–96
Women (16–65)			
All	15992	16483	3
Economically active	10905	11756	8
Economic activity rate (%)	*68*	*71*	
In employment	9728	10994	13
Full-time	5579	6165	11
Part-time	4135	4828	17
Employment rate	*61*	*67*	
ILO Unemployed	1178	763	–35
ILO Unemployment rate (%)	*11*	*6*	
Economically inactive	5086	4727	–7
Men (16–64)			
All	17541	18038	3
Economically active	15384	15319	0
Economic activity rate (%)	*88*	*85*	
In employment	13612	13835	2
Full-time	13061	12783	–2
Part-time	535	1051	97
Employment rate	*78*	*77*	
ILO Unemployed	1772	1483	–16
ILO Unemployment rate (%)	*12*	*10*	
Economically inactive	2175	2765	28

Source: Labour Market Trends (March 1997) Office for National Statistics, © Crown Copyright 1998

68 to 71 per cent, whereas for men the rate has fallen from 88 to 85 per cent. This means that the *participation* of women in the labour market has increased, while that of men has decreased. The net effect has been an increase in overall labour supply. Considering those in employment, the table allows us to calculate that there has been an overall shift from full-time to part-time work, with an increase of 1.2 million part-time jobs over the period, compared with an increase of 308 000 in full-time jobs. Of the additional part-time jobs, 57 per cent have been taken by women. Although there are only 308 000 extra full-time jobs, the number of women in full-time employment has increased by 586 000. The number of men in full-time employment has accordingly decreased by 278 000. The general pattern of rising *participation rates* for women and falling rates for men is replicated across the OECD area, as indicated in Fig. 7.4.

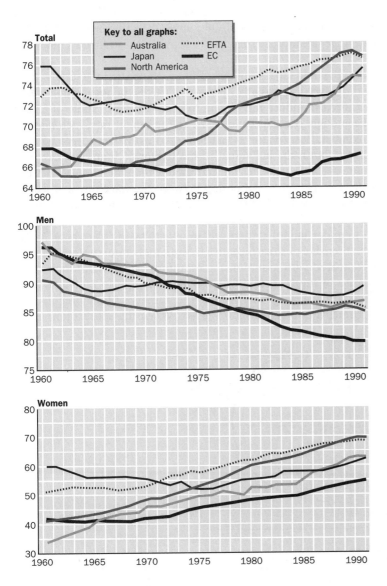

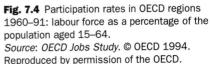

Fig. 7.4 Participation rates in OECD regions 1960–91: labour force as a percentage of the population aged 15–64.
Source: OECD Jobs Study. © OECD 1994. Reproduced by permission of the OECD.

The individual's supply of labour

As noted in Chapter 2, Section 2.3, quantity supplied varies positively with price, *ceteris paribus*. At first sight we might expect the same relationship to hold in the labour market: the greater the reward in terms of the wage rate, the more hours we would expect an individual to be willing to work. However, we must also recognize that the opportunity cost of work is the leisure time that the individual must surrender in order to work. The issue of the individual's supply of labour now becomes the more complex one of balancing the rewards gained from work against the subjective value that he or she places on the leisure that must be given up. Consider the position of someone who is unemployed. Such a person clearly has a lot of free time but only a relatively low income comprising (say) some form of welfare benefit. This means that he or she would be likely to value some extra income gained from work (of which he or she currently has little) more than a few hours of leisure forgone (he or she has leisure in abundance). Thus if a wage rate in excess of benefit is offered, the rational decision is to begin to work. Of course, the difference between the benefit rate and the wage rate must be sufficient to convince the individual that work is worthwhile.

Fig. 7.5 represents the individual's supply of labour. Notice that the supply curve here intersects with the vertical axis at £3 per hour. This is the **reservation wage**: that is, the rate required to induce this person to begin to work. A rate of £2 per hour would not be enough. It might be too close to the benefit rate, such that the opportunity cost of work (lost leisure) is valued more highly than £2 per hour. If the wage rate is £5 per hour, the individual wishes to work 5 hours per day. The £25 he or she earns (5 × £5) is of greater subjective value than the 5 hours of leisure per day forgone. So far, then, the relationship between the wage rate and labour supply is of the expected positive form: the higher the wage rate, the more hours worked.

It is important to understand that there are two effects taking place here. As the wage rate increases, there is a positive incentive to work more hours as the marginal benefit of work compared with leisure increases: the so-called *substitution effect*. However, an increase in the wage rate will also generate a disincentive to work more hours because a higher wage rate reduces the number of hours required to obtain a given income: the so-called *income effect*. When the substitution effect

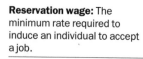

Reservation wage: The minimum rate required to induce an individual to accept a job.

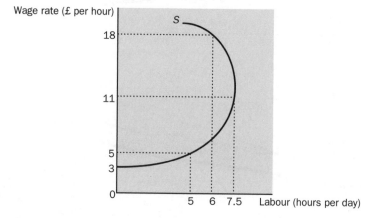

Fig. 7.5 The individual's supply of labour.

dominates, a higher wage rate increases the number of hours that the individual is willing to work. At a wage rate of £11 per hour, the 7.5 hours worked represents the maximum length of the working day desired by our subject (who earns £11 × 7.5 = £82.50 per day). Thereafter, despite higher wages, he or she wishes to work fewer hours, and the supply curve takes on a negative or backward-sloping form. In this situation, the income effect dominates the substitution effect. Quite simply, the individual has reached a point where his or her dwindling leisure time now has a very high subjective value, and further improvements in the wage rate afford the opportunity to maintain a satisfactory income while reducing the number of hours worked.

Another way of putting it is to say that the relatively high income associated with the high wage rate stimulates the individual's demand for all goods and services, including leisure: effectively he or she now has the money to 'buy' more leisure by working less. In Fig. 7.5, when the individual is paid £18 per hour, he or she wishes to work 6 hours per day. Notice that, at this rate, the daily wage of £108 (£18 × 6) does allow our subject to take more leisure while more than preserving his or her income.

The supply of labour to a particular occupation

Having discussed both the supply of labour to the economy as a whole and an individual's supply of labour, we now turn to consider the supply of labour to a particular occupation. Here we need to be aware of two issues.

First, different occupations will offer qualitatively different forms of work. As noted, work on an oil rig is likely to be more dangerous and unpleasant than a 9 to 5 'desk' job. Thus, in order to retain workers, occupations that offer low-quality work must offer higher monetary compensation. This implies some degree of segmentation between different occupations, with *ceteris paribus* higher wages being paid in the more dangerous ones. Clearly, then, different occupations will have different labour supply curves. Supply conditions between occupations may also differ for other reasons. We have already seen for example that variations in natural talent, training and trade union membership may act as constraints on labour supply.

Second, the supply curve for an occupation is likely to be positively sloped such as S in Fig. 7.1. In order to induce an increase in the quantity of labour supplied to a particular occupation, the wage rate will need to be increased.

The elasticity of labour supply

The **elasticity of labour supply** measures the responsiveness of the quantity of labour supplied to a change in the wage rate. The elasticity of supply in a particular occupation will vary according to the degree of skill and training involved and the time period under consideration. For certain highly skilled occupations, such as those in medical practice, it would be difficult or impossible for the quantity supplied to immediately extend following an increase in the wage rate. In these occupations the supply curve will be relatively inelastic. In contrast, for relatively low-skilled occupations such as petrol pump attendants the quantity supplied will be much more responsive to an increase in the wage rate. However, over time labour supply will become more elastic as people acquire the necessary skills to undertake certain occupations.

Elasticity of labour supply:
Measures the responsiveness of the quantity of labour supplied to changes in the wage rate.

7.5 Issues in the labour market: bringing demand and supply together

Skilled and unskilled labour

Let us consider the issue of skill. In Fig. 7.6 the supply curve S_1 represents the supply of unskilled labour. Notice that it has a relatively shallow positive slope, indicating that the supply of labour is not perfectly elastic. At a wage rate W_1 the quantity of unskilled labour supplied is Q_1. A small increase in the wage rate from W_1 to W_2 induces a large increase in the quantity of labour supplied from Q_1 to Q_2.

Next consider the supply curve S_2. This represents the supply of skilled workers. It has a slope slightly steeper than S_1 and lies above it. Why? The position of S_2 reflects the higher wage rate required by skilled workers. If they were paid at the same rate as unskilled workers there would be less incentive for skill acquisition. In order to encourage workers to spend time and money obtaining a skill (which can often necessitate leaving the labour market and paid employment for a period), there have to be adequate rewards. Thus to induce the supply of Q_1 skilled workers requires a wage rate of W_3. The marginally steeper slope of S_2 suggests that the elasticity of supply for skilled workers is not much different from the elasticity of supply of unskilled workers. In both cases, modest increases in the wage rate from W_1 to W_2 (unskilled labour) and W_3 to W_4 (skilled labour) will induce much higher quantities supplied.

Finally, the supply curve S_3 represents the supply curve for highly specialized labour. It lies above both S_2 and S_1 because specialist skills are still more difficult and costly to obtain and therefore require even higher wage rates to make skill acquisition worthwhile. In order to induce the quantity of Q_1 specialists, the wage rate W_5 must be paid. The much steeper slope of S_3 indicates that the elasticity of supply of specialist labour will be relatively low over the same period. An increase in the wage rate from W_5 to W_6 induces an increase in the quantity of labour supplied with specialist skills from Q_1 to Q_2.

Let us now introduce demand into the analysis. In Section 7.3 we saw how the demand for labour reflects labour's marginal revenue product (MRP). The profit-maximizing firm will recruit additional workers up to the point at which the MRP equals the wage rate. The MRP curve is in effect the firm's demand curve for labour.

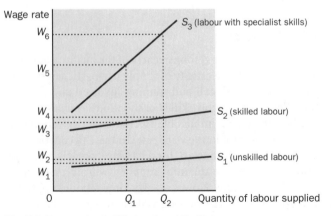

Fig. 7.6 The supply of skilled and unskilled labour.

"I'm afraid we can't afford wages any more, so could you queue up with a bowl . . ."

It follows that if we sum all of the quantities of labour demanded at each wage rate over all firms active in a particular labour market, we arrive at the *demand curve for that market*. We can also distinguish between the market demand for skilled and unskilled labour. Remember that the demand for labour is a derived demand. Firms value labour for its contribution to the production process. It is the case, therefore, that skilled labour will be more valued than unskilled labour because of its greater capabilities as manifested by its marginal revenue product. Accountants sell specialist services, which command a high price, and this justifies the relatively high wage rates they are paid. On the other hand, dry-cleaners sell services that command a relatively low price; accordingly, because workers in this occupation are less productive, their wage rates will be lower. Generally, then, the demand curves for skilled workers will be above those of unskilled workers.

Fig. 7.7 illustrates the point. The curve D_1 represents the demand for unskilled labour. At a wage rate W_1, Q_1 workers are demanded. The demand for skilled labour is represented by the curve D_2. The higher marginal product of skilled labour justifies the payment of a higher wage rate W_2, at which the demand for labour is also Q_1. Thus the wage premium for skilled labour is the distance $0W_2 - 0W_1$.

Let us now combine our analyses of supply and demand. In Fig. 7.8 we reproduce

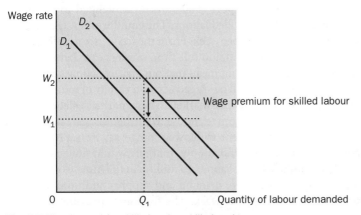

Fig. 7.7 The demand for skilled and unskilled workers.

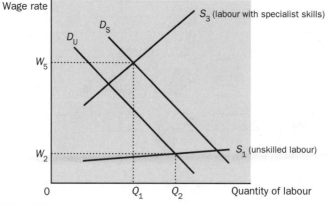

Fig. 7.8 The markets for skilled and unskilled labour.

the supply curves from Fig. 7.6 for unskilled and highly skilled labour and add two demand curves, which correspond to the demand in a market for unskilled (D_U) and highly skilled labour (D_S). For unskilled labour, lower productivity and elastic supply conditions combine to produce an equilibrium wage rate W_2 and quantity Q_2. The higher productivity of highly skilled labour coupled with the wage premium for skill and a much less elastic supply yields a much higher equilibrium wage, W_5. Table 7.2 provides some evidence on the wage rates paid in a variety of occupations, which tends to support this theoretical analysis. From the table we can see that amongst the highest-paid jobs are those in the medical, legal and financial professions. The rewards here reflect both the high prices charged for the services of doctors, solicitors and accountants – the high marginal revenue products of these people – and the fact that there are relatively few of them in the labour market (because their training is very demanding and lengthy). The poorest-paid jobs – kitchen work, waiting, bar work and so on – have much less robust demand and supply conditions. Low marginal revenue products, low skills and relatively elastic supply all combine here to depress wage rates.

Consider, finally, Fig. 7.9. This brings together the theoretical precepts that we have built up on the workings of labour markets and some evidence on the numbers of workers in the UK earning particular wage rates. It is then a representation of some *stylized forms* of labour market conditions that prevail in the UK and a rough estimate of their relative importance. Market type 1 (Fig. 7.9(a)) is intended to typify the demand and supply conditions for unskilled labour. The equilibrium wage we illustrate in this market is an arbitrary £150 per week. From the frequency distribution of UK wage rates we can see that about 1 million full-time workers earn between £140 and £160 per week. This of course does not mean that our stylized labour market is 1 million workers strong. These people will be spread across a variety of industries and regions in what are therefore different labour markets. These markets will however be of the same general form. We could of course choose to further disaggregate market type 1 into a number of subsets that cover a wider wage range: say from £100 to £200 per week. The stylized 'weak demand and supply' markets would now encompass almost 3 million workers (out of a total of about 19 million in full-time work).

For market type 2 (Fig. 7.9(b)), where demand and supply conditions are more robust, the equilibrium wage is £300 per week. The frequency distribution shows that roughly 1.2 million workers are within £10 of this wage rate. Again, if we disag-

Table 7.2 Highest and lowest paid occupations, April 1997; Great Britain[a]

Full time employees on adult rates	Average gross weekly pay (£)
Highest paid	
1. General administrators; national government (senior)	1071.9
2. Treasurers and company financial managers	948.7
3. Medical practitioners	869.8
4. Management consultants, business analysts	775.2
5. Underwriters, claims assessors, brokers, investment analysts	756.2
6. Organization and methods and work study managers	704.4
7. Police officers (inspector and above)	686.7
8. Solicitors	670.4
9. Education officers, school inspectors	667.0
10. Advertising and public relations managers	666.5
Lowest paid	
1. Kitchen porters, hands	159.4
2. Hairdressers, barbers	163.4
3. Waiters, waitresses	165.3
4. Bar staff	171.8
5. Childcare and related occupations	173.4
6. Counterhands, catering assistants	174.5
7. Petrol pump forecourt attendants	176.4
8. Launderers, dry-cleaners, pressers	180.3
9. Retail cash desk and check-out operators	182.9
10. Sewing machinists, menders, darners and embroiderers	184.9

[a]Some industries are not considered due to small sample size and/or large statistical variation
Source: Labour Market Trends (November 1997) Office for National Statistics, © Crown Copyright 1998

gregate this market into subsets that cover the wage range, say, £210 to £400 per week, then the number of workers in our stylized intermediate markets is about 9 million – roughly half of the UK's full time workforce.

Finally, for market type 3 (Fig. 7.9(c)), where demand and supply conditions are the strongest (of those markets considered: we have ignored markets in which the highest wage rates are generated), the equilibrium wage is £600 per week. The frequency distribution shows that about 200 000 people earn between £590 and £610 per week. Disaggregating the market to cover a wider wage range, £500 to £700 per week raises the number of workers included to about 2.5 million. In each of our stylized market diagrams we have given the equilibrium quantity of labour demanded and supplied as Q_n. Given the data in the frequency distribution, these should not be taken as ordinal quantities (Q_1 the smallest etc.) as easily the greatest numbers of workers are employed in our stylized intermediate market(s).

Human capital

Human capital is the reserve of skill and knowledge that a worker can gather. Our discussion so far suggests that it can boost the wage-earning potential of the worker from both the demand and the supply side. On the demand side, it raises the

Human capital: The skill and knowledge that a worker can gather. Note that some forms of human capital will be more valuable than others. The crucial factors are again demand and supply: is what you can do strongly demanded, and how many others can do the same thing?

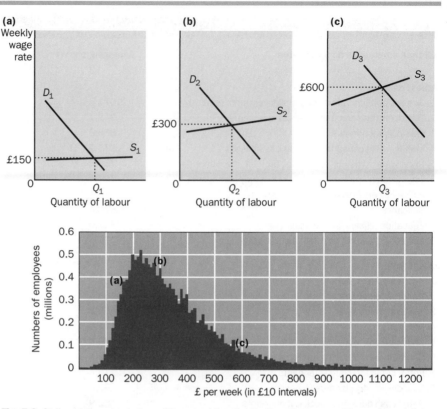

Fig. 7.9 Stylized labour market conditions and the distribution of gross weekly earnings, full-time employees on adult rates, Great Britain, April 1997. (a) Market type 1: relatively weak demand and supply. (b) Market type 2: intermediate demand and supply. (c) Market type 3: relatively strong demand and supply.
Source: Labour Market Trends, November 1997, Office of National Statistics, © Crown Copyright 1998.

worker's marginal revenue product as he or she becomes capable of more challenging tasks. On the supply side it provides the means of entry into a select group of workers, whose relatively small numbers cannot be easily increased. For those who fail to invest in their own human capital or who have in the past invested in what has become the wrong sort of human capital, both earning and employment prospects are relatively poor.

The point is exemplified in Box 7.1. The argument here is that labour market demand and supply conditions in the UK and most other developed countries have moved in favour of those who have invested not just in human capital but in what has turned out to be the *right sort* of human capital. Two important factors underpin this view. First, rapid technological change across all sectors of the economy continues to raise the demand for those with what we might broadly term transferable computing and information technology skills. Second, the chronic decline in industrial and manual work, which itself is partly fuelled by technological change, has rendered traditional craft and 'factory skills' increasingly redundant. In terms of Fig. 7.8, labour markets in the developed world may be dividing into those that are moving towards a situation typified by the curves D_S and S_3 and, unfortunately, those that more readily approximate D_U and S_1.

Box 7.1

Employment opportunity in a changing labour market

Throughout the OECD the employment rate of low skilled and poorly educated workers has been falling since at least the early 1980s; while in the UK and the US there is clear evidence that relative wages of unskilled workers have also been falling. These increases in the relative demand for skilled labour have been accompanied by, and may have directly caused, an increase in the supply of skilled labour. The proportion of people in lower skilled groups has been falling throughout the developed world. The situation is sometimes described as a race between the supply of and the demand for skilled labour. Where the increase in the supply of skilled workers has not been rapid enough to meet the demand for skills, the relative position of skilled workers has been maintained. But in many countries, including the UK over the last twenty years, the increase in the supply of skilled workers has not been rapid enough to meet the increased demand. The relative wages of skilled workers have been bid up – leaving those without skills, and particularly manual workers, in a deteriorating labour market position.

The dramatic decline in employment rates of people with relatively low skills [should also be noted]. The widening gap in job prospects between skilled and unskilled men aged 25 to 49 has been particularly dramatic. Only 5 per cent of prime-age men with a degree are not in work, compared to 33 per cent of those with no qualifications ...

Another long-run trend, intertwined with the decline in the demand for lower skilled workers, has been the shift away from industrial and manual work. Typically, full-time male workers with few educational qualifications, but craft skills specific to their industry , have found their skills made obsolete by structural change. Since the 1960s employment in manufacturing has fallen from around a third of overall employment to around 15 per cent.

There are two main explanations of the deterioration of the labour market prospects of low skilled and manual workers:

- the rapid development and diffusion of new technology, and new forms of work organization, may be biased against those with poor skills; and

- the increase in international trade with countries with a relatively abundant supply of low skilled labour may be putting downward pressure on the demand for low skilled labour in the developed countries.

A wide and expanding academic literature on both these phenomena has highlighted a role for both, but with technological change the more significant.

There is strong evidence that the growth in demand for skilled workers has been associated with the spread of microcomputers and computer-based technologies over the last couple of decades. Although the pace of technological change is certainly not new, it may be that there are particular features of the current wave of technical progress that leave poorly educated workers at a disadvantage relative to those with skills. The tasks which computers currently perform well are routine tasks involving judgement and face to face communication. We would, then, expect to see new technology shifting the relative demand for labour in favour of skilled workers, while increasing the overall levels of growth and productivity.

The best evidence in support of this view is that the increasing demand for skills is very broad-based, occurring within industries and within establishments, rather than just between industrial sectors. Those industries relatively sheltered from international competition have seen changes in the demand for skill, as well as those that are not. Industries with larger investments in research and development, innovation and use of computers have shown the strongest changes in relative demand for skills. There is also evidence that utilization of more skilled workers is complementary with investment in physical capital and the introduction of new technology. The central point here is the evidence suggests the IT revolution, in particular, may be making many traditional unskilled jobs redundant, while increasing the employability of those with skills to make the best use of it.

Box 7.2

A strong link between companies' investment in workers and stock market performance is revealed

By Linda Blimes, Konrad Wetzker and Pascal Xhonneux

It is almost a management truism that companies gain a competitive edge by valuing their workers and investing in them. Yet there is little hard evidence to back this up. In one of the first studies of its kind, our analysis of more than 100 German companies reveals a strong link between investing in employees and stock market performance. Companies which place workers at the core of their strategies produce higher long-term returns to shareholders than their industry peers.

Not every successful company invests a great deal in its employees. However, we found that the shares of companies which focus on their workforce outperform competitors who make human resources a low priority.

The research examined companies in 10 industrial sectors, including car manufacturing, banking and pharmaceuticals, over a seven-year period from 1987 to 1994. 'Employee focus' was divided into two components: traditional human-resource policies and opportunities for 'intrapreneurship' within the company. Both of these are

necessary to produce exceptional shareholder value: employee benefits alone will not do the trick.

The first traditional type of employee focus was measured in four ways:

• Expenditure per employee on training, and continuing levels of training
• Number of layoffs relative to the industry average and efforts to help relocate redundant employees
• Extent to which the corporate philosophy recognizes the contribution of employees as reflected in mission statements and publications
• General human resources policies, including recruitment, performance evaluation and feedback, and promotion opportunities.

'Intrapreneurship' means giving an employee the freedom to take decisions and to maximize the scope for individual initiative within a given job. Four criteria were used to measure the extent to which companies encouraged intrapreneurship:

• Flexible work hours

• Project organization, including the prevalence of teams, number of levels of hierarchy, and independence of working units
• Opportunities for employees to learn skills in new areas, and speed with which a firm can transfer staff to new fields
• Extent to which employees share in company performance through profit-sharing, performance pay and bonuses.

The results are striking. In every industry, those companies which scored most highly on these criteria produced a greater 'total shareholder return' (TSR) than their competitors. TSR is the sum of share price increases and dividends over a given period. The companies receiving the lowest scores also produced the lowest TSR in their sector.

We also looked at the data over a shorter four-year period. Even then, the degree to which a company invests in human resources is still a good predictor of stock market success, with those investing most performing best and vice versa.

Source: The Boston Consulting Group.

While the educational and career choices of individual workers are central to the accumulation of human capital, firms too have an important role to play here. When firms train workers they both enhance the earning potential of those whose skills are upgraded and improve their contribution to the production of goods and services. Recent research in Germany appears to suggest that this is the case (see Box 7.2). Firms that add to the human capital of their employees *ceteris paribus* tend to perform better than those that do not.

Minimum wages

In virtually all developed countries, governments choose to intervene in labour markets to set legally enforceable minimum wage rates. In the 1997 UK general election the commitment of the Labour Party to the principle of a national minimum wage was a major issue. In 1983 a Conservative administration abolished a number of wages councils that had set minimum rates in a number of industries where wage rates are typically low. Why did the Conservatives abolish wage protection, and why was the Labour Party so keen to see it restored? The debate about minimum wages clearly has some normative aspects to it. Many people think it is unfair of employers to pay workers relatively low wages: low wage rates exploit those who do not have the skills to move up in the labour market. Others argue that governments are wrong to interfere in employment arrangements freely entered into by workers and firms. The positive dimension is, however, rather different. The key questions here are:

- Will the establishment of minimum wage rates raise the incomes of low-paid workers?
- What will be the effect of a minimum wage on the level of employment? Will it create jobs or destroy them?

These questions are closely related. Let us see why by first examining the economic case against the imposition of a national minimum wage. We should begin by putting this issue into context. Remember that we are dealing not with one labour market but with many, variously segmented by occupation, geography, industry, gender and so on. Recall also from the frequency distribution in Fig. 7.9 that the majority of the UK's full-time workers are not in markets where relatively low pay dominates. This means that, on the reasonable assumption that a national minimum wage is intended to raise the pay of those at the bottom of the wage range, the minimum wage will be an *irrelevance* in many labour markets. That said, its opponents argue that where it would have an impact, its effect would be to raise the wages of some low-paid workers at the expense of the jobs of other low-paid workers. This conclusion derives from a simple market analysis. If, in a given labour market, there is a relatively low equilibrium wage rate, any attempt to raise wages will cause the quantity of labour demanded to contract and the quantity supplied to extend. The inevitable cost of the improvement in the wage rate is job loss. Referring back to Fig. 7.1, the reader should be able to verify that any wage rate above W_e will produce an excess supply of labour. Moreover, the higher the minimum wage is above W_e, the greater the resultant excess supply of labour. So, the central conclusions are that, in markets where it had an impact, a minimum wage would destroy jobs, improve the wages of those still in work, and lower the incomes of those made unemployed. Finally, we should note the claims of some employers that a minimum wage would spill over into labour markets where it has no formal influence. We have seen how skilled workers require compensation in the form of higher wages for the costs of acquiring those skills. This creates a **pay differential** between skilled and unskilled work. If unskilled workers have their wages boosted by a minimum wage the differential that skilled workers enjoy will be partially eroded. In these circumstances skilled workers may press employers to restore lost differentials. To the extent that they are successful, the impact of a minimum wage may ripple through to labour markets where low pay is not an issue (see Box 7.3).

There are, however, problems with the basic argument that the main economic effect of minimum wage legislation is to destroy jobs. In the first place, it assumes that labour is paid according to the value of its marginal revenue product. This may not always be the case. In Fig. 7.10 the firm's *MRP* curve does not slope smoothly down from left to right in the expected fashion but follows a path with abrupt changes in it. This reflects indivisibilities in the employment of labour. Indivisibilities arise when it is not possible to add relatively small amounts of labour to that already employed. According to Shaw (see source of Fig. 7.10 for reference), this limitation may apply particularly to small firms. Take for example the case of a firm that employs two people who have years of work experience. This sets their marginal revenue product contributions to the firm at a given level. If the firm were to recruit

Pay differentials: Exist where there are wage rate premiums attached to particular kinds of work. The most common pay differentials are between skilled and unskilled work.

Maximum worry on minimum wage

...Labour's commitment to a minimum wage is unsettling a growing proportion of smaller companies. Peter Risdale, chief executive of Tulchan, which operates the Jumpers and Sock Shop Chains, is unequivocal: 'Our major preoccupation at the moment is what the minimum wage is going to be.' Uncertainty is disrupting investment plans for a complete refurbishment of Sock Shop in the next six months, he says. 'If the minimum wage is not set at a sensible level, we go bust. £4 is too high.'

A study by Reed Personnel Services, which is broadly in favour of a minimum wage, found that among 341 businesses employing no more than 100 people, 39 per cent said they would be 'affected' at £4 per hour. At £3 per hour, the figure was just 14 per cent.

Labour has simply said the hourly level would be set in consultation with a low-pay commission. Tony Bradley, head of policy at the Birmingham Chamber of Commerce, dislikes the uncertainty. 'We would be a lot more relaxed if we knew what the level was,' he says.

Dominic Johnson, senior adviser at the Confederation of British Industry, points out that the very lowest-paid work almost exclusively in small companies. He says government data suggests that two-thirds of those earning less than £2.50 work for businesses employing fewer than 25 people. 'There will be a restructuring in the medium term from small to large companies across the low-paying sectors, because the small players won't have the economies of scale.'

A minimum wage also bodes ill for the sector's much vaunted job-creating capacity, according to employers. Ruth Lea, head of policy at the Institute of Directors observes: 'Either people will be laid off, or small businesses will not create the jobs they otherwise might have done.' Service-based industries, which cannot easily automate or improve productivity, believe they would be the most obvious casualties.

However, small manufacturers are also increasingly concerned as they fear a knock-on effect on their wage bills as workers seek to maintain differentials. Bradley says: 'It's an emotive subject. Our members are concerned, not because they are paying lousy wages, but because they fear that the unions will use it as a lever to drive all wages up.' The boss of one small engineering company has told him that he would simply shut down. 'His lowest-paid workers already earn £6.50. But he's worried he'd be hit by the differentials sweeping through,' he adds.

Some, however, would welcome a floor. Tony Banks, chief executive of Tradesource, a Corby-based publisher and printer with 42 staff, says: 'We need relatively skilled people. But a lot of our smaller competitors are not paying those sort of levels. A minimum wage might actually reduce some of our competition.'

Source: Financial Times 29 April 1997

a third worker who is inexperienced, his or her *MRP* would be at a level below that of the first two and not, as we have previously assumed, merely on a downward-sloping *MRP* curve. In terms of Fig. 7.10 the *MRP* of the first two workers is at W_3, while that of the third is at W_1. Now, if the wage level set in the market is W_2, the firm will set demand at Q_2 and not employ the third worker because his or her *MRP* is below the wage: this individual's cost of employment would be above the revenue he or she brought in. Notice, however, that the *MRP* of the first two workers is above the market wage level. The point here is that a minimum wage could be set at any level above the market wage and up to W_3, without causing the firm to reduce its demand for labour. That government-led changes in wage rates might not have any pronounced impact on the demand for labour is also borne out by experiences in the UK and elsewhere. Thus the noted Conservative abolition of wages councils in 1983 has produced no evidence that new jobs have been created in the affected industries as a result. Moreover, minimum wage legislation in the USA appears not to be a drag on what is generally acknowledged to be one of the most dynamic labour markets in the world.

One point of agreement between those who anticipate that the national mini-

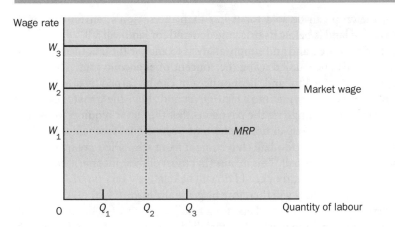

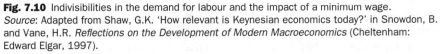

Fig. 7.10 Indivisibilities in the demand for labour and the impact of a minimum wage.
Source: Adapted from Shaw, G.K. 'How relevant is Keynesian economics today?' in Snowdon, B. and Vane, H.R. *Reflections on the Development of Modern Macroeconomics* (Cheltenham: Edward Elgar, 1997).

mum wage in the UK will destroy significant numbers of jobs and those who think that relatively few jobs will be lost concerns the level at which the minimum is set: the higher the level, the greater the danger that firms will reduce their demand for labour. In Box 7.3 a number of employers and their representatives voice concerns that a minimum wage of £4 per hour would drive them out of business or cause lay-offs. They also worry about the effect on pay differentials. However, at least one employer welcomes a minimum wage that would 'bite' because it would prevent his competitors undercutting his prices by paying their workers less. As to the extent to which a minimum wage would be successful in raising the wages of the low paid, the Institute for Fiscal Studies has recently estimated that a level of £4 per hour would improve the pay positions of 4 in 10 women workers and 1 in 8 men over the first three years of its life.

7.6 Factor incomes and economic rent

Having discussed the labour market in some detail, we now finally and briefly consider the operation of capital and land markets. As noted at the beginning of this chapter, a number of key principles are common to all factor markets. Thus the demand for capital and land is, like that for labour, a derived demand. This means that the notion of marginal revenue product – the change in a firm's total revenue from employing an additional unit of a factor – is again relevant when studying the individual firm's demand for capital and land. It follows that the quantity of capital or land demanded by a profit-maximizing firm will be that which equates the *MRP* of the relevant factor with its price (interest for capital and rent for land). If for example the return from the installation of one more machine by a firm exceeds the rate of interest that the firm must pay on the funds it borrows to make this investment, then the investment should proceed. In other words, the firm's *MRP* of capital is currently above the price of capital, and the firm can therefore make additional profit by raising its demand for capital. However, a farmer who rents an extra field on which to grow more crops will break the rental agreement if he or she finds that

Economic rent: Payment to a factor of production above that necessary to retain it in its present use.

Transfer earnings: The payments to a factor necessary to retain it in its present use.

the price that the crop can be sold for is less than the season's rent on the field. Because the *MRP* of land is below its price the demand for land will fall.

While we used basic demand and supply analysis to analyse the labour market, all factor markets can also be studied using the concept of **economic rent**. This is not the same as rent, the reward to land. Economic rent can be earned by *any* factor of production. It is defined as payment to a factor over and above the **transfer earnings** of that factor. Transfer earnings are the payments that the factor requires to remain in its present use. For example, although the best professional footballers are very well paid, because most join a football club straight from school few are qualified to do much else except play football. This means that most of their income is economic rent. Most alternative jobs that they could do will be relatively very poorly paid. The transfer earnings of footballers will therefore be generally low.

Fig. 7.11 depicts three factor markets: for unskilled labour, for finance capital, and for land. Consider first the market for unskilled labour. Supply here is perfectly elastic because the pool of workers is extremely large. At very high levels of supply it is conceivable that the curve will turn upwards, but for our purposes it remains flat over the relevant range. In this case, the total value of wages paid to labour (the wage rate W_1 multiplied by the number of hours worked) is represented by the rectangle $0W_1AQ_1$. The earnings of labour here are all required transfer earnings: there is no element of economic rent. This is because, for Q_1 hours labour to be supplied, the volume of wages paid must be exactly $0W_1AQ_1$. Given that supply is perfectly elastic, if a lower wage was paid no labour would be forthcoming.

The market for finance capital, however, has normally sloped demand and supply curves: D and S respectively. At the equilibrium interest rate r_e, the demand for and supply of capital is Q_1. The volume of revenue generated for the providers of this amount of capital is the return on it (at the rate r_e). However, notice that the rate r_e is necessary to induce the supply only of the very last unit of capital advanced. All the preceding units of capital would still be supplied at rates between r_e and r_1. This means that, except for the last unit, all capital advanced earns economic rent in the form of unnecessarily high rates of return. The transfer earnings, in this case the combination of interest rates that would be just sufficient to bring forth a supply of Q_1, are given by the quadrilateral r_1AQ_10. Economic rent, in contrast, is represented by the triangle r_1Ar_e.

Finally, consider the supply of land. A given piece of land is in fixed supply, which

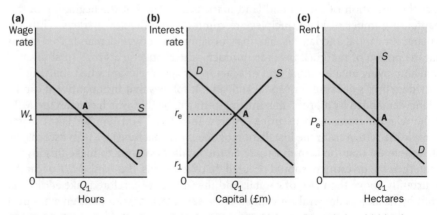

Fig. 7. 11 Economic rent in the markets for (a) unskilled labour, (b) capital and (c) land.

does not vary regardless of the rent paid for it: the land is always supplied. This means the value of the land is wholly dependent upon demand, and all of its earnings take the form of economic rent. This explains why land values are exceptionally high in central London relative to places like central Liverpool. In London, intensive demand is forthcoming from business, government and relatively affluent residents; in Liverpool, the levels of demand from the equivalent sources are much lower. In Fig. 7.11 the market for a given piece of land is in equilibrium at rent P_e, with supply at Q_1. Thus the rectangle $0P_eAQ_1$ is pure economic rent. If rent was halved or even set at zero, the land would still be in supply; there are no minimum transfer earnings necessary to induce its supply.

The significance of economic rent lies in its influence on the potential earnings of factors of production. Where no economic rent is earned, as in our unskilled labour market example, factor returns are effectively fixed by *supply considerations* at the level of transfer earnings. There is no scope for improvement unless supply conditions change. At the other extreme, where earnings are all economic rent, returns are wholly *demand driven*. If demand increases then so, commensurably, does economic rent. As modern Premiership footballers know from their own experience, this can be hugely advantageous. Even a moderately talented Premiership footballer can now enjoy millionaire status. How is this possible when only a few years ago such rewards were unthinkable? The answer is that, as noted, footballers' wages are mostly economic rent and therefore demand driven. The last and most crucial piece in the jigsaw is that the demand for footballers has suddenly ballooned because of the amounts that television companies are willing to pay for the right to screen top football matches. Should programme commissioners grow lukewarm about football, the rewards for footballers will fall back again.

■ Summary

◆ Factor markets, like the markets for goods and services, are governed by the laws of supply and demand. Demand in factor markets is a derived demand: it is dependent upon the demand for the output that factors produce.

◆ The labour market is segmented because of barriers to labour mobility. Labour may be prevented from moving freely between different market segments by the presence of *inter alia* skill or training requirements, the need for natural ability, trade unions, distance, poor information, and discrimination.

◆ In the short run, the firm's demand for labour is regulated by the level of the wage. The firm will employ labour up to the point at which the marginal revenue product (*MRP*) of labour and the wage are equal. In the long run, changes in the price of capital and technological advances can affect the *MRP*, which is also the firm's demand curve for labour.

◆ The supply of labour in an economy is governed overall by the rate of population growth. It is also conditioned by a range of social and institutional factors affecting participation rates. In most industrialized countries the participation rates of women have been rising, while those of men have fallen.

◆ The supply of labour to a market will be positively sloped. The elasticity of labour supply is dependent upon time and the possibility of new workers acquiring the skills or aptitudes necessary to join the market.

◆ The highest market wage rates will be paid to workers in occupations for which there is a strong demand and relatively inelastic supply.

◆ Investing in the right sort of human capital gives workers the best chance of earing a relatively high wage, though it makes sense for firms too to invest in their workers.

◆ In industrial countries such as the UK, minimum wage legislation has no relevance in many labour markets. While, theoretically, minimum wages may help the low paid at the expense of job destruction, the case is not incontrovertible. There is little evidence that they significantly impede the functioning of market processes.

◆ The concept of economic rent helps us to understand why factors in inelastic supply can earn relatively high returns.

■ Key terms

◆ Net advantages
◆ Natural ability
◆ Barriers to labour mobility
◆ Segmented labour markets
◆ Bargaining power
◆ Derived demand
◆ Marginal revenue product
◆ Economically active
◆ Participation rates
◆ Reservation wage
◆ Substitution and income effects
◆ Elasticity of labour supply
◆ Human capital
◆ Minimum wage
◆ Economic rent
◆ Transfer earnings

■ Self-test questions

True (t) or false (f)

1. Generally, wage levels are determined by the interaction of demand and supply.

2. Labour is a fixed factor of production.

3. The marginal revenue product curve is the firm's demand curve for labour.

4. An increase in the price of its output will cause the marginal revenue product curve of a firm to shift to the left.

5. In the advanced economies over the last 30 years the participation rates of women in the labour market have increased while those for men have decreased.

6. The reservation wage is the wage at which people decide to move between jobs.

7. When the income effect dominates, the individual's supply of labour will fall as the wage rate increases.

8. Accountants, solicitors and other professionals are highly paid because they are relatively few in number *and* because of the high prices paid for the services that they offer.

9. The economic case is clear: minimum wages legislation destroys jobs.

10. Economic rent is payment to a factor of production above that necessary to retain it in its present use.

Complete the following sentences by inserting the missing word(s)

1. The demand for labour is a ____ demand.

2. The additional output produced by a worker is called the ____.

3. The quantity of labour demanded by a firm equates the marginal revenue product of labour with the ____.

4. The individual's supply of labour is subject to ____ and ____ effects.

5. The minimum rate required to induce an individual to accept a job is called the ____.

6. The elasticity of labour supply measures the responsiveness of the quantity of labour supplied to changes in the ____.

7. The reserve of skill and knowledge that a worker can gather is called ____.

8. The argument that wage levels in a particular occupation are too low is a ____ argument.

9. The payments necessary to retain a factor in its present use are called ____.

10. When the earnings of a factor are composed entirely of economic rent, they are entirely driven by ____.

◼ Questions for discussion

◆ Why is the concept of labour market segmentation useful in explaining wage rate variation between occupations?

◆ Why is the demand for labour a derived demand, and how does this influence our analysis of the demand for labour by a firm?

◆ Which factors govern the supply of labour in an economy?

◆ Which factors govern the supply of labour to the German building industry? (Hint: labour migration may be important here.)

◆ Your ability to read this book is in part a reflection of the skills of the primary school teachers who taught you to read. Why should a job as socially, culturally and economically important as teaching young children be so poorly rewarded relative to the jobs done by Alan Shearer, 'Sting' and Jeffrey Archer?

◼ Further reading

Penn, R., M. Rose and J. Rubery (eds) *Skill and Occupational Change* (Oxford: Oxford University Press, 1994). Presents the findings of detailed research on the nature of job change in the UK in the 1980s.

Paterson, I. and L. Simpson, 'The economics of trade union power', in N.M. Healey (ed.) *Britain's Economic Miracle: Myth or Reality?* (London: Routledge, 1993). Provides a concise review of labour market reforms in the UK in the 1980s.

Michie, J. and J. Grieve Smith (eds) *Unemployment in Europe* (London: Academic Press, 1994). Documents the growth of unemployment in Europe and considers the policy options for tackling it. This book may also be used to further explore some of the issues discussed in Chapter 11.

Rees, T. *Women and the Labour Market* (London: Routledge, 1992). Considers the reproduction of gender inequalities in the workplace and explores their implication for policy.

▮ Internet links

The *Policy Studies Institute* (PSI) is an independent organization that undertakes research into public policy. One of the PSI's research groups looks at employment issues. All of the PSI's work can be accessed via its Web site at: **http://www.psi.org.uk/index.htm**

The *International Labour Organization*, founded upon the basis of humanitarian concerns for the rights of workers and now also concerned to promote full employment and the raising of living standards, has a Web site with some online information and a wealth of sources of further reading on labour market issues. The site is at: **http://www.ilo.org/**

Distribution of Income

CHAPTER 8

Key issues

▶ How can the distribution of personal incomes be measured?

▶ How can the degree of inequality in the distribution of personal incomes be measured?

▶ What are the major sources of inequality?

▶ How is the pattern of inequality modified by government expenditure and taxation?

8.1 Introduction

In the preceding chapters we focused our discussion on the question of whether a competitive market system will result in an efficient allocation of resources. In Chapter 3 we discussed how, given certain conditions, the level of output produced in a free market will be socially efficient, namely at that point where the marginal social cost of production equals its marginal social benefit. Subsequently, in Chapter 6 we examined the most important cases in which free markets fail to ensure an efficient allocation of resources. You will recall that for many economists market failures arising from monopoly, public goods and externalities provide a rationale for

state intervention in free markets. In this final chapter of the first part of the book we broaden our discussion beyond the achievement of efficiency and consider the question of *social equity*. At the outset it is important to stress two points.

- First, there is no reason to assume that an efficient system will necessarily result in a socially fair or equitable distribution of output between its members.

- Second, views about the equity of how income is distributed between members of society depend upon personal value judgements, and must therefore be considered separately from the question of efficiency. Although, as we saw in Chapter 1, it is sometimes difficult to separate positive from normative economics, the controversy over what is a fair distribution of income is clearly a part of normative economics. While claims for state intervention to redistribute income can be made on the grounds of fairness or equity, equity questions cannot be answered by reference to efficiency arguments.

In what follows we consider: how the distribution of personal incomes can be measured (Section 8.2); how the degree of inequality in the distribution can be measured (Section 8.3); the major sources of inequality (Section 8.4); and finally how the pattern of inequality is modified by government expenditure and taxation (Section 8.5). We begin with a discussion of how the distribution of personal incomes can be measured.

8.2 Measuring the distribution of personal incomes

To illustrate how the distribution of personal incomes can be measured we take an example of income distribution in a Western industrialized economy, namely the United Kingdom. In the UK the *main* source of information on the distribution of income is the annual Survey of Personal Incomes (SPI) conducted by the Inland Revenue. This survey is based on income tax returns of a sample of tax units: that is, single persons over school-leaving age and not at school, or married couples. Income is defined to include income from employment, self-employment, investments, pensions, social security benefits, and some items of income in kind (luncheon vouchers, for example). Data derived from the SPI suffer from a number of deficiencies. For example, tax units have an incentive to under-report their incomes in order to reduce their tax liability. Furthermore, as the SPI provides only information on taxable income and benefits, information on non-taxable income and benefits has to be obtained from other sources. In the UK the other main source of information is the Family Expenditure Survey (FES), which collects information on all sources of income of a random sample of households, and examines their expenditure patterns.

Table 8.1 presents the distribution of personal incomes, both before and after tax, in the UK for the financial year 1984–85, the last year when official statistics on income distribution in the UK were published. The table divides the population into *deciles* or ten equal-sized groups, after the population has been placed in rank order according to income. For example, the top 10 per cent of the population earned 29.5 per cent of total income (before tax) and 26.5 per cent of total income (after tax) in 1984–85. Conversely the bottom 10 per cent of the population received only 2.3 per cent of total income (before tax) and 2.7 per cent of total income (after tax).

Table 8.1 The distribution of personal incomes before and after tax in the UK, 1984–85

Decile group	Percentage shares of income	
	Before tax	After tax
Top 10	29.5	26.5
11–20	16.8	16.6
21–30	13.0	13.0
31–40	10.3	10.4
41–50	8.2	8.6
51–60	6.6	7.1
61–70	5.4	6.0
71–80	4.4	4.9
81–90	3.5	4.2
91–100	2.3	2.7

Source: Economic Trends (November 1987) Office for National Statistics, © Crown Copyright 1998

Table 8.2 Distributions of personal incomes before and after tax in the UK (1984–85) expressed as cumulative percentages

Population		Total income	
		Before tax	After tax
Bottom	10	2.3	2.7
	20	5.8	6.9
	30	10.2	11.8
	40	15.6	17.8
	50	22.2	24.9
	60	30.4	33.5
	70	40.7	43.9
	80	53.7	56.9
	90	70.5	73.5
	100	100.0	100.0

Source: Economic Trends (November 1987) Office for National Statistics, © Crown Copyright 1998

Table 8.2 presents the distribution of personal incomes, before and after tax, in the UK for the financial year 1984–85 expressed as *cumulative* percentages. For example, the bottom 40 per cent of the population received 15.6 (i.e. 2.3 + 3.5 + 4.4 + 5.4) per cent of total income (before tax) and 17.8 (i.e. 2.7 + 4.2 + 4.9 + 6.0) per cent of total income (after tax), while the bottom 80 per cent of the population received 53.7 per cent of total income (before tax) and 56.9 per cent of total income (after tax).

8.3 Measuring inequality in the distribution of personal incomes

The conventional way of illustrating the degree of *inequality* in the distribution of personal incomes is the so-called **Lorenz curve**. Fig. 8.1 depicts the Lorenz curve of the before-tax income distribution in the UK for the financial year 1984–85 using the data presented in the first two columns of Table 8.2. In Fig. 8.1 the cumulative percentage of the population is measured on the horizontal axis, while the cumulative percentage of total income that the population receives is measured on the vertical axis. In line with Table 8.2, the cumulative percentages begin with the bottom group (that is, at the origin, zero per cent of the population receive zero per cent of total income) and continue until the entire population must earn 100 per cent of total personal income. The 45° line, 0B, which shows points of equality between the two axes, is called the line of complete or perfect equality. The degree of inequality can be gauged by the extent to which the Lorenz curve deviates from the line of complete equality. If incomes were shared out equally (that is, 10 per cent of the population received 10 per cent of total income, 20 per cent of the population had a 20 per cent share of total income, and so on), the Lorenz curve would coincide with the line

Lorenz curve: Graphs the cumulative percentage of total income received against the cumulative percentage of the population, beginning with the bottom group.

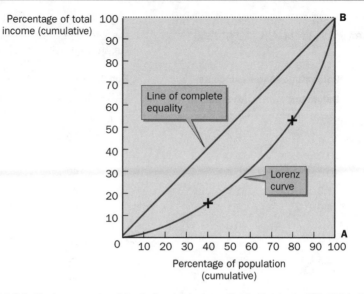

Fig. 8.1 The Lorenz curve of the before-tax income distribution in the UK, 1984–85.

of complete equality. Alternatively if all income was received by just one person and everyone else received nothing then the Lorenz curve would coincide with the line 0AB. In this latter extreme hypothetical case there would be complete inequality in the distribution of personal incomes. In Fig. 8.1 the two points marked by crosses on the Lorenz curve show for example that the bottom 40 per cent of the population received 15.6 per cent of total income, while the bottom 80 per cent of the population received 53.7 per cent of total income (see also Table 8.2). At any point along the horizontal axis the vertical difference between the Lorenz curve and the line of complete equality indicates the degree of inequality in the income distribution. The further the Lorenz curve is from the line of complete equality, the greater is the degree of inequality.

The *overall* degree of inequality in the distribution of personal incomes can be measured by calculating the so-called **Gini coefficient** or ratio. The Gini coefficient can be found by dividing the area between the Lorenz curve and the line of complete equality (0B) by the total area below the line of complete equality (triangle 0BA in Fig. 8.1). The Gini coefficient ranges from a minimum value of zero to a maximum value of unity. If there was no inequality the Lorenz curve would coincide with the line of complete equality, and the Gini coefficient would be equal to zero. Conversely, if there was complete inequality the Lorenz curve would coincide with the line 0AB, and the Gini coefficient would be equal to unity. The Gini coefficient can also be expressed as a percentage, in which case it is calculated by multiplying the coefficient or ratio by 100 (as is the case in Table 8.3). In this situation the Gini coefficient would again be equal to zero if there was complete equality but would be equal to 100 if there was complete inequality. Regardless of how the measure is presented, the larger the value of the Gini coefficient the greater the overall degree of inequality in the distribution of personal incomes. For example, the Gini coefficient for the after-tax income distribution in the UK for 1984–85 was 36 compared with 41 for the before-tax income distribution, suggesting a greater degree of inequality in the distribution of before-tax, compared with after-tax, income.

Gini coefficient: Measures the overall degree of inequality in the income distribution.

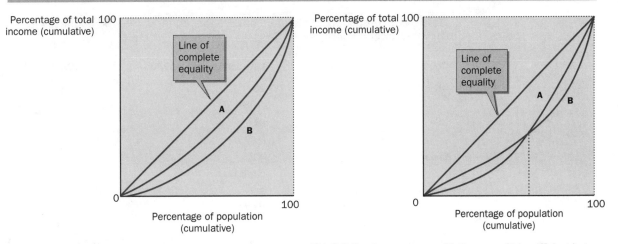

Fig. 8.2 Two Lorenz curves.

Fig. 8.3 Two Lorenz curves with the same Gini coefficient but with different patterns of inequality.

While the Gini coefficient seeks to measure the overall degree of inequality, it is important to exercise some caution in making comparisons between two distributions. Where one Lorenz curve lies completely inside another we can say unambiguously that there is more equality throughout the *entire* income distribution depicted by the Lorenz curve that lies closest to the line of complete equality. For example, as illustrated in Fig. 8.2, the income distribution depicted by Lorenz curve A is more equal throughout its entire range than that depicted by Lorenz curve B. In this example, the value of the Gini coefficient for income distribution A would be smaller than that for income distribution B. If, however, two Lorenz curves intersect while both income distributions might have the same Gini coefficient, they would exhibit different patterns of inequality with more and less equality at different parts of their distributions. For example, in Fig. 8.3 while there is less equality in the bottom part of the income distribution depicted by Lorenz curve A than in curve B (that is, before the point of intersection of the two curves), there is more equality in the top part of the income distribution depicted by Lorenz curve A than in curve B (that is, beyond the point of intersection of the two curves). It is also important to note that international comparisons of income distributions are very difficult to make, not least because different countries often use different methods of collecting data and adopt different definitions of income based on different income units. Trying to compare levels of inequality between developed and developing countries is particularly problematic.

Table 8.3 presents Gini coefficients of income for seven industrialized countries in the early 1970s, late 1970s/early 1980s, and the late 1980s. Leaving aside the noted problems of comparing data across countries, reference to Table 8.3 reveals two interesting features. First, over the entire period of those countries that experienced a rise in inequality (namely the UK, USA and Australia) the increase in inequality was much larger in the UK. For example, between 1981 and 1988 the Gini coefficient in the UK rose by 25 per cent. In contrast, both the USA and Australia experienced a much smaller increase in inequality, while over the entire period Finland and France actually experienced moves towards greater equality. Second, with the notable exception of France, the rankings across the countries cited remained remarkably stable over the period concerned. For example, despite the dramatic rise in inequality

Table 8.3 Gini coefficients of income for seven industrialized countries in the 1970s and 1980s[a]

Country	Early 1970s	Late 1970s/early 1980s	Late 1980s
UK	27	28	35
	(1977)	(1981)	(1988)
USA	36	37	40
	(1973)	(1979)	(1989)
Canada	n.a.	40	40
	Slight fall	(1981)	(1988)
France	38	36	37
	(1975)	(1979)	(1984)
Australia	34	37	39
	(1974)	(1983)	(1988)
Sweden	30	29	n.a.
	(1972)	(1981)	Slight rise
Finland	27	21	20
	(1971)	(1981)	(1985)

[a]After-tax income measure used for the UK, USA, Sweden and Finland. Before-tax income measure used for Canada, France and Australia.
Source:Gregg, P. and S. Machin 'Is the UK rise in inequality different?' in Barrell, R. *The UK Labour Market* (Cambridge: Cambridge University Press, 1994)

in the UK during the 1980s, inequality in the UK in the late 1980s still lay at a lower level than in the USA, Canada, France and Australia.

8.4 Sources of inequality

Having discussed how the distribution of personal incomes is measured in the UK (with illustrative data for the financial year 1984–85) and also how the degree of inequality can be measured, we next consider the major sources of inequality.

Table 8.4 presents the distribution of before-tax income in the UK by source for 1984–85. Reference to Table 8.4 reveals the marked differences in the composition of income at different points of the income distribution. In the top half of the distribution the main source of income is derived from employment and self-employment. For example, the top 25 per cent of the population (who received 53 per cent of total income) derived three quarters of their income from employment and one-tenth from self-employment. As we move from the top to the bottom half of the distribution the main source of income changes from employment and self-employment to state benefits. For example, the poorest 25 per cent of the population (who received only 8 per cent of total income) derived less than a quarter of their income from employment and self-employment, and approximately two thirds from National Insurance retirement pensions and other taxable and non-taxable benefits.

Table 8.4 reveals that overall income from employment and self-employment constituted by far the largest component of total personal income, accounting for 72

Table 8.4 Distribution of before-tax income in the UK by source for 1984–85

Quantile group (and quantiles)	Source of before-tax income (%)						
	Employment	Self–employment	Investment	Occupational pensions and annuities	NIRP[a]	Non-taxable benefits	Total[b]
Top 1 % (over £31 380)	57	26	14	2	1	1	100
Top 25 % (over £9720)	75	10	8	3	2	3	100
Next 25 % (£5480–£9720)	69	7	6	6	6	6	100
Next 25 % (£3160–£5480)	38	4	7	7	25	20	100
Bottom 25 % (up to £3160)	23	1	8	3	30	34	100
	64	8	7	4	8	9	100

[a]NIRP includes National Insurance retirement pensions and taxable benefits.
[b]Due to rounding figures may not exactly sum to 100.
Source: Economic Trends (November 1987) Office for National Statistics, © Crown Copyright 1998

per cent of total (before-tax) income in 1984–85. Given that income earned from employment and self-employment constitutes the largest component of total personal income, the degree of inequality can be explained in large part by differences in wages and salaries. In the previous chapter we discussed the causes of wage differentials between occupations. You will recall that differences in earnings reflect among other things:

- differences in natural ability
- differences in education and training
- differences in bargaining power
- differences in hours worked
- differences in the relative pleasantness of jobs
- differences in mobility.

We next turn to consider how the pattern of inequality is modified by government expenditure and taxation.

8.5 Government policy and redistribution

Earlier in Section 8.3 we alluded to the fact that in the UK taxation policies tend to reduce the overall degree of inequality in the distribution of personal incomes. The **progressive** nature of the income tax system ensures that the shares at the top of the distribution are reduced while those at the bottom are increased. For example, Table 8.1 reveals that in 1984–85 the largest difference between before-tax and after-tax income shares occurred in the top decile group, whose percentage share of income was reduced from 29.5 to 26.5. In this section we consider more fully the effect of government expenditure and taxation on the pattern of inequality in the UK. The discussion that follows is based on an article published in *Economic Trends* (March 1997), which examines how the distribution of income amongst households in the

Progressive tax: One that takes a larger percentage of income from people as their incomes rise.

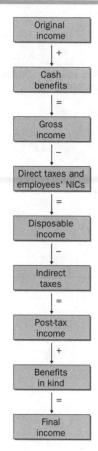

Fig. 8.4 Stages of redistribution of household income.
Source: Economic Trends (March 1997), Office for National Statistics, © Crown Copyright 1998.

UK during 1995–96 was modified by government expenditure and taxation. In contrast to the data presented in Tables 8.1 and 8.2 the main source of data presented in Tables 8.5–8.7 is the Family Expenditure Survey (rather than the SPI), which covers a sample of households (rather than tax units).

Fig. 8.4 depicts a flow diagram of the various ways in which government expenditure and taxation affects the distribution of income amongst households. The first stage in considering redistribution is to start with the total income of households before any government intervention takes place. In Fig. 8.4 total income derived from employment, occupational pensions, investments and other non-government sources is referred to as original income. The addition of various cash benefits to original income yields gross income. Cash benefits themselves can be divided between contributory (e.g. state retirement pensions, unemployment benefit) and non-contributory types (e.g. income support, child benefit, housing benefits). Subtracting direct taxes and employees' National Insurance contributions (NICs) from gross income yields disposable income. Direct taxes are defined here to include not only income tax but also council tax/domestic rates and water charges. Subtracting households' payments of indirect taxes (such as VAT) from disposable income yields post-tax income. Finally, adding benefits in kind to post-tax income yields final income. Benefits in kind involve certain goods and services provided by the government to households either free (at the time of use) or at subsidized prices. The two largest items are health and education services; imputations of the benefits derived from these and other items (such as travel subsidies) are based on the estimated costs of providing them, and are attributed to households according to estimates of different households' use of such goods and services.

Before we consider the effects of government expenditure and taxation on the distribution of income amongst households in the UK we should comment on the need for adjustment to allow for household composition. As households differ in their composition, and in consequence make different demands on resources, income needs to be adjusted to take account of household size, family composition and age of children. The data presented in Tables 8.5–8.7 have been adjusted accordingly and refer to households ranked by so-called 'equivalized' disposable income. Table 8.5 reveals how the tax–benefit system modifies income shares when households are divided into *quintiles* or five equal-sized groups. For example, households

Table 8.5 Percentage shares of total household income for all households in the UK, 1995–96

Quintile group	Original income	Gross income	Disposable income	Post-tax income
Bottom	2.6	7.4	7.9	6.9
Second	7	11	12	12
Third	15	16	17	16
Fourth	25	23	23	23
Top	50	43	40	43
All households	100	100	100	100
Gini coefficient	52	36	33	37

Source: Economic Trends (March 1997) Office for National Statistics, © Crown Copyright 1998

Table 8.6 Percentage shares of total household income for non-retired households in the UK, 1995–96

Quintile group	Original income	Gross income	Disposable income	Post-tax income
Bottom	3.0	6.9	7.4	6.4
Second	10	12	13	12
Third	17	17	17	17
Fourth	25	23	23	23
Top	45	41	40	42
All non-retired households	100	100	100	100
Gini coefficient	44	35	32	37

Source: Economic Trends (March 1997) Office for National Statistics, © Crown Copyright 1998

in the top quintile group received 50 per cent of original income. Taking into account cash benefits reduced the top group's share to 43 per cent of gross income. Allowing for direct taxes and employees' National Insurance contributions further reduced the top group's share to 40 per cent of disposable income. In contrast the bottom quintile group's 2.6 per cent share of original income rose to 7.4 per cent of gross income and 7.9 per cent of disposable income once cash benefits and direct taxes and employees' National Insurance contributions were taken into account respectively. For all households taken together cash benefits contributed most to the reduction in income inequality. This is illustrated most forcefully by the fall in the Gini coefficient from 52 for original income to 36 for gross income.

Given that approximately 42 per cent of households in the bottom two quintile groups are retired and that the pattern of both their income and their expenditure is very different from that of non-retired households, it is useful to present the effects of the tax–benefit system on the income shares of non-retired (Table 8.6) and retired households (Table 8.7) separately. Table 8.6 reveals how the tax–benefit system

Table 8.7 Percentage shares of total household income for retired households in the UK, 1995–96

Quintile group	Original income	Gross income	Disposable income	Post-tax income
Bottom	3.6	10.3	10.4	9.2
Second	6	13	14	14
Third	10	16	17	17
Fourth	19	21	21	21
Top	61	40	38	39
All retired households	100	100	100	100
Gini coefficient	66	29	27	31

Source: Economic Trends (March 1997) Office for National Statistics, © Crown Copyright 1998

modifies the shares of income for non-retired households. For example, non-retired households in the bottom quintile group received only 3.0 per cent of original income compared with 45 per cent of those in the top quintile group. Once cash benefits and direct taxes and employees' National Insurance contributions are taken into account, the share of the bottom quintile group rose to 7.4 per cent of disposable income and that of the top group fell to 40 per cent. Table 8.7 reveals the extent to which the tax–benefit system modifies the shares of income for retired households. As is the case both for all households taken together and for non-retired households, cash benefits contributed most to the reduction in income inequality amongst retired households. The Gini coefficient fell from 66 for original income to 29 for gross income. Finally, comparison of the Gini coefficients noted in Tables 8.6 and 8.7 reveals a greater degree of equality in the distribution of original income among non-retired than among retired households, but a greater degree of equality in the distribution of gross, disposable and post-tax income among retired than among non-retired households.

8.6 Concluding remarks

Controversy exists over the desired pattern of inequality in the distribution of personal incomes. Some see a certain amount of inequality as essential to the efficient functioning of a market system and fear that if the government significantly reduces the existing pattern of inequality, through the tax–benefit system, it will undermine incentives and have an adverse effect on output and growth. Others see the existing pattern of inequality as being morally unjust and a source of social conflict. At the beginning of this chapter we stressed that views about the equity of how income is distributed in society depend upon value judgements and are a part of normative economics. The equity question and what role the government should play in influencing the degree of inequality are sources of perennial political controversy.

■ Summary

◆ Views concerning the equity of the distribution of income between members of society depend upon value judgements and are part of normative economics.

◆ The degree of inequality in the distribution of personal incomes can be illustrated by means of the Lorenz curve. The degree of inequality can be gauged by the extent to which the Lorenz curve deviates from the line of complete equality.

◆ The overall degree of inequality in the distribution of personal incomes can be measured by calculating the Gini coefficient. The coefficient ranges from a minimum value of zero (complete equality) to a maximum value of unity (complete inequality).

◆ In the UK there exist marked differences in the composition of income at different points of the income distribution. In the top half of the distribution the main source of income is derived from employment and self-employment, while in the bottom half it is derived from state benefits. Overall, income from employment and self-employment constitutes by far the largest component of total personal income, and in consequence the degree of inequality can be explained in large part by differences in wages and salaries.

◆ There are a number of ways in which government expenditure and taxation affect the distribution of income amongst households. In the UK, cash benefits contribute most to the reduction in income inequality.

◆ Controversy exists, and will continue to exist, over the desired pattern of inequality in the distribution of personal incomes. Some fear that government policies to further reduce inequality may undermine incentives and adversely affect output and growth; others advocate greater equality on the grounds of social equity.

Key terms

◆ Social equity
◆ Distribution of personal incomes
◆ Deciles
◆ Lorenz curve
◆ Line of complete equality
◆ Gini coefficient
◆ Quintiles

Self-test questions

True (t) or false (f)

1. Deciles divide the population into five equal-sized groups.

2. If incomes were shared out equally the Lorenz curve would coincide with the line of complete equality.

3. The closer the Lorenz curve is to the line of complete equality, the greater the degree of inequality.

4. The Gini coefficient can range in value from a minimum of -1 to a maximum of $+1$.

5. The smaller the value of the Gini coefficient, the greater the overall degree of inequality in the distribution of personal incomes.

6. Where two or more income distributions have the same value for their Gini coefficient, they necessarily exhibit the same pattern of inequality across their entire distributions.

7. A tax system is progressive if individuals pay a larger percentage of income in taxes as their incomes rise.

8. Cash benefits contribute most to the reduction in income inequality in the UK.

Complete the following sentences by inserting the missing word(s)

1. The issue of fairness or equity is a _____ issue.

2. The diagram that depicts the cumulative percentage of total income received against the cumulative percentage of the population, beginning with the bottom group, is called the _____.

3. The degree of inequality in the distribution of personal incomes can be gauged by the extent to which the Lorenz curve deviates from the ____.

4. In the hypothetical case where there was perfect equality in the distribution of personal incomes the ____ would coincide with the ____.

5. The overall degree of inequality in the distribution of personal incomes can be measured by calculating the ____.

6. The Gini coefficient would have a value of ____ if there was complete equality in the distribution of personal incomes, and a value of ____ if there was complete inequality.

Exercise

1. Using data presented in Table 8.2 draw the Lorenz curve of the after-tax income distribution in the UK for 1984–85. How does the curve you have drawn differ from the Lorenz curve of the before-tax income distribution shown in the text?

■ Questions for discussion

◆ Explain why views about the equity of how income is distributed between members of society must be considered separately from the question of efficiency.

◆ How can the degree of inequality in the distribution of personal incomes be illustrated graphically?

◆ How can the degree of inequality in the distribution of personal incomes be measured?

◆ What are the main sources of inequality in the UK?

◆ How is the pattern of inequality modified by government expenditure and taxation?

■ Further reading

Hills, J. (ed.) *New Inequalities* (Cambridge: Cambridge University Press, 1996). Examines the changing distribution of income and wealth in the UK over the last two decades.

The Objectives of Macroeconomic Policy

CHAPTER 9

Key issues

▶ What are the main objectives of macroeconomic policy?

▶ What is the nature of each of these objectives and how can they be measured?

▶ What are the costs of failing to achieve each objective?

▶ What potential conflicts exist between the main objectives of macroeconomic policy?

Contents

9.1 Introduction

The first half of this book dealt with microeconomics. It will be recalled that this involves the study of the behaviour and performance of individual units within the economy, such as the individual market, consumer, firm, and worker. **Macroeconomics**, the subject matter of the second half of the book, is concerned with the study of the behaviour and performance of the economy as a whole. Thus, for example, the microeconomic focus upon the level of output in particular markets is generalized at the macro level into an analysis of the overall or *aggregate* level of output produced in the economy. Similarly, micro analyses of the number of people employed in particular markets are in macro terms transformed into concerns about the total levels of employment and unemployment in the economy. Other central areas of macroeconomic interest include economic growth, inflation, and the balance of payments. **Macroeconomic policy** is concerned with the attempts of policymakers to influence the behaviour of such macroeconomic aggregates in order to improve the overall performance of the economy. As subsequent chapters will make clear, there is much debate and controversy surrounding the appropriate mix of policies required to improve economic performance.

While macroeconomics takes in the complete picture of the way in which the economy works, it is important to recognize that such a broad approach is also associated with the loss of some detail. An analysis of the general trend in the level of unemployment, for example, inevitably glosses over possible unevenness in its

Macroeconomics: The study of the economy as a whole.

Macroeconomic policies: Those used by governments to try to influence overall economic performance.

Chancellor Gordon Brown: keeping the economy on course?

distribution. Thus in both the UK and the EU as a whole there are long-established concerns over sharp differences in regional unemployment rates. This kind of problem is not immediately apparent from an inspection of aggregate data on unemployment. Similarly, though policies that result in an increase in national output are usually to be applauded, we might also have a legitimate interest in how the extra output is shared out. The macro focus tends to neglect this in its preoccupation with the output total.

The purpose of this chapter is to provide an introduction to the four *main* objectives of government macroeconomic policy – namely, the attainment of:

- a stable and satisfactory rate of economic growth
- a high and stable level of employment
- a low and stable rate of inflation
- medium-term balance of payments equilibrium

In each case we describe the nature of the objective and indicate why it is thought to be desirable. We also briefly consider the extent to which these policy goals can be achieved simultaneously. The chapter concludes with a brief historical overview of the changing policy priorities that have operated at the macro level since the end of the Second World War.

9.2 Economic growth

Economic well-being or *welfare* is a decisively materialist concept. In a micro context we have seen that the amount of goods and services that an individual is able to consume is the exclusive criterion of satisfaction: 'more is better'. At the macroeconomic level a similar logic applies: the greater the level of output produced and consumed in an economy, the higher will be its living standards in relation to a given population. One way of measuring overall economic performance is to aggregate – just add up – the value of goods and services produced in a country over a given time period, usually a year. The total that results is known as the **gross domestic product** or **GDP**. While we shall leave a discussion of the three different ways by which GDP can be measured to Chapter 10, Section 10.2, it is nevertheless useful to note that the GDP of an economy is equivalent to the total income paid to the factors of production in contributing to the overall production of goods and services.

Gross domestic product (GDP): The total value of goods and services produced in a country by the factors of production located in that country.

Real GDP: The value of gross domestic product measured in terms of the prices that prevailed in some particular base year; also known as GDP in constant prices.

Economic growth: An increase in real GDP over time.

Economists use data on **real GDP** to measure economic growth. Real GDP measures GDP at the prices prevailing in some particular base year. Fig. 9.1 depicts the movement of real GDP (at 1990 prices) for the UK economy since 1948, showing the change in the actual *volume* of goods and services produced. We can make two observations concerning the way in which real GDP has changed over this period. First, the established trajectory of real GDP is clearly upwards. This means that over the long term domestic output and income in the UK have tended to increase incrementally. **Economic growth** refers to an increase in real GDP, while the annual percentage change in real GDP is known as the rate of economic growth.

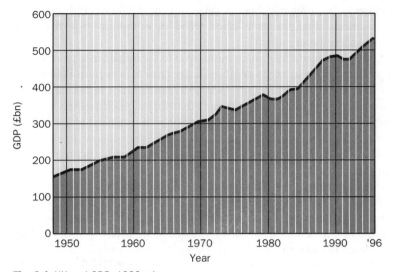

Fig. 9.1 UK real GDP, 1990 prices.
Source: Economic Trends.

As we shall see, *long-term* growth in output can be observed in most economies (Table 9.1 describes the growth performances of the G7 economies since 1970), and reflects changes in factors such as the form and use of technology in new capital equipment, refinements in the organization of production, and increases in the supply of labour.

Second, however, it is evident from Fig. 9.1 that there are a number of periods when the real GDP growth path moves decisively away from its long-term trend. In some cases real GDP actually falls, indicating a reduction in the output total in comparison with earlier achievements. For the UK, periods of negative growth can be observed following the quadrupling of oil prices by the Organization of Petroleum Exporting Countries (OPEC) in 1973–74 and the second OPEC oil price increase in 1979, together with the introduction of the Conservative government's anti-inflation strategy at the start of the 1980s. The most recent period of **recession** occurred in 1991–92, when real GDP fell in successive years by 2.0 and 0.5 per cent respectively. There are also several instances of relatively rapid economic growth, or boom, when real GDP moves sharply above its trend. In the period 1985–88, for example, real GDP in the UK grew at an annual average rate of 4.5 per cent.

The presence of a long-term growth trend mixed with such short-term fluctuations gives rise to the question of what is a desirable or appropriate rate of economic growth. If rapid growth generally equates with strongly rising living standards, should government policy not have as one of its prime objectives the pursuit of as fast a rate of growth as is possible? Similarly, given that severe recessions are associated with falling output and a drop in the standard of living as fewer goods and services are produced and consumed, should governments not seek to avoid such episodes at all costs? In answering these questions it is important to be clear about certain constraints under which government policy operates in both the long and the short term. As noted, the long-term growth path reflects, amongst other things, the technological and organizational sophistication of production, together with the volume of inputs – such as labour – that it is able to command. Because of their very

Recession: Entails a decline in real GDP that lasts for at least two consecutive quarters of a year.

nature, governments can influence these so-called *supply-side* factors only gradually over time. This means that the established trend in economic growth can be conditioned upwards only very slowly.

In contrast, *short-term* growth is much more open to the influence of government policy. Thus governments may try to engineer faster growth in periods before elections in order to curry favour with voters. Why then can they not sustain the rate of expansion over a longer period? One answer is that they are constrained by other macroeconomic policy objectives. A high rate of growth, for example, results in higher incomes, some of the increases in which people may choose to spend on imported goods and services from abroad. If the higher import bill is not matched by increased export earnings, a balance of payments deficit problem may emerge. As we shall see, balance of payments deficits must ultimately be corrected, and therefore a more moderate rate of economic growth may have to be actively sought. Periods of rapid expansion can also be associated with higher rates of inflation, and again policy to trim the rate of economic expansion might be necessary in order to help bring inflation down towards more tolerable levels. It is interesting to note that the historically high rates of growth experienced in the UK in the late 1980s were associated with both balance of payments and inflationary problems, and that these were subsequently addressed by the 1991–92 recession.

Though governments are constrained from operating the economy at short-term growth rates far above the long-run growth trend, it will be equally evident that there is no advantage in accepting meagre expansion below this trend. Slower short-term growth will only entail marginal increases in output and income for the economy as a whole and – in consequence – minimal improvements in living standards. Moreover, if growth becomes negative it is likely to be associated with higher levels of unemployment as falling output prompts firms to reduce the number of people they employ.

If there are constraints on the extent to which the rate of economic growth can be raised in the short term, and it is also recognized that slow growth may have some serious disadvantages, what then can be said about the objective of macroeconomic policy in respect of growth? Generally it is accepted that governments should aspire to a *satisfactory* rate of economic growth. As a policy target 'satisfactory growth' may appear a little vague or imprecise, but let us briefly consider its meaning in the context of earlier discussion. A wildly variable rate of economic expansion, oscillating between rapid growth (which has to be curtailed because of its adverse inflationary and/or balance of payments implications) and severe recession (which is associated with rising unemployment and falling living standards), would clearly not be desirable. This suggests that a satisfactory rate is one that is economically sustainable in the light of the broader framework of macroeconomic objectives.

G7: The group of seven main industrial economies in the world: the USA, Japan, Germany, France, Italy, UK, and Canada.

The comparative performance of similarly advanced industrial economies might also be considered to be important when attempting to assess the adequacy of a given growth rate. Table 9.1 compares real GDP growth rates for the so-called **G7** group of the world's largest industrial economies: the USA, Japan, Germany, France, Italy, the United Kingdom, and Canada. It is apparent from the data contained in the table that the Japanese economy has the best record of real output growth amongst these countries over the past 25 years. The United Kingdom's performance is the poorest of the seven, and as such may be considered to be unsatisfactory in relative terms.

Table 9.1 Growth in real GDP for the G7, 1970–96

	USA	Canada	Japan	France	Germany	Italy	UK
1970	–	2.6	10.2	5.7	5.1	5.3	2.3
1971	3.1	5.8	4.3	4.8	3.1	1.9	2.0
1972	4.8	5.7	8.2	4.4	4.2	2.9	3.5
1973	5.2	7.7	7.6	5.4	4.7	6.5	7.4
1974	–0.6	4.4	–0.6	3.1	0.1	4.7	–1.7
1975	–0.8	2.6	2.9	–0.3	–1.2	–2.1	–0.7
1976	4.9	6.2	4.2	4.2	5.5	6.5	2.8
1977	4.5	3.6	4.7	3.2	2.5	2.9	2.4
1978	4.8	4.6	4.9	3.3	3.5	3.7	3.5
1979	2.5	3.9	5.5	3.2	4.1	5.7	2.8
1980	–0.5	1.5	3.6	1.6	1.0	3.5	–2.2
1981	1.8	3.7	3.6	1.2	0.1	0.5	–1.3
1982	–2.2	–3.2	3.2	2.5	–1.0	0.5	1.7
1983	3.9	3.2	2.7	0.7	1.7	1.2	3.7
1984	6.2	6.3	4.3	1.3	2.8	2.6	2.3
1985	3.2	4.8	5.0	1.9	2.3	2.8	3.8
1986	2.9	3.3	2.6	2.5	2.3	2.8	4.3
1987	3.1	4.3	4.1	2.3	1.4	3.1	4.8
1988	3.9	4.9	6.2	4.5	3.6	3.9	5.0
1989	2.5	2.4	4.7	4.3	3.7	2.9	2.2
1990	0.8	–0.2	4.8	2.5	5.7	2.2	0.4
1991	–1.0	–1.8	3.8	0.8	5.0	1.1	–2.0
1992	2.7	0.8	1.0	1.2	2.2	0.6	–0.5
1993	2.2	2.2	0.3	–1.3	–1.2	–1.2	2.1
1994	3.5	4.2	0.6	2.8	2.9	2.2	4.3
1995	2.0	2.3	1.4	2.1	1.9	2.9	2.0
1996	2.4	1.5	3.6	1.5	1.3	0.7	2.1

Source: International Monetary Fund *International Financial Statistics Yearbook* (1997)

9.3 Unemployment

An internationally recognized definition of unemployment considers the **unemployed** to be people of working age who are jobless but who are both available for work and actively seeking employment. Note that the definition requires *active* participation in the labour market on the part of the unemployed: the unemployed person's situation must impact upon overall market processes. The **unemployment rate** is the proportion of the total labour force (the total of those employed and unemployed) who are currently out of work.

Unemployment is measured at a point in time. Whether or not the level of unemployment changes over time depends on flows into and out of a pool of un-employed labour. As illustrated in Fig. 9.2 there are six main inflows. Four of these inflows involve people previously employed who become unemployed because they are made redundant, are fired or sacked, are temporarily laid off, or voluntarily quit

Unemployed people: Those available for work and who are actively seeking jobs but cannot find them.

Unemployment rate: The percentage of the labour force unemployed.

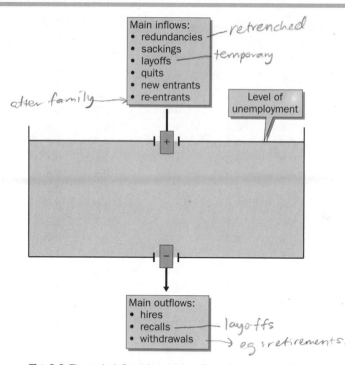

Fig. 9.2 The main inflows into and outflows from a pool of unemployed labour.

their existing job. Two further inflows into the pool of unemployed labour involve people not previously in the labour force and who are now looking for work: new entrants (such as school leavers) and re-entrants (such as people who have raised a family and are now returning to the labour force). There are three main outflows from the pool of unemployed labour. Some people previously unemployed find new jobs; some who have been temporarily laid off are recalled; others withdraw from the labour force (upon retirement, for example, or because, disheartened at the prospect of ever finding work, they stop actively seeking employment).

Table 9.2 summarizes the recent experience of unemployment in the G7 economies. Three points emerge from the trends evident in the table. First, the best and most consistent record is that of Japan. The Japanese unemployment rate over the whole period remains below 3.5 per cent. Second, amongst the European countries, though all rates increased during the 1980s in particular, unemployment in Germany has been lower than the general levels experienced in the UK, France and Italy. Finally, unemployment in the USA has also been relatively stable but at a higher average rate than in Japan. We should also emphasize that the data in the table conveys only the broadest picture of the course of unemployment in each country. The more detailed nuances of its distribution by age, gender, social class, and locale must be left to finer, more disaggregate analyses.

Unemployment is a serious policy problem for both economic and social reasons. Economics, as we know from Chapter 1, is concerned with resource allocation: how are a society's resources being used? Are they being used as well as they might be? Unemployment means that a proportion of one particular resource, perhaps the most important one, labour, is not put to any use whatsoever. This waste is compounded by the need to devote still more resources, such as the money tied up in the

Table 9.2 Standardized unemployment rates for the G7, 1970–96 (per cent of total labour force)

	USA	Canada	Japan	France	Germany[a]	Italy	UK
1970	4.8	5.6	1.1	2.5	0.8	5.3	3.0
1971	5.8	6.1	1.2	2.7	0.9	5.3	3.6
1972	5.5	6.2	1.4	2.8	0.8	6.3	4.0
1973	4.8	5.5	1.3	2.7	0.8	6.2	3.0
1974	5.5	5.3	1.4	2.8	1.6	2.9	5.3
1975	8.3	6.9	1.9	4.0	3.6	5.8	4.3
1976	7.6	7.1	2.0	4.4	3.7	6.6	5.6
1977	6.9	8.1	2.0	4.9	3.6	7.0	6.0
1978	6.0	8.3	2.2	5.2	3.5	7.1	5.9
1979	5.8	7.4	2.1	5.8	3.2	7.6	5.0
1980	7.0	7.5	2.0	6.2	2.9	7.5	6.4
1981	7.5	7.5	2.2	7.4	4.2	7.8	9.8
1982	9.5	10.9	2.4	8.1	5.9	8.4	11.3
1983	9.5	11.9	2.6	8.3	7.7	8.8	12.4
1984	7.4	11.2	2.7	9.7	7.1	9.4	11.7
1985	7.1	10.5	2.6	10.2	7.1	9.6	11.2
1986	6.9	9.5	2.8	10.4	6.4	10.5	11.2
1987	6.1	8.8	2.8	10.5	6.2	10.9	10.3
1988	5.4	7.7	2.5	10.0	6.2	10.9	8.6
1989	5.2	7.5	2.3	9.4	5.6	10.9	7.2
1990	5.5	8.1	2.1	8.9	4.8	10.3	6.9
1991	6.8	10.3	2.1	9.4	4.2	9.8	8.8
1992	7.4	11.3	2.2	10.4	4.6	9.8	10.1
1993	6.8	11.2	2.5	11.7	7.9	10.2	10.4
1994	6.0	10.3	2.9	12.2	8.3	11.1	9.6
1995	5.5	9.4	3.1	11.6	8.2	12.1	8.7
1996	5.4	9.7	3.3	12.4	9.0	12.0	8.2

[a] Up to and including 1992 data concern West Germany; all Germany thereafter.
Source: *OECD Economic Outlook* (various issues). Reproduced by permission of the OECD

benefits system, to alleviate the plight of the unemployed; and by the loss of tax revenue to the state that unemployed people would contribute if they had jobs. Far better, from an economic perspective, to have a situation in which all who are willing to work have the opportunity to do so. In such circumstances, the welfare or well-being – defined by higher incomes and consumption levels – of individuals who might otherwise be unemployed is raised.

For society as a whole, greater employment means more people producing more output and thereby adding to real GDP. The spectacular contemporary growth performance of the Japanese economy and the low Japanese unemployment rate are not a coincidence. Conversely, lower employment means fewer people producing less output and thereby reducing real GDP. For example, for the US economy, it has been estimated that every 1 per cent increase in unemployment reduces the level of real output by 2.25 per cent.

The social and economic problems associated with unemployment fall into two main categories: those that impact directly upon the unemployed themselves and those that are borne by society as a whole. The first and most obvious burden of unemployment for the individual is financial hardship. Though there is relatively wide variation in the benefit levels set in, for example, the major European countries, in most cases the benefits paid to the unemployed are substantially below the average level of wages. Low incomes may be the precursor of a further set of difficulties for the unemployed and their families: poor standards of health and educational under-achievement, for example. Long-term unemployment in particular is also recognized to have significant psychological consequences, such as increased stress and low self-esteem, for those it afflicts. The wider social costs of unemployment arise because a proportion of the population is, or may perceive itself to be, economically and socially disenfranchised from the mainstream. If some people feel excluded from society and the kinds of material welfare that it appears to offer to the majority then a range of consequences may emerge: increases in political and racial tension and rising crime and delinquency have all been associated with higher levels of unemployment.

Unemployment is clearly a serious macroeconomic problem, and the objective of policy in this area, noted at the beginning of the chapter, is to maintain a high and stable level of employment. However, the notion of **full employment** does not mean that every member of the working population will always be in a job. Clearly, in a dynamic and changing economy, as new industries emerge and older ones mature, there will be a periodic refocusing of employment opportunity. This is likely to give rise to structural unemployment (see Chapter 11, Section 11.3) as some workers, newly released from declining industries, may not have the skills and aptitudes demanded by employers in industries that are growing and offering new employment opportunities. Over time the required skills can be learned, and people can then move back into work. In this sense, structural unemployment may be considered to be a consequence of changes that inevitably occur in a dynamic economy. Similarly, it might be expected that, even in the absence of any structural economic shifts, a competitive labour market will embrace a fair degree of fluidity as people move from job to job, seeking promotion, new challenges or new working environments. In the midst of the many job changes that are constantly taking place in the economy, some people will find themselves temporarily unemployed or between jobs for a short period: this is known as frictional unemployment (see Chapter 11, Section 11.3).

In a competitive and ever-changing economy some unemployment is inevitable: the question is, how much? In the UK, for example, full employment in the 1950s and 1960s was associated with an achieved level of unemployment of around 2.5 to 3 per cent. However, since the mid-1970s the UK, along with most of the G7 economies, has experienced a significant rise in the level of unemployment. As is evident from Table 9.2, this is particularly the case for the (cited) European economies in the 1980s. In Chapter 11 we consider possible reasons why unemployment has risen, what level is now believed to be consistent with full employment, and the range of policies open to governments to reduce unemployment.

Full employment: A situation in which all unemployment is frictional and structural.

Inflation: A situation in which the overall or general level of prices rises over time.

Inflation rate: The rate at which the general level of prices increases; expressed as a percentage on an annual basis.

9.4   Inflation

Inflation is a process of continually rising prices. The **inflation rate** in an economy thus denotes the pace at which the price of goods and services on average has risen over a given period of time. Though negative inflation (deflation) is possible, the experience in most economies since 1945 is that of positive inflation. As for other macroeconomic variables, inflation is calculated on an annual basis. Inflation is measured by reference to movements in an **index** of prices. A wide range of price indices may be used, including the Retail Price Index (which seeks to measure movements in the cost of a 'basket' of goods and services bought by a typical household), the Index of Producer Prices, and the implicit GDP deflator (which seeks to measure movements in the prices of all goods and services produced by dividing GDP valued at current prices by GDP at constant prices). All index numbers relate to a particular base year, e.g. 1990 = 100. Once an index has been constructed the *rate* of inflation can be measured by calculating the percentage change in the index from one year to the next. For example, if an index stood at a value of 120 in 1992 and at a value of 135 in 1993, then between 1992 and 1993 prices on average would have risen at a rate of 12.5 per cent. The rate of inflation between 1992 and 1993 is calculated as follows: $((135-120)/120) \times 100 = 12.5$ per cent. If the index stood at 148.5 in 1994, then although the average level of prices would have risen, the rate of inflation would have fallen to 10 per cent: $((148.5-135)/135) \times 100 = 10$ per cent.

Table 9.3 describes the inflation performances of the G7 economies since 1970,

Price index: A measure of the average level of prices of a set of goods and services relative to the prices of the same goods and services in a particular base year.

Table 9.3 Consumer prices for selected economies, 1970–96 (per cent)

	USA	Canada	Japan	France	Germany	Italy	Mexico	Iceland	UK
1970	5.8	3.4	7.7	5.2	3.4	5.0	na	13.6	6.4
1971	4.3	2.8	6.1	5.5	5.3	4.8	na	6.6	9.4
1972	3.3	4.8	4.5	6.2	5.5	5.7	na	9.7	7.1
1973	6.2	7.6	11.7	7.3	6.9	10.8	na	20.6	9.2
1974	11.1	10.9	24.5	13.7	7.0	19.1	na	42.9	16.0
1975	9.1	10.8	11.8	11.8	6.0	17.0	na	49.1	24.2
1976	5.7	7.5	9.4	9.6	4.6	16.7	15.8	28.9	16.5
1977	6.5	8.0	8.2	9.4	3.7	19.3	29.1	30.3	15.8
1978	7.6	8.9	4.2	9.1	2.7	12.4	17.5	43.8	8.3
1979	11.3	9.1	3.7	10.8	4.0	15.7	18.2	44.4	13.4
1980	13.5	10.2	7.8	13.6	5.4	21.2	26.4	58.5	18.0
1981	10.3	12.4	4.9	13.4	6.3	19.3	27.9	51.8	11.9
1982	6.1	10.8	2.7	11.8	5.2	16.4	58.7	50.2	8.6
1983	3.2	5.8	1.9	9.6	3.3	14.9	102.3	84.0	4.6
1984	4.3	4.3	2.3	7.4	2.4	10.6	65.3	30.9	5.0
1985	3.5	4.0	2.0	5.8	2.1	8.6	57.8	32.0	6.1
1986	1.9	4.2	0.6	2.7	–0.1	6.1	86.2	22.1	3.4
1987	3.7	4.4	0.1	3.1	0.2	4.6	131.8	18.3	4.1
1988	4.1	4.0	0.7	2.7	1.3	5.0	114.2	25.7	4.9
1989	4.8	5.0	2.3	3.6	2.8	6.6	20.0	20.8	7.8
1990	5.4	4.8	3.1	3.4	2.7	6.1	26.7	15.5	9.5
1991	4.2	5.6	3.3	3.2	3.6	6.5	22.7	6.8	5.9
1992	3.0	1.5	1.7	2.4	5.1	5.3	15.5	4.0	3.7
1993	3.0	1.8	1.2	2.1	4.5	4.2	9.8	4.0	1.6
1994	2.6	0.2	0.7	1.7	2.7	3.9	7.0	1.6	2.5
1995	2.8	2.2	–0.1	1.7	1.8	5.4	35.0	1.7	3.4
1996	2.9	1.6	0.1	2.0	1.5	3.8	34.4	2.3	2.4

Source: OECD Economic Outlook (various issues). Reproduced by permission of the OECD

together with, for comparative purposes, those of Iceland and Mexico. From the table, it is evident that the lowest and most stable inflation rates have been achieved by Germany and Japan. Indeed, in 1986, the general price level in Germany actually fell, if only by the smallest of margins. The rates quoted in the table are averages for each economy as a whole. Thus the inflation rate for a given economy in a particular year cannot be taken as a literal record of the pace of price change for every, or indeed any, good or service: it is simply a reasonably accurate approximation of what is going on. This is another example of the loss of detail associated with analysis at the macro level.

The experience of inflation amongst the G7 since 1970, as depicted in Table 9.3, is quite varied. In contrast to the noted capacity for inflation control in Germany and Japan, the performance of the UK and Italy, for example, with rates close to or above 20 per cent in 1980, is quite poor. However, even the worst G7 experience pales beside that of Iceland and Mexico. The inflation rates of these two countries in the 1980s are noteworthy in respect of the absolute size of the figures involved – a rate of 131.8 per cent for Mexico in 1987, for example – and, in addition, for their *variability*. This is a characteristic feature of very high inflation: it appears to be more prone to substantial oscillation.

We now turn to consider the significance of inflation: why and at what rates might it be considered a problem? Take first a hypothetical situation in which the agents in an economy – consumers, employers, workers, government and others – are aware of the future course of prices. In this case, the rate of inflation could be said to be **perfectly anticipated**, and it would be possible to effect movements in other nominal variables such that real economic circumstances remained unchanged. Thus if the rate of price inflation turned out to be as expected, say 15 per cent over a future period, equivalent increases in the money value of wages, benefit levels and other incomes would leave the real purchasing power of people receiving such incomes unchanged. The inflation, even though relatively high, would not appear to have any 'concrete' impact. In fact, economists identify two problems that can still occur even if inflation can be perfectly anticipated in this way: so-called 'shoe leather' and 'menu' costs.

Shoe leather costs arise because, in the presence of inflation, cash is continually losing its real purchasing power. This gives people an incentive to hold as little cash as possible and to put their money instead into a bank or some other financial institution where it will earn interest. However, because they need cash for everyday purchases, people will be continually withdrawing small amounts from their accounts, wearing out shoe leather on each visit to the bank or cashpoint. Of course, shoe leather is a metaphor for the general costs of inconvenience and administration associated with many cash withdrawals. *Menu costs* reflect the time and resources used in continually repricing goods and services in shops, vending machines, parking meters and so on, in line with the prevailing inflation rate. Given the relatively moderate inflation rates experienced in most Western industrial economies since the Second World War, there is general agreement that such shoe leather and menu costs are relatively small. However, such costs become more significant as economies begin to experience more rapid rates of inflation. While shoe leather and menu costs would arise even in the hypothetical case of inflation being perfectly anticipated, in reality inflation is **imperfectly anticipated** – for example, the actual rate of inflation turns out to be higher than expected – and, as a result, an additional more important set of costs arises.

Perfectly anticipated inflation: Inflation is perfectly anticipated when the actual rate of inflation is equal to the anticipated or expected rate of inflation.

Imperfectly anticipated inflation: Inflation is imperfectly anticipated when the actual rate of inflation differs from the anticipated or expected rate of inflation.

As suggested from the experiences of Mexico and Iceland recorded in Table 9.3, inflationary surges, unless checked, can develop a momentum of their own, and may eventually lead to extremely rapid rates known as **hyperinflation**. The most widely known instance of hyperinflation occurred in Weimar Germany in the 1920s, where, at its height, the annual rate climbed to 1 billion per cent. Now, given that the market is perhaps *the* central institution of competitive capitalism and that markets are coordinated by price signals, it follows that the extreme distortion of prices by cumulatively higher rates of inflation is a direct challenge to the integrity of the capitalist system itself. To put this another way, consider a situation in which money is constantly and quickly drained of its value. As soon as income is earned the imperative will be to spend it before its purchasing power is diminished. At the same time there will be frantic pressures on all social groups to negotiate and struggle for higher money incomes in order to try to offset imploding real incomes. The apocalyptic consequences for economy and society of the intensification of this kind of process, as inflation surges ever higher, are not difficult to imagine: ultimately, the payments system would collapse, leaving exchange to be coordinated by the process of barter.

Inflation does not need to reach 'hyper' proportions for it to be sufficient to distort and weaken the way in which markets work. The famous American economist Milton Friedman has argued that as the rate of inflation increases so too does its variability. Greater variability of inflation generates more *uncertainty* as to what the actual rate will be at any given time. This makes it more difficult for economic agents to distinguish between changes in the general price level and changes in the **relative prices** of different goods and services. Accordingly, economic agents will make mistakes. For example, higher prices in a market might prompt firms to enter, in the anticipation of higher profits. The overall level of output in the market increases accordingly, but if price rises are occurring right across the economy and there is no new or extra demand present, unsold stocks pile up. The possibility of errors of this sort breeds distrust as to the reliability of price signals, and encourages economic agents to spend time and resources unproductively trying to discern what is really going on. Ultimately then markets become less efficient than they would otherwise be in the absence of high and rising inflation, and Friedman argues that lower output and higher unemployment are the inevitable results. Friedman also suggests that similar consequences follow when increased uncertainty induced by higher rates of inflation makes economic agents more cautious: they become more reluctant to take the consumption and investment decisions that would occur in periods of greater price stability.

A second major problem associated with a high rate of inflation concerns the damage visited upon international competitiveness. An economy that experiences rapid increases in prices will find it more difficult to trade successfully in an environment where its trading partners enjoy more moderate rates of inflation. Very simply, the price of its exports will be rising faster than the price of substitutes in foreign markets; and at home the price of domestic goods will be rising faster than the price of imports. *Ceteris paribus*, this means that the balance of trade in goods and services for the more inflationary economy will deteriorate and, as we explain in the next section of this chapter, trade deficits, where imports surge ahead of exports, cannot be sustained in the medium term. What is crucial here then is not the rate of inflation *per se* but the rate of inflation experienced in one country relative to that experienced elsewhere.

Hyperinflation: Arises when the rate of inflation is extremely high for more than a year.

Relative price: The ratio of the price of one good to the price of another good; expressed as the number of units of one good that one unit of another good will buy.

When inflation is imperfectly anticipated it raises a further set of redistributive problems because of its differing impacts upon different groups of people in society. In financial markets, for example, inflation helps borrowers but penalizes lenders. Just as inflation drains money of its value, so it reduces the real value of debt. A sum borrowed at the beginning of a period of high inflation will be worth much less in real terms when the debt comes to be subsequently repaid. For those in debt this is clearly a substantial boon: they can borrow and spend now but the real value of the sum they have to repay in future will be diminished in direct proportion to the inflation rate. Similarly, the expected real value of the interest paid on a debt will be eroded when inflation turns out to be higher than anticipated. For lenders, the implications are reversed: inflation reduces the real value of their capital tied up in loans, and it similarly erodes the real value of interest earnings when inflation is imperfectly anticipated. Overall, then, inflation has the effect of redistributing income from lenders to borrowers.

Unanticipated inflation has similar redistributive effects among other groups in society. For example, it disadvantages those with incomes that were fixed in less inflationary times. Thus people who are retired may have saved capital to provide for their old age. If inflation diminishes the real value of their savings, and of any income stream that they derive from such savings, they will be severely disadvantaged because they have no further access to other sources of income, such as wages, which may be easier to adjust for inflation. At the same time wage earners, if they are in a strong enough bargaining position, may actually increase the real value of their incomes if they can negotiate an increase in their money wages above the rate of inflation. Here, redistribution would be from the non-waged to the waged. Generally, in distributive terms, we may conclude that inflation injures those who are unable to defend or raise their real incomes and advantages those in debt or who have the capacity to revise their real income levels.

Given the range of real economic problems associated with inflation, what kind of inflationary target should governments adopt? Zero inflation or price stability would be the most ambitious target, and some governments do have aspirations in this direction. The German central bank (the Bundesbank), for example, reflecting the experiences of the Weimar period, is constitutionally charged with protecting the value of the Deutschmark. However, more realistically, governments tend to have as an objective a low and stable rate of inflation. This confronts both the dangers of spiralling price increases and the uncertainty that arises from high and variable rates of inflation.

9.5 The balance of payments

The **balance of payments** is a record of the transactions that take place between the residents of one country and the rest of the world over a given period. As for other macroeconomic variables, the balance of payments is usually measured on an annual basis. Balance of payments transactions come in a variety of forms. The most obvious category is trade in goods and services. Imports and exports of goods are known as *visible* trade, while service transactions are called *invisible* trade. Other balance of payments transactions include: foreign borrowing and lending; buying and selling financial assets such as shares abroad; and buying and selling real assets such

Balance of payments: A record of a country's international transactions.

as firms in international markets. A full discussion of the various components of the balance of payments accounts can be found in Chapter 16, Section 16.2.

Why are balance of payments considerations an important element of macro-economics? To help answer this question, think about the range of goods you will use or consume today. Many of the clothes you are wearing, for example, will have been manufactured abroad, probably in the Far East as well as in other parts of the EU. The television you watch tonight might be Japanese and the bed you sleep in Swedish. This kind of exercise gives us some idea of how interdependent most of the world actually is. We live in an international economy, which is characterized by increasing openness (we prefer 'international economy' rather than 'global econo-my' for reasons we explain in Chapter 17). This means that more and more of the output that individual economies produce is being sold in other countries. For the most part, such openness, because it is associated with increasing market accessibil-ity, faster economic growth and wider consumer choice, is viewed very positively.

Table 9.4 illustrates the increasing openness of the world's major industrial economies over the postwar period. The data express the combined money value of exports and imports as a percentage of nominal GDP: that is, GDP valued in the prices ruling in each year. Though some economies, the USA and Japan for example, have a lower relative dependence on trade, all except Japan have seen a growth in openness over the period in question. For the European nations of Germany, France and Italy, the increase is particularly marked. This probably reflects their collective participation in the long process of economic integration that began in the 1950s.

We can identify two main reasons why such openness is likely to increase still further over the next decade and beyond. First, economic integration is gaining momentum. In particular parts of the world, formerly separate economies or groups of economies are coalescing to form unified or single markets and free trade areas. The single market in Europe, for example, provides for the free movement of both goods and services and factors of production amongst all European Union member states. Prior to the establishment of the European Economic Community (EEC) in 1957 the countries of Europe were much more fragmented, with a host of restric-tions on both the range and form of cross-border transactions that their citizens were permitted to engage in. Now, for economic purposes at least, we are all citizens of the single market rather than of our respective economies. Similarly, the North American Free Trade Area (NAFTA), created in 1993, binds together the economies

Table 9.4 Openness for the G7 1950–1992 (exports+imports / nominal GDP, per cent)

	1950	1955	1960	1965	1970	1975	1980	1985	1992
USA	8.5	9.0	9.4	9.5	11.4	16.4	21.1	18.0	21.9
Canada	41.2	39.7	36.0	38.4	42.9	47.2	55.1	54.5	54.0
Japan	18.2	20.3	21.1	19.7	20.3	25.6	28.3	25.6	18.0
France	28.2	26.5	27.0	25.8	31.1	37.0	44.3	47.2	44.9
West Germany	19.7	29.0	35.2	35.6	40.4	46.5	53.3	61.5	60.0
Italy	18.6	20.2	25.8	27.2	32.8	41.1	46.5	46.1	39.6
UK	46.6	44.9	43.5	39.5	45.3	53.6	52.3	56.9	48.9

Source: Penn World Tables

of the USA, Canada and Mexico into a unified market, which has no internal barriers to trade, although separate markets in factors of production, such as labour, continue to exist.

The second factor promoting accelerated openness in world markets is the liberalization of many of the former centrally planned economies such as China, Vietnam, and those in eastern Europe. Markets in these economies are increasingly open to Western investment and goods, and the West itself is available as a potentially lucrative market for the outputs that the reforming economies produce. Indeed, for the more dynamic of the eastern European states such as Hungary, the Czech Republic and Poland, there is the very real prospect of complete integration with the European single market in the not too distant future.

Because of the high and increasing degree of openness in world markets, balance of payments issues are clearly a significant macroeconomic issue. What then are the policy objectives that arise in this area? In order to simplify the discussion we shall concentrate here on the balance of payments as represented by trade in goods and services. Initially, three possibilities arise for the balance of payments position of an economy:

- deficit, where the total value of imports exceeds the value of exports
- surplus, where export revenues are greater than the total import bill
- balance, where the values of exports and imports are roughly equal.

In the case of a deficit, it follows that domestic residents have an appetite for imports that is not matched by their ability to sell goods and services abroad: they are, in other words, net importers. At this point, the fact that different currencies are involved in international trade becomes significant. Exports are a means of generating the reserves of foreign currency or foreign exchange necessary to pay for imports. If the residents of a country are collectively net importers, then it follows that they have a need to acquire foreign currency to pay for imports that is not matched by the level of foreign currency earnings that their exports currently generate: they have, in other words, a foreign currency 'gap'. This gap can be filled in two ways. Either residents can draw on currency reserves that they have accumulated in previous periods, or they can borrow the foreign currency that they require. Now, while both courses of action are possible in the short term neither is sustainable indefinitely: foreign currency reserves and the goodwill of lenders are both finite. This means that balance of payments deficits cannot be sustained in the medium term because of the exhaustion of the supplies of foreign currency necessary to finance them: a persistent balance of payments deficit is therefore a policy problem.

A surplus on the balance of payments has the effect of augmenting the reserves of foreign currency held in the domestic economy. Because domestic residents are net exporters, it follows that they will be more than meeting the foreign currency requirements of their current level of imports. The extra foreign currency that their net exports generate, because it is not immediately needed, is simply added to any existing reserves. A balance of payments surplus might thus appear to be relatively attractive, particularly when the positive knock-on effects of strong export demand on economic growth and domestic employment levels are also taken into consideration. However, this is not the whole story. A consistent surplus and the piling up of foreign currency reserves also represent missed consumption opportunities: it would be possible for domestic residents to comfortably finance more imports – and thereby raise their welfare – from the revenues generated by current export performance. Alternatively they could increase investment abroad and/or raise overseas aid. A balance of payments surplus therefore, even though it might represent export dynamism, is in itself no real achievement. A surplus can also be a sign of considerable economic weakness. In a recessionary period, when real GDP grows more slowly, the capacity to import is constrained by a slowdown in the growth of income. At the same time, assuming export markets are unaffected – their strength is in part a function of foreign incomes – the balance of payments may improve sharply (that is, move away from deficit) but clearly this is far from any kind of achievement. Further caveats concerning the desirability of balance of payments surplus are considered in Chapter 16.

Given that a deficit is a problem and a surplus is hardly laudable, it follows that the objective of policy in respect of the balance of payments is *balance in the medium term*. Balance equates the import-derived foreign currency demands of domestic residents with their export-derived foreign currency earnings. This means that there is no foreign currency 'gap' to be filled, nor any potential consumption or investment forgone. The emphasis is on balance over the medium term, rather than every year, because individual years' deficits and surpluses have the effect of cancelling each other out.

Finally in this section we briefly consider the relationship between the balance of payments and the other objectives of macroeconomic policy. To some extent this has been anticipated by earlier discussion. We have already indicated for example that improvements in the balance of payments can be achieved from the implementation of domestic austerity measures: if domestic residents are made poorer by the onset of recession they cannot afford to buy as many imports as in previous periods. We also noted in our discussion of growth that a rapidly expanding economy with rising income levels will usually be associated with a deterioration in the balance of payments: in other words a movement towards or into deficit. Such links between the balance of payments and other macroeconomic targets give rise to a wider definition of the notion of balance of payments balance or *equilibrium*. We may consider the balance of payments to be in a desired equilibrium over a period of years if a balance is achieved without the need for slower growth, with all its attendant disadvantages, to make this happen. In Chapter 16 we offer further revisions of this definition.

9.6   A brief overview of macroeconomic policy since 1945

It is a commonplace that economic ideas are *reactive* in that they change and develop to confront new or emergent economic problems. If the macroeconomic objectives we have discussed are, broadly speaking, met for many economies over a sustained period, then there will be little pressure to search for new forms of understanding and policy: economists and governments will seemingly have 'got it right'. However, when targets are missed, perhaps disastrously so, there will be an obvious need to revise the thought behind and conduct of macro policy.

The first major instance of this kind of shift in macroeconomic thinking and action occurred as a result of the **Great Depression** of the early 1930s. During this

Depression: A very severe and prolonged recession.

period, output and employment in most of the world's major industrial economies fell dramatically. For example, in the USA, real GDP fell by 35 per cent between 1929 and 1933, with unemployment reaching a peak of 25 per cent in 1933. Previously, though cycles of fast and slower growth had been experienced, economic progress had proceeded relatively smoothly on a generally uninterrupted upward path. This meant that the prevailing economic orthodoxy of classical economics, seemingly having 'got it right', was not open to serious challenge. The Great Depression offered hugely changed circumstances and the opportunity for the advancement of radically different theory and policy.

As a response to the 'new' economic problems posed in the 1930s, the British economist John Maynard Keynes wrote *The General Theory of Employment, Interest and Money*. This book, published in 1936, contained the seeds of a revolution in macroeconomics; indeed, it is often credited as the first work to be framed in a conscious macro dimension. Keynes argued that governments, through managing the total or aggregate demand for the output of an economy, could vanquish depression and produce full employment (see Chapter 11, Section 11.3 for a much more detailed explanation of this approach). Keynes's work proved to be exceptionally influential in both academic and government circles to the extent that during the 1950s and 1960s both macroeconomic thought and policy came to reflect the broad thrust of his views. Moreover, his influence was not confined to the UK; rather it assumed the proportions of a new ruling orthodoxy in all of the advanced Western economies. Keynesian economics or Keynesianism – as the new approach became known – set its sights firmly on maintaining a high and stable level of employment in order to avoid the social, economic and political costs of unemployment. Accordingly, as governments absorbed and put into practice Keynesian ideas, the major short-term policy objective of the early postwar period became full employment. As we have seen, there is a correlation between higher levels of employment and faster short-term economic growth, and so growth too became an objective associated with Keynesianism. However, recall our earlier qualification that growth over the longer term is much less open to the influence of government policy.

What of the other macroeconomic objectives under Keynesianism? We have noted that the balance of payments can act as a constraint upon the successful attainment of both employment and growth objectives. When more people are employed and incomes are rising quickly there will be a consequent increase in imports without any necessary compensatory movement in exports. In this situation the balance of payments will worsen. Because balance of payments deficits cannot be tolerated beyond the medium term, it may prove necessary to trim the growth rate and accept higher levels of unemployment. The final policy objective – inflation – tended to remain comfortably low in most economies for the period of the 1950s through to the mid-to-late 1960s when Keynesianism was dominant, and therefore following the problem–response notion introduced at the beginning of this section, the issue of inflation was not the focus of a great deal of attention. Where slightly faster inflation did provoke mild concern, it tended to be addressed as a constraint on employment and growth in a similar manner to the balance of payments.

Keynesianism was coincident with an era known as the postwar boom. This lasted from the end of the Second World War until about 1970. The postwar boom was characterized by the general experience in most economies of historically rapid rates of economic growth, full employment and low inflation. Whether or not Keynesianism can be credited with some or all of these achievements is, however, a matter of

Table 9.5 Indicators of UK macroeconomic performance (average percentage change)

	1950-59	1960-69	1970-79	1980-89
Economic growth	2.5	3.3	2.3	2.2
Inflation	4.2	3.5	12.6	7.5
Unemployment	1.6	2.0	4.1	11.1

Source: *Economic Trends*, Office for National Statistics, © Crown Copyright 1998

some dispute. The period since 1970 has been one in which economic progress has faltered somewhat. Growth rates have been lower, unemployment higher on average and, in particular, inflation has been higher and more variable. For example, reference to Table 9.5 reveals that the overall performance of the UK economy has been very disappointing in the post-1970 period. Furthermore, the inflationary surge experienced in major Western economies at the end of the 1960s and beginning of the 1970s was so radically different from the gradual rates that prevailed during the postwar boom that it served to undermine the Keynesian orthodoxy, clearing the ground for a second comprehensive revision of macro thought and policy.

The changed economic circumstances after 1970 served to expose two major weaknesses in Keynesian theory. First, in its understandable preoccupation with unemployment, Keynesianism had tended to neglect inflation both as a phenomenon that needed explanation and as a problem for policy. Second, in its limited theorization of inflation, Keynesianism posed it as an 'alternative' to unemployment: in other words, economies could suffer from high unemployment or high inflation but not both at the same time. The new 1970s phenomenon of **stagflation** thus provided a set of circumstances for which Keynesianism had no ready analysis or answers.

It should be clear that a theoretical approach that could explain the emergence of virulent inflation rates and higher unemployment would challenge Keynesianism for the economic high ground. This is what the revived doctrine of monetarism, associated with the work of Milton Friedman, actually did. As we shall discuss in Chapter 12, Section 12.2, Friedman has argued that inflation is essentially determined by the rate of monetary growth relative to the rate of real output growth, and has stressed the need for monetary control to combat inflation. Moreover, if inflation is kept low and stable by government policy, then it is suggested that markets can be relied upon to produce favourable outcomes in respect of the other three macroeconomic variables introduced in this chapter. To a great extent, the view that many governments have distilled from this approach over more recent years is that inflation should be accorded priority in respect of the conduct of macroeconomic policy.

In summary, then, the postwar period up to the 1970s was successively dominated by two different macroeconomic perspectives, which gave rise to two sets of policy imperatives. During the postwar boom the work of Keynes inspired an approach that emphasized the policy problem of unemployment; since the 1970s the work of Friedman has shifted the policy consensus firmly towards the control of inflation. This refocusing of policy has been paralleled by a move away from the Keynesian management of aggregate demand in favour of Friedmanite monetary growth rules

Stagflation: Situation where high unemployment and high inflation occur simultaneously; a combination of stagnation and inflation.

and the management of the supply side of the economy – areas we shall explore more fully in subsequent chapters.

◼ Summary

◆ Macroeconomics involves the study of the economy as a whole. Macroeconomic policy is concerned with the efforts of policymakers to influence the behaviour of four key variables: the rate of economic growth, the level of unemployment, the rate of inflation, and the balance of payments position. We must recognize that macroeconomic policy objectives in respect of each of these variables cannot be pursued independently. For example, efforts to raise the rate of economic growth in the short term must be tempered with an acknowledgement of its potentially negative effects upon inflation and the balance of payments.

◆ Failure to achieve macroeconomic objectives carries a variety of consequences. Attaining slower rates of economic growth than desirable will entail only modest increases in general living standards and may be associated with rising unemployment. In turn, unemployment carries economic and social costs. It wastes scarce human resources, and it inflicts poverty and a sense of hopelessness on the unemployed. Inflation is economically undesirable as it can distort and undermine a central feature of capitalist resource allocation: the price mechanism. It also disadvantages those on fixed incomes, and may threaten the trading position of the economy as a whole. Finally, adverse balance of payments positions may necessitate actions that undermine other objectives. For example, balance of payments deficits usually require some moderation in the rate of economic growth.

◆ There is a strong correlation between the emergence of new macroeconomic problems and the development of macroeconomic thought and policy. Since 1945 macroeconomic policy has been dominated successively by the development and application of first Keynesianism and then monetarism. Keynesianism promoted the widespread involvement of the state in many aspects of the economy. Monetarism demands much more circumspect forms of state intervention.

◼ Key terms

◆ Macroeconomics
◆ Macroeconomic policy
◆ Economic growth
◆ Unemployment
◆ Full employment
◆ Inflation
◆ Hyperinflation
◆ Balance of payments surplus and deficit
◆ Balance of payments balance
◆ Keynesianism

◆ Postwar boom

◆ Stagflation

◆ Monetarism

■ Self-test questions

True (t) or false (f)

1. Macroeconomics is concerned with the study of the behaviour and performance of the economy as a whole.

2. Economists use nominal GDP data to measure economic growth.

3. Whether or not the level of unemployment rises or falls over time depends on the extent to which flows into a pool of unemployed labour are counterbalanced by flows out of it.

4. Full employment is a situation in which all unemployment is frictional and structural.

5. Inflation is a process whereby the price of all goods and services increases at the same rate over time.

6. In the hypothetical case of inflation being perfectly anticipated, there are no costs of inflation.

7. The main costs of inflation arise when inflation is imperfectly anticipated.

8. The balance of invisible trade measures the difference between the value of goods exported and imported.

9. A persistent balance of payments deficit will act as a constraint on the achievement of other macroeconomic objectives, and is a policy problem.

10. Stagflation involves a situation in which high unemployment and high inflation occur simultaneously.

Complete the following sentences by inserting the missing word(s)

1. Economic growth entails an increase in ____ GDP over time.

2. The ____ is the name given to the seven main industrial countries in the world.

3. Unemployed people are those available for work and are ____ seeking jobs but cannot find them.

4. When the actual rate of inflation is equal to the anticipated or expected rate of inflation, inflation is said to be ____.

5. When the rate of inflation turns out to be higher than anticipated it ____ borrowers and ____ lenders.

6. A situation where a country experiences an extremely high rate of inflation for over a year or more is referred to as ____.

7. The balance of payments is a record of a country's ____.

8. When a country exports more goods and services than it imports its balance of payments on such transactions will be in ____.

9. The birth of modern macroeconomics can be traced back to the publication in 1936 of *The General Theory of Employment, Interest and Money* written by ____.

10. The two schools that dominated macroeconomics in the postwar period up to the 1970s were ____ and ____.

Exercises

1. Using data presented in Table 9.1, plot a graph of the rate of economic growth (vertical axis) experienced over the period 1970–96 (horizontal axis) for any one of the countries listed.

2. Taking the same country as that chosen in completing exercise 1, use data presented in Table 9.2 to plot a graph of the rate of unemployment (vertical axis) over the period 1970–96 (horizontal axis).

3. Again taking the same country, use data from Table 9.3 to plot a graph of the rate of inflation (vertical axis) over the period 1970–96 (horizontal axis).

4. From inspection of the three graphs you have drawn, does there appear to be any evidence to suggest that there exists a relationship between any of these three key indicators of macroeconomic performance?

Questions for discussion

◆ Why are fast rates of economic growth not necessarily desirable?

◆ Why is unemployment an economic and social problem?

◆ What problems does inflation in an economy pose for particular social and economic groups?

◆ Why is a surplus on the balance of payments undesirable?

◆ What is the link between economic performance and the development of economic thought and policy?

Further reading

Peston, M.H. *The British Economy: An Elementary Macroeconomic Perspective* (2nd ed.) (Oxford: Philip Allan, 1984). Offers a succinct and engagingly written guide to macroeconomics in the context of the performance of the British economy.

Johnson, C. and S. Briscoe *Measuring the Economy* (Harmondsworth: Penguin, 1995). Provides a well-written guide to understanding British official statistics on the macroeconomy.

Internet links

The UK Treasury has an excellent Web site, which offers lots of information and discussion about the performance of the UK economy. The site also provides reviews of wider economic issues such as European economic integration. The site can be found at: **http://www.hm-treasury.gov.uk/**

Economic Growth

CHAPTER 10

Key issues

▶ How is economic growth measured?

▶ What is the link between economic growth and living standards?

▶ What factors determine economic growth over time?

▶ Why do standards of living vary so widely between countries?

Contents

10.1 Introduction

Economic growth is the source of *sustained* increases in material living standards over time. Over long periods of time short-term fluctuations in output are dominated by the growth of **potential output** as the productive capacity of an economy increases. Not only is economic growth important for raising living standards but so too is the rate of growth actually achieved in an economy. Even small differences in growth rates can make a tremendous difference to the growth of living standards and the level of potential output over the course of a few decades. As a rough rule of thumb the number of years it takes for an economy to double its productive capacity can be found by dividing 72 by its rate of growth. For example, an economy will take approximately 36 years to double its output of goods and services if its growth rate is 2 per cent, but only 18 years if its growth rate is 4 per cent.

In this chapter we discuss what factors determine the *long-run* rate of growth in output using a model developed in the 1950s and 1960s. However, we begin with a discussion of how economic growth is measured, and the link between growth and living standards.

10.2 Measuring economic growth

Economists use data on gross domestic product (GDP) to measure economic growth. GDP, which is the total value of goods and services produced in a country by the factors of production located in that country, regardless of who owns these factors, can be measured in three different ways.

Potential output: The maximum output that can be produced in an economy, given its factor endowments, without generating inflation; also known as full employment output.

"There's an encouraging increase in the number of new reports saying there's an encouraging increase in the signs of economic recovery"

First, GDP can be measured by aggregating the value of **final output** of new goods and services (cars, videos, food, haircuts, etc.) produced within an economy over a given time period (usually a year). The output method involves summing the *net* output of all industries in the economy by estimating the *value added* by each industry to the final output of goods and services produced. For example, the value added by the car industry can be defined as the value of cars produced minus the value of its inputs (iron and steel, glass, etc.) from other industries. For the economy as a whole, imports are inputs and are therefore excluded from GDP, while exports are included in GDP.

Second, GDP can also be measured by summing the incomes paid to the factors of production (that is, the wages of labour, profits of capital, and rent of land and property) used to produce the total output of goods and services. The income method involves measuring GDP at factor cost: that is, what it costs to pay the factors of production that are used to produce the total output of goods and services.

Finally, GDP can be measured by adding together the expenditure made on final goods and services, including expenditure by foreigners on exported goods and services, and excluding purchases of imported goods and services from abroad by domestic residents. The expenditure method initially measures GDP at market prices: that is, the prices at which final goods and services are purchased. Subtracting indirect taxes on expenditure and adding subsidies provides a measure of GDP at factor cost in line with those obtained from the output and income methods.

One further adjustment is required to GDP to provide a measure known as **gross national product (GNP)**, the main measure of national income or national output in a country. As noted above, GDP measures the total value of goods and services produced in a country by the factors of production located in that country *regardless* of who owns them. If net property income (that is, receipts of income from assets and property owned and held abroad minus corresponding payments made to overseas residents) is added to GDP it provides a measure known as gross national product.

The relationship between the three methods of measuring GDP can be visualized using a circular flow of income diagram (see Fig. 10.1). For ease of exposition, we

Final output: Comprises goods and services that are sold to their ultimate users.

Gross national product (GNP): The value of final goods and services produced by domestically owned factors of production.

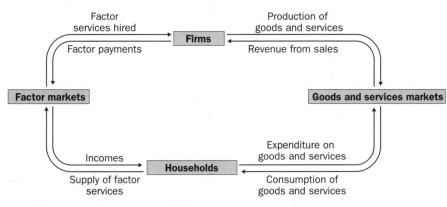

Fig. 10.1 The circular flow of income.

assume initially that there is no government sector or foreign trade sector. In our highly simplified economy there are only two sectors that contribute to the flow of goods and services: firms and households. Households consume a range of goods and services produced by firms. In order to produce these goods and services firms hire the services of factors of production (labour, capital and land) in factor markets from households. Payments made by firms to the factors of production (wages, profits and rent) flow as incomes to households. Households then spend their incomes on the goods and services produced by firms in goods and services markets. Household expenditure flows back to firms in the form of revenue that firms receive from the sales of final goods and services to households. In Fig. 10.1 a real flow of factor services, and of goods and services, repeatedly circulates around the economy in a clockwise direction between households and firms. This real flow is matched by corresponding repeated money flows of incomes and expenditure from firms to households in an anticlockwise direction. If households spent *all* their incomes on firms' final output of goods and services, and firms used *all* the revenue they received from such sales to buy factor services from households, then income would continuously flow around the economy at an unchanged level.

We now drop our initial simplifying assumptions and consider how this circular flow of income is affected when an economy has both a government sector and a foreign trade sector. In doing so we find that there are three main injections of income into the circular flow depicted in Fig. 10.1. First, firms sell some of their output abroad to foreigners. Clearly the revenue from such export sales, X, enters into the circular flow as an injection of income. Second, government expenditure, G, on the purchase of goods and services is an injection of income into the circular flow. Such expenditure includes both current expenditure on goods and services (such as expenditure on the incomes paid to public sector employees) and capital expenditure (such as expenditure on hospital building). Transfer payments (such as expenditure on unemployment benefits), which are transfers between different sections of the community, are excluded as they are not paid out in return for the production of goods and services. Third, private-sector investment expenditure, I, enters the circular flow as an injection of income. Such expenditure includes purchases of fixed investment (for example in plant and machinery), inventory investment (such as increases in stocks of finished goods that have not yet been sold), and residential investment (that is, purchases of new houses). Total injections of income into the circular flow therefore consist of private-sector investment expenditure, I, government expenditure, G, and exports, X.

Just as there are three main injections of income into the circular flow so too are there three main withdrawals from the circular income flow depicted in Fig. 10.1. First, both households and firms purchase imported goods and services, M, from abroad. Such expenditure is a withdrawal from the circular flow of income. Second, households and firms are unable to spend all the income they receive via the circular flow since they have to pay taxes, T, to the government. Third, some income is taken out of the circular flow through savings, S. Total withdrawals from the circular income flow consist of savings, S, taxes, T, and imports, M. If injections are greater than withdrawals, the level of income will rise, and *vice versa*. Income will circulate at an unchanged level only when total injections are exactly matched by total withdrawals. The importance of this equilibrium condition will be discussed more fully in Chapter 11, Section 11.3. In summary, the sum total of value added by all industries in the economy is equal to the sum total of all incomes derived from producing the total output of goods and services by factors of production and the sum total of expenditure made on the final output of goods and services produced in the economy. The output, income and expenditure methods are merely different ways of measuring the same circular flow illustrated in Fig. 10.1 after allowing for injections and withdrawals.

Finally in this section it is important to stress that, while economists use data on GDP to measure economic growth, economic growth refers to an increase in real GDP. The money or nominal value of GDP may change from one year to the next because of a change in the quantity of goods and services actually being produced and/or a change in the price of goods and services. **Nominal GDP** measures GDP at the prices prevailing at the time. Real GDP measures GDP at the prices prevailing in some particular base year. GDP at constant prices (real GDP) will change only if there has been a change in the quantity of goods and services actually produced. As noted in Chapter 9, Section 9.2, economic growth can be defined as an increase in real GDP, while the annual percentage increase in real GDP indicates the rate of economic growth.

Let us now turn to consider real GDP as a proxy measure or indicator of living standards.

10.3 Real GDP, living standards and welfare

As we have seen, real GDP provides a simple measure of the overall economic performance of a country in terms of its material output of goods and services. However, a more reliable indicator of average personal living standards is provided by data on real GDP *per capita*. Real GDP per capita is real GDP divided by the total population of the country. For any given level of real GDP the smaller the population the more goods and services are available for each person in the economy. Real GDP per head will remain constant only if real GDP is growing at exactly the same rate as the population of the country. If the real GDP of a country is growing at a slower rate than its population then real GDP per head will fall, and *vice versa*. As we shall discuss in Section 10.4, the rate at which a country's population grows can help to explain its standard of living.

While real GDP per capita figures provide a rough indicator of average living

Nominal GDP: The value of gross domestic product measured in terms of the prices prevailing at the time; also known as GDP in current prices.

standards they don't tell us anything about the *distribution* of income (see Chapter 8) in a country, or how that distribution changes over time. This is an important consideration that needs to be borne in mind when using real GDP per capita figures as an indicator of average personal living standards. Real GDP per capita figures would provide a reliable measure of what each person in the economy actually received only if income was equally distributed among the total population of a country.

Aside from these qualifications it is also important to reflect briefly on whether figures on real GDP and real GDP per capita provide a complete picture of economic welfare and quality of life in a country. Here we consider two main problems. First, data on real GDP do not include non-market activities, such as leisure. People's happiness depends not only on the consumption of material goods and services but also on the amount of time spent at leisure. Second, data on real GDP do not include the output of negative externalities (see Chapter 6, Section 6.4) such as pollution, traffic congestion and noise, which have an adverse effect on happiness and the welfare of people living in a country. In summary, given these two most fundamental omissions, it is important to remember that figures on real GDP provide only a *crude* measure of national economic welfare.

Let us now turn to consider what factors determine an economy's rate of economic growth over time.

10.4 The Solow growth model

The best framework to start studying economic growth is provided by a model that was developed in the 1950s and 1960s by Robert Solow, Professor of Economics at Massachusetts Institute of Technology. For his important and influential work on the theory of economic growth Solow was awarded the Nobel Prize in Economics in 1987. As we shall now go on to discuss, the Solow growth model identifies what factors determine growth in output over time and also sheds light on some of the reasons why standards of living (real GDP per person) vary so widely between countries. Our starting point is consideration of the aggregate production function that forms the bedrock of the model.

The aggregate production function

The **aggregate production function** is a function that relates the quantity of aggregate output that can be produced to a *given* quantity of factor inputs. This relationship can be written as

$$Y = A(t) \, F(K, N) \tag{10.1}$$

where Y is real output, $A(t)$ represents technological know-how at time t, and F is a function that relates real output to K, the quantity of capital inputs, and N, the quantity of labour inputs. Real output will increase over time if there is an increase in the quantity of factor inputs (capital and/or labour) and/or there is an increase in the productivity of capital and labour inputs (that is, an increase in output per unit of factor input) due to an increase in technological know-how.

At the outset it is important to highlight three key properties exhibited by the neoclassical production function used by Solow in his analysis. First, factor inputs of labour and capital can be smoothly *substituted* for each other in the production process. In other words, firms can use more capital inputs and fewer labour inputs, or

Aggregate production function: A functional relationship between the quantity of aggregate output produced and the quantities of inputs used in production.

Diminishing returns: Occur when successive increases in the use of a factor input, holding other factor inputs constant, eventually result in a fall in the additional output derived from a unit increase in that factor input.

Constant returns to scale: The proposition that a proportionate increase in all factor inputs leads to the same proportionate increase in output.

Capital–labour ratio: The amount of capital per worker; the ratio of the quantity of capital inputs to the number of workers.

vice versa, to produce the same quantity of output. Second, factor inputs experience **diminishing returns**. For example, as first discussed in Chapter 5, while an increase in the quantity of labour inputs with the quantity of capital inputs held constant will result in an increase in real output, output will increase at an ever-declining rate. Similarly, diminishing returns will result from increase in the capital stock to a fixed labour force. Third, it is assumed that the aggregate production function exhibits **constant returns to scale**. Constant returns to scale mean that when all factor inputs increase in some proportion, real output will increase in that same proportion. For example, if both the quantity of labour and capital inputs were doubled, the amount of real output produced would also be doubled.

Given the assumption of constant returns to scale, then for a given technology we can express the aggregate production function in per capita terms. As such output per worker, Y/N, will depend on the amount of capital input per worker, K/N, or what is sometimes referred to as the **capital–labour ratio**. This relationship is depicted in Fig. 10.2, and can be written as:

$$Y/N = A(t)\, f(K/N) \tag{10.2}$$

The astute reader will have noticed that in order to highlight that the aggregate production function is expressed in terms of output and capital input *per worker* we use a small letter *f* in equation (10.2) rather than the capital letter *F* used in equation (10.1).

The aggregate production function depicted in Fig. 10.2 relates output per worker, Y/N, to the amount of capital input per worker, K/N, for a given technology at a point in time t. For example, with a given technology at time t_0, y_0 output per worker ($Y/N = y$) can be produced with k_0 capital input per worker ($K/N = k$). The decreasing slope of the aggregate production function reflects diminishing returns to increases in the amount of capital input per worker. In other words, increases in capital input per worker result in increases in output per worker, but at an ever-declining rate. Finally, it is important to note that technological change over time (e.g. from t_0 to t_1) would shift the aggregate production function upwards, increasing output per worker for a *given* amount of capital input per worker. For example, as illustrated in Fig. 10.2, technological change would allow a higher level of output per worker, y_1, to be produced with k_0 capital input per worker.

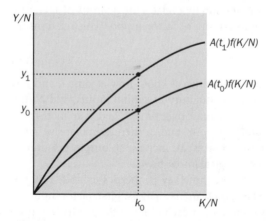

Fig. 10.2 An aggregate production function relating output per worker to capital input per worker.

The steady state

We now turn to consider the long-run *equilibrium* or steady-state growth rate within the neoclassical model developed by Solow. From equation (10.1) it can be seen that growth in output over time depends on both the rate of technological change and the rate at which factor inputs (the capital stock and the labour force) grow over time. One of the most important implications of the Solow growth model is that the economy reaches a steady state in the long run. A long-run equilibrium or **steady state** occurs when output per worker and capital input per worker are constant or unchanging over time. In the simplest case when there is no change in the state of technology, output, Y, capital input, K, and labour input, N, all grow at the same rate.

In Fig. 10.3 a steady state in the long run is achieved at point X with a constant level of output per worker, y_0, and a constant amount of capital input per worker, k_0. Steady state is achieved at the intersection of the steady-state investment line, I, and the saving curve, S. Each point along the steady-state investment line indicates how much investment per worker is *required* to keep the amount of capital input per worker *constant* after taking account of labour force growth and the need to replace the fraction of the capital stock that wears out each year due to depreciation. The line slopes upwards because the faster is labour force growth (and depreciation), the more investment per worker is needed to equip new workers with the current level of capital input per worker and replace depreciating capital. The saving curve, S, which represents saving per worker, has the same shape as the per-worker production function because saving is assumed to be proportional to income in the Solow model. As capital input per worker increases, output per worker increases resulting in an increase in saving per worker. All saving is assumed to be channelled into investment so that saving and actual investment are equal at all times, maintaining goods market equilibrium.

In Fig. 10.3 the steady-state level of capital input per worker k_0 is achieved at point X, the intersection of the steady-state investment line, I, and the saving curve, S. Reference to Fig. 10.3 reveals that if capital input per worker is below k_0 then saving per worker is greater than investment per worker necessary to maintain capital input per worker constant. As the extra savings are invested and converted into

Steady state: A situation in which output per worker and capital input per worker are no longer changing.

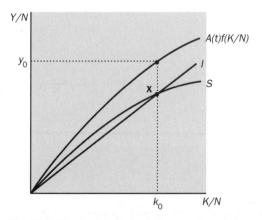

Fig. 10.3 Steady state in the Solow growth model.

capital, capital input per worker will rise towards k_0. Conversely, if capital input per worker is above k_0, then saving per worker is less than the amount of investment per worker required to maintain capital input per worker constant, and capital input per worker will fall towards k_0. In the steady state the positive effect of investment (determined by saving) on the amount of capital input per worker balances the negative effects of labour force growth and depreciation. When capital input per worker is constant at k_0, output per worker is also constant at y_0 over time. In this simple case, output, Y, capital input, K, and labour input, N, all grow at the same rate and all ratios are constant: that is, the steady state.

The model we have outlined allows us to examine the relationship between a nation's output per worker and factors such as its saving rate, labour force growth and rate of technological progress. We first consider what the Solow growth model predicts will happen following an increase in the nation's saving rate. Suppose the economy is initially in steady state with capital and labour inputs growing at the same rate with a steady-state capital input per worker established where the steady-state investment line, I, and saving curve, S_0, intersect. In Fig. 10.4 this initial situation is achieved at point X with k_0 capital input per worker and y_0 output per worker. Assuming that saving is channelled into actual investment, an increase in the saving rate will *initially* increase the rate of capital formation. In the absence of any change in the rate of growth of the labour force or in technological progress, an increase in the rate of capital formation will result in an increase in the amount of capital input per worker. In terms of Fig. 10.4 an increase in the saving rate will raise the saving curve from S_0 to S_1 and capital input per worker will rise from k_0 to k_1 until the economy reaches a new steady state at point Y. Once the economy has made the adjustment from point X to point Y there will be no further increases in either capital input per worker or output per worker. In the new steady state both capital input per worker and output per worker will be stable. The Solow model predicts that countries with higher saving rates will have higher steady-state levels of capital input per worker and therefore higher levels of output per worker, giving a higher standard of living. However, the model predicts that, while an increase in the saving rate will lead to a *temporary* period of faster growth (when output per worker is increasing from y_0 to y_1), it will not affect the long-run equilibrium or steady-state growth rate. Once the new equilibrium has been reached the rate of capital formation and growth rate

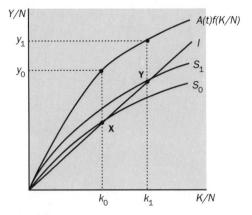

Fig. 10.4 The effects of an increase in the saving rate on capital input per worker and output per worker.

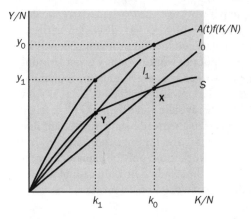

Fig. 10.5 The effects of an increase in the rate of growth of the labour force on capital input per˙ worker and output per worker.

in output will have returned to their initial levels equal to the rate of growth of the labour force.

We finally turn to briefly consider the effects of a change in the rate of growth of the labour force (Fig. 10.5) and technological change (Fig. 10.6) in the Solow growth model. In Fig. 10.5 the economy is initially in steady state at point X with a steady-state capital input per worker k_0 established where the saving curve, S, and steady-state investment line, I_0, intersect. If the rate of growth of the labour force increases, the amount of investment per current member of the labour force will have to rise to maintain a given capital input per worker. In other words, an increase in the labour force growth rate will cause the steady-state investment line to pivot up to the left from I_0 to I_1. In the new steady state, point Y, the level of capital input per worker is lower (k_1), generating a lower level of output per worker (y_1). The Solow model consequently predicts that countries with higher rates of growth in their labour force will have lower steady-state levels of capital input per worker and therefore lower levels of output per worker.

Fig. 10.6 illustrates the effects of an improvement in technology on capital input per worker and output per worker. In Fig. 10.6 the economy is initially in steady state

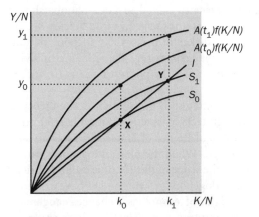

Fig. 10.6 The effects of an improvement in technology on capital input per worker and output per worker.

at point X with a steady-state capital input per worker k_0 established where the saving curve, S_0, and steady-state investment line, I, intersect. As discussed earlier, an improvement in technology shifts the aggregate production function upwards from $A(t_0) f(K/N)$ to $A(t_1) f(K/N)$, increasing output per worker for any given amount of capital input per worker. Since saving per worker is assumed to be proportional to output per worker, the saving curve also shifts upwards from S_0 to S_1 at any given amount of capital input per worker. A new steady state will eventually be reached at point Y where the new saving curve, S_1, intersects the steady-state investment line, I, with a higher level of capital input per worker, k_1, and output per worker, y_1. In the Solow model, *sustained* growth of output per worker can only be explained by technological progress. The model predicts that in the steady state both capital input per worker and output per worker grow at the rate of technological progress.

10.5 The new endogenous growth models

During the 1970s, economists' interest in the theory of long-run economic growth waned, largely because of a number of problems with the Solow growth model. Here we highlight two such problems. The first is that technological change is **exogenous**. As the Solow growth model does not explain or consider the determinants of technological change, it provides no insight into how government policy could raise the long-run equilibrium growth rate of output. Although government policies can influence the saving rate (via tax incentives, for example), as we have seen, the model predicts that a (policy-induced) increase in the saving rate will only lead to a *temporary* period of faster growth, and will not affect the long-run equilibrium growth rate. The long-run equilibrium growth rate depends on the rate of growth of the labour force and technological change, both of which are exogenous.

The second problem with the Solow growth model concerns the non-**convergence** of levels of per capita income of advanced industrial nations and poor nations over time. If technological change is freely available, poor nations should be able to close the gap in living standards between themselves and industrial nations by using the technology developed in industrial nations. Moreover, poor nations have less capital input per worker and in consequence their marginal product of capital is higher than in advanced industrial nations. Higher returns to capital in poor nations should attract foreign investment and cause their capital stock to grow more quickly than in industrial nations. As a result, output per worker in industrial and poor nations should converge over time. However, rather than converging, the difference in living standards between advanced industrial nations and the poorest nations (in Africa, for example) has widened.

The late 1980s witnessed a resurgence of interest by economists in the theory of long-run economic growth. The leading architects of what is commonly referred to as the new endogenous growth theory are Paul Romer of Stanford University and Robert Lucas Jr of the University of Chicago. While the new endogenous growth models are highly technical and are beyond the scope of this text it is useful to briefly outline some of the main ideas involved. Endogenous growth models have extended the basic Solow growth model by making the rate of technological change **endogenous**. In addition, they have abandoned the assumption that all nations have the same access to technological opportunities. Some models of endogenous growth, for

Exogenous: Describes a variable that is not explained within a particular model; its value is taken as given.

Convergence: The tendency for output per worker in different countries to converge over time.

Endogenous: Describes a variable that is explained within a particular model.

example, stress the accumulation of **human capital** – the knowledge and skills of a nation's workers – as a key to achieving economic growth.

In these models the level of output per worker depends on *both* the amount of physical capital input per worker and human capital input per worker. Poor nations with little human capital cannot hope to catch up industrial nations simply by accumulating physical capital. So different levels of investment in human capital – through training and education – help to explain the lack of convergence of per capita income levels and growth rates over time. Other models of endogenous growth stress endogenous innovation in which the development of 'ideas' for new goods is seen as the key to achieving economic growth. Poor nations may therefore fail to catch up with industrial nations because of 'idea gaps'. Overall, the new endogenous growth literature has helped explain the difference in living standards among nations, and has given insights into how government policy can influence long-term growth rates by, for example, encouraging education, training, capital formation and research and development.

> **Human capital:** The knowledge and skills of workers in an economy.

Box 10.1

Sources of US economic growth 1929–82 (per cent)

Annual growth rate of output	2.9
Percentage of growth due to:	
Growth in labour input	32
Growth in labour productivity	
Education per worker	14
Capital	19
Technological change	28
Economies of scale	9
Other factors	−2

Source: Denison, E.F. *Trends in American Economic Growth* (Washington, DC: The Brookings Institution, 1985)

Some indication of the relative importance of various sources of economic growth is contained in a study by Edward Denison of

Trends in American Economic Growth over the period 1929–82. Denison's findings concerning the sources of US economic growth over this period are summarized above. Between 1929 and 1982 real output grew at an annual rate of 2.9 per cent. Denison estimated that 32 per cent of US economic growth over this period was due to growth in the quantity of labour input, while 68 per cent came from growth in labour productivity, itself due to four main factors. According to Denison's estimates 28 per cent of US economic growth was due to technological change (the most important influence on labour productivity), 19 per cent resulted from capital formation, 14 per cent was due to increased education per worker, and 9 per cent resulted from economies of scale.

10.6 Concluding remarks

Economic growth is the result of extremely complex processes involving economic, political and institutional considerations. As a starting point only in this chapter, we have examined a model that identifies *some* of the main determinants of economic growth over time. Like all economic models the Solow growth model simplifies reality and omits many important considerations. Nevertheless, as we have seen, the model sheds light on *some* of the reasons why standards of living vary so widely between countries. The recent resurgence of interest in the theory of long-run growth has produced more sophisticated models in which the rate of technological change is endogenous. These models provide a rationale for governments to adopt policies that encourage education, training, capital formation and research and development in order to increase the economy's productive capacity. Despite these further insights, exactly what role the government can and should play in encouraging growth remains the subject of intense controversy.

▊ Summary

◆ Economists use data on GDP to measure economic growth. GDP itself can be measured in three different ways, each of which can be visualized using a circular flow of income diagram.

◆ Economic growth can be defined as an increase in real GDP. The annual percentage increase in real GDP measures the rate of economic growth.

◆ Real GDP per capita figures provide only a rough indicator of average living standards as they don't tell us anything about the distribution of income in a particular country or how that distribution may have changed over time. Quality of life and economic welfare are affected by a number of factors, including leisure and the output of negative externalities, which are omitted from figures on real GDP.

◆ Real output will increase over time if there is an increase in the quantity of factor inputs and/or in the productivity of inputs.

◆ In the Solow growth model a long-run equilibrium or steady-state growth rate occurs where output, capital input and labour input all grow at the same rate. The model allows us to examine the relationship between a nation's output per worker and its saving rate, labour force growth and rate of technological progress. *Ceteris paribus*, an increase in the saving rate, a decrease in the rate of growth of the labour force, or an improvement in technology increases the level of capital input and output per worker. The long-run equilibrium growth rate depends on the rate of growth of the labour force and technological change, and is not affected by a change in the saving rate. As both the rate of growth of the labour force and technological change are exogenous the Solow model provides no insight into how government policy could raise the long-run equilibrium growth rate of output.

◆ New endogenous growth models help to explain the lack of convergence of per capita income levels and growth rates over time, and provide a number of insights into how government policy can influence the long-run growth rate.

▊ Key terms

◆ Economic growth
◆ GDP
◆ Real GDP per captia
◆ Aggregate production function
◆ Quantity and quality of factor inputs
◆ Solow growth model
◆ Steady state growth
◆ Convergence

◆ Endogenous growth models

◆ Human capital

Self-test questions

True (t) or false (f)

1. It will take approximately 24 years for an economy to double its productive capacity if its growth rate is 3 per cent.

2. Economists use data on real GDP to measure economic growth.

3. Real GDP per capita figures provide a rough indicator of average living standards of people in a country.

4. Real GDP per capita will fall when the real GDP of a country is growing at a faster rate than its population.

5. The Solow growth model predicts that countries with higher rates of growth in their labour force will have higher levels of output per worker.

6. According to the Solow growth model the long-run equilibrium or steady-state growth rate depends on the saving rate.

7. In the Solow growth model sustained growth of output per worker depends on technological progress.

8. Endogenous growth models have extended the basic Solow growth model by making the rate of technological change endogenous.

9. According to endogenous growth models differences in the level of investment in human capital can help to explain the lack of convergence of output per worker in different countries.

Complete the following sentences by inserting the missing word(s)

1. The three main injections into the circular flow of income are ____, ____ and ____.

2. The three main withdrawals from the circular flow of income are ____, ____ and ____.

3. Real GDP divided by the total population of a country is known as ____.

4. Given the two most important omissions of ____ and ____, figures on real GDP can provide only a partial picture of economic welfare and quality of life in a country.

5. As a result of ____ increases in capital input per worker result in increases in output per worker, but at an ever-declining rate.

6. A situation in which output per worker and capital input per worker are constant or unchanging over time is known as ____.

7. In the Solow growth model both the rate of growth of the labour force and technological change are ____.

8. The leading architects of the new endogenous growth theory are ____ and ____.

9. Economists refer to the knowledge and skills of workers in an economy as ____.

Questions for discussion

◆ What is GDP and how can it be measured?

◆ How far do real GDP figures give a guide to economic welfare?

◆ According to the Solow model what effect will each of the following have on the level of output per worker:
  (i)   an increase in the saving rate
  (ii)   an increase in labour force growth
  (iii) a technological improvement?

◆ Explain why the saving rate does not affect the steady-state growth rate in the Solow model.

◆ What determines the long-run equilibrium growth rate in the Solow model?

◆ Explain why according to the Solow model sustained growth of output per worker depends on technological progress.

◆ What are the main problems with the Solow growth model?

Further reading

Crafts, N. and G. Toniolo (eds) *Economic Growth in Europe Since 1945* (Cambridge: Cambridge University Press, 1996). Provides a fascinating re-examination of the topic of economic growth in Europe after the Second World War.

Unemployment: Causes and Cures

CHAPTER 11

Key issues

▶ Is the cause of, and cure for, unemployment to be found inside or outside the labour market?

▶ What are the main theories that economists have put forward to explain unemployment?

▶ How can governments reduce unemployment?

▶ How have economists sought to explain the substantial rise in unemployment that has taken place in the EU since the 1970s?

Contents

11.1 Introduction

In Chapter 9, Section 9.3 we discussed the nature and measurement of unemployment, together with its economic, social and political costs. While there is a general consensus that the maintenance of a high and stable level of employment is an important objective of macroeconomic policy, there is considerable controversy over why unemployment exists and what governments can do to reduce it. This chapter looks at the debate over the causes of, and cures for, unemployment. At the outset it is worth emphasizing that the central question that underlies this continuing debate is whether the cause of unemployment is largely to be found *inside* or *outside* the labour market. If unemployment is essentially due to imperfections in the labour market, then government policy to reduce unemployment needs to be directed to alleviate such imperfections. If the cause of unemployment is largely to be found outside the labour market – because of insufficient spending in the goods market – then government policy needs to be directed to stimulate aggregate demand in the economy.

Historically, economists have applied many adjectives to the term unemployment. These include voluntary, involuntary, classical/real wage, frictional/search, structural/mismatch and demand-deficient/cyclical, to name but a few. In addition, some economists refer to a natural rate of unemployment, while others prefer to speak of a non-accelerating inflation rate of unemployment. It is hardly surprising, given such a plethora of terms and concepts, that students often find the issue of unemployment one that is particularly difficult to get to grips with. In attempting to shed light on the controversy over the causes of – and appropriate cures for – unemployment, we shall trace how economists from the nineteenth century through to the present day have put forward new and often controversial theories to explain unemployment. In tracing the history of unemployment theory in this way it is possible to identify the development of five main approaches within mainstream economics:

- the classical approach
- the orthodox Keynesian approach
- the monetarist approach
- the new classical approach
- the new Keynesian approach.

11.2 The classical approach

In the nineteenth century, economists adhering to the so-called classical approach (see Chapter 1, Section 1.4) maintained that so long as money wages and prices were flexible, and free to adjust, the labour market would always tend to clear at full employment equilibrium. Given a perfectly competitive labour market, anyone able and willing to work could do so at the ruling market-clearing equilibrium real wage rate. This situation is illustrated in Fig. 11.1, where the aggregate demand for labour, D_L, equals the aggregate supply of labour, S_L, at the market-clearing equilibrium real wage rate, W/P_e, and employment, N, is at its full employment level, N_F. Now, if the real wage rate is initially set at W/P_1, above its market-clearing level, the supply of labour, N_2, exceeds the demand for labour, N_1. Competition among the excess supply of unemployed workers $(N_2 - N_1)$ to find work would then lead to a reduction in money wages and hence a reduction in the real wage rate (assuming prices remain unchanged) until such time as full employment was restored.

In classical analysis, Say's law (named after the French economist Jean-Baptiste Say) guaranteed that aggregate demand would be sufficient to absorb the full

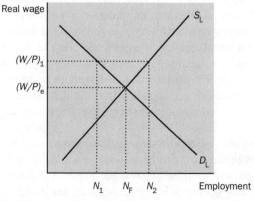

Fig. 11.1 The classical approach.

employment level of output produced. According to this law, 'supply creates its own demand' in that the act of production yields income that will be sufficient to purchase *whatever* level of output is produced. Given a competitive labour market, in which full employment was the normal state of affairs, Say's law ruled out the possibility of any deficiency of aggregate demand: demand would always be sufficient to purchase the full employment level of output produced. Aside from some short-term temporary unemployment, which may occur as the real wage rate adjusts to its new market-clearing level following a change in demand or supply conditions in the labour market, the *only* source of unemployment in this classical approach is *voluntary unemployment*, which arises because there are people who, while they are capable of working, for various reasons choose not to work.

How then did classical economists explain the mass unemployment experienced in Western economies in the 1930s? Classical economists attributed the persistence of such mass unemployment to the downward inflexibility of money (and real) wages due to the actions of trade unions, and argued that full employment would be restored only if money (and real) wages were cut to their market-clearing level. In Fig. 11.1 *classical unemployment*, or what is sometimes referred to as *real wage unemployment*, occurs when the real wage rate is kept too high, resulting in an excess supply of labour equal to $N_2 - N_1$ at $(W/P)_1$. In this situation unemployment exceeds the level that would prevail at the market-clearing real wage rate $(W/P)_e$.

Keynes attacked the classical explanation of the cause of unemployment and also the solution that classical economists put forward to solve the problem. In his *General Theory of Employment, Interest and Money*, published in 1936, he put forward a new, and at the time revolutionary, theory that provided a very different explanation of, and remedy for, the then-prevailing severe unemployment. In contrast to classical economists, Keynes placed the cause of the mass unemployment of the 1930s *outside* the labour market: he argued that it was in fact essentially rooted in a deficiency of aggregate demand in the goods market. In Keynes's view, the cure for unemployment required government intervention to increase aggregate demand in order to restore the economy to its full employment level of output. We now turn to discuss the Keynesian approach to unemployment in more detail.

11.3 The orthodox Keynesian approach

Keynesians have traditionally identified three main types or categories of unemployment: frictional, structural, and demand-deficient unemployment. **Frictional unemployment** occurs because it will take time for a newly unemployed person to obtain information on job vacancies and find a new job. Because frictional unemployment occurs when individuals are changing jobs and searching for new employment, it is also sometimes referred to as **search unemployment**. Even though there will be search costs involved (loss of earnings, expenditure on postage and telephone calls, etc.), such behaviour is entirely rational, as newly unemployed individuals will need to spend time familiarizing themselves with both the pecuniary and non-pecuniary features of available jobs. What can the government do to reduce this type of unemployment? Measures that reduce the search time moving between jobs will reduce the amount of frictional unemployment. One way to reduce search time is to improve the provision of information about employment opportunities via official job centres. In the UK, for example, the continued existence and growth of

Frictional unemployment:
Arises because it takes time for workers to search for suitable jobs; also known as search unemployment.

private employment agencies suggests that there is considerable scope to improve information on the availability of job opportunities in the official system.

Structural unemployment occurs, as the name implies, because of structural changes that take place in the economy. These changes involve underlying shifts in *both* demand (for example changing patterns of demand for goods produced by different industries) and supply (for example changes in the state of technology). Because of such changes some industries and regions will contract, while others expand. As labour is not perfectly mobile (see Chapter 7), some industries and regions will experience unemployment, while others face labour shortages. In the contracting sectors, more individuals will be looking for jobs than there are job opportunities available: in these sectors an excess supply of labour will exist. In contrast, in the expanding sectors of the economy, new job opportunities will outstrip the supply of individuals looking for jobs: in these industries an excess demand for labour will prevail. Because structural unemployment arises from a mismatch of skills and geographical job opportunities, following underlying changes in demand and supply, it is also sometimes referred to as **mismatch unemployment**. What can the government do to reduce this type of unemployment? One way to reduce both the extent and duration of structural unemployment is to design policies aimed at improving the occupational mobility of labour (retraining programmes, for example) and geographical mobility of labour (such as providing financial assistance to help cover the costs of moving from one area to another). In addition, policy measures that encourage new/old firms to locate/relocate in areas of high unemployment (e.g. via grants) will help to reduce the amount of structural unemployment.

We now turn to consider the third main type or category of unemployment: **demand-deficient unemployment**, or what is sometimes referred to as **cyclical unemployment**. In the Keynesian approach, the level of real national income/output and hence employment is *largely* determined by the level of aggregate expenditure or demand in the economy. The economy may therefore come to rest at less than full employment equilibrium because of a deficiency of aggregate expenditure. In contrast to the classical model, the Keynesian view is that less than full employment equilibrium is the *normal* state of affairs. Let us now examine why this is the case.

In Chapter 10, Section 10.2, we discussed the three ways in which national income can be measured: each of these can be conceptualized using the circular flow of income. You will recall that aggregate expenditure or **aggregate demand (AD)** is the sum of the following major categories of expenditure: consumer expenditure, C, investment expenditure, I, government expenditure, G, and expenditure on net exports, $(X - M)$. More formally, we can express this in the following way:

$$AD = C + I + G + X - M \quad \leftarrow GDP \ ? \tag{11.1}$$

In order to explain why within the simple Keynesian model the level of real output and employment is essentially determined by aggregate demand and why the economy may come to rest at less than full employment equilibrium, we first need to consider briefly what determines each of these components of aggregate demand.

Consumer expenditure

In the Keynesian model the main determinant of aggregate consumer expenditure is held to be the level of national income: the higher the level of national income, the higher the level of total consumer expenditure undertaken. This aggregate

Structural unemployment: Arises from a mismatch between the skills or location of existing job vacancies and the present skills or location of the unemployed; also known as mismatch unemployment.

Demand-deficient unemployment: Arises because aggregate demand is insufficient to provide employment for everyone who wants to work at the prevailing real wage; also known as cyclical unemployment.

Aggregate demand: The total planned expenditures of all buyers of final goods and services.

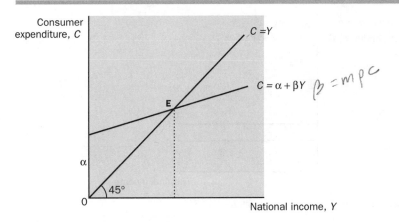

Fig. 11.2 The consumption function.

consumption – aggregate income relationship, which is known technically as the consumption function, is depicted in Fig. 11.2.

In Fig. 11.2 consumer expenditure, C, and national income, Y, are shown on the vertical and horizontal axes respectively. The 45° line shows points of equality between the two axes. In consequence, where the consumption function crosses the 45° line at point E consumption equals income ($C = Y$). The reader may have spotted that in order to further simplify our discussion we have drawn a linear consumption function. This allows us to express the relationship between aggregate consumer expenditure and national income in the form of an equation of a straight line:

$$C = \alpha + \beta Y \qquad\qquad\qquad (11.2)$$

In this equation the intercept, α, shows the level of aggregate consumer expenditure undertaken independently of the level of national income. Such expenditure is said to be exogenous or **autonomous** consumer **expenditure**, and depends on factors such as the level of wealth. The important point to note about autonomous consumer expenditure is that it is *not* determined by the level of national income. Returning to the equation of a straight line, the slope of the consumption function, β, indicates the extent to which consumer expenditure changes when national income changes. Economists refer to this coefficient as the **marginal propensity to consume**. This is an important coefficient, as you will come to see when we discuss the Keynesian approach to business cycles in Chapter 13, Section 13.3.

Investment expenditure

What determines the level of investment expenditure undertaken in the economy? The main determinants of investment expenditure include the rate of change of current sales, expectations about future sales and factor prices, the cost of capital equipment, and the rate of interest. *Ceteris paribus*, investment expenditure will tend to rise following an increase in the rate of change of current sales, an upward revision of business expectations about the future profitability of investment, a fall in the cost of capital equipment, or a fall in the cost of borrowing funds to finance such expenditure, and *vice versa*. In the simple Keynesian model investment expenditure is assumed to be autonomously or exogenously determined. Because in Fig. 11.3 it is assumed to be independent of the level of national income, investment expenditure is depicted as a horizontal line.

Autonomous expenditure: Expenditure that does not depend on the level of national income.

Marginal propensity to consume: The change in consumption expenditure resulting from an additional unit of income.

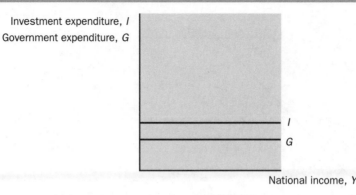

Fig. 11.3 Investment and government expenditure.

Government expenditure

Having considered briefly the main determinants of consumer expenditure and investment expenditure, we now need to comment on government expenditure. For the purposes of constructing the Keynesian model it is sufficient to note that government expenditure, like investment expenditure, is assumed to be independent of the level of national income. Such expenditure depends on government policy. In consequence, government expenditure is also depicted as a horizontal line in Fig. 11.3.

Net export expenditure

Finally, we need to consider what determines net export expenditure. The three main determinants of the level of export and import expenditure are income, relative prices, and non-price factors such as tastes. These determinants are discussed more fully in Chapter 16, Section 16.2. At this point in our discussion we shall focus on how income affects expenditure on imports and exports. The income variable relevant to imports is domestic national income. As national income rises, some part of this increase will be spent on buying more imports from abroad. This positive relationship between imports and national income is illustrated in Fig. 11.4. The slope of the import function depicts the **marginal propensity to import**, and indicates the extent to which import expenditure changes when national income changes. In contrast, the income variable relevant to exports is not domestic national income

Marginal propensity to import: The change in import expenditure resulting from an additional unit of income.

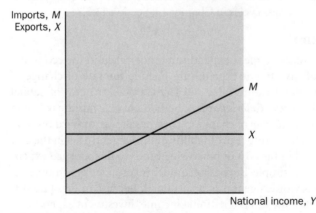

Fig. 11.4 Import and export expenditure.

but rather income in the rest of the world. *Ceteris paribus*, as world income increases, the demand for a country's exports will increase. Because exports are determined independently of the level of domestic national income, the export schedule in Fig. 11.4 is depicted – as it is for investment and government expenditure – as a horizontal line.

[handwritten margin note: World income ↑ demand for country's export ↑.]

The equilibrium level of national income in the Keynesian model

Having briefly discussed what determines each component of aggregate demand, we are now in a position to consider what determines the equilibrium level of national income in the Keynesian model, and why the economy may come to rest at less than full employment equilibrium. This analysis is illustrated in Fig. 11.5.

The 45° line in the top half of Fig. 11.5 shows points of equality between aggregate demand (vertical axis) and aggregate output or national income (horizontal axis). Where aggregate demand and aggregate output are equal ($AD = Y$) firms will be selling all the goods they produce, and in such circumstances there will be no tendency for income to change. We encountered this equilibrium condition in a slightly different form in Chapter 10, Section 10.2, where we explained how the level of income will only remain unchanged when injections ($G + I + X$) are matched by leakages ($T + S + M$). The three main injections of investment expenditure, government expenditure and gross export expenditure are assumed to be determined independently of national income, while consumer expenditure increases as national income increases. In consequence the aggregate demand schedule shown in Fig. 11.5 slopes

[handwritten margin note: T = taxes, S = savings, M = imports]

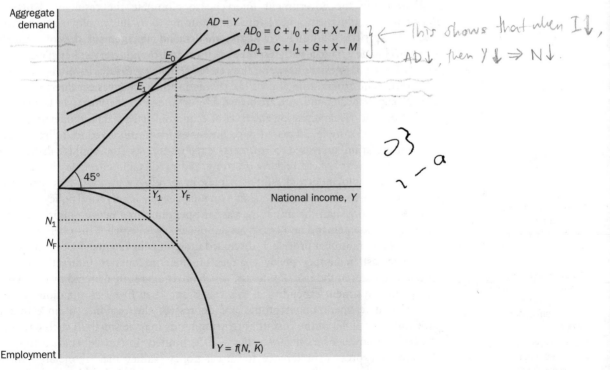

[handwritten margin note: ← This shows that when I↓, AD↓, then Y↓ ⇒ N↓.]

Fig. 11.5 The Keynesian model.

upwards to the right. The equilibrium level of national income is established where the aggregate demand schedule crosses the 45° line: that is, where aggregate demand, AD, equals aggregate supply, Y.

Let us assume that the economy is initially operating at its full employment equilibrium level of national income, Y_F, with aggregate demand equal to AD_0: that is, where AD_0 crosses the 45° line at point E_0. By referring to the bottom half of Fig. 11.5, which shows the short-run aggregate production function, we can trace the implications of the level of income (determined by aggregate demand) in terms of the level of employment: in this case full employment, N_F. Now suppose investment expenditure decreased from I_0 to I_1, causing the aggregate demand schedule to shift downwards from AD_0 to AD_1. Investment expenditure might decrease because of a downward revision of business expectations of the future profitability of investment. In his *General Theory* (1936), Keynes suggested that investment could be influenced by tides of irrational pessimism and optimism, which he referred to as a change in investors' 'animal spirits', causing large swings in the state of business confidence. Following the fall in investment and associated fall in aggregate demand, a new equilibrium level of national income, Y_1, would be established where AD_1 crosses the 45° line at point E_1. Reference to the bottom half of Fig. 11.5 reveals that the level of employment, N_1, required to produce the new equilibrium level of national income, Y_1, is now below its full employment level. In other words, at Y_1, aggregate demand is insufficient to provide employment for everyone who wants a job, resulting in so-called *involuntary unemployment*. The reader should note that income and employment will be affected in the same manner, *ceteris paribus*, following an autonomous decrease in consumer expenditure, government expenditure or net export expenditure.

How could the government intervene to eliminate the resultant demand-deficient unemployment and restore the economy to its full employment income level (Y_F, N_F)? The solution lies in **aggregate demand management**: the government needs to change its stance with respect to its fiscal and/or monetary policy. Traditionally, orthodox Keynesians have emphasized **fiscal policy** measures involving changes in government expenditure and/or tax payments. Such changes act *directly* on the level of aggregate demand, and are believed by orthodox Keynesians to be both more predictable and faster acting on the level of economic activity than monetary policy measures. For example, increased government expenditure or reduced direct taxation (stimulating increased consumers' expenditure as households' disposable income increases) is held to have a strong and predictable effect on the level of income and employment as the initial increase in spending leads to successive rounds of further increases in expenditure. Following such expansionary fiscal policy, income will rise by more than the initial increase in spending, to a new equilibrium level where aggregate demand and aggregate supply are again equal. This phenomenon, known as the multiplier process, is discussed more fully in Chapter 13, Section 13.3.

In contrast, **monetary policy** changes are held to operate indirectly mainly through changes in the rate of interest, which affect aggregate demand by causing a change in investment expenditure. In a recession, when firms' expectations about profitable investment opportunities are depressed, the response of investment expenditure to a fall in the cost of borrowing funds may be small. In such circumstances, the power of monetary policy will be limited. In consequence, orthodox Keynesians express a preference for fiscal policy, rather than monetary policy measures, to restore full employment.

Aggregate demand management: The use of fiscal and monetary policies to influence the level of aggregate demand.

Fiscal policy: Entails measures that alter the level and composition of government expenditure and taxation.

Monetary policy: Entails measures that alter the money supply and/or interest rates.

At this stage it would be useful to draw together our discussion of the Keynesian approach to unemployment and consider the three main types of unemployment within the context of the labour market. The demand for labour, D_L, comprises the level of employment, N, plus the level of vacancies, V, while the supply of labour, S_L, comprises the level of employment, N, plus the level of unemployment, U:

$$D_L = N + \textcircled{V} \rightarrow \text{level of Vacancy} \tag{11.3}$$
$$S_L = N + \textcircled{U} \rightarrow \text{level of unemployment} \tag{11.4}$$

It follows that when the labour market clears and the demand for labour, D_L, equals the supply of labour, S_L, then vacancies, V, will equal unemployment, U. In this situation all unemployment will fall in the category of frictional and structural unemployment (i.e. non demand-deficient unemployment), and demand-deficient unemployment will equal zero. As illustrated in Fig. 11.6, this occurs at a real wage rate, W/P_0, at the intersection of D_L and S_L. Now suppose as before that investment expenditure decreases, causing output and employment to fall. As the aggregate demand for goods and services within the economy falls, the demand curve for labour will shift to the left from D_L to D_L^*, resulting in demand-deficient unemployment at the prevailing real wage rate, W/P_0. This would be an *additional* source of unemployment on top of any existing frictional or structural unemployment. Note that in Fig. 11.6, there are N_F workers willing to work at the prevailing real wage rate, W/P_0, but demand from firms (which in our example have collectively cut investment) would produce a level of employment of only N_1. This demonstrates that Keynesian demand-deficient unemployment occurs when there is an excess supply of labour at the ruling wage rate: in other words, when the real wage rate is above the market-clearing wage rate. Now the important point to make about demand-deficient unemployment is that its cause lies *outside* the labour market: people who want to work cannot find jobs not because they are in a search process (which would involve frictional unemployment), or because they need retraining to take jobs in new industries (which would involve structural unemployment), but because there are not enough jobs to go around: the demand is not there to sustain them. Finally, we should again emphasize that, in the Keynesian view, it is of course possible for all three types of unemployment to exist simultaneously.

The Keynesian approach to unemployment stands in bold contrast to the classical approach discussed earlier. In the classical approach full employment is determined

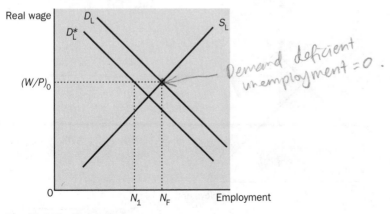

Fig. 11.6 The Keynesian approach.

within the labour market, with Say's law ruling out the possibility of any deficiency of aggregate demand. As long as money wages and prices are free to adjust, classical economists argued that the labour market would clear, with any excess supply of labour being eliminated by downward pressure on the real wage rate. Why then does the labour market fail to clear in the Keynesian approach? The answer to this question lies in the assumption made by Keynes that workers would not be prepared to accept a cut in money wages when there is unemployment. The reason he advanced for this is that workers are concerned to maintain their real wage *relativities*. Workers would strongly resist a cut in money wages that affected only their section of the workforce because such a cut would adversely affect their real wage relative to other workers. Given the assumption that money (and hence real) wages tend to be sticky in a downward direction, the labour market will fail to clear. Furthermore, cutting everybody's wages would fail to restore labour market equilibrium. According to Keynes a generalized cut in wages would merely reduce aggregate 'effective' demand in the economy and result in a further fall in output and still higher unemployment. In the orthodox Keynesian approach both the cause of, and cure for, unemployment are to be found largely outside the labour market.

11.4 The monetarist approach

The monetarist approach to unemployment derives from the highly influential work of the famous American economist Milton Friedman, who in his Presidential Address to the American Economic Association in 1967 coined the term the **natural rate of unemployment**. According to Friedman, the natural rate – or what can alternatively be thought of as the long-run *equilibrium* rate of unemployment – depends on both the structure of the economy and the institutions within it. He specifically highlights such factors as market imperfections in the labour and goods markets, the cost of gathering information on job vacancies and labour availabilities, and the costs of mobility as determinants of the natural rate of unemployment.

Natural rate of unemployment: The rate of unemployment that exists when the labour market is in equilibrium; composed of frictional and structural unemployment.

The natural rate of unemployment is associated with equilibrium in the labour market at the market-clearing real wage rate. This situation is illustrated in Fig. 11.7, where the equilibrium or natural level of employment, N_N, is established at the

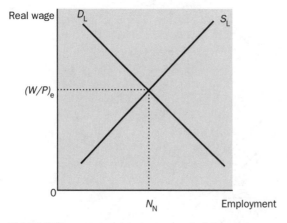

Fig. 11.7 The monetarist and new classical approaches.

market-clearing real wage rate, W/P_e. The natural rate of unemployment corresponds to the amount of unemployment that would exist where the aggregate supply of, and demand for labour, are equal. Although monetarists do not approach unemployment in terms of the sum of various types or categories, it is possible to define the natural rate as a situation where there is no demand-deficient unemployment. Hence the natural rate can be conceptualized as embracing the two main types of non-demand-deficient unemployment: frictional and structural unemployment.

How can the government reduce the natural rate of unemployment in order to achieve higher output and employment levels? Rather than the macroeconomic (demand management) policies favoured by orthodox Keynesians, monetarists advocate that governments should pursue *microeconomic* (supply management) policies designed to improve the structure and functioning of the labour market. Within the labour market any policy that leads to an increase in either the supply of labour (shifting the supply curve to the right) or the demand for labour (shifting the demand curve to the right) will increase the equilibrium level of employment and reduce the natural rate of unemployment. Among the wide range of policy measures that have been advocated are policies designed to:

- increase the incentive to work, for example through tax and social security reforms
- increase the flexibility of wages and working practices, and reduce distortions that prevent the labour market from working efficiently, for example through trade union reform
- increase the geographical and occupational mobility of labour
- increase the efficiency of markets for goods and services (for example, by privatization – see Chapter 6, Section 6.7) and for capital (for example, through the abolition of various controls on activity in financial markets).

Many of these proposed measures are of course highly controversial. For example, the reform of social security or welfare payments to unemployed people entails cutting such benefits. The purpose here is to lessen the relative 'attractiveness' of unemployment in comparison with low-paid work. While this measure might increase the supply of labour (shifting S_L in Fig. 11.7 to the right), raise the equilibrium level of employment, and thereby reduce unemployment, it would also prompt equity or fairness questions about low pay and the impartiality of the state *vis-à-vis* the unemployed and less scrupulous employers.

In summary, given that in the monetarist view the natural or long-run equilibrium rate of unemployment derives essentially from labour market imperfections, reducing the natural rate necessitates measures designed to increase competitiveness in the labour market.

Before turning to discuss the new classical approach to unemployment it is important to note that, while monetarists argue that the labour market will clear in the long run with a corresponding equilibrium or natural rate of unemployment, in the short run actual unemployment may be above or below the natural rate. In other words, for monetarists the labour market may be in disequilibrium in the short run. In the next chapter, when we come to discuss the relationship between inflation and unemployment, commonly referred to as the Phillips curve, you will see how in the short run unemployment may be temporarily reduced below or raised above its natural rate following expansionary or contractionary aggregate demand policies.

However, in the long run, monetarists argue that there is no trade-off between inflation and unemployment. The natural or equilibrium level of employment and unemployment is therefore held to be independent of the level of aggregate demand, and is associated with a stable rate of inflation (see Chapter 12, Section 12.2).

11.5 The new classical approach

During the 1970s a new and highly controversial new classical approach to unemployment emerged. In the USA the most prominent new classical economist is Robert Lucas Jr (University of Chicago), the 1995 Nobel Laureate in Economics, while in the UK the new classical approach is mainly associated with the work of Patrick Minford (Cardiff Business School). In contrast to both Keynesian and monetarist approaches, the assumption underlying the new classical approach to unemployment is that the labour market *continuously* clears. In other words, in line with the classical approach discussed earlier, new classical economists assume that anyone wishing to find work can do so at the market-clearing equilibrium real wage rate: that is, at W/P_e in Fig. 11.7. As we shall discuss in Chapter 13, Section 13.5, in the new classical approach fluctuations in employment are held to reflect voluntary changes in the amount that people want to work. Unemployment is treated entirely as a *voluntary* phenomenon, with those who are unemployed voluntarily choosing not to work at the current market-clearing real wage rate. Moreover, any unemployment that results from trade union bargaining and higher real wages in a particular sector is also considered to be voluntary in that workers have chosen unions to represent them. Viewed in this way, new classical economists argue that those who are unemployed could find jobs if only they were prepared to lower their sights and accept inferior or less well paid jobs.

If all unemployment is regarded as being voluntary, as new classical economists argue, is there anything that governments can do to reduce unemployment? In the new classical view, any policy measure that increases the *microeconomic incentive* for workers to supply more labour will reduce unemployment. For example, it is claimed that by reducing the real value of unemployment benefits, unemployment will fall as unemployed workers spend less time looking for the 'right' job, and as certain low-paid jobs become more attractive, compared with the reduced benefits that can be obtained when out of work, ensuring that fewer job vacancies remain unfilled.

11.6 The new Keynesian approach

During the 1980s a new Keynesian approach to unemployment was developed to challenge the new classical view that unemployment is entirely a voluntary phenomenon. Within the extensive new Keynesian literature a number of models have been put forward to explain why an 'equilibrium' real wage rate can emerge that is above the market-clearing real wage rate. Such models are therefore capable of generating involuntary unemployment in long-run equilibrium. In what follows we shall outline two such new Keynesian explanations of real wage rigidity in the labour market: the efficiency wage and insider–outsider theories.

Efficiency wage model

The essence of efficiency wage theories is that the productivity (effort or efficiency) of workers depends positively on the real wage rate that workers are paid. In consequence it is both profitable and rational for firms to pay a so-called efficiency wage that is above the market-clearing real wage rate. Efficiency wage theories suggest that, even in the face of an excess supply of labour, it will not be in firms' interests to lower the real wage rate, as to do so would lower productivity and raise costs. Before we outline the main reasons why firms may pay an efficiency wage above the market-clearing real wage rate it would be useful to consider the implications of this analysis by reference to Fig. 11.8.

In Fig. 11.8 full employment, N_F, where the aggregate demand for labour, D_L, is equal to and matched by the aggregate supply of labour, S_L, would occur at a market-clearing real wage rate, (W/P_e). If, however, firms pay an efficiency wage $(W/P)^*$ above this market-clearing real wage rate there will be an excess supply of labour $(N_2 - N_1)$, and involuntary unemployment will result. Suppose now that a shock occurs that shifts the aggregate demand for labour to the left from D_L to D_L^*. In this situation, if the efficiency wage remains at $(W/P)^*$ the excess supply of labour will increase from $N_2 - N_1$ to $N_2 - N_3$, and the amount of involuntary unemployment will increase.

Let us now outline the four versions of efficiency wage theory that have been put forward in the literature. First, the *labour turnover model* suggests that quit rates are a decreasing function of the real wage rate paid to workers. In consequence, firms have an incentive to pay an efficiency wage in order to deter workers from quitting and reduce costly labour turnover: for example, the costs involved with hiring and training new employees. At the same time, the existence of involuntary unemployment that results from the payment of an efficiency wage above the market-clearing real wage rate also acts as a disincentive to workers to quit their job.

Second, the *adverse selection model* suggests that workers' abilities and reservation or minimum wage, which would induce them to take a job, are closely connected. In consequence, by paying an efficiency wage, firms will not only attract the best or most productive applicants but will also deter the most productive workers from quitting.

Third, the *shirking model* suggests that in many jobs workers can exercise considerable discretion with respect to how well they perform their job, and that there is

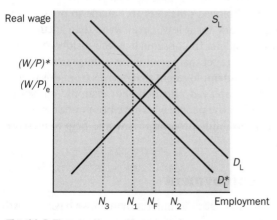

Fig. 11.8 The new Keynesian approach.

a real possibility that some workers will shirk their work effort. Such behaviour may be difficult to detect and/or costly to monitor, especially where teamwork predominates. In a fully employed economy where firms pay the market-clearing real wage rate, the threat of dismissal for workers caught shirking will fail to act as an effective deterrent since they can easily find alternative employment at the same real wage rate. If, however, firms pay an efficiency wage above the market-clearing real wage rate (as depicted in Fig. 11.8) then there will be a disincentive for workers to shirk since if they are caught and are subsequently dismissed they will not readily find employment elsewhere but will join those who are already involuntarily unemployed. In other words, by paying an efficiency wage firms discourage shirking and raise worker productivity or effort. In addition to an efficiency wage acting as a disciplinary device it also allows firms to reduce costs in monitoring workers' performance.

Finally, the *fairness model* suggests that workers' productivity or effort is closely connected to their morale, which is in turn linked to the notion of being treated fairly with respect to pay. By paying an efficiency wage above the market-clearing real wage rate the morale and loyalty of workers will increase and workers will respond by working harder, increasing their productivity.

In the four versions of efficiency wage theory outlined above it is firms who decide to pay an efficiency wage above the market-clearing real wage rate because it is both profitable and rational for them to do so. We next consider a model in which no positive effect of real wages on productivity is assumed, and where the focus shifts away from firms as employers to the power of employees in partially determining wage and employment outcomes.

Insider–outsider model

Within the insider–outsider model of real wage rigidity the so-called *insiders* are the incumbent employees and the *outsiders* are the unemployed workers. The power of insiders arises from labour turnover costs. As mentioned earlier, these costs include hiring and firing costs (such as those associated with advertising and severance pay) and also the costs of training new employees. In addition, the power of insiders is reinforced by the fact that they can refuse to cooperate with or can even harass new employees. As a result, insiders can affect the productivity of new employees. In these circumstances, it is argued that insiders have sufficient bargaining power to raise real wages above the market-clearing rate without the fear of losing their jobs and being undercut by outsiders. Unemployed outsiders are unable to price themselves back into work by offering to work for a lower real wage than incumbent employees, because of the power of insiders. In consequence, the insider–outsider model is able to explain why real wages are set that result in involuntary unemployment. One policy implication to reduce unemployment that derives from this model is to increase the market power of unemployed outsiders. For example, measures targeted at the long-term unemployed (those people who have been out of work for a year or more) such as government retraining programmes would help to increase the power of unemployed outsiders.

Hysteresis effects and unemployment

So far in discussing the new Keynesian approach to unemployment we have focused our attention on various theoretical models that can help to account for the existence of involuntary unemployment as an *equilibrium* phenomenon. In this context equilibrium is defined as a situation where there is no incentive for economic agents to change their behaviour. In other words, as illustrated in Fig. 11.8, equilibrium can occur in the labour market where there is an excess supply of labour and involuntary unemployment persists. We now turn to consider new Keynesian hysteresis theories where the resultant long-run equilibrium level of unemployment is affected by the path taken by the actual level of unemployment.

Earlier, in discussing the monetarist approach to unemployment, we introduced Friedman's concept of a natural rate of unemployment to describe the long-run equilibrium rate of unemployment. We also noted that the natural rate of unemployment is associated with a stable rate of inflation (see Chapter 12, Section 12.2). While aggregate demand shocks can influence the actual rate of unemployment in the short run, in the long run the natural rate is determined by supply-side influences independently of aggregate demand. Rather than refer to the natural rate, many Keynesians prefer to speak of the **non-accelerating inflation rate of unemployment** (**NAIRU**) to describe the long-run equilibrium rate of unemployment that is consistent with stable inflation. However, in marked contrast to monetarists, new Keynesians argue that the natural rate (or NAIRU) *is* affected by the path taken by the actual rate of unemployment. In other words the natural rate (or NAIRU) is affected by the level of aggregate demand.

Why do new Keynesians believe that the natural rate (or NAIRU) is affected by the path taken by the actual rate of unemployment? In order to explain why this is the case suppose the economy is initially operating at its natural rate of unemployment. If the economy experiences, for example, a contractionary aggregate demand shock it may then undergo a prolonged recession. In circumstances where the actual rate of unemployment remains above the natural rate for a prolonged period the natural rate (or NAIRU) will tend to increase because of so-called **hysteresis** effects. Such effects act like a magnet, pulling the natural rate in the same direction. Not only will those who are unemployed suffer a deterioration of their human capital (skills), exacerbating the problem of structural unemployment, but the number of long-run unemployed, who exercise little influence on the wage bargaining process, is also likely to increase. Both forces will raise the natural rate (or NAIRU). Following our discussion based on the insider–outsider model, outsiders will be unable to price themselves back into work even in the face of high and rising unemployment. Thus hysteresis effects provide a strong case for the authorities to stimulate aggregate demand during a protracted recession.

11.7 Unemployment in Europe

While estimates of the natural rate (or NAIRU) diverge, and are themselves fraught with difficulties, most economists agree that the natural rate of unemployment in Europe has increased from around 3 per cent in the 1960s to over 9 per cent in the early 1990s. Some indication of this phenomenon is provided by Fig. 11.9 and Table 11.1. Fig. 11.9 depicts the average standardized unemployment rate in the European Union (EU), the USA and Japan over the period 1970–96. Table 11.1 shows five-year (quinquennial) averages for unemployment in the EU, together with those for selected European countries, the USA and Japan for the five quinquennia over the period 1970–94. Reference to Fig. 11.9 reveals that during the 1970s un-

NAIRU: The rate of unemployment at which inflation is stable.

Hysteresis: The proposition that the equilibrium value of a variable depends on the history of that variable.

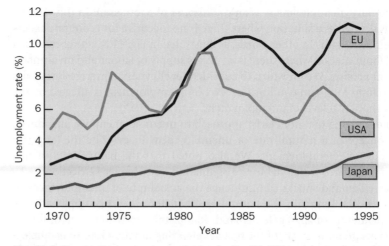

Fig. 11.9 Standardized unemployment rates for the EU, USA and Japan. European unemployment rate between 1970 and 1974 is for Germany, France, Italy, UK, Belgium, Netherlands, Portugal, and Spain. In addition to these eight countries, for the period 1975–96 the data also cover Finland, Ireland and Sweden.
Source: OECD Economic Outlook.

Table 11.1 Quinquennial average unemployment rates (standardized) in the EU, selected European countries, USA and Japan[a]

	EU	Germany	France	Italy	UK	USA	Japan
1970–74	2.9	1.0	2.7	5.2	3.8	5.3	1.3
1975–79	5.2	3.5	4.9	6.8	5.4	6.9	2.0
1980–84	8.9	5.6	7.9	8.4	10.3	8.2	2.4
1985–89	9.9	6.3	10.1	10.6	9.7	6.1	2.6
1990–94	9.6	6.0	10.5	10.2	9.2	6.5	2.4

[a] Per cent of total labour force (correct to one decimal point)
Source: OECD Economic Outlook (various issues). Reproduced by permission of the OECD

employment in the EU rose steadily and by 1979 had roughly caught up with that experienced in the USA. At the start of the 1980s unemployment rose sharply in both the EU and the USA. However, while unemployment fell steadily in the USA after 1983, in the EU it has remained high, and since the early to mid-1980s has been significantly above that experienced in the USA. We now turn to consider how economists have sought to account for the substantial rise in unemployment that has taken place in the EU since the 1970s.

Two main theories have been put forward to explain the rise in European unemployment. One theory explains high European unemployment in terms of labour market rigidities. Among the specific changes that it is alleged have reduced the flexibility of the labour market and resulted in higher unemployment are:

- more powerful trade unions, who by obtaining real wage increases above the increase in the value of output produced per worker, and by imposing restrictions on working practices, limiting firms' ability to adjust to changes in economic circumstances, have raised firms' costs

- higher unemployment benefits, which have acted as a deterrent for the unemployed to find a job, especially for unemployed unskilled workers to take up low-paid jobs

- minimum wage laws, which have made it unprofitable for firms to hire unskilled workers.

Changes in technology it is argued have further reduced the demand for unskilled relative to skilled workers. The term **Eurosclerosis** has been applied to describe such developments. In other words, labour market rigidities are it is suggested leading to the *sclerosis* (a term applied to describe a hardening of the tissues) of the economic system in Europe, resulting in high unemployment. While some of these factors may explain part of the rise in European unemployment in the 1970s, many economists doubt that they offer a plausible explanation of European unemployment experience since the 1980s, when many of these rigidities have been reduced. For example, trade union density (the percentage of the labour force that is unionized), which can be used to proxy trade union power, has declined in most European countries since the early 1980s.

The second main theory explains high European unemployment in terms of hysteresis effects, in that following prolonged periods when actual unemployment has been high the natural rate (or NAIRU) has itself increased. Two episodes are highlighted. First, in the 1970s, unemployment in most European countries rose sharply following the OPEC oil price increases that occurred in 1973–74 and 1979 (see for example the experience of Germany, France and Italy recorded in Table 9.2). Second, in the early 1980s, following the lead given by the Thatcher government in the UK, most European countries sought to reduce inflation via monetary contraction resulting in recession and rising unemployment (see Chapter 12, Section 12.2). For example, reference to Table 9.2 reveals that actual unemployment in the UK rose from 5.0 per cent in 1979 to 12.4 per cent in 1983. In particular, adherents of this second main theory argue that periods of prolonged recession in Europe have led to an increase in the number of long-term unemployed, who not only have lost skills and work habits but also exercise little influence on the process of wage determination (in line with the insider–outsider model). According to this theory, prolonged unemployment has led to an increase in long-term unemployment, which has in turn caused an increase in the natural rate of unemployment (or NAIRU).

What tentative conclusions can be drawn from our overview of unemployment in Europe? Most economists tend to take an *eclectic* position between the two main views we have outlined. They recognize that the substantial rise in European unemployment can be attributed in part to changes in the labour market on the *supply side*, and in part to two major adverse (OPEC) supply shocks and deflationary policies on the *demand side*. In the latter case, the evidence suggests that there are significant output/employment costs involved in reducing inflation (see Chapter 12, Section 12.2), and that such costs can be sustained by hysteresis effects. A major problem facing policymakers in Europe is to reduce persistent unemployment. While some argue that this may require some reform of the unemployment benefit system with respect to the level of benefits, and the duration for which they are paid, it is especially important that *active* labour market policies are pursued that are targeted at the long-term unemployed: for example, retraining programmes, or the payment

Eurosclerosis: A term used to describe the belief that Europe suffers from excessive labour market rigidities.

High unemployment in France prompts demonstrations

of recruitment subsidies to employers who take on long-term unemployed workers. Furthermore, in a prolonged recession where actual unemployment has risen significantly above the natural rate (or NAIRU), governments should seek to stimulate aggregate demand. But the main lesson to learn above all else is not to let unemployment increase in the first place. Once unemployment has been allowed to rise, as it has in the EU, it is extremely difficult to bring down again.

Summary

◆ The central question that underlies the debate over unemployment is whether the cause of, and consequently cure for, unemployment is essentially to be found inside or outside the labour market.

◆ Orthodox Keynesians identify three main types or categories of unemployment: frictional, structural, and demand-deficient. Each type of unemployment requires a different policy solution. In the Keynesian approach the level of employment is largely determined outside the labour market by the level of aggregate demand in the economy. Because aggregate demand may be too low to guarantee full employment, governments need to stimulate aggregate demand to maintain high and stable levels of employment.

◆ Monetarists refer to a natural or long-run equilibrium rate of unemployment, which is independent of the level of aggregate demand and is consistent with a stable rate of inflation. The natural rate depends on a number of factors, and can be reduced by measures that improve the flexibility of the labour market.

◆ In the new classical approach the labour market is assumed to be cleared continuously. Unemployment is treated entirely as a voluntary phenomenon.

◆ New Keynesian economists have put forward efficiency wage and insider–outsider theories to explain the existence of involuntary unemployment as an equilibrium phenomenon. The long-run equilibrium rate of unemployment or NAIRU that is consistent with stable inflation is affected by the level of aggregate demand. Where the actual rate of unemployment remains above NAIRU for a prolonged period, NAIRU will increase because of hysteresis effects.

◆ Two main theories have been put forward to explain the rise in European unemployment. One view focuses on labour market rigidities, which have led to an increase in the natural rate (or NAIRU); the other focuses on hysteresis effects pulling NAIRU up following periods when actual unemployment has been high. What is needed to reduce the present high level of unemployment in the EU is a set of solutions that involve both aggregate supply and aggregate demand policies.

Key terms

◆ Classical/real wage unemployment
◆ Frictional/search unemployment
◆ Structural/mismatch unemployment
◆ Demand-deficient/cyclical unemployment
◆ Natural rate of unemployment/NAIRU
◆ Efficiency wages
◆ Insiders versus outsiders
◆ Hysteresis
◆ Eurosclerosis

▆ Self-test questions

True (t) or false (f)

1. Classical unemployment occurs when the real wage is maintained above the level at which the aggregate demand for labour equals the aggregate supply of labour.

2. Frictional unemployment is also known as search unemployment.

3. Measures that increase the search time moving between jobs will reduce the amount of frictional unemployment.

4. Structural unemployment is also known as cyclical unemployment.

5. Policies that improve the mobility of labour will reduce the amount of structural unemployment.

6. Demand-deficient unemployment is also known as mismatch unemployment.

7. The cause of demand-deficient unemployment lies inside the labour market.

8. The natural rate of unemployment is the rate of unemployment that exists when the labour market is in equilibrium.

9. Governments can reduce the natural rate of unemployment by pursuing macroeconomic policies that stimulate aggregate demand.

10. New classical economists treat unemployment as an entirely voluntary phenomenon.

11. According to new Keynesian economists, it is neither profitable nor rational for firms to pay an efficiency wage that is above the market-clearing real wage rate.

12. New Keynesians argue that NAIRU is affected by the path taken by the actual rate of unemployment.

Complete the following sentences by inserting the missing word(s)

1. Classical unemployment is also known as _____ unemployment.

2. The three main types of unemployment identified by Keynesians are _____, _____, and _____ unemployment.

3. Expenditure that does not depend on the level of national income is referred to as _____ expenditure.

4. When the labour market clears and the aggregate demand for labour equals the aggregate supply of labour all unemployment will fall in the category of _____ and _____ unemployment.

5. In the Keynesian approach the level of unemployment is largely determined outside the labour market by the level of _____ in the economy.

6. The term 'the natural rate of unemployment' was coined by the famous American economist _____.

7. Governments can reduce the natural rate of unemployment by pursuing _____ policies that improve the structure and functioning of the labour market.

8. The four versions of the efficiency wage theory are the _____ model, the _____ model, the _____ model and the _____ model.

9. New Keynesians refer to _____ to describe the long-run equilibrium rate of unemployment that is consistent with stable inflation.

10. The proposition that the equilibrium value of a variable depends on the history of that variable is known as _____.

◼ Questions for discussion

◆ What is frictional unemployment? What policies can help to reduce this type of unemployment?

◆ What is structural unemployment, and how can it be reduced?

◆ What is demand-deficient unemployment? How can the government reduce this type of unemployment?

◆ What determines the natural rate of unemployment? What policies might be used to reduce the natural rate?

◆ Why may firms find it profitable to pay an efficiency wage above the market-clearing real wage rate?

◆ In the insider–outsider model what is the source of insider power?

◆ What is the essential difference between the natural rate of unemployment and NAIRU?

◆ How have economists sought to explain the rise in unemployment that has taken place in the EU since the 1970s?

◼ Further reading

Dawson, G. *Inflation and Unemployment: Causes, Consequences and Cures* (Aldershot: Edward Elgar, 1992). A thoughtful, lucid and comprehensive guide to the issues of both unemployment and inflation.

Layard, R., S. Nickell and R. Jackman *The Unemployment Crisis* (Oxford: Oxford University Press, 1994). An accessible, comprehensive and up-to-date explanation of the causes of, and sources of fluctuations in, unemployment, citing the recent experience of OECD countries.

Vane, H.R. and J.L. Thompson *An Introduction to Macroeconomic Policy* (4th ed.) (Hemel Hempstead: Harvester Wheatsheaf, 1993). Chapters 11 and 12 provide more detailed discussion of fiscal and monetary policy respectively.

◼ Internet links

The *Office for National Statistics* has a Web site that offers micro and macro time series data on line, including data on employment and unemployment. The site is at:
http://www.ons.gov.uk/ons_f.htm
The *Department for Education and Employment* has responsibility for employment issues in the UK. Its Web site offers a series of press releases that describe the changing patterns of employment and unemployment in the UK. The site is at:
http://www.open.gov.uk/index/../dfee/dfeehome.htm

Inflation: Causes and Cures

Contents

Key issues

▶ What causes inflation?

▶ How can the authorities reduce the rate of inflation?

▶ Is it necessary to increase unemployment in order to reduce the rate of inflation?

12.1 Introduction

In Chapter 9, Section 9.4, we defined inflation as a process of continually rising prices, and outlined how it can be measured. In addition we discussed the economic, social and political costs associated with inflation. You will recall that the main costs of inflation arise when inflation is imperfectly anticipated. The purpose of this chapter is to examine the debate over the causes of, and cures for, inflation. This debate can be conveniently divided into two main explanations of inflation involving monetarist and non-monetarist views. We begin our discussion with the monetarist explanation, which embodies two of the most famous relationships that exist in macroeconomics: the quantity theory of money, and the (expectations-augmented) Phillips curve.

12.2 The monetarist view

The quantity theory of money: old and modern

The monetarist view of inflation is best summarized by Milton Friedman's pronouncement that '... inflation is always and everywhere a monetary phenomenon in the sense that it can be produced only by a more rapid increase in the quantity of money than in output.' This belief is embodied in the quantity theory of money, a body of doctrine concerned with the relationship between the money supply and the general price level.

The traditional quantity theory, which has taken a variety of forms, has a long history dating back to before the seventeenth century. Rather than discuss any one particular formulation of the theory, in what follows we present a stylized version of the old (classical) quantity theory. This stylized version of the old quantity theory of money can be described by the equation

$$MV = PY \tag{12.1}$$

where M = the nominal money supply, V = the income velocity of circulation of money during a given time period (the average number of times money circulates throughout the economy in exchange for final output), P = the average price of final output, and Y = the real quantity of final output produced during a given time period.

By definition, the nominal money supply multiplied by the average number of times it circulates in exchange for final output *must* be equal to the average price of the final output multiplied by the real quantity of final output produced during a given time period (see Box 12.1). To turn an identity into a theory we must discuss what determines each of the four variables M, V, P and Y. Classical economists argued that the authorities controlled the nominal supply of money in the economy. So M was determined independently of V, P and Y in the quantity theory relationship. The income velocity of money was thought to depend on institutional factors, such as the length of the payments period, and was also treated as being independent of the other variables. As institutional factors were held to change slowly over time, V was assumed, for practical purposes, to be constant.

Box 12.1

The quantity theory of money: a numerical example

To illustrate the postulated relationship between the money supply and the general price level suppose the values of M, V, P and Y are as follows:

- M, the nominal money supply = £90 000
- V, the income velocity of circulation of money = 4
- P, the average price of final output = £3, and
- Y, the real quantity of final output produced = 120 000 units.

Within our stylized version of the quantity theory:

$$MV = PY$$
$$£90\,000 \times 4 = £3 \times 120\,000$$

Now suppose that the authorities decide to increase the nominal money supply by 10 per cent from £90 000 to £99 000. With V and Y held constant then a 10 per cent increase in the money supply will lead to a 10 per cent increase in the average price of final output to maintain the quantity theory relationship. In other words:

$$MV = PY$$
$$£99\,000 \times 4 = £3.30 \times 120\,000$$

Turning to the right-hand side of the quantity theory relationship, classical economists believed that the level of real output was determined by real forces, such as the supply of factors of production. Furthermore, they believed that output would always return to full employment in the long run. In consequence, Y was assumed to be constant at the full employment level of output. Given these assumptions classical economists argued that in the *long run P*, the average price of final output, would be determined solely by the supply of money, and that any change in the money supply would lead to a proportionate change in the general price level. For example, with V and Y assumed to be constant, a 10 per cent rise in the money supply would lead to a

Inflation: too much money chasing too few goods?

10 per cent rise in the general price level (see Box 12.1). Classical economists thereby postulated a purely monetary explanation of the determination of the general price level and its rate of change: inflation. In the latter case the old quantity theory relationship can be rewritten and expressed in terms of percentage rates of change. Maintaining the assumption that V and Y are constant we obtain the old quantity theory prediction that, in the long run, the rate of inflation, $\dot{P}$, is determined by, and equal to, the rate of growth of the money supply, $\dot{M}$:

$$\dot{P} = \dot{M} \tag{12.2}$$

In the mid-1950s Friedman reformulated the old quantity theory of money relationship. Although his restatement of the theory was in the first instance a theory of the demand for money, the modern quantity theory of money provides the basis for the monetarist explanation of inflation. In contrast to the old quantity theory, in which V and Y were assumed to be approximately constant over time, in the modern quantity theory V and Y are held to be *stable* and *predictable* in the long run. Once the assumption that Y is constant is relaxed, then in the long run the rate of inflation is determined by, and equal to, the rate of growth of the money supply minus the rate of growth of real output:

$$\dot{P} = \dot{M} - \dot{Y} \tag{12.3}$$

The policy proposal that follows from this modern quantity theory approach is that the authorities should seek to control the rate of growth of the money supply, in line with the underlying rate of growth of real output, in order to ensure long-term price stability.

Our discussion so far has focused on how, according to the monetarist view, the rate of monetary expansion essentially determines the rate of inflation in the long run. We now turn to consider how, in the short run, the effects of a change in the rate of monetary expansion are divided between changes in output and inflation. This involves an examination of the relationship between unemployment and inflation, commonly referred to as the Phillips curve.

The original Phillips curve

In 1958 the results of a *statistical* investigation undertaken by Phillips into the relationship between unemployment (U) and the rate of change of money wages ($\dot{W}$) in the United Kingdom, over the period 1861–1957, were published in *Economica*. Phillips found evidence of a *stable* relationship between these two variables that appeared to have existed for almost a century. The negative (non-linear) relationship between unemployment and wage inflation is depicted in Fig. 12.1. The estimated average relationship indicated that when the level of unemployment was approximately 5.5 per cent the rate of change of money wages was zero. Furthermore, at an unemployment level of approximately 2.5 per cent the rate of change of money wages was approximately 2 per cent, which was roughly equal to the then-average growth of productivity (output per worker). In consequence a 2.5 per cent level of unemployment was compatible with price stability. For this reason the Phillips curve is presented in some textbooks with price (rather than wage) inflation on the vertical axis, with the curve cutting the horizontal axis at an unemployment level of 2.5 per cent.

Now Phillips's study was, as noted above, a statistical investigation, and the economic rationale for the curve was provided by Lipsey in an article subsequently published in *Economica* in 1960. Utilizing standard demand and supply analysis, which we first encountered in Chapter 2, Lipsey argued that money wages will rise when there is an excess demand for labour. Moreover, the greater the extent of excess demand for labour the faster the rate or speed at which money wages will increase.

Phillips curve: The relationship between the inflation rate and the unemployment rate.

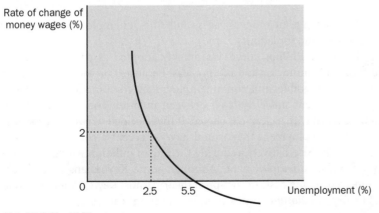

Fig. 12.1 The Phillips curve.

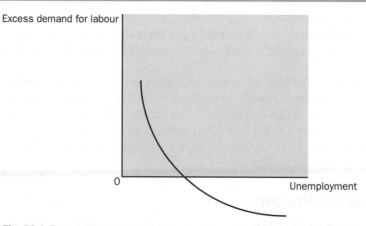

Fig. 12.2 The relationship between excess demand for labour and unemployment.

While it is straightforward to illustrate a state of excess demand diagrammatically, it is more problematic to actually measure excess demand for labour. To get round the problem that excess demand for labour is not directly observable Lipsey used the level of unemployment as a proxy or surrogate measure for excess demand in the labour market. He postulated that a negative (non-linear) relationship exists between excess demand and unemployment, as shown in Fig. 12.2. Reference to Fig. 12.2 reveals that when the demand for and supply of labour are equal (that is, excess demand is zero) there will still be, as discussed in Chapter 11, some positive amount of unemployment. As excess demand for labour increases, unemployment will fall (for example as vacancies increase and jobs become easier to find), but by increasingly smaller amounts. Unemployment will never actually fall to zero because of various factors such as those individuals who change their jobs and who will be unemployed while they are searching for new employment.

A combination of two postulated hypotheses, namely that the rate of increase in money wages depends positively on excess demand for labour, and that excess demand for labour and unemployment are negatively related, provided the economic rationale for the Phillips curve shown in Fig. 12.1.

The Phillips curve can also be described by the equation

$$\dot{W} = f(U) \tag{12.4}$$

where $\dot{W}$ = rate of change of money wages, and U = unemployment (a proxy measure for excess demand for labour).

During the 1960s the Phillips curve was quickly adopted as part of the then-prevailing Keynesian economic orthodoxy, not least because it provided the authorities with a menu of possible inflation–unemployment combinations for policy choice. Given the apparent *stable trade-off* between inflation and unemployment policymakers were faced with a clear-cut choice. If they decided to run the economy at a lower level of unemployment they would have to accept a cost in terms of a higher rate of inflation. Alternatively, reducing the rate of inflation would involve a cost in terms of higher unemployment. Although some Keynesians argued that inflation was caused by rising costs (a cost-push theory), most Keynesians adhered to a **demand-pull** theory of **inflation**. In this view, inflation was caused by an excess demand for goods and services when the economy was at, or above, full employment.

Demand-pull inflation:
Inflation caused by an excess demand for goods and services when the economy is at or above full employment.

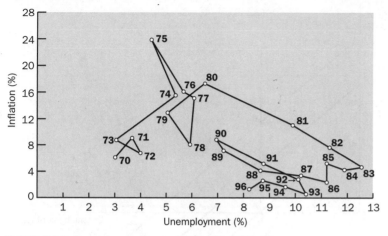

Fig. 12.3 Inflation and unemployment in the UK, 1970–96.
Source: OECD Economic Outlook (various issues).

By the late 1960s the original Phillips curve had broken down. Fig. 12.3 illustrates the breakdown of any stable relationship between inflation and unemployment with data for the UK economy over the period 1970–96. Reference to Fig. 12.3 reveals that the UK economy (as has been the case in other Western economies) has experienced at various times a simultaneous increase in both the rate of inflation and unemployment (so-called stagflation). Broadly speaking, economists reacted to the breakdown of the original Phillips curve in one of two main ways. Some Keynesian economists abandoned the demand-pull theory of inflation and turned to a **cost-push** theory of **inflation** (see Section 12.3 below). Other economists sought to modify the demand-pull theory by arguing that inflation is caused by excess demand *and* expectations of future rates of inflation. We first turn to discuss the expectations-augmented Phillips curve and how this fits into the monetarist view of inflation.

The expectations-augmented Phillips curve

In Chapter 7 we discussed how within orthodox microeconomic analysis of the labour market the demand for, and supply of, labour are specified in real, not money, terms. In other words, although money wages are set in wage negotiations, what really matters to both firms as employers and workers as employees is the real wage that is negotiated. In addition, given that wage bargains are struck for an advance period (for example lasting for one year), the rate of inflation expected throughout the period of the contract has a crucial bearing on the real wage negotiated. In the light of these considerations, Friedman augmented the original Phillips curve with the expected rate of inflation as an additional variable determining the rate of change of money wages.

The introduction of the expected rate of inflation as an additional variable that determines the rate of change of money wages modifies the original Phillips curve. As we shall now discuss, the expectations-augmented Phillips curve implies that there is no longer a single unique Phillips curve; rather there exist a whole family of **short-run Phillips curves**. Each short-run Phillips curve is associated with a different expected rate of inflation. As the expected rate of inflation increases, the short-run

Cost-push inflation: Inflation caused by cost increases even though there are no shortages of goods and services and the economy is below full employment.

Short-run Phillips curve: Depicts the relationship between inflation and unemployment that exists for a given expected rate of inflation.

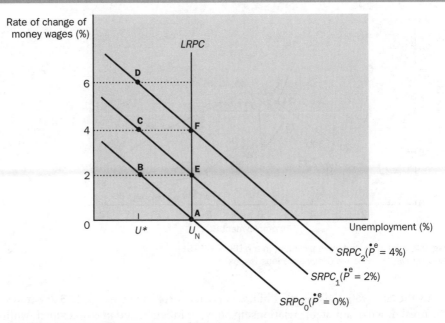

Fig. 12.4 The expectations-augmented Phillips curve.

Phillips curve will shift upwards. In other words, each level of unemployment corresponds to a unique rate of change of real wages. This analysis is illustrated in Fig. 12.4 where both to simplify the analysis and for ease of diagrammatic presentation two assumptions are made:

- Productivity growth remains constant at zero, with the result that firms will pass on any wage increases in the form of price increases, in order to maintain their profit margins.

- The short-run Phillips curves are linear.

Fig. 12.4 maintains the same axes as the original Philips curve of Fig. 12.1 and shows three short-run Phillips curves, each associated with a different expected rate of inflation, and a *vertical long-run Phillips curve (LRPC)* at the natural rate of unemployment, U_N. Suppose the labour market is initially in equilibrium (that is, there is zero excess demand) at the natural rate of unemployment (see Chapter 11, Section 11.4) with a zero rate of increase in money wages. Assuming productivity growth is zero, a zero rate of increase in money wages, $\dot{W}$, will be matched by a zero rate of increase in prices, $\dot{P}$, and the expected rate of increase in prices, $\dot{P}^e$, will also be zero. In this situation the real wage is constant as the rate of increase in money wages is exactly equal to the rate of increase in prices. Furthermore, inflation is perfectly anticipated with the actual and expected rates of inflation equal at zero. In Fig. 12.4 this initial situation is indicated by the short-run Phillips curve $SRPC_0$, which cuts the horizontal axis at point A, at the natural rate of unemployment.

Now, suppose that the government decides to increase aggregate demand in the economy by embarking on a policy of monetary expansion in an attempt to maintain unemployment below U_N at U^*. As firms increase their production to meet the increase in aggregate demand for goods, the demand for labour will increase, and money wages will start to rise at a rate of 2 per cent. Given recent experience of zero actual and expected inflation rates workers will interpret the 2 per cent increase in their money wages as a 2 per cent increase in their real wages and respond by increasing the supply of labour. As the demand for and supply of labour increases, unemployment will fall from U_N to U^*, a movement along the short-run Phillips curve ($SRPC_0$) from point A to point B. Assuming productivity growth is zero, a 2 per cent rate of increase in money wages will lead to a 2 per cent rate of increase in prices. Sooner or later workers will start to adapt their expectations of future inflation in the light of such changed circumstances and take their revised expectations into consideration when negotiating money wage increases. As individuals fully revise their expectations of inflation upwards from zero to 2 per cent the short-run Phillips curve will shift upwards from $SRPC_0$ to $SRPC_1$. In other words once the 2 per cent rate of actual inflation is fully anticipated ($\dot{P} = \dot{P}^e = 2$ per cent) money wages will have to increase at a rate of 4 per cent in order to achieve the 2 per cent increase in real wages necessary to maintain unemployment at U^*: that is, point C on $SRPC_1$.

In this situation the authorities will have to increase further the rate of monetary expansion in order to finance the 4 per cent rate of wage and price inflation. As individuals revise upwards their expectations of inflation the short-run Phillips curve will again shift upwards, this time from $SRPC_1$ to $SRPC_2$. At an expected inflation of 4 per cent money wages will have to increase at a rate of 6 per cent, in order to achieve the 2 per cent rise in real wages required by the continued existence of excess demand in the labour market at U^*: that is, point D on $SRPC_2$. In this situation the authorities will have to increase the rate of monetary expansion still further in order to finance the 6 per cent rate of wage and prices inflation, and so on.

In summary, in the monetarist view inflation is *initiated* by excessive monetary expansion, which leads to excess demand in the labour market. This causes a rise in money wages, which firms then pass on to consumers in the form of higher prices. Expectations of further price increases lead to increased wage claims, resulting in an inflationary 'wage–price' spiral. In the monetarist view, the chain of causation runs from changes in the money supply (and its rate of expansion) to changes in prices (and their rate of increase, namely inflation). As we shall discuss in Section 12.3 below, in the non-monetarist view this chain of causation is reversed.

Policy implications

One of the main policy implications that follows from this analysis is that any attempt to *maintain* unemployment below the natural rate will result in an accelerating rate of inflation, which can be financed only by accelerating monetary growth. If, however, the authorities refuse to increase continuously the rate of monetary expansion unemployment will return to U_N, and in line with the quantity theory of money, in equilibrium in the long run, the rate of monetary expansion will equal the rate of inflation ($\dot{P} = \dot{M}$). At U_N the real wage will be restored to its original level, and there will be no disturbance in the labour market. Joining together all such points of equilibrium (points A, E, F etc.), a vertical long-run Phillips curve ($LRPC$) is obtained at the natural rate of unemployment. In summary, monetarists argue that while an inflation–unemployment trade-off exists in the short run along a given short-run Phillips curve, once economic agents have fully adjusted their inflationary expectations the trade-off disappears, resulting in a vertical long-run Phillips curve at the natural rate of unemployment. The natural or equilibrium level of unemployment is associated with a stable (or non-accelerating) rate of inflation, which is itself determined by the rate of monetary expansion.

Before we consider the policy implications of reducing inflation it is useful to note that the expectations-augmented Phillips curve can be described by the equation

$$\dot{W} = f(U) + \dot{P}^e \tag{12.5}$$

where $\dot{W}$ = rate of change of money wages, U = unemployment, and $\dot{P}^e$ = the expected rate of inflation. When the economy is in equilibrium at the natural rate of unemployment and there is no excess demand for labour, the rate of increase in money wages, $\dot{W}$, will equal the rate of increase in prices, $\dot{P}$, and the expected rate of increase in prices $\dot{P}^e$. In this situation the real wage will be constant. The vertical long-run Phillips curve traces a locus of possible points where inflation is perfectly anticipated (that is, $\dot{W} = \dot{P} = \dot{P}^e$) at the natural rate of unemployment. The intersection of the short-run Phillips curve ($SRPC_0$) with the vertical long-run Phillips curve at point A represents our initial starting point, where the rate of wage and price inflation, and the expected rate of inflation, are all equal to zero. Points E and F represent other potential long-run equilibrium situations.

Let us now turn to consider the output–employment costs of reducing inflation. As we have seen, in the monetarist view inflation is essentially a monetary phenomenon propagated by excessive monetary growth. It follows from this analysis that inflation can be reduced only by slowing down the rate of monetary expansion. Reducing the rate of growth of the money supply will in the short run result in an increase in the level of unemployment above the natural rate. The extent and duration of the rise in unemployment depend on two main factors: whether the authorities pursue a policy of rapid or gradual monetary contraction, and the speed at which economic agents revise their expectations of inflation downwards in the light of changed circumstances. We illustrate why this is the case in Fig. 12.5.

In Fig. 12.5 we assume that the economy is initially operating at point A, with a 6 per cent (stable) rate of wage and price inflation (determined by a 6 per cent rate of monetary expansion), and that unemployment is at its natural level, U_N. At point A,

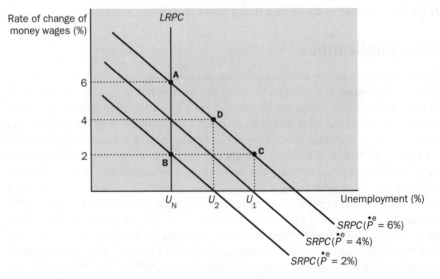

Fig. 12.5 The unemployment costs of reducing inflation.

which is both a short-run and long-run equilibrium position, inflation is perfectly anticipated, with the actual and expected rates of inflation equal at 6 per cent. Now suppose the authorities decide that they want to reduce the rate of wage and price inflation to 2 per cent and move to point B on the long-run Phillips curve (*LRPC*). One option open to the authorities would be to rapidly reduce the rate of monetary expansion from 6 per cent to 2 per cent in order to attain their new inflation target of 2 per cent. Such a policy stance would initially result in a relatively large increase in unemployment from U_N to U_1: that is, an initial movement along the short-run Phillips curve associated with an expected rate of inflation of 6 per cent, from point A to point C. As the rate of wage and price inflation fell individuals would revise their expectations of inflation downwards, and the short-run Phillips curve would shift downwards. Eventually unemployment would return to U_N and a new short-run and long-run equilibrium would be established at point B.

Alternatively the authorities might choose to gradually reduce the rate of monetary expansion from 6 per cent to 4 per cent and thereafter from 4 per cent to 2 per cent. Such a policy stance would involve a smaller initial increase in unemployment above the natural rate from U_N to U_2: that is, an initial movement along the short-run Phillips curve, associated with an expected rate of inflation of 6 per cent, from point A to point D. The short-run Phillips curve would, as before, shift downwards as individuals revised their expectations of inflation downwards in line with the fall in the actual rate of wage and price inflation. As the authorities gradually reduced the rate of monetary expansion further from 4 per cent to 2 per cent, they would reduce inflation to their target of 2 per cent, and eventually unemployment would return to U_N. In contrast to the policy option of rapid **disinflation**, sometimes referred to as **cold turkey**, reducing inflation by **gradual** monetary contraction would take longer. Recognition of this has led some economists to advocate the use of supplementary policy measures, such as prices and incomes policy (see Section 12.3), to accompany gradual monetary contraction. Such supplementary policy measures would speed the adjustment process to a lower rate of inflation *if* they succeeded in reducing individuals' expectations of inflation. The faster individuals revise their expectations of inflation downwards, the shorter the period of time for which unemployment will remain above the natural rate following a decrease in the rate of monetary expansion. Of particular importance in this context is the *credibility* of any anti-inflation strategy pursued by the authorities.

Keynesians, monetarists and new classicists

We now turn to highlight four important differences between Keynesians, monetarists and new classicists with respect to the expectations-augmented Phillips curve and the policy implications that derive from it.

First, *nowadays* while most Keynesian economists accept that the long-run Phillips curve is vertical, some Keynesians believe that there is a long-run trade off between inflation and unemployment, although one that is less favourable (steeper) than that predicted by the short-run Phillips curve. As such they argue that the long-run (non-vertical) Phillips curve still offers the authorities a menu of possible inflation–unemployment combinations for policy choice.

Second, in contrast to monetarists and new classicists, Keynesian economists tend to be more favourably disposed towards the use of **prices and incomes policy** as an anti-inflationary weapon. Some Keynesians advocate the *temporary* use of prices

Disinflation: Entails a decrease in the rate of inflation.

Cold turkey: Involves a rapid and permanent reduction in the rate of monetary growth aimed at reducing the rate of inflation.

Gradualism: An approach to disinflation that involves a slow and gradual reduction in the rate of monetary growth.

Prices and incomes policy: Entails measures that establish guidelines or controls for wage and/or price increases.

and incomes policy as a supplementary policy measure to accompany gradual monetary contraction. Other Keynesians, who assign a role to wage increases made independently of the state of excess demand, advocate the *permanent* use of prices and incomes policy as an anti-inflationary weapon. In the latter case, if the long-run (non-vertical) Phillips curve could be shifted downwards by the adoption of a prices and incomes policy, the trade-off between inflation and unemployment could be improved, allowing the authorities to achieve a lower rate of inflation at any given target level of unemployment.

Third, in marked contrast to monetarists and new classicists, new Keynesians argue that the natural rate of unemployment (or, as discussed in Chapter 11, Section 11.6, what they would prefer to refer to as NAIRU) is affected by the path taken by the actual rate of unemployment. In other words, new Keynesians argue that the natural rate (NAIRU) is affected by the level of aggregate demand. If, following monetary disinflation, the economy experiences a prolonged recession, the natural rate or NAIRU will tend to increase as hysteresis effects pull the long-run Phillips curve to the right.

Fourth, in contrast to the views held by most Keynesians and monetarists, new classicists do not see the need to follow a policy of gradual monetary contraction in order to reduce inflation. According to the new classical view, the unemployment costs associated with monetary disinflation will be non-existent or negligible provided policy is **credible.** If the authorities announce a reduction in the rate of monetary growth and the policy announcement is believed to be credible, rational economic agents would immediately revise their expectations of inflation downwards in line with the anticipated effects of monetary contraction on the rate of inflation. In terms of Fig. 12.5, inflation would be reduced from 6 per cent to 2 per cent without any increase in unemployment. So the short-run Phillips curve associated with a 6 per cent expected inflation would immediately shift downwards to that associated with a 2 per cent expected inflation: that is, the economy would immediately adjust from point A to point B on the long-run Phillips curve. In such circumstances, the authorities might just as well announce a rapid reduction in the rate of growth of the money supply in order to reduce inflation to their new target rate. If, however, there is widespread scepticism that the authorities are not fully committed to disinflation through monetary contraction, individuals will not adjust their inflation expectations downwards. In such a situation the unemployment costs involved with the adjustment process will be more severe than the case where the authorities have no such credibility problem.

The monetarist view that inflation can be reduced only by slowing down the rate of monetary expansion had an important bearing on the course of anti-inflation policy pursued in many countries during the 1980s. For example, in the UK the Conservative government elected into office in 1979 sought to reduce progressively the rate of monetary growth in order to achieve its overriding economic policy objective of reducing the rate of inflation. As part of its medium-term financial strategy (see Box 12.2), first introduced in the March 1980 Budget, the Thatcher government announced declining targets for monetary growth. Such targets reflected an *explicit* acceptance of the monetarist view that a reduction in monetary growth is both necessary and sufficient to reduce the rate of inflation. At the same time the pre-announcement of declining monetary growth targets reflected an *implicit* acceptance of the view that economic agents form their expectations of inflation rationally and would quickly revise their inflationary expectations downwards, thereby minimizing the unemployment costs associated with monetary disinflation.

Credibility: The degree to which people believe the authorities' announcements about future policy.

Box 12.2

The medium-term financial strategy of the Thatcher government

In May 1979 a Conservative government under the leadership of Mrs Margaret Thatcher was elected to office in the UK. The new administration made reducing inflation the overriding objective of its economic policy. This objective was conditioned by its belief that a high rate of inflation increases uncertainty, impedes economic efficiency, discourages investment, and adversely affects international competitiveness (see Chapter 9, Section 9.4). In order to reduce inflation the government first introduced in 1980 its so-called medium-term financial strategy (MTFS), which embraced both monetary and fiscal policy. The strategy involved the pre-announcement of declining targets for both the rate of growth of the money supply and the **public sector borrowing requirement** (PSBR) for a number of years ahead. In the former case, as noted in the text of the chapter, the targets set for the rate of growth of the money supply reflected: (i) an explicit acceptance of the monetarist view that inflation can *only* be reduced by slowing down the rate of monetary expansion and (ii) an implicit acceptance of the view that economic agents form their expectations of future rates of inflation rationally (a view largely associated with new classical macroeconomics – see Chapter 14, Section 14.5). From the mid-1980s onwards the government gradually changed its strategy towards setting monetary growth targets, in that they no longer occupied the centre stage in the implementation of monetary policy, and with entry into the exchange rate mechanism of the European Monetary System in October 1990 (see Chapter 16, Section 16.6) the UK economy witnessed the formal end of what the media at the time dubbed 'Thatcher's monetarist experiment'.

The targets set for the **PSBR** within the MTFS reflected a number of views held by the Conservative government:

- an implicit acceptance of the (controversial) view that there exists a stable and predictable relationship between the size of the PSBR and monetary growth
- that the long-term credibility of its anti-inflation strategy by monetary targeting depended on its reducing the PSBR
- a desire to avoid excessive upward pressure on interest rates through sales of government bonds for fear of crowding out private-sector investment in the economy (see Chapter 14, Section 14.4)
- a desire to reduce the size of the public sector and provide scope for cuts in income tax to increase the incentive to work.

For more detailed and highly accessible accounts of the Thatcher monetarist experiment in the UK the reader is referred to Keegan, W. *Mrs Thatcher's Economic Experiment* (Harmondsworth: Penguin, 1984) and Smith, D. *The Rise and Fall of Monetarism* (Hardmondsworth: Penguin, 1987).

Public sector borrowing requirement (PSBR): The amount of money the public sector (central government, local authorities and nationalized industries) has to borrow after taking into consideration its total expenditure and revenue.

Table 9.3 reveals that the Thatcher government achieved some measure of success in reducing inflation in the UK in the early 1980s. Between 1979 and 1983 inflation fell from 13.4 per cent to 4.6 per cent, and most economists agree that the domestic monetary (and fiscal) policies pursued contributed substantially to reducing the rate of inflation in the UK. However, most economists also agree that the restrictive domestic policies pursued made a significant contribution to the rise in unemployment experienced in the early 1980s. Table 9.2 reveals that between 1979 and 1983 unemployment rose from 5.0 per cent to 12.4 per cent.

Prima facie evidence from other economies also suggests that the unemployment costs of reducing inflation are not insignificant. For example, the pursuit of restrictive monetary policy in the US economy in the early 1980s was also associated with deep recession. Tables 9.2 and 9.3 reveal that, while inflation fell from 11.3 per cent to 3.2 per cent in the US economy between 1979 and 1983, over the same period unemployment rose from 5.8 per cent to 9.5 per cent. Most economists agree that the restrictive domestic policies pursued contributed significantly to the rise in US unemployment, along with other contributory factors including the second oil price shock.

Inflation as an international monetary phenomenon

So far we have discussed the monetarist view of inflation implicitly in the context of a closed economy in which no international trade takes place. In a closed economy (or an open economy operating under flexible exchange rates – see Chapter 16, Section 16.5), the domestic rate of inflation is held to be determined by the domestic rate of monetary expansion relative to the rate of growth of domestic real output. However, in a regime of fixed exchange rates, such as the Bretton Woods system (see Chapter 16, Sections 16.5–16.6) which operated from the mid 1940s until the early 1970s, inflation is viewed as an international monetary phenomenon. Under a regime of fixed exchange rates, monetarists argue that nations are linked together in a world economy in which the aggregate world money supply (and its rate of change) determines world prices (and their rates of change). Domestic monetary expansion will influence the domestic rate of inflation only to the extent that it influences the rate of growth of the world money supply and in consequence the rate of growth of world prices. An increase in the world rate of monetary expansion (due to rapid monetary expansion by either a large country relative to the rest of the world, or a number of small countries simultaneously) would create excess demand and result in inflationary pressure throughout the world economy. On the basis of this analysis monetarists have argued that the acceleration of inflation that occurred in Western economies in the late 1960s was primarily the consequence of an increase in the rate of monetary expansion in the USA to finance increased expenditure on the Vietnam War. As such, inflationary pressure initiated in the USA was then transmitted to other Western economies via the US balance of payments deficit.

For an economy operating under a regime of flexible exchange rates monetarists argue that a country's domestic rate of inflation will be determined, as in the case of a closed economy, by its domestic rate of monetary expansion (relative to the rate of growth of domestic real output). If the domestic rate of monetary expansion in an economy is greater than that in the rest of the world, then it will experience a faster domestic rate of inflation compared with that prevailing in other countries, and its currency will depreciate.

Having discussed the monetarist view of inflation in some detail we now turn to discuss the second main conflicting explanation of inflation: the non-monetarist view.

12.3 The non-monetarist view

In contrast to the monetarist view, in the non-monetarist view (also sometimes referred to as the cost-push or sociological explanation of inflation) wage increases are regarded as the initiating force of inflation. Furthermore such wage increases can occur *independently* of the state of demand and supply conditions in the labour market. Adherents to this view argue that there exist various social pressures that lead to largely *exogenous* wage increases. Given these social pressures, the common theme in the non-monetarist approach is that, because wages are such an important component of firms' costs of production, if money wages continually rise at a faster rate than the growth of productivity then an inflationary wage–price spiral will result, in a similar manner to that analysed in the monetarist view. In the absence of monetary expansion, unemployment will increase as inflation reduces the real value of the money supply. Proponents of the non-monetarist view argue that, in the past, governments have increased the money supply in order to prevent unemployment from rising. This response by the government explains, in this view, the strong correlation between changes in the money supply and changes in prices. In contrast to the monetarist view, in the non-monetarist view causation runs from changes in prices to changes in the money supply, rather than the other way round.

In what follows we outline some of the social pressures that, it is alleged, lead to wage increases and initiate the inflationary process. Two examples will suffice. First, some writers argue that class conflict is inevitable in a capitalist society and that inflation results from the struggle between workers and capitalists as each group strives to achieve a bigger share of national income for themselves. If workers succeed in securing wage increases above productivity growth, capitalists' profit margins will be reduced. In order to maintain the share of profits in national income capitalists will react by increasing their prices. Workers then react by pressing for wages increases, resulting in the familiar inflationary wage–price spiral. The more workers' aspirations for real income growth exceed productivity growth the faster will be the ensuing inflation. Second, some writers suggest that inflation results from the attempts of unions to improve or maintain their members' position in the league table of wages. If one union succeeds in improving its *relative* wage position, other unions seeking to restore or improve on the previous order of wage differentials will react by pushing for wage increases. Such a process will lead to leapfrogging as each union tries to improve its relative wage position, resulting in an inflationary wage–price spiral.

In the two examples of the non-monetarist view cited above, the common theme is that trade unions continually push for increases in money wages above the growth of productivity. Such wage increases feed into price increases, which in turn lead to further wage increases, and so on. If this is the case then it is important to ask why firms are willing to accede to such inflationary wage claims. The usual answer given to this question by adherents of the non-monetarist view is that the balance of power in negotiating wage increases has tended to move away from firms in favour of unions. Among the reasons put forward to explain this is that increased welfare benefits have enabled workers to resort to longer periods of strike action if their wage claims are not met. Furthermore, given the changing nature of the production process, firms are more willing to accede to claims for wage increases rather than resist and face 'costly' strike action. As production has become more capital intensive in many industries, firms have become more vulnerable to disruption of their whole production process by a small number of workers threatening strike action. In addition, greater foreign competition has meant that in the event of strike action output may be lost as customers turn to foreign markets. In these circumstances it is argued that it is less costly for firms to give in to wage claims than to face the severe costs that result from strike action, which disrupts the production process.

The non-monetarist view of inflation outlined above emphasizes rising wage costs as the initiating force of the inflationary process. Before considering the policy implications of this view, mention should also be made of the role of increases in other production costs in triggering higher prices. Some writers have drawn attention to rising costs of imported raw materials and fuels, which firms pass on to consumers in the form of higher prices. As domestic prices rise, unions demand money wage increases in order to maintain their members' real wages. As a result, an inflationary wage–price spiral develops, which is then accommodated by monetary expansion in order to prevent a rise in unemployment. In particular the two oil price hikes that occurred in 1973–74 and 1979 are highlighted as triggering the high rates of inflation experienced in many Western economies in the mid 1970s and early 1980s (see Table 9.3).

Policy implications

Let us now turn to examine the policy implications of this non-monetarist view of inflation. Given the belief that money wage increases or other increased costs of production initiate inflation, the introduction of a *permanent* prices and incomes policy is seen as the best way to control the inflationary spiral. Such a policy involves implementing a series of *direct controls* or rules that govern the extent that wages and prices can increase. For example, for wage increases not to be inflationary, money wage increases need to be controlled to ensure that they do not exceed the average increase in productivity. Past policy has traditionally focused on *wage control*, rather than income control, in part because other forms of income, such as dividends and interest, are much more difficult to influence.

Despite the simple logic behind the introduction of prices and incomes policy, such a policy involves a number of potentially important problems, and is not without its critics. In what follows we outline four main difficulties associated with prices and incomes policy. First, there are a number of problems involved with the implementation of both a wages and a prices policy. For example, both workers and firms may find ways of evading wage and price controls respectively. Second, a wages policy operates *outside* the market mechanism, and in consequence may result in a misallocation of resources. For example, firms in growth industries may find it difficult to expand production if they are not allowed to offer wage increases that are necessary to attract additional workers required. Third, if a prices and incomes policy is accompanied by excessive monetary expansion the policy will ultimately be doomed to failure. Unless the extreme view is taken that excess demand never affects wages and prices, excessive monetary expansion must result in inflationary pressures, which will inevitably lead to the breakdown of a policy seeking to control wage and price increases. Fourth, while a prices and incomes policy may succeed in moderating the rate of wage and price increase during the period in which it is operated, once the policy is relaxed, or breaks down, wages and prices may subsequently 'catch up' by increasing at a faster pace.

12.4 Concluding remarks

In this chapter we have presented two competing explanations of the cause of, and cure for, inflation. In the monetarist view the cause of inflation is excessive monetary expansion – a case of 'too much money chasing too few goods'. Since governments cause inflation they also have it within their power to reduce inflation through monetary contraction. In contrast, in the non-monetarist view, inflation is caused primarily by largely exogenous wage increases, which arise from various social pressures. In this view the best way to control inflation is through the introduction of prices and incomes policy. While our presentation has highlighted the difference between these two competing explanations it is important to note that some economists take an eclectic or compromise stance, suggesting that inflation can be caused by both excessive monetary expansion and various cost-push pressures. Indeed the consensus view is that while *sustained* inflation is not possible without excessive monetary expansion, *temporary* bouts of inflation can be attributed to non-monetary causes arising from the supply side of the economy.

Summary

◆ The debate over the causes of, and cures for, inflation can be divided between two main competing explanations involving monetarist and non-monetarist views.

◆ In the monetarist view the rate of inflation, in the long run, is determined by the rate of monetary expansion relative to the rate of growth of real output. While an inflation–unemployment trade-off exists in the short run, in the long run the Phillips curve is vertical at the natural rate of unemployment. The natural rate of unemployment is associated with a stable rate of inflation, which is itself determined by the rate of monetary expansion.

◆ In the short run monetary disinflation results in an increase in the level of unemployment above the natural rate. How much unemployment increases depends on whether the authorities pursue a policy of rapid or gradual monetary contraction and how quickly inflation expectations are revised downwards. *Prima facie* evidence from the UK and US economies in the early 1980s suggests that the unemployment costs of monetary disinflation are significant.

◆ Under a regime of fixed exchange rates inflation can be regarded as an international monetary phenomenon.

◆ In the non-monetarist view of inflation wages increases, which can occur independently of labour market conditions, are seen as the initiating force of an inflationary wage–price spiral. As the balance of power in negotiating wage increases has changed in favour of trade unions firms have become more willing to accede to claims for wage increases. Prices and incomes policy is seen as the best way to control the inflationary spiral according to proponents of the non-monetarist view.

◆ Some economists take an eclectic stance between the monetarist and non-monetarist views, and argue that inflation can be caused by both excessive monetary expansion and various cost-push pressures.

Key terms

◆ Quantity theory of money
◆ Phillips curve
◆ Inflation–unemployment trade-off
◆ Expectations-augmented Phillips curve
◆ Monetary disinflation
◆ Gradualism versus cold turkey
◆ Credibility
◆ Cost-push inflation

◆ Prices and incomes policy
◆ Eclecticism

■ Self-test questions

True (t) or false (f)

1. The quantity theory of money is a doctrine concerned with the relationship between the money supply and the price level.

2. Classical economists believed that, in the long run, a change in the money supply would lead to a proportionate change in output.

3. The Phillips curve depicts the relationship between inflation and unemployment.

4. Phillips found no evidence of a stable relationship between inflation and unemployment.

5. Friedman augmented the original Phillips curve with the expected rate of inflation as an additional variable determining the rate of change of money wages.

6. The short-run Phillips curve will shift upwards as individuals revise their expectations of inflation downwards.

7. Attempts to maintain unemployment below the natural rate of unemployment will result in a stable rate of inflation.

8. Gradualism is an approach to disinflation that involves a rapid and permanent reduction in the rate of monetary growth.

9. The output/employment costs of reducing inflation will be lower the faster economic agents revise their expectations of inflation downwards in the light of changed circumstances.

10. According to the new classical view, the unemployment costs associated with disinflation will be non-existent or negligible provided the policy of announced monetary contraction is credible.

11. In the non-monetarist view of inflation, rising wage costs are regarded as the initiating force of the inflationary process.

12. In the non-monetarist view of inflation, the chain of causation runs from changes in the money supply (and its rate of expansion) to changes in prices (and their rate of increase).

13. In the non-monetarist view of inflation, the introduction of a permanent prices and incomes policy is seen as the best way to control inflation.

14. Some economists argue that inflation can be caused by both excessive monetary expansion and various cost-push pressures.

Complete the following sentences by inserting the missing word(s)

1. 'Inflation is always and everwhere a ____ phenomenon.' (Friedman).

2. In the modern quantity theory of money, V and Y are held to be ____ and ____ in the long run.

3. The trade-off between inflation and unemployment is depicted by the ____.

4. In providing a theoretical rationale for the Phillips curve, Lipsey argued that money wages will rise when there is an ____.

5. Inflation, if caused by an excess demand for goods and services when the economy is at or above full employment, is referred to as ____.

6. The expectations-augmented Phillips curve analysis implies that there are a whole family of short-run Phillips curves, each associated with a different ____.

7. Monetarists argue that in the long run the Phillips curve is ____ at the ____ rate of unemployment.

8. In the non-monetarist view of inflation, wage increases can occur ____ of the state of demand and supply conditions in the labour market.

9. The non-monetarist view of inflation is also sometimes referred to as the ____ or ____ explanation of inflation.

10. In the non-monetarist view of inflation, the best way to control inflation is to introduce measures that establish guidelines or controls for wage and/or price increases. Such measures are referred to as ____.

11. Wages policy operates ____ the market mechanism and may result in a misallocation of resources.

12. ____ inflation is not possible without excessive monetary expansion.

Exercise

1. Fig. 12.3 illustrates the breakdown of any stable relationship between inflation and unemployment for the UK economy over the period 1970–96. In a similar fashion, using data presented in Tables 9.2 and 9.3, plot the relationship between inflation and unemployment for the US economy over the same period.

◼ Questions for discussion

◆ In what sense is inflation always and everywhere a monetary phenomenon?

◆ Is there a trade-off between inflation and unemployment?

◆ What are the main differences between Keynesians, monetarists and new classicists with respect to the expectations–augmented Phillips curve?

◆ What factors determine the unemployment costs of reducing inflation?

◆ What initiates inflation in the non-monetarist view?

◆ What are the main problems that may arise in implementing prices and incomes policy?

◆ How is the strong correlation between changes in the money supply and changes in prices explained in the monetarist and non-monetarist views of inflation?

◆ What are the main differences between the monetarist and non-monetarist views of inflation?

◼ Further reading

Dawson, G. *Inflation and Unemployment: Causes, Consequences and Cures* (Aldershot: Edward Elgar, 1992). A thoughtful, lucid and comprehensive guide to the issues of both inflation and unemployment.

Friedman, M. *Unemployment versus Inflation?* (London: Institute of Economic Affairs, 1975). A very clear and accessible evaluation of the Phillips curve written by the most famous living economist in the world.

Vane, H.R. and J.L. Thompson *An Introduction to Macroeconomic Policy* (4th ed.) (Hemel Hempstead: Harvester Wheatsheaf, 1993). Chapters 3 and 12 provide more detailed discussion of the role of money and monetary policy respectively.

■ Internet links

The Bank of England *Inflation Report* offers an assessment of inflation pressures and prospects for the UK economy. Summaries of the Inflation Report are available on the Internet at: **http://www.coi.gov.uk/coi/depts/GBE/GBE.html**

For other economies, inflation issues will also be subject to a watching brief by *their* central banks. Links to a large number of the world's central banks are provided by the Bank for International Settlements at: **http://www.bis.org/cbanks.htm**

Business Cycles: Causes and Control

CHAPTER 13

Key issues

▶ What are business cycles?

▶ What are the main theories that economists have put forward to explain business cycles?

▶ Can the authorities control business cycles?

Contents

13.1 Introduction

The purpose of this chapter is to examine the debate over the cause and control of business cycles. At the centre of the debate lie a number of fundamental questions, most notably:

- Is the economy inherently stable?
- What is the main source of shocks that affect the economy?
- How long does it take for the economy to self-equilibrate once subjected to a shock?
- Can the authorities intervene to reduce fluctuations in economic activity?

In attempting to answer these questions it is possible to identify the development of five main approaches within mainstream economics:

- the Keynesian approach
- the monetarist approach
- the new classical approach
- the real business cycle approach
- the political business cycle approach.

Before considering each of these approaches in turn we first need to describe the main features of business cycles.

13.2 Main features of business cycles

The **business cycle** (or trade cycle as it is sometimes called) can be defined as periodic fluctuations in the pattern of economic activity. While recurrent cycles in a number of aggregate economic series such as employment, consumption and investment can be observed, the business cycle is usually defined as deviations of output (real GDP) from its secular or long-term trend path. Fig. 13.1, which depicts a stylized business cycle using this definition, can be used to describe the main features of business cycles.

The *period* of the cycle, or length of time it takes to complete a full cycle, can be measured by the time gap between any two points at the same stage of the cycle. Reference to Fig. 13.1 reveals that it may be measured by the time between successive:

- troughs, e.g. A and E
- peaks, e.g. C and G
- upcrosses (of the trend), e.g. B and F
- downcrosses (of the trend), e.g. D and H.

Only in the hypothetical case of a *perfectly* regular cycle depicted in Fig. 13.1 will these alternative measures of the period of the cycle coincide. The *amplitude* of the cycle, which gives an indication of the severity of the cycle, may be measured by the total difference of successive peaks and troughs from the trend path of output, e.g. $c + e$ or $e + g$. Note that the amplitude of the cycle will remain constant only where the deviations of output above and below the trend are perfectly regular from one time period to the next, as depicted in Fig. 13.1. In practice, cycles will vary in both their timing and their amplitude.

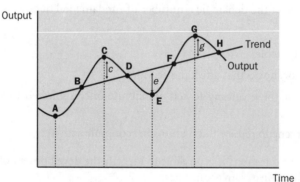

Fig. 13.1 A stylized business cycle.

Fig. 13.1 can also be used to distinguish between the different phases of the cycle. The *expansionary phase* refers to the movement from a trough or lower turning point (such as point A) to a successive peak or upper turning point (such as point C) in the cycle, while the *contractionary phase* refers to the movement from a peak (such as point C) to a successive trough (such as point E). The terms 'boom' and 'slump' are also often used in connection with the business cycle. These terms refer to the periods of rapid expansion (boom) and contraction (slump) before the movement

Business cycle: Involves fluctuations in aggregate economic activity; in particular movements in output around its trend.

The ups and downs of the business cycle are sometimes compared to a roller coaster

of output from the trend begins to flatten out near the top and bottom of the cycle respectively. Note also that with respect to the contractionary phase of the cycle the term 'recession' is generally used to describe a slowdown in the growth rate of output below the trend growth rate, while the term 'depression' is usually reserved for the most severe recessions.

Having described the main features of business cycles we are now in a position to consider alternative explanations of the cause of the cycle. Before considering the five main approaches to the cause and control of cycles it is important to stress that, unlike the stylized cycle depicted in Fig. 13.1, in practice business cycles are characterized by recurrent fluctuations in output/real GDP from its trend of varying length and amplitude. Furthermore, this pattern of behaviour is also observed in a number of other aggregate economic series. While controversy exists over the duration of cycles, economists usually have in mind short cycles of approximately 3–10 years in length when they refer to the business cycle.

13.3 The Keynesian approach

Keynesians believe that the economy is *inherently unstable* and is subject to erratic shocks, which cause it to fluctuate between periods of rapid expansion and contraction. The erratic shocks that cause these fluctuations in economic activity are attributed primarily to a change in autonomous expenditures, most notably investment. Furthermore, Keynesians contend that after the economy has been subjected to some disturbance, it can take a long time to return to the neighbourhood of full employment/potential output.

In the Keynesian approach the expansionary and contractionary phases of the business cycle are explained by the interaction of the multiplier process and the

Multiplier: The ratio of the change in income to a change in autonomous expenditure.

accelerator. Let us now examine why periods of economic expansion and contraction, once begun, tend to develop their own momentum. Starting from a position of less than full employment, suppose there occurs an increase in the amount of autonomous investment expenditure undertaken in the economy. An increase in investment expenditure will result in an increase in employment in firms that produce capital goods. Newly employed workers in capital goods industries will spend some of their income on consumer goods. The rise in demand for consumer goods will lead to increased employment in consumer goods industries and result in further rounds of expenditure. In consequence, an initial rise in autonomous investment produces a *more than* proportionate rise in income: a process known as the **multiplier** (see Box 13.1). The rise in income will *induce* a further increase in investment as new capital equipment is needed to meet the increased demand for output. Since the cost of capital equipment is usually *greater than* the value of its annual

Box 13.1

The multiplier: an algebraic derivation and numerical example

Consider first a hypothetical economy in which there is no government sector or international trade undertaken. The output, Y, of such an economy would be split between the production of consumption, C, and investment, I, goods:

$$Y = C + I \qquad (13.1)$$

Let us further assume that investment expenditure is autonomously determined, while consumer expenditure depends positively upon income. As discussed in Chapter 11, Section 11.3, the form of the consumption function can be represented by a simple linear equation:

$$C = \alpha + \beta Y \qquad (13.2)$$

If we substitute equation (13.2) into equation (13.1) we obtain

$$Y = \alpha + \beta Y + I \qquad (13.3)$$

Rearranging equation (13.3) and factorizing we obtain

$$Y(1 - \beta) = \alpha + I \qquad (13.4)$$

Finally dividing both sides of equation (13.4) by $(1 - \beta)$ we obtain

$$Y = \frac{1}{1 - \beta}(\alpha + I) \qquad (13.5)$$

Equation (13.5) determines the equilibrium level of income. The multiplier is given by

$$\frac{1}{1 - \beta}$$

and is equal to the reciprocal of 1 minus the marginal propensity to consume, β. Alternatively in this hypothetical economy,

with no government or foreign trade, the multiplier is equal to the reciprocal of the marginal propensity to save. For example, with a marginal propensity to consume of 0.8 (and by definition a marginal propensity to save of 0.2) the multiplier would be equal to 5. Following a change in investment, income will change (ΔY) by some multiple of the original change in investment expenditure, ΔI. For example, if investment expenditure increased by £2 million, income would increase by £10 million: that is $\Delta Y = \Delta I \times 5$.

The above analysis needs to be modified if we consider an economy with a government sector that engages in international trade. While an initial increase in investment spending will lead in exactly the same way to successive rounds of increased expenditure, some part of the *extra* income will be withdrawn, not only in the form of savings (marginal propensity to save), but also on import spending (marginal propensity to import) and taxes paid to the government (marginal tax rate). The multiplier will in consequence depend on the fraction of income withdrawn from the circular flow (see Chapter 10, Section 10.2) via savings, imports and taxes, and can be generalized as

$$\frac{1}{w}$$

For example, if the fraction of income withdrawn, w, from the circular flow is 0.5, then the multiplier will be equal to 2. Finally, it is interesting to note that the same multiplier process will apply following a change in exports or government expenditure.

output, new investment will be greater than the increase in output that brought it about. This latter phenomenon is referred to as the **accelerator** (see Box 13.2). The *interaction* of the multiplier process and the accelerator explains why periods of economic expansion or contraction will tend to develop their own momentum. Following an initial increase in autonomous investment, the rise in income due to the multiplier process will be reinforced by an increase in new investment, via the accelerator, which will in turn have a further multiplier effect on income and so on.

Although the interaction of the multiplier process and the accelerator can explain both the expansionary and contractionary phases of the cycle, the Keynesian approach requires the addition of *ceilings* and *floors* to account for turning points in the cycle. Periods of rapid expansion cannot continue indefinitely. As the economy approaches its full employment or potential output 'ceiling', the rate at which income/output increases will slow down because of resource constraints. As the rate of increase in income slows down this leads to a reduction in new investment, through the operation of the accelerator (see Box 13.2), which in turn leads to a fall in income, through the multiplier process, and so on. The cycle now passes into its contractionary phase as it moves from an upper turning point to a lower turning point. The movement of output from trend will eventually flatten out near the bottom of the cycle. The contractionary phase of the cycle will be reversed when the economy

Accelerator principle: The theory that the level of net investment depends on the change in output.

Capital–output ratio: The ratio of the amount of capital to the amount of output produced by it.

Box 13.2

The simple accelerator theory of investment: a numerical example

The relationship between output, Y, and the amount of capital, K, required to produce it can be described by the equation:

$$K = \alpha Y$$

The **capital-output ratio**, α, is also referred to as the accelerator coefficient. New investment, I, will be required to increase the capital stock, ΔK, to meet an increase in output/sales, ΔY:

$$I = \Delta K = \alpha \Delta Y$$

The following numerical example illustrates the 'simple' accelerator theory of investment:

1 Year	2 Output, Y	3 Required capital stock, K	4 Change in output, ΔY	5 Change in required capital stock, ΔK
1	£50	£150	£0	£0
2	£51	£153	£1	£3
3	£53	£159	£2	£6
4	£56	£168	£3	£9
5	£61	£183	£5	£15
6	£63	£189	£2	£6
7	£64	£192	£1	£3
8	£64	£192	£0	£0

Columns 2 and 3 show that the value of capital equipment is three times the value of annual output produced and sold. The capital–output ratio is fixed at 3:1. An increase in the production and sales of annual output requires new investment to increase the required capital stock. Columns 4 and 5 show that new investment is proportional to the change in output sales. For example, as sales of annual output increase by £5 from year 4 to year 5, new investment of £15 is required. Reference to columns 4 and 5 also reveals that as the increase in sales of annual output slows down in years 6 and 7, new investment falls.

hits a 'floor'. Sooner or later, as the existing capital equipment wears out, it will fall to a level where it needs replacing in order to produce the current sales/production of annual output. New investment for replacement orders will, through the interaction of the multiplier and accelerator, start the expansionary phase of the cycle again and so on.

What are the implications of the Keynesian approach for **stabilization policy** and the control of business cycles? Given the belief that the economy is inherently unstable and is not rapidly self-equilibrating, Keynesians stress the *need* to stabilize the economy. Furthermore, in their view, governments *can* and therefore *should* use **discretionary** aggregate demand (especially fiscal) policies to offset fluctuations in autonomous expenditures (such as private sector investment) and stabilize the economy (see Chapter 11, Section 11.3, and Chapter 14, Section 14.2).

13.4 The monetarist approach

In contrast to Keynesians, monetarists believe that the economy is *inherently stable*, unless disturbed by erratic monetary growth. Most of the actually observed instability is attributed to fluctuations in the money supply induced by the authorities. Furthermore, monetarists contend that, when subjected to some disturbance, the economy will return fairly rapidly to the neighbourhood of the natural level of output and employment. The dominant position assigned to monetary shocks in determining the course of economic activity is embodied within the quantity theory approach to macroeconomic analysis. In Chapter 12, Section 12.2, we discussed how the effects of a change in the rate of monetary expansion are divided between real and nominal variables in the monetarist view. You will recall that this involves a distinction between short-run and long-run effects. While an inflation–unemployment trade-off exists in the short run, in the long run the trade-off disappears. In the monetarist view, changes in the rate of monetary growth result in short-run fluctuations in output and employment around their natural levels. However, in the long run the trend rate of monetary growth only influences movements in the price level and other nominal variables.

The monetarist view that monetary shocks are the dominant cause of business cycles is based on two kinds of empirical evidence. The first kind of evidence is the empirically observed tendency for monetary changes to *precede* changes in economic activity. One of the earliest studies concerning the timing of monetary changes was undertaken by Milton Friedman in the late 1950s. In his study, Friedman compared rates of monetary growth with turning points in the level of economic activity. On the average of 18 non-war cycles in the USA since 1870, he found that peaks in the rate of change of the money supply had preceded peaks in the level of economic activity by an average of 16 months; and troughs in the rate of change of the money supply had preceded troughs in the level of economic activity by an average of 12 months. While accepting that timing evidence such as this is by no means decisive, monetarists argue that it is *suggestive* of an influence running from monetary changes to changes in economic activity.

The second kind of evidence to support the monetarist belief that monetary shocks are the dominant cause of business cycles was presented by Milton Friedman and Anna Schwartz in their influential study of the *Monetary History of the United*

Stabilization policies: Policies aimed at stabilizing output and employment at or near their full employment or natural levels by influencing the level of aggregate demand.

Discretionary policy: Arises when the authorities are free to vary the strength of fiscal and/or monetary policy in any way they see fit in order to achieve their desired objectives.

States, 1867–1960 published in 1963. In this work they found that the rate of growth of the money supply had been slower during cyclical contractions than during cyclical expansions in the level of economic activity. Indeed, the only times when there was an appreciable *absolute* fall in the money stock coincided with the six *major* US recessions identified over the period examined. Examining the specific historical circumstances surrounding events, Friedman and Schwartz concluded that the factors producing the absolute fall in the money supply during these major recessions were mainly independent of contemporary or prior changes in nominal income and prices. In other words, monetary changes were the *cause*, rather than the consequence, of all major American recessions.

For example, Friedman and Schwartz argue that the severity of the Great Depression, 1929–33, was due to a dramatic decline in the money stock. Between October 1929 and June 1933 the money stock in the USA fell by about a third. An initial mild decline in the money stock from 1929 to 1930 was, they argue, converted into a sharp decline by a wave of bank failures beginning late in 1930. Those bank failures produced a loss of faith on the part of both the public, in the banks' ability to redeem their deposits, and banks, in the public's willingness to maintain their deposits with them. In Friedman and Schwartz's interpretation of events, the Federal Reserve System could, by adopting alternative policies, have prevented the banking collapse and the dramatic fall in the money stock that coincided with the period of severe economic contraction.

Given the belief that the main cause of economic fluctuations is policy-induced changes in the rate of monetary growth, monetarists advocate that the authorities should pursue a monetary **rule**, rather than attempt to use monetary policy in a discretionary manner. Several rules have been suggested, the best known of which is Friedman's rule that the authorities should pursue a *fixed* rate of monetary growth in line with the long-run growth potential of the economy. Note that a monetary growth rule is not submitted as a panacea for fluctuations in the level of economic activity. While instability may arise from sources other than the mismanagement of the money supply, monetarists believe that by avoiding sharp swings in monetary policy the authorities can remove the main source of economic disturbances. Even when the economy is subjected to shocks that can be identified as arising from other sources, monetarists argue against the use of discretionary monetary policy to stabilize the economy.

Their fear that discretionary monetary policy could turn out to be destabilizing is based on a number of arguments including the length and variability of time lags associated with monetary policy, and the inflationary consequences of maintaining unemployment below the natural rate, a problem compounded by uncertainty over what precise value to attribute to the natural rate (see Chapter 12, Section 12.2, and Chapter 11, Sections 11.4 and 11.7). In the former case, monetarists argue that stabilization policy could in reality make economic fluctuations more severe because, by the time monetary policy changes affect economic activity, the underlying state of the economy may have changed making the measures adopted inappropriate (see Chapter 14, Section 14.3).

In summary, given their belief that the economy is inherently stable and is rapidly self-equilibrating, monetarists question the need to stabilize the economy via discretionary aggregate demand policies. Furthermore, even if there were a need, they tend to argue that discretionary aggregate demand policies cannot, and therefore should not, be used to stabilize the economy.

Rules: Involve prespecified guidelines that determine the conduct of policy.

13.5 The new classical approach

During the 1970s a new classical approach to explaining business cycles was developed. This approach derives largely from the influential work of Robert Lucas Jr of the University of Chicago, who was awarded the Nobel Prize in Economics in 1995. The theory developed by Lucas and other leading new classical economists is similar to the monetarist explanation in that business cycles are viewed as being primarily caused by monetary shocks. However, in the new classical approach it is *unanticipated monetary shocks* that are the dominant cause of business cycles. As we shall now discuss, in the new classical *equilibrium theory* economic agents respond optimally to the prices they perceive, and markets continuously clear.

Consider an economy that is initially in a position where output and employment are at their natural levels. Suppose the authorities *announce* that they intend to increase the money supply. According to the new classical approach, rational economic agents would take this information into account in forming their expectations and fully anticipate the effects of the announced increase in the money supply on the general price level. In this situation output and employment would remain unchanged at their natural levels. Now suppose that the authorities *surprise* economic agents by increasing the money supply without announcing their intentions. In this situation firms and workers with *incomplete information* would *misperceive* the resultant increase in the general price level as an increase in relative prices and respond by increasing the supply of output and labour respectively. A central element of this approach is the structure of information available to economic agents. To illustrate the role that incomplete information plays in the new classical approach we focus on the supply decisions of firms.

A firm's production plans are made on the basis of information on the price of its output. When a firm experiences a rise in the current market-clearing price of its output it must decide how to react to the rise. Where the price rise reflects a real increase in demand for its product the firm should respond to the increase in the current price of its output *relative* to the price of other goods, by increasing production. In contrast, where the change in price merely reflects a *nominal* increase in demand across all markets, producing a *general* increase in prices, no supply response is required. In other words, a firm is faced by what is referred to as a *signal extraction problem* in which its supply response depends on its distinguishing between relative and absolute price changes. In the new classical approach it is assumed that a firm has information both on the current price of its own goods and on prices in the limited number of markets in which it trades. However, information on the general price level for other markets becomes known only after a time lag. Suppose an unanticipated monetary shock occurs, which leads to an increase in the general price level and therefore in prices in all markets throughout the economy. In this situation individual firms with incomplete information will, it is argued, misperceive the increase in the current price of their goods as an increase in the relative price of their output and respond by increasing their output.

Why will output and employment remain above (or below) their natural levels for a succession of time periods? The fact that output and employment levels in any one time period are correlated with their preceding values can be explained by the inclusion of an accelerator mechanism in the analysis. As before, consider an economy that is initially in a position where output and employment are at their natural levels. Following an unanticipated monetary shock, which causes an unexpected rise in prices, firms will respond by increasing output. In a situation where no spare capacity exists, new investment will be required to increase the capital stock in order to produce extra output following the perceived real increase in demand for firms' output. Given the durability of capital goods, errors made in one time period will in consequence continue to affect output in subsequent time periods.

What are the implications of the new classical approach for stabilization policy and the control of business cycles? The new classical approach suggests that changes in monetary or fiscal policy can affect output and employment only if they are unanticipated. For example, suppose the money supply is determined by the authorities according to some rule, and the public *knows* the rule and bases its behaviour and decision-making on the anticipated growth of the money supply. In this situation the authorities will be unable to influence output and employment, even in the short run, by pursuing a systematic monetary policy. Only departures from a known monetary rule, resulting from policy errors made by the monetary authorities or unforeseen changes in policy, will have real effects because they are unanticipated. Any attempt to influence output and employment by random or non-systematic aggregate demand policies would, it is argued, only increase the variation of output and employment around their natural levels and increase uncertainty in the economy. Stabilization policy would be beneficial only in two situations. First, if the authorities had superior information, compared with the private sector, then they could exploit this information to influence the economy. Second, if the authorities were able to react to shocks more quickly than the private sector, there would be scope for discretionary intervention to stabilize the economy. Nevertheless, having noted these two possible situations, it is the case that the new classical approach, in line with the monetarist approach, maintains a non-intervention position with respect to macroeconomic policy.

The early 1980s witnessed the demise of the 'monetary surprise' version of the new classical approach to business cycles. A number of criticisms of the new classical approach were voiced, involving both theoretical and empirical failings. In the former case, for example, critics of the approach drew attention to the fact that both aggregate price level and money supply data are published within a short time lag and are readily available to economic agents. Given the availability of such data, they questioned how business cycles could be caused by supposed information gaps. In the latter case, the results of a number of empirical tests suggested that both unanticipated *and* anticipated money supply shocks have real output and employment effects. The depth of the recessions in both the USA and the UK in the early 1980s (see Table 9.2 and Chapter 12, Section 12.2), following announced monetary disinflation policies, provided further ammunition for the critics that systematic monetary policy has real effects. Criticisms of the monetary surprise version of the new classical approach led a number of economists who were sympathetic to the 'equilibrium' approach to develop a new version in which business cycles are predominantly caused by persistent real (supply-side) shocks, rather than by unanticipated monetary (demand-side) shocks, to the economy. This approach, which is largely associated with the work of American economists, most notably Finn Kydland of Carnegie Mellon University and Edward Prescott of the University of Minnesota, is commonly referred to as the real business cycle approach.

13.6 The real business cycle approach

According to proponents of the real business cycle approach, business cycles are driven by persistent *supply-side shocks* to the economy. These *random* supply-side shocks can originate from such sources as changes in raw material or energy prices, natural disasters, the development of new products, and the introduction of new techniques of production. Despite the wide variety of potential supply-side shocks most real business cycle models are based on the premise that these shocks mainly result from *large* random fluctuations in the rate of technological progress. In the real business cycle approach, observed fluctuations in output and employment are *equilibrium* phenomena and are the outcome of rational economic agents responding *optimally* to unavoidable changes in the economic environment. Furthermore, observed fluctuations in output are viewed as fluctuations in potential output, not as deviations of actual output from the trend. In the real business cycle approach the distinction between actual and potential output is abandoned. Given the belief that the economy is subjected to large random fluctuations in the rate of technological progress, the fluctuating path of output over time follows a so-called **random walk** and is nothing more than a continuously fluctuating full employment/potential output equilibrium. The approach therefore integrates business cycle theory with the theory of economic growth.

What are the implications of the real business cycle approach for stabilizing economic fluctuations? As fluctuations in output and employment are held to reflect the **Pareto-efficient** responses to a succession of supply-side shocks hitting the economy, the approach provides no role for monetary and fiscal policies for stabilization purposes. On the one hand, monetary factors are regarded as being irrelevant in explaining such fluctuations, with monetary policy having no influence on real variables. On the other hand, attempts to stabilize fluctuations in output and employment through fiscal policy would, it is claimed, reduce welfare because government taxation and spending policies would distort output and employment from the optimal amounts chosen by firms and workers.

The real business cycle approach to business cycles, and the implication that stabilization policy has no role to play, is *highly* controversial and has been subjected to a number of criticisms. Two examples will suffice. First, most economists question whether supply shocks are large enough or frequent enough to explain observed aggregate fluctuations in output and employment. With the exception of the two OPEC oil price shocks that occurred in 1973–74 and 1979, it is difficult to identify adverse supply shocks that are powerful enough to explain major recessions, especially episodes such as the Great Depression in the 1930s. The idea that major recessions are caused by technological *regress* strikes many critics as being particularly implausible. Second, real business cycle models assume wage and price flexibility so that markets continuously clear and equilibrium always prevails. Critics of the new classical approach have put forward a variety of reasons to explain wage and price stickiness that prevent continuous market clearing. For example, as discussed in Chapter 11, Section 11.6, new Keynesians have put forward various explanations of real wage rigidity in the labour market that can account for the existence of involuntary unemployment as an equilibrium phenomenon. Indeed, most economists believe that demand shocks, arising from changes in monetary policy, can have significant real effects in the short run, because of the nominal price and wage rigidities that characterize actual economies.

Random walk: The path of a variable whose changes over time are unpredictable.

Pareto efficiency: A situation in which it is impossible to make someone better off without making someone else worse off; also known as Pareto optimality.

13.7 The political business cycle approach

In the **political business cycle** approach business cycles are policy induced, and reflect the objectives of politicians either in terms of getting re-elected or in terms of ideological/partisan differences.

Consider first the possibility of a political business cycle resulting from a government manipulating the state of the economy just before an election, in order to improve its chances of being re-elected. This particular approach, which is associated with the work of William Nordhaus in the mid-1970s, is based on the beliefs that the main goal of political parties is winning the next election, and that the state of the economy has a strong influence on voters. As an election approaches, the government pursues expansionary policies (for example increasing its expenditure and/or reducing taxes) in order to reduce unemployment and gain votes. Once it is re-elected contractionary policies will be required to dampen down inflationary pressures, which arise as output rises above its full employment/potential level. As inflation subsides and unemployment increases, the stage is set once again for the government to engineer expansionary policies to reduce unemployment and gain popularity before the next election. Changes in macroeconomic policy produce a political business cycle.

Although this approach is intuitively appealing, it suffers from a number of weaknesses. Three examples will suffice. First, the approach would seem to be more appropriate for countries with fixed election dates, such as the USA, rather than countries where election dates are variable, such as the UK. Second, the approach implies that in a two-party system political parties will offer similar policies to attract voters at the centre of the political spectrum (so-called median voters) and ignores the fact that political parties are likely to have ideological or partisan aims in addition to that of obtaining power. Third, the approach implies that voters are myopic or shortsighted and do not learn from past experience that politicians generate a pre-election boom, followed by a post-election slump.

Since the mid-1980s interest in the political business cycle approach has been rekindled, most notably by the work of Alberto Alesina of Harvard University. Alesina has put forward a partisan model in which political parties do not pursue a simple vote-maximizing strategy, and differ in their priorities and preferences. In particular, right-wing parties are assumed to attach more importance to keeping inflation in check than left-wing parties, who care more about unemployment. Voters know that given such priorities parties will pursue different policies when they are in office. In this model, what drives the cycle is the fact that election results are unknown before they occur. Wage contracts set before an election will be determined by the rate of inflation expected after the election. The expected rate of inflation will depend on which party is expected to form the next government. For example, if wage negotiators expect that a left-wing government currently in office will be re-elected, they will form contracts that have a high expected rate of inflation built into them. If a right-wing party then gains office it will tighten monetary policy in order to reduce inflation. In a situation where contracts cannot be instantly re-negotiated unemployment will rise. The opposite sequence of events would follow if a right-wing government in office was replaced by a left-wing party. In this case, after the election a left-wing government would expand the economy and reduce unemployment. In both cases, once inflation expectations had adjusted to the new situation, at a later stage in the government's term of office output and employment

Political business cycle: Entails fluctuations in the level of output and employment caused by the manipulation of the economy for electoral gains or due to partisan differences.

would return to their natural levels (see the discussion of the expectations-augmented Phillips curve in Chapter 12, Section 12.2). Unlike Nordhaus's political business cycle model, which predicts a pre-election boom and a post-election slump, Alesina's partisan model predicts a slump after a change in policy regime to a right-wing government and a boom after a change of regime to a left-wing government.

The political business cycle approach provides another reason for those economists who favour giving central banks greater independence, enabling monetary policy to be conducted free from consideration of electoral gain and partisan influences (see Chapter 14, Box 14.1).

13.8 Concluding remarks

In this chapter we have outlined five main approaches to the business cycle. Four of these approaches suggest that cycles are primarily caused by demand shocks. In the Keynesian approach the main cause of cycles is changes in autonomous expenditures. Monetarists emphasize changes in the rate of monetary growth as the main source of cycles, while the new classical approach highlights unanticipated monetary shocks as the dominant cause of cycles. The political business cycle approach ascribes the existence of cycles to government macroeconomic policy. In contrast to these approaches proponents of the real business cycle approach suggest that business cycles are primarily caused by supply shocks. While our presentation has highlighted the differences between these competing explanations it is important to remember that many economists take an eclectic stance, recognizing that no one key causal factor can account for all business cycles. Some cycles will be triggered by demand shocks, others by supply shocks. On some occasions demand and supply shocks will *both* be important. Whether governments cause cycles and what policies they should pursue to reduce fluctuations in economic activity remain highly controversial issues. In the next chapter we turn to consider more fully the issue of stabilizing the economy.

Summary

◆ The business cycle can be defined as deviations in output from trend. Cycles that vary in both their timing and their amplitude involve expansionary and contractionary phases, and upper and lower turning points.

◆ In the Keynesian approach the main cause of business cycles is fluctuations in autonomous expenditures. Expansionary and contractionary phases are explained through the interaction of the multiplier process and the accelerator, while ceilings and floors account for turning points in the cycle. Keynesians believe that governments need to, can and therefore should stabilize the economy.

◆ In the monetarist approach the main cause of business cycles is held to be monetary actions, which result in changes in the rate of growth of the money supply. Monetarists argue that, by pursuing a monetary growth rate rule, the authorities can remove the major source of economic disturbances.

◆ In the new classical approach unanticipated monetary shocks are the dominant cause of business cycles. Surprised by such shocks economic agents, with incomplete information, mistake general price changes for relative price changes and react by changing the supply of output and labour. Governments can influence output and employment only by pursuing random or non-systematic monetary policy. New classicists claim that such policy will, however, only increase the variation of output and employment around their natural levels, and increase uncertainty in the economy. In line with the monetarist approach, the new classical approach maintains a non-interventionist position with respect to macroeconomic policy.

◆ In the real business cycle approach business cycles are primarily caused by persistent real supply shocks to the economy, mainly large random fluctuations in the rate of technological progress. Fluctuations in output and employment are held to reflect the optimal response of economic agents to such shocks. Because cycles are due to a succession of supply shocks hitting the economy, there is no role for the government to stabilize fluctuations in output and employment through aggregate demand policies.

◆ The political business cycle approach suggests that cycles are policy induced and reflect the objectives of politicians either in terms of getting re-elected or in terms of partisan differences.

◆ No one key factor can account for all business cycles. On some occasions demand and supply shocks will both be important.

Key terms

◆ The period of the cycle
◆ The amplitude of the cycle
◆ Expansionary and contractionary phases
◆ Multiplier process
◆ Accelerator
◆ Multiplier–accelerator interaction
◆ Ceilings and floors
◆ Monetary shocks
◆ Monetary rule
◆ Unanticipated monetary shocks
◆ Signal extraction problem
◆ Real shocks
◆ Politically induced cycles
◆ Partisan priorities and preferences

Self-test questions

True (t) or false (f)

1. The business cycle entails recurrent cycles in a number of aggregate economic series.

2. Business cycles will vary both in their timing and in their amplitude.

3. In the Keynesian approach monetary shocks are the dominant cause of business cycles.

4. Keynesians contend that the economy will rapidly self-equilibrate after being subjected to some disturbance.

5. In the monetarist approach the main cause of business cycles is fluctuations in autonomous expenditures.

6. Monetarists argue against the use of discretionary monetary policy to control the business cycle.

7. In the new classical approach supply-side shocks are the dominant cause of business cycles.

8. The new classical approach maintains a non-interventionist position with respect to macroeconomic policy.

9. Proponents of the real business cycle approach make a distinction between actual and potential output, acknowledging that output fluctuates around its long-term trend.

10. According to the real business cycle approach business cycles are primarily caused by demand shocks.

11. According to the political business cycle approach business cycles are caused by government manipulation of the economy for electoral gains or because of partisan differences.

Complete the following sentences by inserting the missing word(s)

1. The business cycle can be defined as deviations of output (real GDP) from its ____.

2. The movement from a trough to a successive peak is referred to as the ____ of the cycle, while the movement from a peak to a successive trough is referred to as the ____ of the cycle.

3. In the Keynesian approach the expansionary and contractionary phases of the business cycle are explained by the interaction of the ____ and the ____.

4. The process whereby an increase in autonomous expenditure produces a more than proportionate increase in income is known as the ____.

5. In the monetarist approach ____ are the dominant cause of business cycles.

6. Friedman has advocated that the authorities pursue a ____ rate of monetary growth in line with the long-run growth potential of the economy.

7. The new classical approach to explaining business cycles derives largely from the influential work of ____.

8. In the new classical approach ____ monetary shocks are the main cause of business cycles.

9. Proponents of the real business cycle approach argue that business cycles are driven by persistent ____ to the economy.

10. The real business cycle approach is largely associated with the work of two American economists, namely ____ and ____.

11. Nordhaus's political business cycle model predicts a pre-election ____ and a post-election ____.

▪ Questions for discussion

◆ What is the main cause of business cycles in the Keynesian approach?

◆ How are the expansionary and contractionary phases of the business cycle explained in the Keynesian approach?

◆ What is the main cause of business cycles in the monetarist approach?

◆ Compare and contrast the main policy implications of the Keynesian and monetarist approaches for the control of business cycles.

◆ What is the main cause of business cycles in the new classical approach?

◆ What role does incomplete information play in the new classical approach to explaining business cycles?

◆ What is the main cause of business cycles in the real business cycle approach?

◆ What role is there for stabilization policy in the new classical and real business cycle approaches?

◆ What is the main cause of business cycles in the political business cycle approach?

■ Further reading

Morgan, B. and J.R. Shackleton 'The ups and downs of business cycle theory' in Shackleton, J.R. (ed.) *New Thinking in Economics* (Aldershot: Edward Elgar, 1990). Provides a deftly written survey of business cycle theory.

Friedman, M. *The Counter-Revolution in Monetary Theory* (London: Institute of Economic Affairs, 1970). An accessible non-technical discussion, which places the monetarist counter-revolution in historical perspective, and describes the central propositions of monetarism.

■ Internet links

The Bank of England's Web site offers a wealth of information and commentary on the performance of the British economy. The site can be found at: **http://www.bankofengland.co.uk/**

Stabilizing the Economy

Key issues

▶ Why do economists disagree over the issue of whether the authorities need
to, can and should stabilize the economy?

▶ Should macroeconomic policy be operated at the discretion of the authorities
or on the basis of rules?

▶ What are the main problems encountered by policymakers in implementing
stabilization policy?

14.1 Introduction

In the preceding three chapters we have examined the debate over the causes of and
appropriate responses to unemployment, inflation, and the business cycle. Given the
nature of our discussion, it should be evident that there is much controversy
between macroeconomists over these important issues. The purpose of this present
chapter is to draw together a number of themes addressed in Chapters 11–13 and to
consider the ongoing debate over stabilization policy aimed at keeping output and
employment at or near their full employment or natural levels by influencing the
level of aggregate demand. In particular, we shall focus on the controversy of
whether, in their conduct of macroeconomic policy, the authorities should be given
discretion to change the strength of fiscal and monetary policy in the light of particular
economic circumstances at the time, or whether monetary and fiscal policy should
be conducted by rules.

14.2 Discretionary policy and policy rules

Before proceeding to discuss alternative views on stabilization policy we need first to
highlight the difference between discretionary policy and policy rules.

Discretionary policy takes place where the authorities are given the *freedom* to
vary the strength of fiscal and/or monetary policy in any way they see fit in order to
achieve their desired objectives. In monitoring the course of the economy, policy
may be changed either: (i) frequently in an attempt to maintain output and employ-

ment at, or near, their full employment or natural levels – so-called *fine tuning*; or (ii) occasionally in response to a large divergence in output and employment from their full employment or natural levels – so-called *rough tuning*. In contrast, where policy is conducted by rules, the authorities are *committed* to follow a *prespecified* rule that determines the conduct of fiscal and/or monetary policy.

Rules themselves may or may not be linked to changes in economic conditions. With a **passive policy rule** the prespecified rule for the policy instrument is not linked to prevailing economic circumstances. An example of a passive monetary policy rule is one where the authorities are committed to pursue a *constant* rate of monetary growth. Whatever the state of the economy the authorities would pursue a given fixed rate of monetary growth of say 3 per cent per annum. An **activist policy rule**, however, involves feedback from the state of the economy to the policy instrument. An example of an activist monetary policy rule would be one where the money supply is targeted to grow at a rate of say 3 per cent per annum if unemployment is 6 per cent, but monetary growth is automatically increased (or decreased) by 1 per cent per annum for every 1 per cent by which unemployment rises above (or falls below) 6 per cent. If unemployment rose to 8 per cent, monetary growth would be increased to 5 per cent. Conversely, if unemployment fell to 4 per cent, monetary growth would be reduced to 1 per cent. Both active and passive policy rules tie the hands of the authorities to pursue prespecified rules without leaving them any discretion to change the strength of fiscal and/or monetary policy.

As we shall now go on to discuss, the debate over stabilization policy critically depends on whether one views the economy as being inherently unstable, and subject to frequent shocks, which lead to inefficient fluctuations in output, employment and inflation; or whether one views the economy as being naturally stable. Broadly speaking, those economists who subscribe to the former view emphasize the need for stabilization policy, and argue that the authorities should be given discretion to use fiscal and monetary policy to offset shocks and keep output and employment close to their full employment or natural levels. Other economists who subscribe to the latter view tend to question the need for stabilization policy and favour rules over discretion, blaming ill-conceived policies for inefficient departures of output and employment from their natural levels experienced from time to time.

14.3 The Keynesian view

In the *orthodox* Keynesian view, the economy is *inherently unstable*, experiencing frequent shocks, which lead to inefficient fluctuations in output, employment and inflation. The main source of the disturbances that cause these fluctuations in economic activity is attributed to aggregate demand shocks. Furthermore, orthodox Keynesians contend that, after being subjected to such disturbances, the economy will not rapidly self-equilibrate and will take a long time to return to the neighbourhood of full employment output. Given these beliefs, orthodox Keynesians stress the need for stabilization policy, and argue that the authorities *can* and therefore *should* use discretionary fiscal and monetary policies to stabilize the economy.

Using the Keynesian model first introduced in Chapter 11, Section 11.3, we can illustrate how the authorities would, via discretionary policy activism, seek to stimulate the economy after it had been subjected to some contractionary aggregate demand shock and to deflate the economy when it was overheating. In Fig. 14.1 we

Passive policy rule: A prespecified rule for the conduct of policy not linked to prevailing economic circumstances

Activist policy rule: A prespecified rule for the conduct of policy that is linked to the state of the economy; also known as a feedback rule.

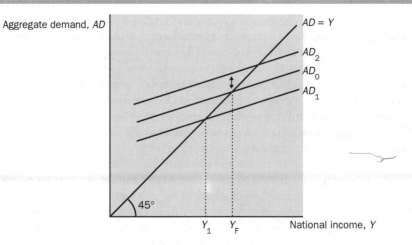

Fig. 14.1 Stabilization policy in the orthodox Keynesian model.

assume that the economy is initially operating at its full employment level of output, Y_F. Following some contractionary aggregate demand shock, which shifts the aggregate demand curve from AD_0 to AD_1, the economy could, if left to its own devices, come to rest below full employment at Y_1 for a prolonged period of time. Orthodox Keynesians argue that by taking appropriate corrective action (that is, expansionary fiscal and/or monetary policy), which offsets the contractionary shock and shifts the aggregate demand curve back from AD_1 to AD_0, the authorities can stabilize the economy at or close to its full employment level. Alternatively, the economy might be subjected to an expansionary aggregate demand shock, which shifts the aggregate demand curve from AD_0 to AD_2, causing the economy to overheat as aggregate demand exceeds national income at the full employment level of output. The resulting *inflationary gap*, indicated by the arrows in Fig. 14.1, would require deflationary fiscal and/or monetary policy to close the gap and offset the expansionary shock, shifting the aggregate demand curve back from AD_2 to AD_0.

In both situations analysed above, it is clearly important that the authorities exert the *correct dosage* of stimulus or restraint. Consider for example the former case of the economy experiencing a contractionary aggregate demand shock. If the authorities fail to stimulate aggregate demand sufficiently the economy will come to rest below its full employment equilibrium. In contrast, if the authorities overstimulate aggregate demand beyond that required to establish full employment, then an inflationary gap will ensue. While acknowledging this potential problem, orthodox Keynesians believe that the authorities can and therefore should use discretionary fiscal and monetary policies to stabilize the economy at or close to their full employment levels. Indeed, in the 1950s and 1960s, when Keynesian economics was the conventional wisdom, many Western governments attempted to fine-tune their economies using discretionary aggregate demand policies. However, by the late 1960s/early 1970s many Western governments began to experience a steady rise in unemployment and inflation (see Tables 9.2 and 9.3), leading some economists to question the ability of conventional Keynesian economics to deal with the problem of so-called stagflation.

Before discussing subsequent developments associated with monetarist and new classical views, which provide a critique of discretionary policy activism involving fine tuning, we need to mention the views of *new* Keynesians. New Keynesians accept that the economy is not as unstable as once believed. Nevertheless they argue that the economy does experience shocks, from both the demand side *and* the supply side, which cause undesirable and inefficient economic fluctuations. In line with orthodox Keynesians they therefore recognize the need for stabilization policy, and believe that the authorities can and therefore should use discretionary aggregate demand policies to stabilize the economy. However, unlike orthodox Keynesians, new Keynesians do not support what they regard as over-ambitious attempts to fine-tune the macroeconomy, and have instead championed the case for rough tuning. In particular, as discussed in Chapter 11, Section 11.6, hysteresis effects provide new Keynesians with a strong case that the authorities should stimulate aggregate demand during a prolonged recession.

14.4 The monetarist view

During the late 1960s and early 1970s a monetarist counter-revolution took place (most notably in the USA), which led to an ongoing debate over stabilization policy. As outlined in Chapter 13, Section 13.4, monetarists, in stark contrast to Keynesians, believe that the economy is *inherently stable*, unless disturbed by erratic monetary growth. Furthermore they contend that, when subjected to some disturbance, the economy is rapidly self-equilibrating, and will return fairly quickly to the neighbourhood of the natural level of output and employment. Given these beliefs monetarists question the need for stabilization policy involving the management of aggregate demand. Even if there were a need, they argue that discretionary fiscal and monetary policies cannot, and therefore should not, be used to stabilize the economy. We now consider more fully the monetarist case against discretionary policy activism.

While monetarists accept that fiscal policy can be used to influence the level of output and employment in the short run, they argue that in the long run fiscal expansion (for example an increase in government expenditure) will replace or crowd out components of private sector expenditure so that real income remains unchanged at its natural level. **Crowding out** will be complete where private sector expenditure is reduced by the same amount that government expenditure is increased, so that the long-run government expenditure multiplier is zero. The monetarist view contrasts with the Keynesian view in which an increase in government expenditure will, through the multiplier process (see Box 13.1), lead to an increase in income by some multiple of the original change in government expenditure.

A number of reasons have been put forward to explain why crowding out may occur. Two examples will suffice. First, crowding out may arise as a direct result of the way in which an increase in government expenditure is financed: a so-called financing effect. Consider the case where an increase in government expenditure is financed by increased sales of government bonds. In order to induce the public to buy more government bonds, the rate of interest on new bond issues will have to increase. When the cost of borrowing funds rises, the level of private sector investment will be reduced as firms cancel investment projects that they had planned to finance by borrowing before interest rates increased. Second, crowding out may occur in an open economy operating under a regime of fixed exchange rates (see Chapter 16, Section 16.5) because of a price level effect. If the domestic price level

Crowding out: Entails the reduction in private sector expenditure that results following an increase in government expenditure.

Permanent income: The average income that people expect to receive over a period of years in the future; also known as normal income and average expected income.

increases following an increase in government expenditure and the exchange rate is fixed, exports will become less competitive with foreign-produced goods, while imports will become more competitive with domestically produced goods (see Chapter 16, Section 16.2). In other words, an increase in government expenditure will result in a fall in exports and an increase in imports.

In discussing fiscal policy we have so far considered only why monetarists typically argue that an increase in government expenditure will in the long run replace or crowd out some components of private-sector expenditure. We next need to consider why monetarists question the likely impact of tax changes as a stabilization instrument. In contrast to the Keynesian view, in which consumption expenditure depends on current income, Milton Friedman has argued that consumption spending depends on **permanent** (long-run average) **income** that people expect to receive. Tax changes that people believe will be in effect for only a year or two will have only a negligible effect on permanent income. In consequence, temporary tax changes will have only a small effect on consumption, and are useless for stabilization purposes. Finally, turning to monetary policy, as discussed in Chapter 12, Section 12.2, monetarists argue that discretionary monetary policy can also influence output and employment, but again only in the short run. In the long run, monetary policy can determine only nominal variables and their rates of change.

If both fiscal and monetary policy can influence output and employment in the short run, why are monetarists against discretionary policy activism? In summary, monetarists argue that because of numerous problems associated with stabilization policy (including time lags, forecasting errors, and uncertainty) the authorities should refrain from attempting to stabilize the economy in the short run, by discretionary aggregate demand management policies, for fear they may do more harm than good.

We first examine how, given the existence of time lags, it is possible for discretionary policy activism to be destabilizing. In discussing time lags in the conduct of stabilization policy it is customary to divide the lags into an inside lag and an outside lag. The *inside lag* is the period of time that it takes to initiate a policy change, such as a tax cut or an increase in the money supply. The *outside lag* is the time between an initiated policy change and its influence on the economy.

The inside lag can be divided into two components: a recognition lag, and an administrative lag. The *recognition lag* is the time lag between when a disturbance or shock affects the economy and when the authorities recognize that some kind of corrective action is needed. This lag will be the same for both fiscal and monetary policy. The *administrative lag* is the time lag between recognizing that action is required, and actually planning and implementing the corrective policies. Unlike the recognition lag, the administrative lag will not be the same for fiscal and monetary policy. In the USA, the administrative lag associated with fiscal policy is longer than that for monetary policy. While monetary policy actions can be implemented fairly swiftly by the Federal Reserve System, most fiscal policy changes require the approval of both Houses of Congress, and the legislative process involved can sometimes be painfully slow. For example, in the 1960s an income tax cut first proposed in 1962 by President Kennedy, in order to stimulate the American economy, was not actually implemented until 1964. In contrast, in the UK, the legislative process required to implement fiscal policy changes is much quicker as long as the government in office enjoys a parliamentary majority.

Once a policy change has been implemented we move on to the outside lag.

Unlike the inside lag, the outside lag is a *distributed* lag in that the effects of a policy change on the economy will be spread out over time. A policy change such as a tax cut or a change in the money supply will not lead to an immediate increase in spending and employment in the economy, and its effects are likely to continue over several periods. The length of the outside lag will vary depending on a number of factors, including the state of the economy at the time when the policy change is implemented, the way the private sector responds to the policy change, and whether fiscal or monetary policy changes are implemented. In the latter case, for example, it is generally accepted that monetary policy has a relatively long outside lag. Monetary policy works through interest rate changes, which in turn influence investment spending in the economy. Given that many firms will plan new investment far in advance, their response to interest rate changes is likely to be slow, and may take many months. Because of the length of the inside lag associated with fiscal policy (especially in the USA) and the length and variability of the outside lag associated with monetary policy (see Chapter 13, Section 13.4), monetarists argue that any attempt to use discretionary fiscal and/or monetary policy to stabilize the economy could do more harm than good. This possibility is illustrated in Fig. 14.2.

Fig. 14.2 depicts a situation where output is initially at its full employment or natural level, $\bar{Y}$. At time t_0, a disturbance affects the economy, which reduces output below $\bar{Y}$. However, given the inside lag, it is not until time t_1 that the authorities actually implement an expansionary policy. There then follows a further outside time lag before the initiated policy change starts to affect the economy at time t_2 and thereafter. Without discretionary stabilization policy output would return to $\bar{Y}$ by time t_3. With discretionary stabilization policy output rises above its full employment/natural level. At time t_4 the authorities initiate contractionary policy, which again only begins to affect the economy after a further period of time has elapsed. With stabilization policy output now falls below its full employment/natural level at time t_5 and thereafter. It can be seen that, in this example, because of time lags stabilization policy has actually destabilized the economy, resulting in more severe fluctuations in output than would otherwise have occurred if the authorities had not engaged in activist discretionary policy intervention.

In addition to the problems raised by time lags, uncertainty over both the size of policy multipliers associated with fiscal and monetary policy in the short run and what precise value to attribute to the natural rate of unemployment makes it possible

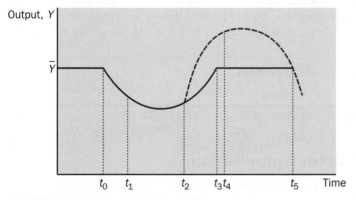

Fig. 14.2 Time lags and stabilization policy.

for discretionary policy activism to be destabilizing. In the latter case, given the belief that the long-run Phillips curve is vertical, any attempt to maintain unemployment below the natural rate by discretionary aggregate demand policies will result in accelerating inflation (see Chapter 12, Section 12.2). In consequence, monetarists advocate that discretionary aggregate demand policies should be replaced by some form of monetary rule. Finally, it is interesting to note that, in addition, some monetarists justify their position that policy is best conducted by rules rather than discretion for fear that opportunistic politicians cannot be trusted not to use activist discretionary policy to manipulate the economy for political gain.

14.5 The new classical view

The 1970s witnessed the development of the new classical approach to macro-economics, an approach that cast further doubt on whether traditional Keynesian aggregate demand policies can be used to improve overall economic performance and stabilize the economy.

Underlying the new classical model of the macroeconomy is the joint acceptance of three main tenets:

- rational expectations
- the assumption that all markets in the economy continuously clear
- the Lucas surprise supply function.

Rational expectations assumes that agents make the best use of all available in-formation – including information on current and prospective policies – to form their forecasts or expectations of the future value of a variable. For example, if economic agents believe that the rate of inflation is determined by the rate of mon-etary expansion then they will make the best use of all publicly available information on rates of monetary expansion in forming their expectations of future rates of in-flation. The Lucas surprise supply function states that output only deviates from its natural level in response to deviations of the actual price level from its expected value. As discussed in Chapter 13, Section 13.5, in the absence of price surprises, which arise from incomplete information, output will remain at its natural level. The combination of the rational expectations hypothesis, the assumption of continuous market clearing and the Lucas surprise function produces a number of important implications for macroeconomic policy. In what follows we outline three insights associated with the new classical approach, which are relevant to the debate over stabilization policy:

- the policy ineffectiveness proposition
- the time inconsistency of discretionary policy
- the Lucas critique of traditional methods of policy evaluation.

Rational expectations approach: Assumes that people make the best use of all available information to forecast the future.

Policy ineffectiveness proposition

In line with monetarists, new classicists believe that the economy is inherently stable, and that when subjected to some disturbance will quickly return to its natural level of output and employment. While the main source of disturbances is attributed to monetary shocks in both approaches, according to the new classical view only *unanticipated* monetary shocks affect output and employment, and then only in the short run (see Chapter 13, Section 13.5). Furthermore, rational economic agents will react very quickly to aggregate demand shocks, returning the economy to its long-run equilibrium in a very short period of time. Not only is stabilization policy totally unnecessary but the authorities will also be unable to influence output and employment, even in the short run, by pursuing systematic aggregate demand policies. According to the so-called **policy ineffectiveness** proposition, which was first put forward in the mid-1970s by Thomas Sargent and Neil Wallace, anticipated monetary policy will be completely ineffective. The proposition implies that only random or arbitrary policy actions undertaken by the authorities have real effects, because they cannot be anticipated by rational economic agents. However, given that such actions would only increase the variation of output and employment around their natural levels and increase uncertainty in the economy, the policy ineffectiveness proposition provides new classicists with a strong argument against discretionary policy activism and in favour of rules.

Time inconsistency

In the mid-1970s the influential work of Finn Kydland and Edward Prescott on the problem of time inconsistency of policy provided another argument in the case for fixed rules over discretion. In some situations, in order to influence the expectations of private decision-makers, the authorities may announce that they intend to pursue a particular policy or course of action. However, once private decision-makers have reacted to the announced policy, the authorities may then be tempted to renege on their previous announcement. **Time inconsistency** describes a situation in which an announced policy that is optimal today may not remain optimal in subsequent periods once private decision-makers have adjusted their behaviour accordingly. The problem of time inconsistency can be illustrated with a simple example. To encourage students to work hard a lecturer announces that his course will end with a hard exam. After students have responded by studying hard and learning the course material, the lecturer may then be tempted to cancel the exam in order to avoid marking the exam scripts.

In macroeconomics one of the best examples of the problem of time inconsistency concerns the Phillips curve trade-off between inflation and unemployment. In Chapter 12, Section 12.2, we discussed how the expectations-augmented Phillips curve implies that while the long-run Phillips curve is vertical at the natural rate of unemployment, there exists a whole family of short-run Phillips curves, each associated with a different expected rate of inflation. For example, as the expected rate of inflation decreases, the short-run Phillips curve will shift downwards so that, for any given rate of unemployment, inflation will be lower the lower are expectations of inflation.

In Fig. 14.3 we assume that the economy is initially operating at point A with a 4 per cent rate of inflation and unemployment at its natural rate, U_N. Now suppose that the authorities want to reduce inflation to zero per cent and move to point B on the long-run Phillips curve (*LRPC*). The authorities announce a policy of monetary contraction in order to reduce expectations of inflation held by workers and firms.

Policy ineffectiveness: The proposition that anticipated changes in monetary policy have no effect on output and employment.

Time inconsistency: Involves the temptation of policy-makers to deviate from a previously announced policy once private decision-makers have adjusted their behaviour to the announced policy.

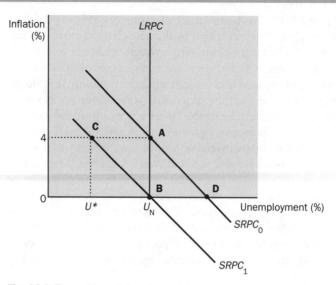

Fig. 14.3 The problem of time inconsistency.

However, once workers and firms have reduced their inflation expectations, shifting the short-run Phillips curve downwards from $SRPC_0$ to $SRPC_1$, the authorities will have an incentive to renege or cheat on their previously announced policy and implement expansionary monetary policy in order to reduce unemployment. By exercising their discretionary powers and engaging in monetary stimulus the authorities can create an 'inflation surprise' and move to point C on $SRPC_1$. Point C is unsustainable, however, since unemployment, U^*, is below its natural rate, U_N, and the actual rate of inflation is greater than expected. As rational economic agents revise their inflation expectations upwards, shifting the short-run Phillips curve back from $SRPC_1$ to $SRPC_0$, the economy will return to point A on the $LRPC$ with an *inflationary bias*.

In situations where the authorities have such discretionary powers and have in consequence an incentive to cheat, the credibility of announced policies will be significantly weakened. Aware that the authorities may be inconsistent over time, workers and firms are likely to distrust policy announcements. In circumstances where the announced policy of monetary contraction lacks credibility, agents will not revise their inflation expectations downwards. If the authorities actually carry out their announced policy, unemployment will rise above the natural rate: that is, a movement along $SRPC_0$ from point A to D.

The implication of the analysis we have discussed is that economic performance may be improved if discretionary powers are taken away from the authorities, and the authorities make a commitment to pursue a fixed monetary growth rate rule. In this case, policy will be seen to be credible, and agents will reduce their inflation expectations downwards, making possible a policy of lower inflation without higher unemployment. The inflationary bias present when the authorities are given discretion in the way they conduct monetary policy has led some economists to advocate giving the responsibility for anti-inflation policy to a central bank that is *independent* from the government. In Box 14.1 we discuss the relationship between central bank independence and inflation performance.

Central bank independence and inflation performance

A number of economists have undertaken research that has examined the relationship between central bank independence and macroeconomic performance in advanced industrial countries for the period from the 1950s to the late 1980s. These studies have uncovered two main results. First, there appears to be no relationship between central bank independence and real macroeconomic performance, such as average unemployment and real output growth. Second, there is a striking inverse relationship between central bank independence and inflation performance. More central bank independence is strongly associated with lower, and more stable, inflation. Countries with more independent central banks – such as the USA, Switzerland, and Germany – have experienced the lowest average inflation. In contrast, countries with less central bank independence – such as Spain, Italy and New Zealand – have experienced higher average inflation.

No doubt with these findings in mind, and also to help establish the credibility of monetary policy, a number of countries over recent years have given a higher degree of independence to their central banks. For example, in the early 1990s the central bank of New Zealand was given greater independence *and* accountability for its actions. In the latter case, if the head of the central bank of New Zealand fails to fulfil pre-agreed low inflation targets, he/she is fired. Interestingly, since being given greater central bank independence (and accountability) New Zealand has achieved lower inflation performance. More recently Gordon Brown, the Chancellor of the newly elected Labour Government in the UK, announced in May 1997 that the Bank of England would be given responsibility for setting interest rates. Although the Chancellor would set the inflation target, the Bank of England would have 'operational independence' in deciding interest rates to meet the inflation target. In short, giving central banks more independence acts as a pre-commitment to policies favouring lower average rates of inflation.

Lucas critique

In 1976 the leading new classical economist Robert Lucas Jr put forward a further criticism of traditional policy evaluation, which is popularly known as the **Lucas critique**. In order to understand the significance of this critique we must first explain briefly the role of a macroeconometric model in providing forecasts and simulations of the effects of policy changes. A macroeconometric model consists of a set of equations that describe the behaviour of the economy as a whole. The estimated numerical values for the parameters of the model, such as the marginal propensity to consume, are themselves based on past behaviour. Once constructed, macroeconometric models can be used not only to provide forecasts of the future course of key macroeconomic variables, such as output, unemployment and inflation, but also to study the effects of various policy changes on these variables. Lucas however argues that traditional macroeconometric models should not be used to predict the consequences of alternative policy changes, since the parameters of such models may change as economic agents adjust their expectations and behaviour in response to the policy change.

Robert Lucas Jr, b. 1937

One example of the Lucas critique concerns the role of rational expectations in determining the output/employment costs of reducing inflation. According to the new classical view the output/employment costs of monetary disinflation will be non-existent or negligible provided a policy change is credible. If the authorities announce a reduction in the rate of monetary expansion and the policy announcement is believed to be credible, rational economic agents will immediately revise their expectations of inflation downwards in line with the anticipated effects of

Lucas critique: The argument that traditional policy evaluation may be misleading as it fails to take into account that people may change their expectations and behaviour when policy changes.

Adaptive expectations approach: Assumes that people's expectations of the future value of a variable are based solely on recently observed values of that variable.

monetary contraction on the rate of inflation (see Chapter 12, Section 12.2). New classicists claim that traditional estimates of the output/employment costs of reducing inflation are unreliable because they do not take into account the way in which agents adjust their expectations and behaviour to a policy change. The traditional approach incorporates **adaptive expectations**, where economic agents form their expectations of the future value of a variable solely on the basis of recent past values of the variable. For example, agents' expectations of inflation will depend solely on past inflation and will not change following a policy change. In consequence, new classicists argue that traditional policy evaluation overestimates the output/employment costs of reducing inflation because it is subject to the Lucas critique. In summary, the Lucas critique has cast doubt on the reliability of traditional estimates of the impact of various policy changes on key macroeconomic variables.

14.6 The real business cycle view

While both monetarists and new classicists question not only the need for stabilization policy but also whether the authorities can stabilize output and employment by discretionary policy intervention, a much more radical view emerged in the 1980s associated with the real business cycle approach to economic fluctuations. As discussed in Chapter 13, Section 13.6, according to this approach economic fluctuations are the optimal response of the economy to supply shocks. In consequence, there is no role for the authorities to stabilize fluctuations in output and employment through conventional aggregate demand policies.

14.7 Concluding remarks

In this chapter we have outlined various views concerning the ongoing debate over stabilization policy. Two main views can be identified. One view, held by orthodox Keynesians and new Keynesians, is that the authorities need to, can and therefore should stabilize the economy using aggregate demand policies. Even though nowadays most Keynesian economists accept that the long-run Phillips curve is vertical, they justify discretionary policy intervention to stabilize the economy on the following grounds: the period of time required for the economy to return to the natural rate of unemployment having been subjected to some shock or disturbance; and the potential to identify and respond to major shocks that periodically hit the economy. The other main view, held by monetarists and new classicists, is that there is no need for stabilization policy involving the management of aggregate demand, and that in any case discretionary fiscal and monetary policies cannot and therefore should not be used to stabilize the economy. Given the divide between these two broad groupings of economists, the debate over stabilization policy is likely to continue and remain a controversial area within macroeconomics.

Summary

◆ One of the key questions that divide macroeconomists is whether the authorities need to, can and therefore should stabilize the economy at or near the full employment or natural level of output by influencing the level of aggregate demand.

◆ Discretionary policy takes place in circumstances where the authorities are free to vary the strength of fiscal and/or monetary policy in any way they see fit at the time. In contrast the authorities may be committed to follow a prespecified rule that determines the conduct of fiscal and/or monetary policy. Rules may or may not be linked to prevailing economic circumstances.

◆ The debate over stabilization policy critically depends on whether one views the economy as being inherently unstable or naturally stable. While both orthodox Keynesians and new Keynesians subscribe to the former view, arguing that there is a need for stabilization policy, new Keynesians regard attempts to fine-tune the macroeconomy as being overambitious, and instead advocate rough tuning.

◆ Both monetarists and new classicists, believing the economy to be inherently stable, question the need for stabilization policy involving the management of aggregate demand. Highlighting a number of problems associated with stabilization policy, most notably those associated with time lags, monetarists argue that discretionary policy activism may make matters worse, and advocate that discretionary aggregate demand policies should be replaced by some form of monetary rule. New classicists' support for rules over discretion is based on the insights provided by policy ineffectiveness, the problem of time inconsistency and the Lucas critique.

◆ In the real business cycle approach there is no role for stabilization policy.

Key terms

◆ Discretionary policy
◆ Fine tuning and rough tuning
◆ Policy rule: active and passive
◆ Inflationary gap
◆ Crowding out
◆ Inside and outside lags
◆ Rational expectations
◆ Policy ineffectiveness
◆ Time inconsistency
◆ Macroeconometric model
◆ Lucas critique

Self-test questions

True (t) or false (f)

1. An example of discretionary policy is the situation where the authorities are given the freedom to increase government expenditure during a recession.

2. Policy rules tie the hands of the authorities to pursue prespecified rules for fiscal and/or monetary policy.

3. Keynesians stress the need for stabilization policy, and argue that the authorities can and should use discretionary fiscal and monetary policies to stabilize the economy.

4. New Keynesians suggest that shocks from both the demand side and supply side of the economy can cause undesirable and inefficient economic fluctuations.

5. Monetarists argue that discretionary fiscal and monetary policies can be used to stabilize the economy.

6. According to monetarists an increase in government expenditure will, in the long run, crowd out some components of private sector expenditure so that real income remains unchanged at its natural level.

7. According to the new classical policy-ineffectiveness proposition, anticipated monetary policy changes will have no effect on output and employment.

8. In the new classical view economic agents form their expectations in line with the adaptive expectations approach.

9. The problem of time inconsistency of policy has provided another argument in support of fixed rules over discretion.

10. According to the real business cycle view the authorities can stabilize fluctuations in output and employment using discretionary fiscal and monetary policies.

Complete the following sentences by inserting the missing word(s)

1. Frequent intervention by the authorities to maintain output and employment at, or near, their full employment or natural levels is known as ____.

2. A ____ policy rule is one in which the prespecified rule is not linked to the state of the economy.

3. Keynesians contend that the economy is inherently ____.

4. Orthodox Keynesians stress the need for discretionary ____ policies to stabilize the economy.

5. The period of time it takes to initiate a policy change is referred to as the ____ lag.

6. The time lapse between an initiated policy change and its influence on the economy is referred to as the ____ lag.

7. Monetarists contend that the economy is inherently ____.

8. According to the new classical view only ____ monetary shocks affect output and employment and then only in the ____.

9. New classical economics is an approach based on the three assumptions of continuous market clearing, incomplete information, and ____.

10. The argument that traditional policy evaluation may be misleading, as it fails to take into account that people may change their expectations and behaviour when policy changes, is known as the ____.

■ Questions for discussion

◆ What is the difference between discretionary policy and policy rules?

◆ Why do economists disagree over the issue of whether discretionary policy activism is needed to stabilize the economy?

◆ What are the main areas of agreement and disagreement between orthodox Keynesians and new Keynesians with respect to stabilization policy?

◆ What are the main arguments put forward by monetarists against discretionary policy activism?

◆ Why do new classicists believe that systematic aggregate demand policies will be ineffective?

◆ What is the problem of time inconsistency?

◆ What is the Lucas critique?

◆ State and justify your position in the rules versus discretion debate.

Further reading

Stewart, M. *Keynes and After* (3rd ed.) (Hardmondsworth: Penguin, 1986). An excellent non-technical introduction to Keynesian economics and monetarism.

Marin, A. *Macroeconomic Policy* (London: Routledge, 1992). Examines the central tenets of the Keynesian and monetarist schools in a clear and non-technical manner.

Shaw, G.K. *Rational Expectations* (Brighton: Wheatsheaf Books, 1984). A concise, lucid and analytical introduction to rational expectations and its implications.

Internet links

The *Institute for Fiscal Studies* (IFS) is an independent centre for economic policy research. Most of its work is available on the Internet. Amongst other things, it offers comprehensive coverage of the UK budget, including the opportunity to access its forecasting software so that users can play at being the Chancellor of the Exchequer. The IFS Web site is at: **http://www1.ifs.org.uk/index.htm**

International Trade

Contents

Key issues

▶ Why do countries trade?

▶ Can all countries gain from trade?

▶ How have patterns of trade changed since 1945?

▶ How has trade policy unfolded since 1945?

15.1 Introduction

International trade is simply the extension of the market process across international boundaries: the buying and selling of goods and services in foreign markets rather than in the domestic economy. To begin our discussion of international trade it is useful to consider the following three basic questions:

- What advantages does trade offer over and above the confinement of economic activity to the domestic market alone?
- What is the economic basis for trade?
- Is trade always a mutually advantageous process, or are some economic agents potentially disadvantaged by it?

The advantages of trade

The most obvious advantage of international trade is that it provides mutual access to a range of goods and services that might otherwise be denied to domestic populations. The residents of Germany, for example, cannot easily produce and consume tropical fruits or lie on a tropical beach on holiday except through trade: the German economy and German factors of production are not suited to the production of either of these things, so demand for them must be met from abroad. More significantly, many economies have no means whatsoever of meeting certain basic material consumption needs out of domestic resources. Ireland, for example, has no independent recourse to oil or even coal; both of these important fuels have to be imported. This, the *consumption* motive for trade, is not restricted solely to items

Visible trade: containers full of goods ready for shipping

that are beyond the powers of the domestic economy to produce. A growing number of countries have industries that sell their outputs into the markets of rival foreign producers. For example, French cars are sold in Britain and British cars are bought in France. Some British residents clearly prefer French cars to those produced at home, and *vice versa*. Such preferences for foreign goods over their domestically produced counterparts may simply reflect differences in taste but can also be based on price or quality factors. Whatever the motivation, trade makes much wider consumption choices possible in comparison with those available under *autarky* (meaning self-sufficiency).

If trade opens up new opportunities for consumption, what of its effects upon *production*? It should be clear that goods and services sold abroad provide incomes and employment for those who produce them. As we shall see, the relatively rapid rates of economic growth enjoyed by the advanced industrial countries in the two decades after the Second World War, together with the recent exceptional growth performances of the newly industrializing countries of the Pacific Rim such as South Korea, have their basis at least in part in the growth of international trade. There is a close affinity between success in foreign markets and domestic economic progress, which is perhaps best expressed by the phrase 'export-led growth'. Of course trade also gives access to the global range of raw materials upon which production rests. As few countries, if any, are completely self-sufficient in raw materials, trade provides the vital conduit through which the earth's resources can be put to productive use.

The economic basis for trade

Having briefly reviewed the advantages of international trade, we now introduce the fundamental economic principle upon which it is rests. This, the notion of *specialization and exchange*, is associated with the work of the British (classical) economists Adam Smith and David Ricardo.

In his book *An Inquiry into the Nature and Causes of the Wealth of Nations*, published in 1776, Smith argued that labour can be made more productive by dividing it up amongst specialist tasks. He famously used the example of pin-making to demonstrate that a group of workers, each with a particular and complementary skill in which they are well versed, will collectively be much more productive than they would be if each alone tried to master the full repertoire of pin-making skills. In other words, it is better to be adept at a small range of tasks than to undertake many with questionable competence. As for individuals, Smith declared, so for nations. It is appropriate for countries to limit the range of economic activities to those to which they are *best suited*, and to engage in trade (exchange) to obtain those goods and services that they desire but cannot or choose not to produce.

Smith also provided a rationale for **free trade**, unregulated and unchecked by government interference. This too proceeds from an analysis of the individual. Recall from Chapter 1 our description of Smith's defence of *laissez-faire* and the free market. The argument here was that individuals will freely enter into transactions that benefit them: hence the greater the number of transactions, the greater the benefit. At the international level the same reasoning applies: the greater the volume of trade, the greater the benefit derived by those engaging in it. Thus trade should be allowed to flourish unconstrained. Note the mutually supportive link here between the notion of an **international division of labour** (nations specializing in what they are best at) and the argument for free trade. In a free and open international economy, countries will be motivated to push their productive specialisms as far as they are able, utilizing to the full factors of production in the most appropriate ways.

Ricardo's contribution to this analysis, published in his book *On The Principles of Political Economy and Taxation* in 1817, was to demonstrate that *all* countries can gain from specialization and exchange and not just those that have reached a certain level of economic development. In such circumstances there are no sustainable arguments to confound the general case for free trade. We review the Ricardian concept of **comparative advantage**, which is at the heart of this thesis, in Section 15.2 below.

Some negative consequences of trade

The free trade arguments advanced by Smith and Ricardo have become a cornerstone of modern economic orthodoxy, but this is not to say that international trade is not without its problems or that the case for *managed* trade can find no advocates. Later in this chapter we shall provide some examples of instances in which the international division of labour has shifted over time between nations. In such circumstances, countries with long-standing specialisms in the production of particular goods can find themselves 'outcompeted' in those specialisms by emergent rivals. This situation requires that the newly uncompetitive nations shift factors of production out of their threatened specialisms and reallocate them to uses in which they retain or can develop a competitive edge. However, while in theory the reallocation of resources can proceed in a smooth and timely manner, the reality is usually rather different and may involve bankruptcies and unemployment in industries with deteriorating competitiveness. This is because opportunities for the reinvestment of capital and re-employment of labour in new sectors usually emerge slowly and not at a pace sufficient to offset the original industrial decline. This kind of *adjustment problem* may give rise to calls for domestic industries to be protected by governments from the full force of international competition that completely free trade

---

Concept

Free trade

Free trade implies an absence of government regulation in the international markets for goods and services.

Concept

International division of labour

The international division of labour describes patterns of specialization in the production of goods and services between nations.

Comparative advantage: The ability of a country to produce a commodity at a lower opportunity cost, in terms of other commodities forgone, than another country.

Concept

Protectionism

Protectionism occurs where the principle of free trade is compromised. Usually, protectionist policies are implemented by governments concerned to promote domestic industries over their foreign rivals.

would unleash. We examine the contemporary validity of this position in Section 15.5 of this chapter.

15.2   The theory of comparative advantage

Ricardo's theory of comparative advantage suggests that all countries will have some particular efficiency in the production of a good or service relative to another country. This means that every country can gain from specialization and trade. It does not matter if a given national economy is economically advanced or backward in comparison with its neighbours: it can still find an appropriate avenue of production upon which to concentrate.

At the time of its publication, Ricardo's work, together with that of Smith, constituted a radical attack on the prevailing philosophy of international trade, namely **mercantilism**. Mercantilists argued that the key to national prosperity was the accumulation of gold and silver bullion. Bullion was of itself manifest wealth, but it could also be used to finance wars with other foreign powers. The key to the accumulation of bullion was strong export performance – in order to maximize the inflow of gold and silver arising from payments for goods sold abroad – together with import restraint to minimize bullion outflow. The mercantilists also argued that the state had a duty to implement policies to promote exports and protect domestic industry from import penetration; both were a means of furthering national prosperity. Note that this establishes mercantilism as a profoundly interventionist philosophy. Finally, in the mercantilist view, international trade could only ever be attractive to one group of nations: those consistent net exporters, following an aggressive trade policy, who accumulated bullion and were prosperous. In contrast, other nations, less successful in the drive for exports, tended to lose bullion and were economically enfeebled.

Ricardo thought that this conceptualization of strong nations carving out overseas markets at the expense of the weak was wholly mistaken. Indeed he argued that there were no economically strong or weak nations in the mercantilist sense: all were possessed of a comparative advantage in the production of some good or service. The truly striking element in his approach, compared with what had gone before, was to demonstrate that, as a consequence of the existence of comparative advantage, international trade could no longer be considered to be a 'zero sum game' in which the strong nations elbowed aside the weak. Instead, trade was a 'positive sum' process, which actually raised the production and consumption possibilities of participant nations, leaving them *all* better off.

The theory of comparative advantage is best explained with the help of a simple example. We begin by identifying two countries, Germany and the Ukraine, each of which, fully using the resources available to it, can produce some combination of two goods: cameras and beer. Let us assume that the *production possibilities* in Table 15.1 apply: Germany, in other words, can produce either 20 million cameras or 20 million units of beer (in a given time period) if all its resources are allocated to either camera or beer production respectively, or some combination of both products in between these two values. Similarly the Ukraine can produce either 5 million cameras or 15

> **Concept**
>
> **Mercantilism**
>
> Mercantilism was an economic philosophy advanced by merchants and politicians prior to the rise of industrial capitalism. Mercantilism emphasized the importance of accumulating bullion from balance of trade surpluses, and advocated tariffs and other protectionist measures to achieve that end.

Table 15.1 Hypothetical production possibilities

	Cameras		Beer
Germany ⟶	20 million units	*or*	20 million units
Ukraine ⟶	5 million units	*or*	15 million units

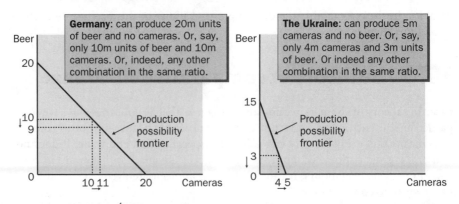

Fig. 15.1 Production possibility frontiers.

million units of beer or some combination in between. Fig. 15.1 graphs the possible production combinations for both countries, assuming, for ease of exposition, constant returns to scale.

For each country we can now express the opportunity cost of one good in terms of the other. Recall that opportunity cost refers to the amount of one good that must be given up in order to obtain a given increase in the output of the other good. In the case of Germany it can be seen for example that the opportunity cost of producing 1 camera is 1 unit of beer (20 million cameras would 'cost' 20 million units of beer; 20m ÷ 20m = 1). Therefore to produce 1 million more cameras (for example from 10 million to 11 million), 1 million units of beer must be sacrificed (for example from 10 to 9). In the Ukraine, however, the opportunity cost of the amount of beer that must be forgone to produce one more camera is higher. Here the maximum of 5 million cameras that can be produced would cost the forgone production of 15 million units of beer. Thus the opportunity cost of a camera in the Ukraine is 3 units of beer (15m ÷ 5m = 3). To produce 1 million more cameras (for example from 4 million to 5 million), 3 million units of beer must be sacrificed (that is, from 3 million to zero).

This means that Germany can produce cameras at a lower opportunity cost in terms of beer production that must be forgone than the Ukraine. Germany, in other words, has a comparative advantage in camera production over the Ukraine. Conversely, it is apparent that the Ukraine has a comparative advantage in beer production over Germany. In Germany each extra unit of beer produced involves the loss of 1 camera; but in the Ukraine it is possible to produce 3 extra units of beer for the loss of a camera (that is, the opportunity cost of producing 1 unit of beer is the loss of a third of a camera). In opportunity cost terms the Ukraine can produce beer at a lower opportunity cost than Germany. In other words it has a comparative advantage in beer production over Germany.

The different opportunity costs suggest that there is scope for specialization in the two countries. Germany could produce only cameras, at which it appears adept, and no beer, while the Ukraine could do the reverse. Each country would be producing the commodity in which it has a comparative advantage (that is, at the lowest opportunity cost) in comparison with the other country. We now need to demonstrate that in this situation there is scope for trade between Germany and the Ukraine that is mutually advantageous. Consider Germany first. Suppose the German economy produces *only* cameras: 20 million of them, some of which it wishes to exchange for beer from the Ukraine. The crucial issue is the exchange ratio that needs to be agreed. We know that to obtain one unit of beer in Germany there is a 'price' to be paid of one camera. If Germany could persuade the Ukraine to let it have say 2 units of beer per camera, then this would represent a huge improvement on what was available domestically. The obvious question now concerns the receptiveness of the Ukraine to this offer. In the Ukraine, the opportunity cost of producing a camera is 3 units of beer. If Germany offers to exchange its cameras for only 2 units of beer this is a very acceptable arrangement for the Ukraine. It would be advantageous for the Ukraine to produce only beer (that is, 15 million units) and to exchange some of its beer production for German cameras. The important point to notice is that there is a different international exchange ratio (or price) for cameras and beer compared with that prevailing in the two domestic economies.

Table 15.2 summarizes the position of both countries in autarky (that is, no trade) with an arbitrary division of production between the two goods. Note the total output levels for cameras and beer in this situation: 19 million cameras and 8 million units of beer. We shall now consider complete specialization in both countries, where some of the output of each is traded at an exchange ratio of 2 units of beer per camera. Again, the volumes traded are selected arbitrarily simply for illustrative purposes. The results are summarized in Table 15.3. Here it can be seen that both countries have gained from the process. In Germany camera consumption has remained at the same level as in autarky but the consumption of beer has doubled from 5 to 10 million units. In the Ukraine camera consumption has increased by 1 million units and beer consumption by 2 million units. World production and consumption has increased by 1 and 7 million units of cameras and beer respectively.

It is evident then that specialization and exchange has indeed improved the consumption positions of both countries, and Ricardo's critique of the mercantilist view – that countries can gain through trade only at the expense of their rivals – appears

Table 15.2 Germany and the Ukraine in autarky

	Production and consumption	
	Cameras (millions)	Beer (millions of units)
Germany	15	5
Ukraine	4	3
'World' output in autarky	19	8

Table 15.3 Specialization and trade

	Produces	Exports	Imports	Consumes
Germany	20m cameras	5m cameras ⟷	10m beers	15m cameras ; 10m beers
Ukraine	15m beers	10m beers ⟷	5m cameras	5m cameras ; 5m beers
'World' output and consumption after trade			⟶	20m cameras; 15m beers

Absolute advantage: The ability of a country to produce more of a particular commodity than another country, using an equal quantity of factor inputs.

vindicated. Similarly, the Ricardian case for free trade is equally well founded. Note that in our example Germany is capable of producing more of *both* commodities than is the Ukraine. It is said to possess an **absolute advantage** in the production of both. Adam Smith had originally supposed that trade could only take place between countries that had an absolute advantage in the production of particular goods. Ricardo's great contribution was to show that the important criterion was the existence of comparative, not absolute, advantage. Now, because all countries have a comparative advantage in something, all may gain from the trade process. This means that free trade is in the interest of all countries and that, as a corollary, its inverse – the kind of protectionism recommended by the Mercantilists – is inimical to the general economic good.

15.3 Reflecting on comparative advantage: further developments in trade theory

The basic message that emerges from the theory of comparative advantage is very clear: the best way to organize the international economy is to allow specialization and trade to flourish. Yet there are still some questions that our description of the principle so far has left unanswered.

- Are there really *no* problems whatsoever with the trade process in the Ricardian view?

- What kind of factors determine a country's comparative advantage?

- How are we to reconcile Ricardo's expectation of specialization with the fact that, as noted, many countries produce the *same* commodity (the car was the example used earlier) and sell it in each others' markets?

To begin with the first of these questions, it is the Ricardian case that for each country as a whole trade offers no threats, only opportunities. However, Ricardo himself acknowledged that for some groups inside the national economy problems could arise as a result of free trade. His specific reference was to the losses that free trade might visit upon British landowners at the end of the Napoleonic wars in 1815 (recall that Ricardo's book was published in 1817). War had raised British food prices to the benefit of the landowners on whose property the food was produced. Because free trade threatened to open the British market to imports of cheaper foreign food, landowners were in favour of the protection, by government, of the domestic food market. However, a second British interest group – the newly emerging manufacturing class – wanted a liberal trading environment that would allow them to profit from open overseas markets. Ricardo's suggested compromise was that the free-trade-enriched manufacturers should compensate the disadvantaged landowners. In this way internal objections to the effects of trade could be overcome and its larger benefits secured. We consider the modern parallels to this situation in Section 15.5 on trade policy.

What of the *source* of comparative advantage? In his original formulation Ricardo highlighted the importance of *labour productivity* as the key determinant of a country's specialization decision. The more productive its labour becomes in the fashioning of one particular commodity as against an alternative, the lower the opportunity cost of the commodity. Returning to our earlier example (summarized in Table 15.1 and Fig. 15.1), consider the impact of a fivefold increase in productivity in the German camera industry. Instead of 20 million cameras in a given time period it is now able to produce 100 million cameras. We assume that conditions in the German beer industry are unchanged. Formerly, the opportunity cost of a camera was 1 unit of beer. Now, given the improvement in camera industry productivity, one camera costs only a fifth of a unit of beer (20m ÷ 100m = 1/5). If the Ukraine is still happy to trade at the existing international ratio of 1 camera for 2 units of beer, then the leap in German camera productivity provides the basis for an even better deal for the Germans. Domestically, they can now get only 1/5 of a unit of beer for every camera they sacrifice (instead of one unit as previously) but internationally they can still obtain 2 beers per camera; and they're producing many more cameras.

Although the concept of comparative advantage still survives as the underlying essence of modern international trade theory, Ricardo's emphasis on labour productivity as its (sole) source has fared less well. In particular, given the existence of a number of factors of production, it seems reasonable to question the validity of elevating only *one* factor as a means of explaining patterns of trade. This concern eventually prompted a further important step in the development of trade theory with the emergence, in the 1920s, of the **Heckscher–Ohlin model** of international trade, named after its Swedish originators. The Heckscher–Ohlin model supposes that a country's comparative advantage will reflect its particular *endowments* of factors of production. Because, globally, factors are not evenly spread, the basis for specialization and exchange is established. For example, those countries that are richly endowed with fertile land will find it beneficial to devote resources to the production of agricultural output. For countries with a relative abundance of labour, specialization in the production of labour-intensive goods and services will be preferable. The advantage of this kind of approach is that it has expectations that appear to conform to some very obvious real-world general trading patterns. 'Land-rich' countries such as New Zealand and Brazil do tend to specialize in outputs that exploit their natural resource endowments, while a country such as Japan, which has fewer natural resources but a relative abundance of capital (in the shape of technologically advanced factories and machines), specializes in manufactured goods. Unfortunately, despite the stamp of realism that the Heckscher–Ohlin model appears to possess, its formal construction required that only *two* factors of production could be considered, rather than the four that microeconomic theory identifies. The preferred two factors were labour and capital. Despite such simplification, the model was still regarded as an advance upon the foundations provided by Ricardo.

In 1947 the central hypothesis of the Heckscher–Ohlin model was subjected to a famous test by an economist named Leontief. Using a model of the US economy Leontief expected to be able to demonstrate specialization by the USA in capital-intensive goods, and therefore that US exports were similarly capital intensive. Given that the USA was by far the most technologically advanced nation in the world at that time, this was a reasonable hypothesis. However, Leontief's results were the reverse of those anticipated. His work suggested that the USA was an exporter of labour-intensive goods and an importer of capital-intensive goods; in other words, the USA was *not* specializing in the production of goods that required the use of its most abundant factor. Yet because the Heckscher–Ohlin model was supported by an apparent wealth of casual empirical evidence concerning the kind of international division of labour noted above, economists, including Leontief himself, were

> ## Concept
>
> ### Heckscher–Ohlin model
>
> The Heckscher–Ohlin approach to international trade holds that a country's production and trade specialisms will reflect its particular factor endowments.

Concept

Leontief paradox

The Leontief paradox refers to the finding by the economist Leontief that, for the USA, the predictions of the Heckscher–Ohlin model did not appear empirically verifiable.

Concept

Inter-industry trade

Inter-industry trade refers to the tendency for countries to trade the same kinds of goods and services.

Concept

Product life cycle theory

Product life cycle theory understands patterns of international trade by referencing the development of commodities over time. As they move from a stage of innovation through to maturity, products have different international geographies of production, and therefore varying trade patterns.

reluctant to dismiss it, and his findings subsequently became known as the **Leontief paradox**.

This impasse between an intuitively defensible model and apparently contradictory empirical evidence subsequently resulted in a number of analyses that attempted to reconcile the two. The most widely accepted of these have usually involved some acknowledgement that comparative advantage must have its roots in something a little more complex than two simple categories of labour and capital. For example, Leontief thought that his results might be explained by the higher *quality* of labour in the USA. This subsequently became known as the human capital argument, and rests upon the proposition that the relatively heavy investment in education and training that takes place in the advanced economies makes labour there much more productive than elsewhere. The specialization of the USA in labour-intensive industries, as discovered by Leontief, can therefore be explained by the abundance of high-quality labour in the USA. In this sense there is no paradox: it is just that the basis of comparative advantage is indeed more complex than the formalities of the Heckscher–Ohlin model can allow. The model itself, with due deference to its Ricardian foundations, remains the central element of orthodox trade theory in modern economics.

In our third question reflecting upon comparative advantage, we raised a further facet of real-world trade complexity. In his original formulation Ricardo argued that countries specialize in particular goods, which they then trade for different goods that the domestic economy either cannot or chooses not to produce. The Heckscher–Ohlin model was a slightly more sophisticated endorsement of this same view. But of course the world is not that simple. A large proportion of trade takes place between countries in the *same* product lines. As noted, the car industry is an obvious case in point. There is little sign of specialization and exchange of the kind that Ricardo expected here: an increasing number of countries make cars and sell them to each other. Trade between nations in the same goods is known as **inter-industry trade**, and the rapid increase in this kind of activity in the postwar period has prompted the most recent developments in trade theory.

Although it might at first appear that the growth of inter-industry trade serves to undermine the traditional Ricardian approach, with its emphasis on the development of patterns of specialization, this is not the case. Contemporary trade theory recognizes that Ricardo's rather rigid demarcation between 'country A producing good X and country B producing good Y, with trade between them' is increasingly outdated, but it continues to respect the essence of comparative advantage: *that different forms of production will be more efficiently conducted in different places*. Because everywhere is not the same in terms of economic attributes, it makes sense to use some places for one (suitable) form of production and other places for other (suitable) forms.

This kind of approach has provided the basis for a number of new advances in international trade theory. One of these, **product life cycle theory**, describes the relationship between, on the one hand, the initial launch of a new good and its subsequent path to the status of a mature and recognized product and, on the other, its evolving *geography of production*. Let us take the car as an example of the application of this theory. When the car was first invented, the location of its production was constrained by a number of factors. First, as it was a new and expensive good, its market was initially small, and prospective customers needed to be affluent. Second, its technical complexity demanded a skilled labour force. Finally, new car makers may have gained from close proximity to one another: perhaps from sharing information or resources, or simply by 'keeping an eye on the competition'. Taken together, these factors tended to mean that car production was restricted to certain economically advanced locations.

Eventually the car became a mature commodity. Its form was no longer experimental and changing but established and stable. The way in which it was produced changed too. Skilled labour was no longer pre-eminent as the introduction of the assembly line allowed cars to be produced in vast numbers by semi-skilled or even unskilled labour. Such efficient production – taking advantage of scale economies – lowered the price of cars even to within reach of the pockets of the people who made them. Finally, in a large and established market, car manufacturers began to compete much more heavily on price than they had done in the earliest stages of production. These new circumstances meant that the location of production became much more flexible; the old imperatives restricting it to economically advanced locations disappeared, and indeed there were positive benefits to be reaped from seeking out places where costs could be minimized.

The above stylized analysis permits us to grasp the notion of a **shifting comparative advantage**, which favours different locations as a product moves from a stage of innovation to one of maturity. At first, because certain factors – such as skilled labour inputs – are crucial, production must be retained in the innovating areas; for carmaking these are the advanced industrial nations. Later, when other factors become more important upon the maturing of the product, a wider distribution of production is favoured, and may encompass for example less developed country locations. More generally, this kind of approach enables us to understand some of the reasons for the growth of inter-industry trade. If product life cycle theory is applicable to many 'durable' consumer goods then it is possible to conceive of a highly complex patterning of trade (such as actually exists in the real world) that reflects the processes of innovation and maturation of many different products as their production migrates to, and they are exported from, newly appropriate locations. Again, however, we should be aware that the essence of 'locational appropriateness' is captured in Ricardian comparative advantage.

Finally in this section we should emphasize the potential richness of the theoretical path to which this kind of approach to international trade gives rise. We have concentrated here on product life cycle theory as one explanation of inter-industry trade, but there is in addition a range of complementary material that highlights other potentially significant factors. These would include a more systematic review of the interaction between *inter alia* national patterns of investment and innovation, economies of scale and government policy (see guide to further reading at the end of this chapter).

15.4 Patterns of trade since 1945

We referred earlier to the rapid growth in international trade that has occurred since the end of the Second World War. In this section we shall briefly describe the scale of this process and demonstrate its economic importance. We shall also describe the striking changes in the patterns of trade that have emerged over the period.

· Table 15.4 illustrates the positive nature of the relationship between trade and economic growth: the more rapid the annual rate at which trade expands, the faster

Concept

Shifting comparative advantage

Shifting comparative advantage implies that patterns of comparative advantage are not stable over time. Countries may lose and gain comparative advantage in different products.

Table 15.4 World output and trade growth, 1820–1993 (annual average % change)

	Output	Trade
1820–1870	2.2	4.0
1870–1913	2.5	3.9
1913–1950	1.9	1.0
1950–1973	4.9	8.6
1971–1980	4.0	5.0
1981–1987	2.0	2.5
1988–1993	2.5	5.6

Source: Adapted from P. Armstrong, A. Glyn and J. Harrison *Capitalism Since 1945* (Oxford: Basil Blackwell, 1991); GATT (1987); and IMF (1992)

the growth in world output. It is evident from the table that in periods in which the growth in trade has been relatively sluggish, such as 1913–1950, the rate of growth of output has been similarly poor. In contrast, faster trade growth is consistently equated with faster output growth. There is in fact a causal link between these two variables: it is the opening up of new and bigger international markets for goods and services that motivates producers to increase output levels.

In Chapter 9 we described the years 1945–70 as the postwar boom: a period during which most of the advanced economies experienced unprecedented rates of economic growth, together with full employment and low inflation. Table 15.4 indicates the central contribution made by the growth in world trade to this 'golden era'. Between 1950 and 1973 trade grew at an annual average rate of 8.6 per cent, more than double that in any previous period; while output expanded at 4.9 per cent, again about twice the best previous rate. However, it is also evident from the table that the more modest expansion of trade since the beginning of the 1970s has not unexpectedly been associated with slower growth in world output.

If world trade has expanded at a rapid if uneven rate over the postwar period, which particular countries have been the strongest participants in this process? Table 15.5 summarizes the distribution of world merchandise trade since 1970. From the table we can see first that the overall share of the **OECD** nations in trade has remained, at 68 per cent, remarkably stable over the period as a whole, notwithstanding the sharp dip in 1980. This suggests that despite the purported success of

OECD: The Organization for Economic Cooperation and Development, founded in 1961, comprises a group of rich industrialized nations.

Table 15.5 Regional shares in total world merchandise trade (%)

	1970	1980	1992
Americas	22.6	18.8	19.4
USA	13.0	11.0	12.6
Canada	4.4	2.8	3.2
Mexico	0.5	0.8	0.9
Other Americas	4.7	4.2	2.7
Europe	54.2	47.6	46.9
EU	35.9	32.9	37.1
EFTA	6.5	5.4	5.6
Other Europe	11.8	9.3	4.2
Asia	14.1	20.9	27.0
Japan	5.7	6.1	7.2
South Korea	0.4	0.9	2.0
Hong Kong	0.8	1.0	3.0
China	0.7	0.9	2.1
Other Asia	6.5	12.0	12.7
Oceania	2.1	1.3	1.4
Africa	4.4	4.5	2.2
Middle East	2.6	6.9	3.1
OECD	68.1	60.3	68.0
Total	100.0	100.0	100.0

Source: OECD *Main Developments in Trade*. © OECD 1995. Reproduced by permission of the OECD

many less developed countries in the trade process, the international economy is still overwhelmingly the preserve of the advanced economies. There are however clear differences in long-term trade performance between different regional groups, and indeed between individual countries.

Let us concentrate first on the more successful participants in the trade process. The Asian nations for example have managed to almost double their collective share of world trade since 1970. Given that the slowdown in the growth of trade overall has certainly meant that overseas markets have become more keenly contested, this is a remarkable achievement. Japan consistently assumes the largest individual share of any Asian nation, but the prize for the rate of expansion must be awarded to the other three named countries: China's share of world trade has increased threefold since 1970, Hong Kong's has increased almost fourfold, and South Korea's fivefold. Other comparable performances have been recorded by Singapore and Taiwan, though these are not noted in the table. In fact the achievements of the so-called Asian 'newly industrializing countries' (NICs) – Hong Kong, Singapore, South Korea, and Taiwan – in opening up foreign markets have resulted in rates of economic growth consistently above those of any of the established advanced industrial nations. Between 1965 and 1990, for example, the Asian NICs grew at an annual average real income per capita rate of 7 per cent. Over the same period the comparable figures for Japan and the OECD as a whole were 4.2 and 2.4 per cent respectively.

How can the unparalleled expansion in trade shares enjoyed by these particular economies be explained? The answer lies in the Ricardian notion of shifting comparative advantage. These nations have managed to cast off long-established patterns of specialization in favour of others that have allowed them to enter new and growing world markets. In particular, they have shifted resources away from the production of primary commodities (foodstuffs and raw materials) and towards the production of *manufactures*. This has been possible because, as their name suggests, these newly industrializing countries are able to fashion certain kinds of manufactured item more efficiently than the advanced countries. By taking advantage of lower labour costs, for example, the NICs have begun to produce a range of labour-intensive manufactures that they can price extremely competitively in world markets. However, as we shall see, this has posed certain problems for newly *un*competitive industries in the advanced nations.

Of the other major regions in Table 15.5, only the Middle East has managed to raise its share of world trade beyond that which it enjoyed in 1970. The fortunes of countries in this region are closely tied to the price of oil, and the marked rise in trade share up to 1980 reflected the very sharp oil price increases of 1973–74 and 1979. The subsequent fall in oil prices over the 1980s had the effect of trimming back the share of the Middle East in world trade.

The trade performances of the Americas and Europe also repay some scrutiny. Although both their aggregate regional shares in world trade have fallen over the period concerned (and together they accounted for approximately two-thirds of world trade in 1992), subregional performances have been much more varied. For example, while the overall share of the Americas has fallen from 22.6 per cent in 1970 to 19.4 per cent in 1992, more than half of the reduction has been incurred by the 'Other Americas' category, which is entirely composed of the Central and South American nations. In North America the USA has held its share (the world's largest) relatively stable in comparison with a pronounced Mexican gain and a Canadian loss.

In Europe too there is similar unevenness. The EU countries have enhanced their share, while those in **EFTA** have lost ground. The old Eastern Bloc countries that make up most of 'Other Europe' have suffered the most catastrophic fall in trade share, in both absolute and relative terms. The problem here of course has been the exposure of the notoriously uncompetitive formerly state-controlled industries to more open markets. The other notably poor performance revealed in the table is that of Africa, which has seen its share of world trade exactly halved over the period in question. We examine the particular difficulties facing African and other 'less developed' nations in Chapter 17.

We are now aware of the distribution of international trade: we know which countries and regions enjoy most of it and which are enjoying the fastest growth in trade shares. But what of the *pattern* of trade: who trades mostly with whom? Some answers to this question can be found in Table 15.6. The evidence here is that already heavy intra-regional and by implication inter-industry trade processes are increasing. In Europe, for example, 70.9 per cent of international trade was internally retained in 1972; by 1992 this figure had increased to 74.6 per cent. This means that European countries are trading more and more intensively with each other, rather than with nations in some other parts of the world. Now, given that many of the European nations have similarly advanced industrial structures, this also suggests that inter-industry trade is becoming ever more dominant. Similar increases in intra-regional trade are evident in Asia. In the case of **NAFTA**, although its exports to the Americas have fallen slightly from 50.3 to 48.6 per cent, the very existence of this free trade zone implies that further intra-regional and inter-industry trade increases

EFTA: The European Free Trade Association, created in 1960, was a free trade area formed under British leadership to rival the EEC. It has more recently been absorbed by the EU single market.

NAFTA: The North American Free Trade Agreement is a free trade area that covers the US, Canadian and Mexican economies.

Table 15.6 Intra-regional merchandise trade, 1972 and 1992 (%)

1972

Origin	Destination				
	Americas	Europe[a]	Japan	Asia[b]	Other regions
NAFTA	50.3	25.7	8.5	7.1	8.6
EU + EFTA	13.4	70.9	1.1	2.6	12.1
Japan	41.7	17.4		24.5	16.3
Other East Asia[c]	33.8	18.6	19.0	21.7	6.9

1992

Origin	Destination				
	Americas	Europe	Japan	Asia	Other regions
NAFTA	48.6	22.0	9.0	13.1	7.2
EU + EFTA	9.5	74.6	1.9	4.9	9.0
Japan	34.9	21.6		34.5	9.0
Other East Asia	24.7	16.5	13.7	37.9	7.2

[a] EU, EFTA, CEECs, and the NIS (newly independent states). Includes intra-EU and intra-EFTA trade.
[b] Includes all of the Asian continent except the Middle East and the NIS.
[c] Hong Kong, Korea, Chinese Taipei, Singapore, Thailand, Indonesia, Malaysia, Brunei, Philippines and China.
Source: Main Developments in Trade. © OECD 1995. Reproduced by permission of the OECD

are likely. This kind of evidence explains the development of the new and more complex forms of Ricardian trade theory described in Section 15.3: modern trade processes appear to bear little similarity to the simple binary model that Ricardo originally advanced.

15.5 International trade policy

On the basis of the theory and evidence offered so far in this chapter the issue of trade policy should, for all nations, be an uncontentious one. Because it permits the deployment of resources in their most productive uses together with the mutually advantageous exchange of the resulting maximized output, free and unrestricted trade should always be the preferred option. This is one of the cast iron certainties of orthodox economics. Yet *all* nations *do* engage in many forms of protectionism. Indeed, the post-1970 period has been one in which protectionism has become more widespread than at any time since the interwar years. The obvious question arises: if free trade is so mutually advantageous, why protect?

Understanding protectionism

One of the most instructive ways to think about the development of trade policy involves use of the framework provided by *institutionalist economics*. The work of this school was first introduced in Chapter 5 in the context of a discussion of the theory of the firm. In Chapter 5, Section 5.7, we described the institutionalist emphasis – exemplified in the writings of John Kenneth Galbraith – on the evolutionary development of capitalist economies. Very simply, this approach suggests that because the world's economies are not all at the same stage of development they require different kinds of policy to help them flourish. In terms of trade policy this means that for some nations, at particular stages, elements of protectionism are indeed appropriate.

In advancing this view, Galbraith draws on the work of an early institutionalist and critic of Smith and Ricardo: the German economist Friedrich List (1789–1846). List was an advocate of German protectionism in the first half of the nineteenth century. His concern, reflecting the idea of different stages of national economic development, was that the strong industrial base of the then more advanced British economy would suppress the growth of new German industries. The development of the German economy as a whole would therefore be constrained unless its industries could be insulated from their superior British competitors. Such insulation was available through the imposition of tariff-based protection, which would raise the prices of imports from Britain. However, once German industrialization had attained a level of maturity that would permit it to compete on a more equal basis with Britain, then a liberal German trading regime would be appropriate. The important point here is that the form of trade policy that an economy adopts must be appropriate to the particular stage of development of that economy, and as the economy matures so the choice of trade policy will change. This conclusion is clearly at odds with the free trade recommendations of Smith and Ricardo.

As Galbraith notes, such views made List an early advocate of the **infant-industry argument** for protection. This supposes that protection is legitimate in cases where

Concept

Infant-industry argument

The infant-industry argument suggests that nascent domestic industries may need to be protected from mature foreign competitors until such time as they have acquired the necessary scale or expertise to compete openly with them.

industrial development in an economy might be denied because of the presence of superior foreign competition. In these circumstances, protection offers a respite to infant domestic industries until they achieve a degree of maturity and self-sufficiency that allows them to survive and grow independently. Though the infant-industry argument gained wide currency in the nineteenth century, when many economies were industrializing in the wake of the British lead, it is by no means absent from contemporary economic debate. Indeed, it is a curious irony that it is now interest groups in the *advanced nations* that have adopted the idea that temporary protection for acutely threatened domestic industries is a sensible form of trade policy. The notion of shifting comparative advantage, introduced in Section 15.3, is again relevant here.

In Section 15.3 we noted that the basis of the economic success of the newly industrializing countries (NICs) has been the development of new manufacturing industries that are able to compete in world markets against the formerly dominant industries of the advanced nations. The concern in the advanced countries is the loss of jobs, incomes and profits that this more intense competitive environment brings. As an illustration, consider the contents of the *Guardian* newspaper report reproduced in Box 15.1. This example reveals the particular source of shifting comparative advantage as it affects the British textile, clothing and footwear industries:

Box 15.1

50 000 jobs in textiles could go overseas

Fifty-thousand jobs could be lost in the textile and footwear industry by the end of the decade as manufacturers accelerate the transfer of production to the developing world, union leaders warned yesterday.

New job cuts by leading companies have particularly affected the North-west, the Midlands and Scotland. Unions defending 400 000 jobs in Britain's fifth largest manufacturing industry are calling for a long-term commercial strategy.

. . . The unions said recent announcements by industry leaders like Coats Viyella, Claremont, Dewhirsts, Baird and Peter Black's footwear linked job losses with plans to transfer production to areas like North Africa.

In a joint statement, three unions with a combined membership of 150 000 in textiles and footwear said: 'The current stream of announcements is threatening the existence of a major strategic industry.

'We lost hundreds of thousands of jobs in the clothing industry in the 1980s,

and the UK economy cannot afford to lose a further tranche in the 1990s.'

The unions – the general workers' union GMB, the transport union TGWU and footwear employees' union NUKFAT – called on government and the employers 'to stop this flow of job losses becoming a flood.'

They said: 'For our part we are desperate to cooperate in such a plan. Our industry will disappear if action is not taken.'

The unions said that British companies could not compete 'with the appallingly low wages, low skill markets of developing countries without some backing from government.'

British industry pay rates were based on a guaranteed minimum of around £3 an hour. Gross pay of around £4 an hour was achieved with productivity pay. Pay for clothing workers in Morocco – now one of the chief recipients of British orders – was 62p an hour.

The unions named companies planning to move 'significant proportions' of production overseas in the next few years as including Coats Viyella, which is

planning to close 12 UK factories, with the loss of 7750 jobs by the year 2000, as its non-UK production doubles to 40 per cent.

Courtaulds was planning to increase overseas production from 20 to 30 per cent, and Claremonts, which is making 700 Glasgow workers redundant, is increasing production abroad from 15 to 20 per cent. Dewhirsts is also doubling its overseas output from 25 to 50 per cent, said the unions.

'We are talking about exporting even more jobs to countries such as Morocco, Mauritius and the Philippines,' said Des Farrell, national secretary of the GMB. 'This is a very worrying trend.'

. . . The unions are seeking government support both to protect British jobs in international trade negotiations and to increase investment in new technology and training to keep British fashion at the forefront of international quality markets. All sections of the industry should be involved in survival strategy talks.

Source: The Guardian 13 September 1996. © *The Guardian* 1996.

differences in wage rates between the UK and other locations, such as Morocco, where production is now undertaken. Because the textile, clothing and footwear industries are based on relatively low-skill and labour-intensive production techniques, production becomes more efficient if it migrates to lower-wage locations. Though the *Guardian* report concentrates on the worries of the unions about job losses, British firms too may be concerned if output from less developed countries (LDCs) threatens their markets at home or abroad. While some firms may relocate some production overseas as a means of increasing competitiveness, this may not be possible for all firms or for all production. This means that shifting comparative advantage is a problem both for British workers *and* for British firms.

The final paragraph of the report indicates the kind of solution that the unions see as a way forward. On the one hand there is the possibility of using investment in new technology and training to re-establish domestic competitiveness. High-technology production, which demands the utilization of more skilled labour, might be a means of carving out markets for 'quality' output, which low-cost production could not threaten. On the other hand there is the possibility of relying on 'international trade negotiations': in other words, protectionism. Textile trade is in fact an already heavily protected process. Since 1961 textile exports from LDCs to many of the advanced nations, including the whole of the European Union, have been restricted by the operation of a protocol known as the *Multi-Fibre Arrangement* (MFA). The main objective of the MFA has been to prevent the sudden disruption of the established patterns of trade in textiles so that the textile industry in places such as Britain could adjust more slowly to the presence of new and vibrant sources of competition: effectively, the infant-industry argument in reverse. The MFA has always been viewed as a *temporary* form of trade policy, and it is currently due to expire in 2004.

We appear now to have a fairly robust rationale for protection. It appears defensible in cases where new infant industries require less than full exposure to open competition for a period in order that they might mature; and it is also demanded by already mature industries, again temporarily, so that they can become acclimatized to more intense competitive pressures. But where does this leave the 'cast iron' case for free trade? The crucial issue here appears to be the *stability* of comparative advantage. When patterns of international specialization are firmly established and settled, factors of production are reasonably secure: labour, capital, land and enterprise are each valued in their current uses and are rewarded accordingly. There is then no pressure from factors of production for protection. However, when there is the possibility of a significant shift in comparative advantage in a particular industry, such security evaporates. In the case of the infant industry, those with resources committed to a new venture will wish to see their investment safeguarded from aggressive foreign competition; governments too may have an interest in nurturing what may be a strategically important form of production. In older established industries, threatened by new and dynamic forms of foreign competition, the emerging insecurity may be even more fevered. The example of the British textile unions quoted above is a case in point.

What emerges from this discussion is an appreciation that openness in international trade will be championed by those who are in *unchallenged* forms of production, and therefore in a position to gain from trade. For others, coping with shifts in comparative advantage, some resort to protection may be preferred. We can explore this view further by reflecting upon the history of the main vehicle for the development of world trade policy over the postwar period: the General Agreement on Tariffs and Trade (GATT) (1947–94), and its recently created successor body, the World Trade Organization (WTO) (1995–).

The institutions of international trade policy: from GATT to the WTO

The GATT originated in the early postwar years as a means of securing tariff reductions and preventing new tariffs emerging amongst its then 23 signatory countries. The interwar period witnessed a huge escalation in retaliatory tariff protection involving many nations, causing a two-thirds fall in the value of world trade in the early 1930s. As international markets were closed off and world demand fell, producers cut back on the output of goods they could no longer sell and unemployment rose everywhere: the world economy entered its deepest ever *slump*. It was the connection between the slump and high tariffs that motivated the advent of the GATT so soon after the end of the Second World War: nations were determined that they would not repeat their mistakes of the 1930s. (Although a detailed analysis of the 1930s slump is beyond the scope of this book, some suggestions for further reading are given at the end of the chapter.) Initially the GATT was intended solely as an interim measure, which would begin the process of cutting the vast array of tariffs accumulated in the 1930s; it was soon to have been superseded by the creation of a new international trade body. In the event, plans for this organization collapsed and instead the GATT matured from a mere treaty into an organization in its own right. In 1995 the GATT's permanent secretariat in Geneva and its membership in excess of 125 countries or so-called 'contracting parties' were inherited by the WTO. (The GATT actually lives on in treaty form, overseen by the WTO.)

The GATT can be seen to have had three main objectives. These were:

- to prevent an immediate postwar resumption of the kind of protectionism that had done so much damage in the 1930s
- to dismantle the tariff structures built up during this period
- to provide a protocol that would ensure that international trade relations were conducted on an *open* and *multilateral* basis.

In the 1930s too many nations had begun to act unilaterally and bilaterally, segmenting and preserving 'their' markets for themselves and their preferred partners. It was thought that the promotion of a multilateral environment was the natural way to prevent the same thing happening again. The work of the GATT over the postwar period as a whole has largely been conducted in a series of negotiating 'Rounds', each of which has attempted to address an agenda of tariff reduction. The Rounds have also provided a forum for the refinement of rules and codes that the GATT nations agree will govern trading relations between them. We do not need here to go into the detail of each of the *eight* Rounds that took place during the life of the GATT, but it is useful to give a brief overview of the general course of their development.

The first half of the life of the GATT coincided with the postwar boom. As noted, during this period growth rates for the advanced nations were at an historic high and full employment targets were consistently met. These conditions provided a fertile background for the GATT Rounds – six in all – that took place before 1970. Countries are more likely to lower trade barriers and expose domestic industries to international competition if the level of economic activity is generally high. In such circumstances, factors of production released from declining industries will be more quickly absorbed by new and expanding ones.

The longest and most notable of the pre-1970 Rounds was the 1964–67 *Kennedy Round*. Although earlier meetings had succeeded in implementing significant tariff reductions, the Kennedy Round is credited with finally dismantling the tariff structures erected during the 1930s. This was clearly an important milestone in the development of the GATT, as it meant that two out of three of its objectives had been achieved: there had been no resumption of the kind of protectionism that typified trade policy in the 1930s, and the barriers to multilateral trade that had emerged during that decade had now gone. Unfortunately, the Kennedy Round also marked the high point of GATT's achievements. Since 1970 new problems of protectionism have emerged onto the world stage, and it is as yet unclear whether these are resolvable. We emphasize the word 'new' here to distinguish post-1970 protectionism from the 'old' tariff structures of the 1930s. But where has the **new protectionism** come from? Part of the answer lies in the ending of the postwar boom. The benign economic climate associated with strong growth and full employment was replaced after 1970 by a much more sombre one conditioned, in the advanced nations in particular, by much slower growth rates and rising unemployment. Now, whereas the boom period made tariff concessions easier to justify, the new recessionary times made nations much more reluctant to expose their economies to more intense international competition when lower levels of economic activity meant that alternative sources of employment would be harder to find for factors released from uncompetitive industries.

The end of the boom was not the only issue affecting trade policy from the early 1970s; important shifts in comparative advantage were also evident at this time. In particular, the noted tendency of *industrialization* amongst formerly 'less developed' nations was decisively under way. We described earlier how the NICs were able to begin to compete with the advanced nations in certain labour-intensive branches of manufacturing – textiles, clothing, footwear and sports goods are amongst the most typical examples – by using the relatively low-paid labour available to them. This process posed clear difficulties for the equivalent industries in the advanced nations and at a time when the advanced economies as a whole were experiencing an economic slowdown. How then did threatened interests in the advanced nations react? The simple answer is that they lobbied governments for protection from the NICs, but because of the presence and authority of GATT this had to be implemented in a *non-tariff form*. Recall again the difference between the old and the new protectionism. The old protectionism of the 1930s was tariff based; the new protectionism post-1970 is not. In fact the new protectionism assumes a variety of guises. Its object, at root, is to enhance the competitive position of domestic industry *vis-à-vis* its rivals. This means that protection can include measures such as:

- state subsidy (which reduces the costs of production to industry and allows it to lower prices)
- preferential state procurement (where governments make their purchases from domestic industry alone)
- discriminatory administrative action (where imports are discouraged by the imposition of arduous bureaucratic procedures)
- quota restrictions on imports (such as the Multi-Fibre Arrangement discussed earlier)
- 'persuading' exporters to voluntarily limit their exports.

> ### Concept
>
> **New protectionism**
>
> The new protectionism refers to the non-tariff-based protectionism that has emerged in the world economy over the postwar period. It is usually contrasted with the 'old' tariff-based protectionism of the interwar period.

The latter form of new protection – the so-called *voluntary export restraint* (VER) – is particularly insidious. The GATT trade rules explicitly commit member nations to a multilateral philosophy. This makes it very difficult for individual nations to be selected as the targets of protection. For example, Italy cannot legally place restrictions on footwear imports from Indonesia; if it wants to protect its domestic market from Indonesian competition it must discourage footwear imports as a whole. This of course might cause a number of countries to invoke retaliatory measures against Italy. However, if Italy can persuade Indonesia to *voluntarily* limit its exports then this potential problem is solved. A bilateral agreement on the *export* side allows Italy to discriminate against Indonesian imports alone without formally breaking GATT principles. Indonesia might be amenable to this course of action because it presents it with a securely open export market (albeit a smaller one) and for fear of more draconian Italian protection should this option fail. The discriminatory potential of the VER has made it an increasingly popular measure with the advanced nations in the context of shifting comparative advantage. Because they are selectively threatened by particular NICs in particular industries, they require the kind of finely tuned protection that the VER offers. Conversely, the more widespread its use, the greater the threat the VER poses to the multilateral trade framework bequeathed by GATT. Moreover, the VER has increasingly become a tool for the management of trade *between* the advanced nations. For example, Japanese car exports to both Europe and the USA have been periodically limited by VER agreements since the 1980s.

Recognizing the threat to openness in international markets posed by VERs, the most recently completed *Uruguay GATT Round* (1986–94) agreed that they should be phased out over a 10-year period: like the MFA, VERs will be officially illegal after 2004. However, similar intentions have been declared in the past. The MFA itself for example is actually the result of a series of temporary deals, but as each expiry date has approached a new 'temporary' accommodation has been reached: the end result is effectively a *permanent* policy. If protectionist lobbying pressures are intense enough, perhaps similar 'temporary' extensions will be made to the VER framework.

The Uruguay Round was also notable for two other features. First, it provided for the replacement of the GATT with the *World Trade Organization*, the new body that will oversee the implementation of the agreements of the Round and the establishment of a new system for the settlement of trade disputes. Second, the Uruguay Round, for all the popular adulation given to its successful completion, very nearly ended in crisis and collapse. The uncertainty was the result of a long-running dispute between on the one hand the European Union and on the other the USA and a disparate group of food producing countries known as the **Cairns Group**. The European Union, which subsidizes agricultural production heavily, was reluctant to concede the principle of completely free trade in agriculture that the Cairns Group preferred. Ultimately a compromise position acceptable to both sides did emerge, but not before the Uruguay Round had been brought to the brink of disaster.

The significance of this dispute lies less in its own seismic proportions, though these were considerable, than in its general form. Both the EU and the Cairns Group are collective representations of very powerful trading interests, of which there are an increasing number in the international economy. The previously mentioned North American Free Trade Agreement (NAFTA), for example, which came into force in 1994, binds together the markets of the USA, Canada and Mexico; while the Asia-Pacific Economic Cooperation (APEC) forum plans a similar arrangement for

Cairns Group: Comprises Argentina, Australia, Brazil, Canada, Chile, Columbia, Fiji, Hungary, Indonesia, Malaysia, Philippines, New Zealand, Thailand, and Uruguay.

an even larger number of countries, including the USA and Japan, by 2010. Now although such groupings are organized on the basis of *internal* free trade, they offer no similar external commitments, and there is a natural concern, reflecting the experiences of the Uruguay Round, that the segmentation of the international economy into *trading blocs* of this type might provide an environment in which large-scale (inter-bloc) protectionism becomes a distinct possibility. The last time the world economy witnessed equivalent segmentation was in the 1930s, when rampant protectionism did severely threaten the integrity of the world economy.

What implications has this discussion for the debate over free trade? At one level we have the arguments of Smith and Ricardo, who were convinced of its universal merits and whose work still forms the kernel of modern trade theory. Yet at a slightly lower and 'messier' level we have the institutionalist views of those such as List and Galbraith, who find that the tidy framework of comparative advantage can become blurred when real economies, with shifting hierarchies of competitiveness, are considered. Here, pressures for protection from vulnerable factors of production are to be expected. Indeed, as in the infant-industry case, protection may even be rationalized as a means to temporarily stabilize production until its competitive promise is realized. Similarly, in the case of established but weakening industries, such as British textiles (see Box 15.1), temporary protection may allow new sources of competitiveness to be developed or alternative sources of factor employment to emerge.

One way to reconcile the differences between the two approaches might be to suggest that, while open international markets do not imperil the security of factors of production in their strategically established uses, free trade is indeed a preferable arrangement. However, when shifting comparative advantage demands large-scale changes in global patterns of production, then the management, through active trade policy, of this process is required. This seems broadly to be a philosophy embodied in the new World Trade Organization. Although its most basic presumption favours openness in trading relations, the WTO explicitly recognizes the principle of 'fair competition'. This acknowledges that when the effects of shifting comparative advantage are unexpected, or too abruptly or too intensely felt, countries may legitimately take measures to soften such effects. At the same time, the WTO retains significant powers to mediate – for which read 'compromise' – in trade disputes. As such it appears at this early stage in its life to be well positioned to oversee the legitimate and temporary use of protection on its own terms.

◼ Summary

◆ International trade permits economies to push the boundaries of specialization and exchange beyond the confines of their own borders. The Ricardian theory of comparative advantage suggests that all participant economies can gain from trade. This conventional wisdom contrasts strongly with older mercantilist notions that trade is a zero sum game.

◆ The policy implication of comparative advantage is that free trade offers benefits to all trading economies. However, where comparative advantage is shifting, there may be claims for protection arising from threatened interests in particular countries or regions.

◆ Since 1945 international trade policy has been possessed of a broad liberalizing ethos under the auspices of the GATT and latterly the WTO. However, coincidence of the ending of the postwar boom and shifting comparative advantage between the developed and less developed countries have led to the re-emergence of protectionism under a new, non-tariff, guise.

Key terms

◆ International trade
◆ Specialization and exchange
◆ Protection
◆ Mercantilism
◆ Comparative advantage
◆ Shifting comparative advantage
◆ Trade policy
◆ The General Agreement on Tariffs and Trade
◆ Uruguay round
◆ The World Trade Organization

Self-test questions

True(t) or false (f)

1. The notion of comparative advantage suggests that all countries can gain from international trade.

2. Mercantilism has protectionist policy implications.

3. Ricardo highlighted factor endowments as the basis for a country's specialization decision.

4. Economists generally suppose that there is a causal link between growth in trade and economic growth.

5. The Kennedy GATT Round is generally credited with dismantling the last elements of interwar tariff protection.

6. The majority of the world's international trade continues to take place between its richest nations.

7. Africa's share of international trade has grown steadily since 1970.

8. The growth of the Asian NICs can be explained by their success in international markets for primary commodities.

9. Despite the arguments for free trade, most countries engage in some form of protectionism.

10. The World Trade Organization was created by the Tokyo GATT round.

Complete the following sentences by inserting the missing word(s)

1. The prevailing philosophy of international trade, which Smith and Ricardo sought to undermine, was called ____.

2. The fundamental policy implication of comparative advantage is that trade should be ____.

3. Ricardo emphasized _____ as the basis of a country's comparative advantage.

4. The Heckscher–Ohlin approach explains the basis of international trade in terms of countries' _____.

5. The Heckscher–Ohlin approach was challenged by the _____.

6. If foreign competition threatens the development of domestic industry, protection is sometimes justified using the _____ argument.

7. _____ arises where countries trade the same or similar goods and services with one another.

8. World trade in textiles is regulated by the _____.

Questions for discussion

◆ What are the advantages of trade?

◆ Explain the arguments underlying the theory of comparative advantage.

◆ What were the later developments in trade theory that built upon Ricardian notions of comparative advantage?

◆ Describe the major patterns of world trade that have evolved since 1945 and explain the notion of shifting comparative advantage.

◆ Why does protectionism arise and what are its main forms?

Further reading

Jepma, C.J., H. Jager and E. Kamphuis *Introduction to International Economics* (Harlow: Longman, 1996). Chapter 3 of this book offers an elaborate but still approachable treatment of international trade theory.

Kitson, M. and J. Michie, 'Trade and growth: a historical perspective', in J. Michie and J. Grieve Smith (eds) *Managing the Global Economy* (Oxford: Oxford University Press, 1995). Provides a short and very readable historical overview of the links between international trade and national economic performance.

Hoekman, B. and M. Kostecki *The Political Economy of the World Trading System* (Oxford: Oxford University Press, 1995). Discusses the political economy of the world trading system in the context of the newly formed World Trade Organization.

Heidensohn, K. *Europe and World Trade* (London: Pinter). Provides an accessible survey of Europe's trading relations in an integrating world trading system.

Moon, B.E. *Dilemmas of International Trade* (Boulder: Westview Press, 1996). Discusses the theory and practice of protectionism, and makes refreshingly open references to modern-day mercantilism.

Internet links

The *World Trade Organization* offers up to date information on general trade issues as well as its own activities. The WTO can be found at: **http://www.wto.org/**
The World Bank's International Trade Division is a useful source of papers on trade issues. These can be ordered online from its Web site at: **http://www.worldbank. org/html/iecit/iecit.html**

The United Nations Conference on Trade and Development (UNCTAD), established in 1964, is the principal United Nations body dealing with trade and development issues. UNCTAD's main goals are to promote the development of the world's poorer countries and to help integrate the world economy on an equitable basis. UNCTAD's Web site can be found at: **http://unicc.org/unctad/en/enhome.htm**

The Balance of Payments and Exchange Rates

CHAPTER 16

Key issues

▶ What is the balance of payments?

▶ Why does balance of payments imbalance matter?

▶ What are exchange rates?

▶ How are exchange rates determined?

▶ What are the main forms of exchange rate policy?

Contents

16.1 Introduction

Having discussed a number of general issues of international trade, we now turn in this chapter to consider trading relationships of the individual economy. The balance of payments provides both a way of thinking about how a country connects to the wider global environment and a means of measuring that connection. In what follows we first discuss the nature of the balance of payments accounts and notions of balance of payments equilibria and disequilibria, together with a brief examination of the recent balance of payments performances of some selected economies. Because international markets, like all others, are coordinated by price signals, it is necessary to develop an understanding of the role played in the international economy by the different currencies in which prices are quoted. Accordingly, this chapter also offers some discussion of exchange rates and different exchange rate systems.

16.2 The balance of payments accounts

The **balance of payments** accounts record the transactions that take place between the residents of one country and the rest of the world over a given period, usually one year. Such transactions take the form of either trade in *goods and services* or trade in *capital*. These two kinds of transaction give rise to a compartmentalization of the balance of payments accounts. Trade in goods and services is recorded in the *current*

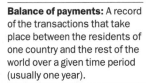

Balance of payments: A record of the transactions that take place between the residents of one country and the rest of the world over a given time period (usually one year).

account, and trade in capital is recorded in the *capital account*. Table 16.1 summarizes the main components of the UK balance of payments accounts.

As is evident from the table, the *current account* has two main components: visible trade in goods and invisible trade in services. Because they are associated with *monetary inflows*, exports of goods produced in the UK are recorded as positive visible trade entries. Imports of goods, because they give rise to *monetary outflows*, are recorded as negative entries. Thus if visible trade is in overall surplus (value of exports greater than value of imports) its value will be positive in nature, reflecting a net monetary inflow from trade in goods, and *vice versa*. Invisible trade includes trade in services, income arising from investments, and transfers. Similar positive and negative entry conventions apply here. The cost of a holiday taken in the UK by a resident from another country is the equivalent of a service export and, because it is associated with a *monetary inflow*, is recorded as a positive invisible trade entry, while the transport cost of shipping using a foreign carrier is a service import (*monetary outflow*) and is recorded as a negative service trade entry. Again, if the value of service exports exceeds the value of service imports, then the resultant invisibles surplus has a positive sign, reflecting a net monetary inflow. If the situation is reversed then the resultant deficit (net monetary outflow) on invisibles will have a negative sign.

Table 16.1 Structure of the UK balance of payments

Current account

Visibles

- Exports of goods (monetary inflow)
- Imports of goods (monetary outflow)

Invisibles

- Services (financial; transport and travel; military services overseas) (inflow and outflow)
- Investment income (interest, profits and dividends) (inflow and outflow)
- Transfers (non-pecuniary and EC contributions) (inflow and outflow)

Capital account

Investment

- Foreign direct investment (FDI) in UK (monetary inflow)
- FDI by UK firms abroad (monetary outflow)
- Portfolio investment by overseas residents in UK (monetary inflow)
- Portfolio investment by UK residents abroad (monetary outflow)

    → Usually considered as long-term flows

Borrowing and lending

- By foreign banks to UK (monetary inflow)
- By UK banks abroad (monetary outflow)
- By foreign non-banking sector to UK (monetary inflow)
- By UK non-banking private sector abroad (monetary outflow)

Use of reserves of foreign currency (inflow and outflow)

Changes in other external general government assets and liabilities (inflow and outflow)

Balancing item

The *capital account* records several kinds of transaction. Consider first those concerned with investment. This can take the form of both foreign direct investment (FDI) (the buying or selling of British and foreign firms) and portfolio investment (the buying or selling of British and foreign share capital). An increase in the UK's FDI and portfolio asset base is indicated by a negative sign (because it denotes a monetary outflow), while a decrease is indicated by a positive sign (because it denotes a monetary inflow). A second form of capital account transaction covers borrowing and lending by the banking and non-banking private sector. Because it is associated with a monetary inflow, borrowing is usually recorded as a positive item, while lending outflows are usually recorded as negative items. However, very occasionally, the repayment of liabilities can result in these signs being reversed. A third form of transaction recorded in the capital account concerns changes in the **foreign exchange reserves** of the Bank of England. For reasons that we will explain shortly, an increase in reserves is recorded as a negative item and a decrease in reserves as a positive one. Finally, the capital account also includes changes in other external general government assets and liabilities. This category includes borrowing by central and local government abroad (an inflow: recorded as a positive item) and lending abroad by central government (an outflow: recorded as a negative item).

There is another way to interpret the structure of the capital account. This entails the identification of two broad elements that we can distinguish by reference to their long-term or short-term nature. Notice from Table 16.1 that investment is usually considered to be a *long-term capital flow*: in other words it is not subject to the same degree of variation as the other recorded capital flows. There is an important reason for this, which is central to a clear understanding of how the balance of payments is made to balance. Investment is in fact an **autonomous transaction** on the balance of payments. 'Autonomous' here refers to transactions undertaken spontaneously *for their own sake*. Both kinds of investment recorded on the capital account obviously originate in the profit-related ambitions of those who make them. All transactions on the current account are also autonomous in nature: a UK resident, for example, buys an import because he or she finds some personal benefit in doing so. Now the remaining items in the capital account are all *short-term* in nature. These are collectively known as **accommodating transactions**, and they are undertaken solely in order to make international trade possible and to make the balance of payments balance. Table 16.2 shows how they work.

Foreign exchange reserves: Stocks of foreign currencies held by central banks.

Autonomous transaction: An autonomous transaction on the balance of payments is one undertaken for its own sake.

Accommodating transaction: An accommodating transaction on the balance of payments is one undertaken for balance of payments purposes.

Table 16.2 How the balance of payments works

Current balance

All are *autonomous* transactions   Net deficit of –£1bn (outflow)

Capital balance

Autonomous transactions (LT investment)   Net deficit of –£1bn (outflow)

Accommodating transactions   Borrowing of +£2bn (inflow)

Balancing item   Zero

Because autonomous transactions are in a combined deficit of –£2bn, accommodating transactions must be made to cover the deficit. Here the suggestion is that the UK must borrow to cover the amount it owes to foreign residents. However, the deficit could alternatively be accommodated using currency reserves.

In Table 16.2 we show a hypothetical deficit of −£1bn for each of the current account and the long-term (LT) investment element of the capital account. Overall then autonomous transactions are in deficit to the tune of −£2bn. This means that economic agents in the UK have sold goods, services, firms, shares and so on abroad worth £2bn less than foreign agents have managed to sell in the UK over the period in question. The −£2bn is in effect a collective debt owed by the UK to the rest of the world: a *net monetary claim*, here on UK residents. How is this debt settled, bearing in mind that foreign residents will want to be paid in their own currencies rather than British pounds sterling? The answer is that payment is facilitated by (positive) accommodating transactions of £2bn. The UK must either borrow the £2bn equivalent of foreign currency that it requires, draw on the reserves of foreign currency that it already holds, or undertake some combination of both. This action leaves the balance of payments accounts as a whole *in balance* (that is, neither in surplus nor in deficit).

What happens if the situation is reversed, and the UK runs a surplus on its autonomous transactions? Here, UK residents have a *net monetary claim on the rest of the world*: foreign residents owe a debt, which must be settled in sterling. In this case the UK can conduct (negative) accommodating transactions, which involve lending the necessary sterling abroad. In addition, or alternatively, the Bank of England may supply sterling abroad in exchange for foreign currencies, thus increasing its reserves of foreign currency (but note that, as suggested, the increase must be by convention represented by a negative sign). Regardless of the precise course of action taken, it should be clear that once again net autonomous transactions are counterbalanced by equivalent net accommodating transactions. In the situation (and its inverse) depicted in Table 16.2 the *balancing item* must be zero. The balancing item, sometimes also referred to as 'errors and omissions', indicates any measurement discrepancies between autonomous and accommodating transactions. In our example there are none, but this is seldom the case in reality. Thus the balancing item permits the balance of payments to balance in an 'accounting' sense.

Table 16.3 describes the actual UK balance of payments position for 1994. Note first that autonomous transactions on current and capital account are indeed counterbalanced by appropriate accommodating transactions, although here the presence of a rather large balancing item complicates matters somewhat. The table also allows us to comment on an element of apparent ambiguity in the balance of payments. It is true in any given period that the balance of payments must balance as overseas debts or receipts are settled, but how does this square with the notions of balance of payments surplus and deficit introduced in Chapter 9, Section 9.5? How can the balance of payments balance and simultaneously be in surplus or deficit? A balance of payments (BP) surplus or deficit in fact refers only to autonomous transactions and then, because investment flows tend to be influenced by long-term factors, to autonomous transactions on the current account. Thus BP surplus or deficit is usually equated with the current account only.

Finally we should note that the notions of BP surplus and deficit introduced here rest on the assumption of a prevailing **fixed exchange rate** system or an environment in which exchange rates are managed by the authorities rather then left to market forces. In Section 16.5 we demonstrate that a market-determined flexible exchange rate system has the effect, in theory, of automatically eliminating BP disequilibria.

Fixed exchange rate: One that is fixed at a predetermined level by intervention by the country's central bank in the foreign exchange market.

Table 16.3 UK balance of payments 1994 (£bn)

Current balance

Visible trade

Exports	–134.5
Imports	–145.1
Net visible trade	**–10.6**

Invisible trade

Service exports	39.5
Service imports	–35.7
Investment income inflow	78.1
Investment income outflow	–67.6
Transfers in	5.4
Transfers out	–10.8
Net invisible trade	**8.9**

Current balance	**–1.7**

Capital balance

£39 billion in autonomous transactions (40.7 – 1.7 = 39)

Investment

FDI in UK	6.7
UK FDI abroad	–16.4
Foreign portfolio investment in UK	31.8
UK portfolio investment abroad (+ve sign indicates a fall in foreign portfolio assets)	18.6
Net investment	**40.7**

Borrowing and lending

UK banks borrowing	47.3
UK banks lending	–49.6
Non-banking borrowing (–ve sign indicates a fall in non-bank borrowing liabilities)	–50.6
Non-banking lending (+ve sign indicates a fall in non-bank lending)	9.8
Net borrowing and lending	**–43.1**

Use of reserves of foreign currency	–1.0

–£44.2 billion in accommodating transactions

Changes in other general government assets and liabilities	–0.1
Capital balance	**–3.5**

Balancing item	5.2

–£44.2 + £39 = £5.2 billion i.e. the value of the balancing item

Source: Central Statistical Office *UK Economic Accounts* (Office for National Statistics) © Crown Copyright 1998

Influences upon the current and capital accounts

What are the main determinants of autonomous current and capital account transactions as depicted in Table 16.1? Which factors influence imports, exports and investment flows?

To take the *current account* first, the demand for imports and exports may be analysed in exactly the same way as the demand for any good or service. In Chapter 2 we demonstrated that a picture of demand – quite literally a picture in the shape of a demand curve – is built up using price as a starting point. Other factors, such as income and tastes, are then admitted for consideration. Following the same process, we can say that the demand for an import will be determined in part by its price relative to the price of home-produced alternatives, which can act as import substitutes. The obvious complication here is that the relative price of imports is influenced by the price-setting decisions of domestic and foreign producers, and by changes in the exchange rate. In the former case, if the price of imports is increasing at a slower rate than that for home-produced alternatives (that is, the rate of inflation in the rest of the world is below that in the home economy) then imports will become more competitive. In considering the influence of the exchange rate on import demand, it will be sufficient to proceed by means of a simple example. Table 16.4 demonstrates the effect of a fall in the sterling exchange rate upon the price, expressed in pounds, of an import from the USA. Because the fall in the pound's value means that more pounds are required to obtain a given amount of dollars, the price of an import from the USA must increase. Assuming that the price elasticity of demand is greater than 1, it follows *ceteris paribus* that a fall in the sterling exchange rate will precipitate a contraction in the demand for imports. Conversely, on the same assumptions, an increase in the sterling exchange rate will be associated with an extension in the demand for imports, as their domestic price falls.

As noted, the level of demand for imports is also affected by changes in domestic incomes. Higher domestic incomes facilitate additional expenditure on goods and services generally, some of which will be on imports. As will be recalled from Chapter 11, Section 11.3, this involves the concept of the marginal propensity to import, which generally implies that the demand for imports varies positively with domestic incomes. Finally, the tastes and preferences of domestic consumers will

---

Table 16.4 The effects of a fall in the exchange rate

On imports:

Initial exchange rate: £1: $4

A pen imported from the USA at $20 will cost £5 (20 / 4 = 5) in the UK

A fall in the value of the pound gives a new exchange rate of £1 : $2

This raises the sterling price of the imported pen to £10 (20 / 2 = 10)

On exports:

Initial exchange rate is again £1 : $4

A watch exported from the UK at £20 will cost $80 (20 × 4 = 80) in the USA

A fall in the value of the pound gives a new exchange rate of £1 : $2

This reduces the dollar price of the exported watch to $40 (20 × 2 = 40)

clearly influence the demand for imports. We should be aware that some hard material judgements fall under this heading. For example, the prodigious increase in the worldwide sales of Japanese cars over the last three decades is certainly grounded on perceptions of quality and reliability as well as the aesthetics of design.

Export demand is similarly governed by the price of exports relative to the prices of goods produced by competitors abroad, by income, and by tastes. To begin with relative prices, we may say that if inflation in the home economy is greater than that prevailing in the rest of the world, then export demand will contract because of declining international competitiveness. Conversely, lower domestic inflation will be associated with improving international price competitiveness and an extension in export demand. The exchange rate also remains an important influence, but in the case of export demand it works in the opposite direction to that described earlier. From Table 16.4 it can be seen that a fall in the exchange rate, because it reduces the number of dollars that have to be exchanged to obtain a given number of pounds, has the effect of lowering the price of UK exports to the USA. Assuming that the price elasticity of demand is greater than 1, it follows *ceteris paribus* that a fall in the sterling exchange rate will precipitate an extension in the demand for UK exports. On the same assumptions, an increase in the sterling exchange rate will be associated with a contraction in the demand for exports, as their price (in foreign markets) rises. Export demand is also a function of *foreign* incomes and tastes. If incomes overseas are rising, or foreign consumer preferences favour exports, then clearly demand will increase and vice versa.

Turning to the *capital account*, it is possible to identify three main influences upon autonomous investment flows: expectations of exchange rate changes, nominal interest rate differentials between countries, and differences in the perceived profitability of investments overseas.

First, where exchange rate changes can be anticipated, it is possible for adroit investors to move out of a currency about to fall in value or into one about to increase in value. In both cases it is possible to reap capital gains as a result. For example, holders of sterling at the time of the European exchange rate mechanism crisis in the autumn of 1992 – which forced down the value of the pound (see Section 16.6) – had they transferred into deutschmarks in time, would have been able to realize a sterling profit as their deutschmarks quickly became worth more in sterling terms. This means that expectations of a fall in the value of a currency will lead to a capital outflow, while expectations of an increase in the value of a currency will be likely to prompt a capital inflow.

Second, because *ceteris paribus* higher domestic nominal interest rates improve the returns on financial assets, it follows that they will be associated with capital inflows. Lower nominal interest rates, presaging poorer returns, will occasion capital outflows.

Finally, a perceived improvement in the profitability of new overseas investments relative to the anticipated returns on new foreign investments in the domestic economy will be associated with a net capital outflow and *vice versa*.

Disequilibria in the balance of payments

We know that there are two ways that the balance of payments can be out of balance: the current account can be either in surplus or in deficit. Neither eventuality is actually a policy problem unless it becomes *persistent*. If a deficit in one year is counterbalanced by a surplus in the next, then over a run of several such years the BP will remain broadly in balance and this, as suggested in Chapter 9, Section 9.5, is the object of policy.

What then is the difficulty posed by a persistent deficit? In such a situation we know that the deficit economy – the UK to continue with our present example – will be piling up net monetary liabilities with the rest of the world for each year for which the deficit persists. The UK must be consistently importing a greater value of imports of goods (visibles) and services (invisibles) than it is exporting. In each year these liabilities are settled (that is, accommodated) by some combination of borrowing from abroad and drawing upon the UK's reserves of foreign currency. *The crucial point is that neither of these avenues of debt settlement can be kept open indefinitely.* A country that tries to run a persistent BP deficit is in effect asking the rest of the world to continually lend it more money, or it is hoping that its foreign currency reserves will never reach the point of exhaustion. In the end, of course, lenders will lose patience and reserves must dwindle away (besides borrowing, the only way to replenish reserves, as we will see, is by running a surplus). A persistent BP deficit is therefore a policy problem because it cannot be sustained, and it may precipitate a crisis of international confidence in the deficit nation.

A persistent surplus appears at first sight to be much less of a problem, and indeed this is usually considered to be the case, not least by some creditor nations themselves as they enjoy the fruits of export-led growth. However, a policy response to persistent surplus may still be required for two reasons. First, BP surplus is associated with the steady accumulation of net monetary claims on the rest of the world. For the surplus country this can involve the acquisition of more and more foreign currency reserves as its credits are settled. Alternatively it may continually make accommodating loans abroad to indebted nations. The point here is that both forms of BP accommodation mean that opportunities for *current consumption* are being sacrificed. The accumulating reserves and the foreign loans could be converted into spending on imports: consumption would be higher at home and BP deficits in other countries would be reduced or eliminated entirely.

The second reason why BP surplus requires a policy response arises from the fact that in balance of payments terms the world economy is a 'zero-sum game': one nation's surplus necessitates concomitant deficits elsewhere. Now, given that the growth of the global economy since 1945 has been predicated on *openness* in trading relationships and general international economic cooperation (see Chapter 15, Sections 15.4 and 15.5), the appearance of significant surpluses and deficits may prompt some countries to seek refuge in highly damaging introspection and even autarky. The rising tide of protectionist sentiment and the re-emergence of isolationist lobbies in the deficit-ridden USA are adequate testament to such dangers.

Finally it is important to emphasize that the balance of payments is not something that policymakers can elevate to the status of an ultimate goal to the exclusion of other macroeconomic considerations. Thus the pursuit of balance of payments balance must be tempered by the competing claims of full employment, price stability, and a satisfactory rate of growth. To grow only slowly, for example, encumbered by high unemployment in order to maintain a given balance of payments position is really no achievement at all.

The balance of payments performance of selected economies

As a means of elaborating upon some of the themes introduced above it will be helpful, in concluding this section, to briefly review the balance of payments performances of some actual economies. Table 16.5 describes the current account positions of the G7 economies since 1990. Notice that the table measures the deficit or surplus on current account in each case as a percentage of GDP. This approach is used because it scales each deficit or surplus in terms of the size of the economy that must accommodate it. The USA for example has a deficit much larger in absolute terms than the UK over the period in question (see Table 16.6), but because the US economy is itself much bigger than the UK economy the relative significance of the USA deficit – as illustrated in Table 16.5 – is not so great.

Table 16.5 shows the major current account debtors amongst the G7 to be Canada, the UK and the USA, while France, Italy and Germany enjoy performances much closer to medium-term equilibrium over the period concerned. Only Japan is in consistent current account surplus. Table 16.6 gives absolute figures for merchandise trade for the G7. Merchandise trade, for the advanced nations usually the largest

Table 16.5 Current balances as a percentage of GDP for the G7

	1990	1991	1992	1993	1994	1995[a]	1996[a]
USA	−1.7	−0.1	−1.0	−1.6	−2.2	−2.4	−2.2
Japan	1.2	2.2	3.2	3.1	2.8	2.3	2.0
Germany	3.3	−1.1	−1.1	−0.8	−1.0	−0.8	−0.9
France	−0.8	−0.5	0.3	0.7	0.6	1.3	1.0
Italy	−1.6	−2.1	−2.3	1.2	1.5	1.9	2.5
UK	−3.5	−1.4	−1.6	−1.9	0.0	−1.1	−1.5
Canada	−3.8	−4.0	−3.7	−4.0	−3.0	−2.5	−1.9

[a] Estimates and projections
Source: OECD *Economic Outlook* (various issues). Reproduced by permission of the OECD

Table 16.6 G7 merchandise trade balances (billions of US$)

	1990	1991	1992	1993	1994[a]
USA	−109	−74	−96	−133	−171
Japan	64	103	132	141	152
Germany[b]	73	25	32	43	53
France	−13	−9	3	9	7
Italy	0	−1	3	33	39
UK	−33	−18	−24	−21	−16
Canada	9	5	6	8	8

[a] Estimate
[b] Data for 1990 and 1992 are for western Germany only.
Source: OECD *Economic Outlook* (various issues). Reproduced by permission of the OECD

single balance of payments component, is trade in goods only. Table 16.6 starkly demonstrates the symmetry between the US merchandise deficit and the Japanese and, to a lesser extent, German merchandise surpluses. Because these are the world's three largest nations (accounting together for approximately 50 per cent of global GNP) it is highly improbable that a large absolute merchandise deficit in one would not be reflected in the counterweight of large surpluses in the others.

We can now relate these real-world balance of payments performances back to our earlier theoretical discussions. There we argued that a persistent balance of payments deficit posed an adjustment problem for the deficit nation. This is certainly the case for the USA, which has in fact been in current account deficit since 1982. Indeed, we might reasonably wonder at the ability of the USA to run a deficit for so long: how has this been possible? Part of the answer lies in the noted size and importance of the US economy. While lesser nations might find their accommodating credit lines running dry in the presence of a persistent balance of payments deficit sooner rather than later, because the USA is responsible for about 25 per cent of global GNP it is deemed to be more creditworthy than most. But this is not to imply that the US deficit is unproblematic. Balance of payments adjustment will be required eventually, and as we have seen this can have painful economic consequences for the adjusting economy. Moreover, as noted, there is evidence that the deficit has prompted a revival of harmful protectionist sentiment in the USA itself. Under a provision in its 1988 Omnibus Trade Bill, the USA reserves the right to take retaliatory protectionist measures against particular countries that it finds to be engaged in unfair trade practices. Japan has been an early target of this so-called 'Super 301' legislation. Such discriminatory action is clearly at odds with the multilateral spirit of the GATT and the WTO (see Chapter 15, Section 15.5), and is of a kind with the pernicious trade policies of the 1930s. The links between strategic balance of payments deficit and surplus in the world economy on the one hand and the re-emergence of protectionism on the other are clear.

16.3 Exchange rates

An **exchange rate** is simply a *price*: the price of one currency expressed in terms of another. At the time of writing (November 1996), one pound sterling is valued at 2.31 German deutschmarks and 1.55 US dollars. These are two of the wide range of current prices at which sterling is bought and sold. Tomorrow, in all likelihood, different prices will prevail. In the remainder of this chapter we shall explain how exchange rates are determined and why they vary over time. We shall also describe the fundamentals of different *exchange rate systems* and their implications for the balance of payments. During this century, two basic forms of exchange rate system have operated: fixed regimes, which have limited the tendency of exchange rates to change; and flexible regimes, which have been much more tolerant of exchange rate variation. We shall examine the relative arguments for these different kinds of arrangement.

16.4 Exchange rate determination

Exchange rate: The price of one currency expressed in terms of another.

Because an exchange rate is a price, it is determined like any other price by the interaction of supply and demand. What then are the influences upon supply and demand in the foreign exchange market? (There are several foreign exchange markets in the world, the largest of which are in London, New York, Singapore and Hong Kong.)

For ease of exposition in what follows we initially limit our discussion to current account transactions. Let us take the French franc as an example. Why would a foreign demand arise for francs? The most simple answer is of course that non-residents of France wish to purchase goods or services from French residents. Because French residents require payment in francs, foreign buyers must obtain (demand) francs in exchange for their own currencies. The supply of francs arises from the purchases of foreign goods and services made by French residents. As foreign suppliers similarly require payment in their own currencies, French residents must obtain these in exchange for (a supply of) francs. In this way, the foreign exchange market can be understood as a mechanism that facilitates the trade process: it allows economic agents resident in different countries holding different currencies to buy and sell goods and services to each other. (As the attentive reader will have noticed, in fact all autonomous transactions on the balance of payments give rise to currency demand and supply in the foreign exchange market.)

A diagrammatic representation of the demand and supply sides of the foreign exchange market for francs is given in Fig. 16.1. Fig. 16.1(a) demonstrates the negative relationship between the demand for francs and the value of the franc expressed in terms of other currencies (that is, the franc exchange rate). As the value of the franc falls (from *a* to *c*), so do the prices of French goods in foreign markets. Assuming that the foreign price elasticity of demand for French goods is greater than 1, this leads *ceteris paribus* to an increase in the foreign demand for French goods and an extension in the quantity of francs demanded (from *b* to *d*). Alternatively, if the franc's value increases, the prices of French goods in foreign markets rise, leading *ceteris paribus* to a fall in the demand for these goods and a contraction in the quantity of francs demanded.

In Fig. 16.1(b) the supply curve for francs is derived in a similar manner. A fall in the value of the franc (again from *a* to *c*) causes the price of foreign goods and services in French markets to rise and therefore the demand for them to fall. Assuming that the French price elasticity of demand for foreign goods is greater than 1, this occasions a contraction in the quantity of francs supplied on the foreign exchanges (from *b* to *d*)

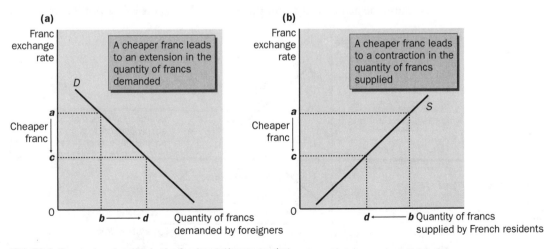

Fig. 16.1 Demand and supply in the foreign exchange market.

as French residents require less foreign currency for imports. Conversely, a rise in the franc's value makes foreign goods in France cheaper, causing an increase in the demand for them and an extension in the quantity of francs supplied.

We can now put the two sides of the foreign exchange market together to see how it works. This is done in Fig. 16.2. The general principles of operation here are identical to those of any normal market. Equilibrium is defined by the intersection of the demand and supply curves. At this point the exchange rate b gives rise to a quantity of francs demanded d and an identical quantity supplied, also d. Because the exchange rate produces an exact fusion of interest between the two sides of the market – no demand is unmet and no supply is ignored – there are no pressures for it to change: hence the equilibrium.

At all other possible exchange rates there can be no such stability. Above the equilibrium exchange rate b a stronger franc gives rise to an extension in the quantity supplied as domestic residents increase their demand for cheaper foreign imports. At the same time, however, the quantity of francs demanded contracts as its higher value makes French exports more expensive in foreign markets. Thus at the exchange rate a, for example, there is an excess supply of francs of the order marked in the diagram. The elimination of excess supply conditions will require a weakening of the franc. As the franc falls in value from a, the quantities demanded and supplied come closer together, but they will not be finally harmonized until the equilibrium exchange rate b has been reached. It should be clear that exchange rates below b, such as c, will stimulate conditions of excess demand. A cheap franc makes French goods more desirable in foreign markets, and therefore foreign residents demand more francs; but it also reduces French interest in imports and thus causes a contraction in the quantity of francs supplied. The unsatisfied demand for francs that now prevails in the market allows the exchange rate to rise. Again, this pressure is fully dissipated only when the equilibrium rate b is attained.

In Fig. 16.2 the demand and supply curves for foreign exchange were derived by reference to the usual market relationships between prices and quantities, with other influences held constant. For the sake of completeness, we should note here that the positions of the curves themselves depend on a range of other relevant factors. Some of these were discussed in our introduction to market dynamics in Chapter 2, and include for example income and tastes. A fall in incomes in the rest of the world would cause the demand curve for the franc to shift to the left as world demand for

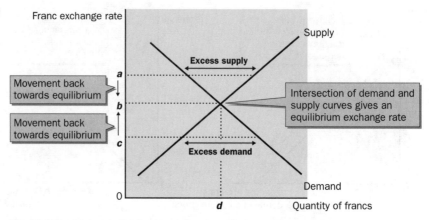

Fig. 16.2 Equilibrium in the foreign exchange market.

all imports fell, whereas a more favourable disposition towards French goods on the part of foreign consumers would shift the franc demand curve to the right as more French goods were sold on world markets. Changes in the domestic interest rate also greatly influence the demand for francs, especially over the shorter run. Because it makes interest bearing assets denominated in francs more attractive (as returns on them become higher), an increase in the French interest rate, compared with that prevailing in the rest of the world, would be associated with a rightward shift in the demand curve for francs. Conversely, a reduction in the French interest rate, because it lowers the attractiveness of franc-denominated interest-bearing assets, would cause the demand curve for francs to shift to the left. Similar considerations will influence the position of the supply curve.

Having explained the process of exchange rate determination and the notion of equilibrium, we need also to understand why exchange rates vary. The underlying connection between trade and the demand and supply of foreign currencies is significant here. If there was no trade, there would be no demand for specifically foreign currency; all material needs and desires could be financed using domestic currency. But there *is* trade. The rest of the world does have a taste, for example, for French wines, and this must involve a foreign demand for francs. Now, which of all the world's currencies would we expect to be in the greatest demand? The obvious answer is the currency of the nation that produces the greatest value of exports. Conversely, there would be less demand for the currencies of nations that exported relatively fewer goods and services.

We are now in a position to understand *secular* movements in exchange rates. ('Secular' is a useful word in this context. It means slow but persistent.) These are explained by the long-term trade performances of nations. Countries that gradually lose shares in world export markets will *ceteris paribus* see demand for their currencies fall. If at the same time these countries maintain healthy appetites for imports, thereby underwriting a consistent supply of their currencies onto the foreign exchanges, then the inevitable outcome will be excess currency supply and **currency depreciation** over the long term. Graphically this would involve something approximating a steady leftward shift of the demand curve for a typical currency, consistently dragging down the equilibrium exchange rate (Fig. 16.3(a)). For nations that are able to improve their shares in world export markets, the concomitant strong currency demand would most likely be associated with long-term **currency appreciation**.

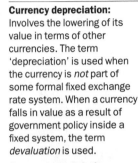

Currency depreciation: Involves the lowering of its value in terms of other currencies. The term 'depreciation' is used when the currency is *not* part of some formal fixed exchange rate system. When a currency falls in value as a result of government policy inside a fixed system, the term *devaluation* is used.

Currency appreciation: Involves an increase in its value in terms of other currencies. The term 'appreciation' is used when the currency is *not* part of some formal fixed exchange rate system. When a currency increases in value as a result of government policy inside a fixed system, the term *revaluation* is used.

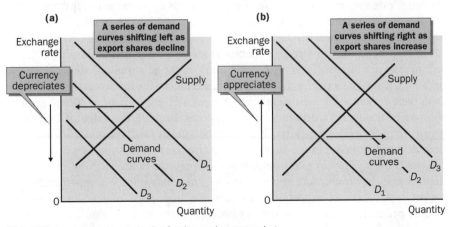

Fig. 16.3 Long-term change in the foreign exchange market.

Graphically, this would involve a steady rightward shift of the demand curve for the typical currency, consistently pulling up the equilibrium exchange rate (Fig. 16.3(b)).

If long-term currency movements can be attributed to trade performance, what of short-term movements? The value of currencies changes on a *daily* basis, and on occasion short-term movements can be very abrupt: how are these to be explained? Short-term currency movements are certainly in part trade related, but the activities of currency speculators can also be an important influence here. Speculation can be a profitable activity for those who are in a position to buy a currency in the anticipation that it will gain in value against other weaker currencies. The increasing size and sophistication of the world's financial markets has facilitated a significant expansion of speculative activity in the last 30 years. Indeed speculation – rather than 'real' trade in goods and services – appears now to be the primary focus of transactions on the world's foreign exchanges. We discuss the implications of this remarkable development in more detail in Section 16.7 below. Of course, government is the other agency that can prompt short-term movements in exchange, particularly through changes in interest rates affecting capital flows. As noted, higher domestic interest rates tend to increase the foreign demand for a currency, thus causing a relatively sharp rise in its value.

16.5 Exchange rate systems

Flexible exchange rates

In Section 16.3 we characterized two general forms of exchange rate system: those that embraced exchange rate flexibility and those that imposed some degree of restriction on exchange rate movements. A flexible system is one that follows free market principles. Exchange rate determination is left entirely to the processes of currency supply and demand described earlier, and governments do not attempt to manipulate the market in order to achieve particular exchange rate outcomes.

A flexible exchange rate system confers a number of advantages upon economies that adopt it. The first and most important of these relates to the balance of payments. We know that one of the central objectives of macroeconomic policy is the achievement of balance of payments balance over the medium term. A flexible exchange rate system automatically provides for this objective without the need for any action whatsoever by policymakers. How? Consider the implications for the foreign exchange market of a balance of payments deficit in, say, the UK. Assuming, for the moment, that all foreign exchange transactions are trade related, the deficit will necessarily be associated with conditions of excess supply of sterling. This is because UK residents will be supplying more sterling to the foreign exchange market than there is demand for. Remember that, here, sterling demand is conditioned by the rest of the world's demand for UK exports. Because the value of imports is greater than the value of exports, there must be a greater volume of sterling supplied than demanded: hence excess supply. By the familiar market processes identified in Fig. 16.2, a currency in excess supply will depreciate in value. Now the sterling depreciation has important implications for the relative price competitiveness of exports and imports. Exports become cheaper in foreign markets, and because import prices rise, import substitutes become more attractive to domestic consumers (see Table 16.4 for an example of this process at work). Assuming that the price elasticity of demand for exports plus imports is greater than 1 (that is, demand is sufficiently price elastic), there will be an improvement in the UK's trade balance. This is known as the *Marshall–Lerner condition*. We must also presume that there are spare resources so that export industries and import-substituting industries are able to respond to the extra domestic demand stimulus that results from the depreciation.

If depreciation facilitated by a flexible exchange rate system impacts upon a deficit in the way described, at what point does the process end? Given that depreciation itself is prompted by, in our example, an excess supply of sterling on the foreign exchanges, it should be clear that this condition will persist so long as the deficit itself is present. This means that the deficit will continue to exert downward pressure on sterling until balance of payments balance is achieved.

A flexible exchange rate also provides an automatic panacea for balance of payments surplus. An excess of UK exports (to continue with our example) over UK imports in value terms gives rise to an excess demand for sterling and an appreciation of the sterling exchange rate. This adversely affects the price competitiveness of UK exports and import substitutes and, on the Marshall–Lerner assumption, worsens the trade balance and erodes the surplus. Again, the process continues until balance of payments balance has been achieved and equilibrium in the market for sterling prevents further appreciation of the currency.

The most famous advocate of the case for flexible exchange rates is the economist Milton Friedman. In his view, flexible rates offer nations the opportunity to enjoy *consistent* balance of payments balance. Friedman argues that any early or 'incipient' (the word he uses) deficit or surplus that might arise will be swiftly dissipated by appropriate corrective exchange rate movements. Flexible rates also offer two other advantages in Friedman's view. First, they allow nations to pursue their own *independent* economic goals in respect of the other objectives of macro policy. As we shall see, membership of a fixed exchange rate system restricts the ability of participant countries to conduct policy autonomously. Second, flexible rates, because they reflect the free interplay of market forces, offer the most appropriate framework for the international allocation of resources through the trade process. The alternative – rates manipulated by governments – Friedman considers to be inimical to the very desirable objective of free trade.

Fixed exchange rates

There are three sets of issues to be explored in respect of fixed exchange rate systems:

- How can rates be fixed in the first place?

- How can a persistent balance of payments deficit be corrected under a regime of fixed exchange rates?

- If exchange rates can be fixed and if balance of payments deficits can be corrected with fixed rates, what are the *additional* merits of fixed systems that might make them preferable to a flexible system?

On the first of these questions it is important to realize that fixity cannot be achieved by simple government decree. As we have seen, there are powerful economic forces at work in the foreign exchange markets; restricting the movement of currencies requires equally decisive countervailing action by the authorities. This can take two broad forms: direct intervention in the foreign exchanges using so-called 'open market operations', or the less direct option of interest rate manipulation.

The fixing of an exchange rate very rarely involves the establishment of a single point away from which a currency is not permitted to move. The usual approach is to define a *target zone* for the currency. The authorities then respond with appropriate measures when market forces threaten to move the currency above or below the zone. Fig. 16.4 depicts a hypothetical case in which for the sake of illustration a target zone has been defined above the market equilibrium. The boundaries of the zone are points *a* and *c* on the vertical axis, while point *b* marks its mid-point and is the central parity of the currency. The market equilibrium here is given by point *d*. Under free market conditions, should an exchange rate emerge somewhere in the target zone, say because of a sudden surge in import demand in the domestic economy (which, remember, would lead to an excess supply of the currency), market forces would tend to drive the rate back down towards the equilibrium at *d*. To prevent this happening and retain an exchange rate above equilibrium the authorities themselves could buy the excess currency supply that is the driving force of the depreciation process. If for example the authorities wished to hold the exchange rate at *b*, they would need to buy the excess supply of currency $y-x$ that arises at this rate. The purchase would of course have to be made using reserves of foreign currency. Alternatively, should market conditions change such that there are excess demand pressures that threaten an appreciation of the currency above the upper limit of the target zone at *a*, then open market operations to sell domestic currency in exchange for additional reserves would have to be undertaken by the authorities. Theoretically then it is possible to hold a currency at any given rate, so long as the associated excess demand or supply of the currency at that rate can be met.

The second policy measure that can be used as an alternative or supplement to open market operations involves the noted use of interest rates. If the German authorities, for example, raise interest rates, investments denominated in deutschmarks become more attractive to overseas investors. This means that they are more likely to demand deutschmarks for investment purposes. The stronger demand for the deutschmark leads to a rise in its value against other currencies. In terms of Fig. 16.4 this would involve a shift in the demand curve to the right such that the demand for deutschmarks is higher at every exchange rate, and a new higher rate

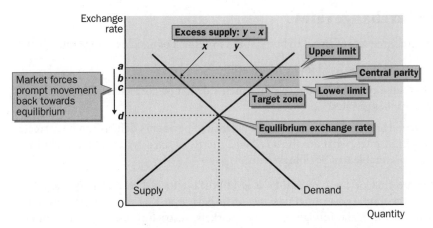

Fig. 16.4 A target zone in the foreign exchange market.

equilibrium is established. Conversely, if the German authorities elected to reduce interest rates, the lower associated demand for deutschmarks would shift the demand curve to the left and force down the exchange rate. The interest rate is therefore a potentially powerful weapon, which the authorities can use to maintain a currency at a selected level in defiance of the will of the market.

It might well be possible to stabilize exchange rates, but how are balance of payments disequilibria to be corrected under more rigid frameworks of this kind? In answering this question, we concentrate upon the most pressing problem of balance of payments *deficit*. There are two possible courses of action open to any deficit economy: expenditure reduction policy or expenditure-switching policy (or, indeed, some combination of both). The aim of **expenditure reduction policy** is to dampen the level of aggregate demand in the domestic economy so that the demand for imported goods and services is reduced. Because the level of exports is unrelated to domestic demand – export demand depends on such factors as foreign incomes, the prices of exports relative to the prices of rival goods produced by competitors abroad, foreign tastes and so on – it follows that the balance of payments position should improve. Moreover, as lower domestic demand may ease domestic inflationary pressures, the international competitiveness of home-produced goods and services should rise, thereby further improving the current account. Domestic demand may be reduced by contractionary monetary or fiscal policy or some combination of both. Unfortunately, dealing with a balance of payments deficit in this way may have deleterious consequences for some of the other major macroeconomic objectives. Thus a lower level of demand is likely to constrain output and effect an increase in unemployment. Recall our caution that balance of payments equilibrium should not be relentlessly pursued at the expense of other goals or objectives.

Turning to **expenditure-switching policies**, the objective here is to encourage overseas residents to buy more exports and to induce domestic residents to purchase home-produced goods and services instead of imports. How are such modifications in consumption behaviour to be achieved? The most obvious method is to *devalue* the domestic currency. This requires the monetary authorities to revise downwards the declared central parity for the currency inside the relevant fixed exchange rate system. Devaluation has the effect of reducing the price of exports in foreign markets as overseas buyers have to part with fewer units of their own currency to obtain a given amount of the devalued currency. The domestic price of imports is simultaneously increased as home consumers must part with more of their currency to obtain a given amount of foreign currency (see Table 16.4 for an illustration). In this way currency devaluation induces relative price changes that favour the products of the devaluing economy. For the devaluation to work – for it to improve the trade balance – two additional conditions must be observed. These were introduced earlier in our discussion of BP adjustment under flexible exchange rates. First, there must be sufficient spare capacity in domestic industries to enable them to respond to greater demand pressures both at home and abroad. Second, the relative price changes themselves must stimulate appropriate behaviour amongst consumers: in other words, there must be a reasonable degree of price elasticity of demand for exports and imports. For a current account deficit to ease following a devaluation, it is generally recognized that the price elasticity of demand for exports plus the price elasticity of demand for imports must be greater than 1 (the noted Marshall–Lerner condition).

It should be clear that the devaluation will also have a positive influence on the

Expenditure reduction policy: Involves reducing the level of aggregate demand in the domestic economy in order to improve the balance of payments position on current account.

Expenditure-switching policies: Policies intended to switch domestic and foreign demand away from foreign goods and towards home-produced goods.

levels of output and employment in the domestic economy, in that demand has been raised. However, there may be a potentially adverse affect on inflation. Rising import prices, particularly for strategically important commodities such as fuel, may introduce cost-push pressures into domestic industry. Finally, we should be aware that there are several additional measures available to governments, which also have expenditure-switching properties. These include import controls, export promotion, and the promotion of domestic industry by fiscal or other means.

Our analysis so far in this section suggests that exchange rates can be fixed, and that balance of payments deficits can be corrected inside fixed rate regimes. Yet in themselves these findings hardly amount to a recommendation of exchange rate fixity; a market-based system also provides for deficit correction. Why then might fixed regimes be actively preferred by policymakers? There are two arguments for exchange rate fixity: the *integration argument* and the *anchor argument*.

The *anchor argument* proceeds by analogy. An economy is thought to gain certain advantages from its ability to issue a single currency that is uniformly acceptable throughout its territory. In Italy, for example, the lira serves equally well in transactions in the north and south of the country and in Sicily and Sardinia. This means that (say) a northern food-processing firm can pay for olive oil from the south in lire and that a Sardinian resident can buy a coffee machine manufactured in the north and also pay in lire. In this way the lira provides *monetary coherence* throughout Italy: all transactions are patently transparent. However, if the four Italian regions just mentioned issued their own individual currencies then a degree of coherence would immediately be lost. The northern oil purchaser would need to obtain southern currency to pay for its olive oil, while the Sardinian resident would require northern currency to pay for the coffee machine. The inconvenience associated with this more complex situation would clearly be much worse were these separate currencies free to fluctuate in value against each other. In fact the more complex the monetary arrangement becomes, the greater the potential fragmentation of the economy. The danger is that producers and consumers may begin to retreat and confine their activities to their own 'monetary region', thus segmenting and impoverishing the competitive process itself. Consumers may not choose to buy what offers them the best value simply because it comes from another region, and the associated transaction might be inconvenient; or the price might be unclear because of currency fluctuations. Economic fragmentation of this sort reduces the exposure of less efficient producers to the full rigours of the competitive process. If greater competition is a desirable objective – and we presume that it is – then the benefit to the Italian economy of the highest possible degree of monetary coherence is clear.

Let us retain the essence of this conclusion and move back to the international level. Different national economies usually have different currencies, which means, in terms of our Italian example, that there is a choice to be made over the *degree of incoherence* that the prevailing international monetary system should have. (We discuss the notable forthcoming case of the EU's single currency below.) On the one hand, fixed exchange rates do not offer the same level of simplicity and transparency that a single currency does; but, on the other hand, it can be argued that they certainly appear preferable to the more uncertain environment often associated with flexible rates.

The second argument for fixed exchange rates is based on the proposition that membership of a fixed regime restricts the freedom that policymakers have to pursue expansionary monetary and fiscal policy. This means that participant economies become *anchored* to a policy of disinflation. Consider the implications of a decision by one member of a fixed system to adopt a relatively loose fiscal and monetary stance compared with those of its partners. Such a shift in policy might be motivated by the need to engineer faster growth and lower unemployment in advance of an election. One unwelcome consequence of reflationary fiscal and monetary policy is likely to be an increase in the rate of inflation. While this might be viewed internally as an acceptable price to pay for the higher level of economic activity that expansion generates, participation in a fixed exchange rate system means that in external terms the policy is impossible to sustain, and indeed must be reversed. This is because the increase in the rate of inflation has negative implications for the international competitiveness of the reflating economy. Faster inflation must mean adverse movements in the relative prices of imports and exports as compared with prices prevailing in the economies of other members of the fixed system. The end result is the likely emergence of a trade deficit for the reflating economy with its fixed system partners. If trade with its partners accounts for a substantial proportion of its overall trade, the reflation will cause an overall trade deficit for this economy.

Now we know from earlier discussion that deficits cannot be sustained in the medium term, so the question arises as to what must be done about this newly derived problem. The key point here is that membership of the fixed system rules out the main form of deficit correction using expenditure-switching policy: currency depreciation. This leaves expenditure reduction as the only available policy option that can be used to deal with the deficit. Expenditure reduction of course involves fiscal and monetary austerity, and thus must reverse the original reflation. It is in this way that fixed exchange rate membership necessarily imposes fiscal and monetary discipline upon participant economies.

Managed rates

Although we have so far framed exchange rate policy in terms of a rather stark choice between market determination and absolute fixity imposed by government, there are several qualifications that must be made here. In the first place there is the third option of the **management** of a floating rate, sometimes referred to in the literature as a 'dirty' float. It is unlikely that the authorities in any country could remain completely indifferent to the behaviour of the exchange rate, and yet this is what the advocates of completely flexible rates recommend. The continuous depreciation of the currency of a deficit nation, for example, would clearly raise concerns over how far it could tolerably sink. Notwithstanding the fact that the strength of a currency is sometimes popularly interpreted as a measure of national economic vitality, a pronounced depreciation would for example have extremely serious inflationary consequences for the domestic economy as the prices of imports with low price elasticities of demand (such as oil) were forced up. Dangers of this kind mean that managed or dirty floating is the more usual alternative to participation in a fixed exchange rate system. In practice, a managed float permits the authorities to intervene in the foreign exchange markets, using direct open market operations, interest rates, or some combination of both, when market imperatives threaten particularly unwelcome currency movements; in all other circumstances the market is the preferred mechanism of control.

Managed exchange rate: One that is influenced by intervention of the country's central bank in the foreign exchange market.

If absolute flexibility is not usually a practical option, what of exchange rate fixity:

can this tend towards the absolute? We have already noted the common use of inter-vention zones around a central exchange rate parity, such as that depicted in Fig. 16.4. This means that *some* movement of rates is possible, but what of the parities them-selves: are they immutably fixed? In terms of the history of actual exchange rate systems the simple answer here is that, in cases where parities have been adjustable, the systems themselves appear more robust than the alternative 'hard' parity systems. In order to illustrate this point we now turn to consider some important examples of actual exchange rate systems.

16.6 Exchange rate systems in practice

In this section we shall review the nature and performance of two major fixed ex-change rate systems: the Bretton Woods system (1945–71), and the European Exchange Rate Mechanism (1979–date). We shall also examine a flexible exchange rate regime: the 'non-system' (1975–date).

The Bretton Woods system

In Chapter 15 we explained how the GATT multilateral trade framework emerged as a response to the chaotic protectionism of the 1930s. Although in trade policy terms the protectionism was tariff based, it also had an exchange rate dimension. This took the form of a series of *competitive devaluations* in which individual countries lowered the values of their currencies in an attempt to encourage domestic economic recovery. However, as with the tariff, devaluation at this time tended to spawn re-taliation rather than recovery, and as more and more countries took part, none was left in a better general economic position than when it started. This kind of back-ground greatly influenced the architects of the postwar international monetary system when they met in Bretton Woods, a small resort town in the US state of New Hampshire, in July 1944.

The Bretton Woods conference gave rise to an agreement that the postwar world economy would be best served by the adoption of a framework of fixed exchange rates. This, it was believed, would both obviate the dangers of a new round of com-petitive devaluations and – on the assumption that trade is enhanced by exchange rate stability – stimulate a general environment in which export-led growth could flourish. The new system was to be based on the US dollar, which was fixed in value by the US authorities against gold (at $35 per ounce). All other currencies in the sys-tem could then be tied to the dollar – and each other – at fixed values. The UK pound, for example, had an initial central parity with the dollar of $4.03. The US dollar was accorded such a pivotal role because of the enormous economic advan-tage that the USA enjoyed over the rest of the world at the end of the war: at this time fully half of the world's output was produced in the USA, and the US Federal Reserve held 67 per cent of the world's gold stock. The purpose of fixing the value of the dollar to gold was to limit the ability of the US authorities to indulge in un-warranted monetary expansion. Because the US commitment to gold meant that all other participants in the system could exchange dollar holdings for gold with the Federal Reserve at $35 per ounce, the US authorities could only issue (print) dollars commensurate with their ability to redeem them from other central banks using gold. The general intention here was to ensure inflation control via sober American monetary policy.

The target zone for the Bretton Woods system was set at 1 per cent, which meant that currencies could fluctuate against each other up to a 1 per cent margin above or below the declared parity. To keep currencies inside their target zones it was recognized that active management of the foreign exchange markets through open market operations would be required. Accordingly, the Bretton Woods agreement established the *International Monetary Fund* (IMF), which would lend participant nations intervention currencies in order that they might fulfil their obligations regarding the stability of their own currencies. The IMF was itself resourced by subscriptions from system members. Finally, and most importantly, it was recognized that currencies would need to be realigned from time to time as, for example, new trading patterns and relationships evolved. Accordingly, the rules of the system permitted devaluations by countries in balance of payments deficit of up to 10 per cent of the value of a currency, but larger movements required IMF approval. Note that a clamour for the right to *revalue* was not anticipated. As we have seen, the pressures upon deficit nations are generally more intense than on those in surplus; moreover, surplus nations are often understandably reluctant to allow revaluation to undermine export-led growth.

In summary, then, the Bretton Woods system was envisaged as one that would provide a framework of stable exchange rates conducive to trade development. Participant nations, with the help of the IMF, would manage their currencies in this spirit but periodic realignments were anticipated in order that changes in real economic circumstances – especially the emergence of persistent balance of payments deficits – could be accommodated.

As we shall see, the actual development of the Bretton Woods system during the 1950s and 1960s differed from this agreed blueprint in some important ways, but the most fundamental element – exchange rate stability – remained in place, and was associated with the most sustained and trade-based economic boom in human history.

Given this kind of achievement, why then did the system not last? One answer is that it became an *overly* fixed exchange rate system: something that its founders had been concerned to avoid. In part this reflected a view that emerged from the IMF that, especially for the most important currencies, *any* movement beyond the agreed target zones was undesirable. More generally, it also became apparent that declared parities were widely interpreted as tokens of economic vitality, to the extent that devaluation came to be associated with national weakness and incompetence on the part of policymakers of the countries experiencing persistent deficits. This had the effect of forestalling those currency realignments that were necessary to the healthy functioning of the system: deficit countries that needed to devalue were reluctant to do so for fear of the consequences of appearing weak, and surplus countries would not revalue because they had no wish to imperil their growth prospects. In this way the Bretton Woods system ossified, unable to make the periodic currency adjustments that would allow the whole currency grid to retain its integrity. Ultimately something was bound to snap, as indeed the US dollar did in 1971.

This brings us to the second and ultimately fatal weakness of the system: the so-called **dollar dilemma**. We know that the US dollar was selected as the system's pivotal currency at the Bretton Woods conference because of the great strength of the US economy at the time. The overwhelming scale of US production also made

Concept

Dollar dilemma

The dollar dilemma referred to the contradictory needs inside the Bretton Woods system for, on the one hand, a sufficient supply of dollars to finance the growth in world trade and, on the other, some constraints on the supply of dollars in order to maintain market confidence in the dollar.

the dollar the world's most heavily demanded currency: dollars were necessary to finance the rest of the world's imports of US goods. The imperatives of postwar reconstruction served only to accentuate this situation. In 1948, to begin to meet the huge demand for dollars, the USA initiated the *Marshall Plan*, a programme of dollar grants to European countries. However, despite this action, what became known as the period of the *dollar shortage* persisted until the end of the 1950s. Thereafter the gap between the supply of and demand for dollars began to be closed by other changes in the US economy itself. There was for example a significant increase in US foreign direct investment. This raised the flow of dollars abroad as US firms opened foreign production facilities. But herein lay the essence of the problem for the Bretton Woods system. What if the outflow of dollars from the USA became so large that it swamped the US capacity – to which it was committed – to continue to redeem dollars using its gold stock? In such a situation the system would fail because the entire exchange rate framework proceeded from the established gold valuation of the dollar. However, the greater availability of dollars was important as it provided the extra volume of *the* key currency necessary to finance the continued unprecedented growth in world trade. In effect this meant that the world economy did not want a dollar shortage, but there were great risks should the shortage turn into a glut. The problem became known as the *Triffin dilemma*, after the economist Robert Triffin, who (presciently) identified it in 1960.

Unfortunately, from the mid-1960s the shortage *did* give way to glut. The most notable cause was the domestic economic expansion associated both with the escalation of the Vietnam War and with President Johnson's 1964 announcement of the 'Great Society' programme. (The Great Society programme involved *inter alia* increases in government spending on education, housing, and measures to tackle poverty.) This served to effect a serious deterioration in the US balance of payments on the current account, resulting in significant increases in dollar holdings by foreign central banks. While confidence in the gold basis of the dollar held, the central banks were happy to accumulate dollar assets; in fact, because they could not obtain sufficient gold for reserve use purposes (as the world supply of gold was growing too slowly), they greatly needed this alternative prime reserve asset. But the threat of a dollar crisis loomed ever larger as these holdings increased. At the beginning of the 1970s a further and even more severe deterioration in the US balance of payments appeared to convince private agents (that is, speculators) in the foreign exchange markets that the dollar would have to be devalued: consequently the dollar was sold heavily in favour of more robust currencies such as the deutschmark and the yen. This meant that the German and Japanese central banks had to buy dollars using their own currencies in order to prevent them from rising in value (they had to meet higher demand with an equivalent increase in supply, in other words). As the following passage illustrates, this very quickly became an impossible task.

On a single day, May 4 1971, the Bundesbank [the German central bank] had to buy $1 billion to hold its dollar exchange rate fixed in the face of the great demand for its currency. On the morning of May 5, the Bundesbank purchased $1 billion during the first hour of foreign exchange trading alone! At that point the Bundesbank gave up and allowed its currency to float. (*Source*: P.R. Krugman and M. Obstfeld, *International Economics* (3rd ed.) (New York: Harper Collins, 1994) p. 549)

This tide of speculation against the dollar continued unabated until 15 August 1971, when President Nixon effectively dissolved the Bretton Woods system by announcing that the USA would no longer honour the agreement to exchange dollars for gold. As the fixed gold value of the dollar was at the very heart of the framework of interconnected currency rates the entire structure simply melted away, ultimately to be replaced by the present **non-system** of flexible exchange rates.

The non-system

Although it had been informally operating for some time, the non-system was officially endorsed by the IMF at a meeting in Jamaica in January 1976. That the IMF survived the demise of the system it was designed to oversee is, together with the spirit of international economic cooperation that this institution embodies, one of the lasting legacies of Bretton Woods. The Jamaica meeting gave permission for the former Bretton Woods participants to assume any exchange rate policy they found appropriate, subject to the exhortation that they should not seek to manipulate exchange rates for unilateral competitive gain: a clear reference to the regrettable currency dispositions of the 1930s. In fact, as we saw in Chapter 9, the major macroeconomic policy preoccupation of this period was not exchange rates and the balance of payments but inflation.

Indeed, it is worth pausing for a moment here in order to explain how the resurgence in worldwide inflation actually *necessitated* a return to a more flexible exchange rate environment. Table 9.3 illustrates the high and uneven incidence of inflation amongst the advanced nations in the 1970s. Compare for example the UK and German experiences. The average inflation rate in the UK from 1973 to 1979 was 16.7 per cent; in Germany over the same period the rate was 4.9 per cent. As we have seen, differing inflation rates have important effects upon the relative international price competitiveness of nations. The high inflation rate in the UK meant lost price competitiveness *vis-à-vis* Germany and other economies with a similar capacity for greater price stability. In a fixed exchange rate system the UK could only regain international price competitiveness by imposing relatively severe expenditure reduction policies. Domestically, this makes the option of expenditure switching much more attractive. The main form of expenditure-switching policy is currency devaluation or depreciation. Now, under fixed exchange rate conditions, it is simply not possible to engineer the *series* of devaluations required to confront the lost international price competitiveness implications of an inflationary environment. To do so would clearly undermine any pretence of exchange rate stability. This means that a period of high and unevenly experienced inflation will tend to prise countries away from an adherence to exchange rate fixity so that they can use currency depreciation both to protect their international price competitiveness and to stave off the need for severe expenditure reducing policies.

Although the non-system provides for exchange rate flexibility this is generally recognized to be a *managed* flexibility. We argued earlier that no country can afford to be entirely indifferent to the behaviour of its exchange rate. Pronounced depreciation can have, for example, severe inflationary consequences for the domestic economy as import prices are forced up, while pronounced appreciation will clearly impinge upon the prospects for exports and growth. It has been a feature of the non-system that exchange rates have at times moved to positions that appear to be at variance with conditions prevailing in, and the longer-term interests of, domestic economies. For example, in 1980–81 the sterling exchange rate climbed rapidly to $2.45 on the back of high domestic interest rates and because North Sea oil caused

Non-system: Refers to the broad system of flexible exchange rates prevailing in the world economy since 1973.

speculators to take a more favourable view of the currency. This in part can help to explain the abrupt contraction in UK manufacturing output of some 20 per cent as firms found themselves less able to compete on price in foreign markets and as the relative price of manufactured imports fell. The recessionary impact on the economy as a whole was of an order not seen since the 1930s. Yet in the sterling crisis of 1984–85 the value of the pound plummeted to $1.04 at its lowest point as speculative sentiment turned sour. The central point here is that there was nothing in the 'real' economy that could justify such wild oscillations in the value of the pound over a relatively short period and the damage they caused. It was this kind of experience that helped to prompt the evolution of forms of collective management of the non-system.

While the misalignment of sterling might be a serious problem for the UK economy, it has limited impact upon the fortunes of the rest of the world. However, this is not true of the US dollar, which, reflecting the absolute size of the US economy, remains the world's most important currency. In the mid-1980s the dollar was generally recognized to be overvalued, given the presence of a large US current account deficit, but contrary to the expectations of currency market theory there was little sign of the necessary and corrective dollar depreciation. This meant of course that in the absence of US expenditure reduction policy the deficit would in all likelihood become even larger. It is at this point that the issue becomes a more generalized one. The intractability of the deficit gave rise to increasingly strident calls from US industrial and labour lobbies for protection, and the major economies recognized that the possibility of a retaliatory trade war existed unless some ameliorative action could be taken. Accordingly the **G5** group of nations, in the 1985 *Plaza Agreement*, declared their collective intention to orchestrate an appropriate managed depreciation of the dollar. This amounted to a general recognition that the non-system could not be coordinated on the basis of market sentiment alone. In 1987 the G5 plus Canada moved a stage further by recognizing – in the *Louvre Accord* – that a greater degree of stability amongst the world's major currencies would bolster the prospects for trade growth, and therefore for general economic expansion. The Accord established undisclosed target zones for the currencies of its signatories. The zones themselves were informed by an awareness of the basic economic circumstances of each economy such that currency levels would be both stable and appropriate.

The European exchange rate mechanism (ERM)

It would seem from the experiences of Bretton Woods and the non-system that both overly fixed and highly flexible exchange rate regimes have limitations. One of the critical failings of the Bretton Woods system was the absence of any formal mechanism of currency adjustment. It had been envisaged that devaluations would periodically occur in order to dissipate evident balance of payments imbalances, but this simply did not happen on a sufficient scale. Similarly, theoretical predictions that the non-system would be typified by smooth, orderly and appropriate currency movements have not been realized, and substantial intervention has occurred as a result. In practice what seems to be required is some kind of compromise between near absolute fixity and limitless flexibility. The ERM, at least for part of its life, can be seen to have been the institutional embodiment of such a compromise. The ERM

G5: The world's five leading industrial nations: the USA, Japan, (the then) West Germany, France and the UK.

is actually the centrepiece of a wider institutional framework: the European Monetary System (EMS). The EMS has two classes of member: full and associate. Full members of the EMS undertake to manage their currencies within the ERM fixed exchange rate grid. Associate members retain their currencies outside the ERM but do participate in the wider institutional framework of the EMS.

The ERM emerged in 1979 as a 'zone of monetary stability in Europe'. It was conceived as a *fixed but adjustable* exchange rate system, which would do two things. First, it would provide the exchange rate stability conducive to trade growth in an integrating EU (see Chapter 2, Section 2.5). Second, by binding the monetary policies of participant nations to the highly successful policy operated by the German Bundesbank, it would provide them with a means of *inflation control*. Recall the *anchor argument* for fixed exchange rates. This suggests that members of a fixed system cannot permit their inflation rates to diverge significantly from the lowest rate in the system. The lost international price competitiveness that would result cannot be ignored, nor can it be regained by devaluation (fixity forbids regular recourse to this option). In fact the only means by which price competitiveness can be restored is by bearing down on inflation, which *must* involve the setting of an appropriately tight monetary policy. In the ERM this reduces to mirroring the monetary policy of the Bundesbank.

The parity grid of the ERM is based on a specially created hybrid currency: the European Currency Unit (ECU). The ECU is a weighted average of the currencies of all member states. The weights accorded to each currency reflect its exchange rate and the importance of its economy in terms of both the size of its national product and the scale of its trade within the EU. Originally the amounts of each currency upon which the weights are based were subject to revision every five years, but they have been unchanged since 1989 and were formally fixed in 1994. Table 16.7 describes the present composition of the ECU in terms of the proportions allocated to each EMS currency. Inside the ERM each central bank declares a parity with the

Table 16.7 The composition of the ECU

	Amount[a]	Weight (%)[b]
Belgian / Luxembourg franc	3.431	8.1
French franc	1.332	19.3
Lira	151.80	9.7
Guilder	0.2198	9.6
Deutschmark	0.6242	30.4
Danish krone	0.1976	2.5
Irish punt	0.008552	1.1
Peseta	6.885	5.2
Drachma	1.44	0.7
Pound sterling	0.08784	12.6
Escudo	1.393	0.8

[a] These amounts have applied since September 1989.
[b] Weights based on exchange rates on 30.10.90.
Source: UK Treasury. Crown copyright is reproduced with the permission of the Controller of Her Majesty's Stationery Office

ECU and through it with all other participant currencies. In this way a parity grid for the entire ERM is formed. The target zone for most currencies was initially set as a 2.25 per cent band (+ or −) around the central parity. In the event of a pair of currencies threatening to move too far apart, *both* central banks are required to intervene in the foreign exchange markets to re-establish the integrity of the target zone. This approach established a degree of *symmetry* in the ERM that had been lacking in Bretton Woods: there, the responsibility for currency defence had fallen primarily upon countries with weaker currencies.

Our main interest here is in the evolution of the ERM. Between 1979 and 1987 the system functioned as intended in a fixed but adjustable manner. In other words the dominant concern was for currency stability within the prescribed limits, but appropriate currency realignments were made from time to time. This meant that the kind of tensions associated with overdue adjustment, which had typified the Bretton Woods system, did not have the chance to build up. However, from 1987, following the advent of the *Basle Nyborg Agreement*, the ERM ossified to produce sets of parities that were in effect *non-adjustable*. This meant that the system had no way to relieve tensions created by exchange rates that became misaligned: they had simply to be defended using the familiar tools of currency management. Ironically, the Basle Nyborg agreement was actually an attempt to strengthen the integrity of the ERM by more forcefully equipping its members to withstand speculative attacks upon their currencies. It established a new protocol of parity defence – facilitating, for example, the coordinated use of interest rate changes – and enhanced the pooled resources available for intervention in the foreign exchange markets. However, the agreement also relegated the option of currency realignment to the status of 'last resort'. Now, insofar as the last resort of realignment fused into a policy of *no* realignment, the ERM became possessed of a fundamental shortcoming as divergent economic performances amongst member states raised inevitable and increasingly stark questions as to the sustainability of established parities.

The integrity of the post Basle Nyborg 'unadjustable' parity grid eventually foundered upon problems associated with the reunification of Germany in 1989. Reunification sparked a huge reconstruction programme in the old East Germany, which was funded by an expansionary fiscal policy in Germany as a whole. Fears that this policy might have inflationary consequences prompted the Bundesbank to operate a tighter – that is, higher interest rate – monetary policy. In turn, higher interest rates had the effect of putting upward pressure on the deutschmark and downward pressure upon other major European currencies such as sterling and the French franc. Eventually the markets seized first upon sterling, and despite heavy intervention by the Bank of England in its favour and the raising of UK interest rates to emergency levels, the pound left the ERM in October 1992, two years after it had belatedly joined. The lira and the Spanish peseta were floated at the same time. The following summer, renewed tensions in the ERM, which again favoured the deutschmark, were dissipated only by a widening of the margins of fluctuation inside the parity grid from ±2.25 to ±15 per cent. Fig. 16.5 illustrates the movement to the (very much) wider band.

The pound plummets after leaving the ERM

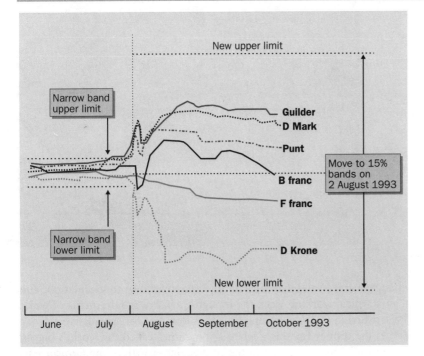

Fig. 16.5 The widening of the ERM band in 1993.
Source: *Bank of England Quarterly Bulletin* (November 1993).

16.7 Currency speculation and exchange rate systems

The three exchange rate systems discussed in the previous section have all fallen victim to speculative forces. In the case of Bretton Woods, the outcome was terminal; for the non-system and the ERM, substantial modifications have had to be made to deter speculation. In this section we briefly consider the relative scale of speculative transactions on the foreign exchange markets, explain the reasons for the rapid growth in speculation over the last 30 years, and consider the arguments for and against speculation as a defensible form of economic activity.

In Section 16.4 we explained that the underlying supply and demand structures of the foreign exchange market were derived from the contours of international trade. A currency is supplied to the market because its (domestic) holders wish to buy imports for which foreign currencies are required; the demand for the currency arises from the foreign demand for domestic output. To buy this output, foreign residents need the domestic currency in which it is priced. Despite the presence of speculative transactions it is still reasonable to interpret the basis of the foreign exchange markets in trade terms because it is trade that guides the long-term movements of currencies. However, the contemporary scale of speculative transactions illustrates their latent and occasionally exercised capacity to engineer substantial shorter-term exchange rate oscillations. It has been recently estimated that trade-based transactions on the foreign exchanges now account for only one-fifth of total

How many of these to the franc?

foreign exchange business, and that most of the rest is given over to speculation. This means that in a typical working week the foreign exchange requirements of world trade can be satisfied in *one day*, leaving the other four free for speculative activity. But where does the money for this – what is sometimes called the world's biggest casino – come from? The answer lies in the spectacular growth of the *Eurocurrency markets* over the last 30 years.

Briefly, the eurocurrency markets grew out of desire on the part of governments, banks and firms to hold currency deposits beyond the regulatory control of issuing authorities. The first example involved dollar deposits by the old Soviet Union in UK banks in London in the 1950s. In the climate of the Cold War the Soviet Union was anxious to keep its dollar reserve beyond the reach of the US authorities. The banks then lent on these dollars in the normal commercial way. In the 1960s, as US banking regulations were tightened, the attraction of the eurodollar market increased. Dollars from this source could be used in ways denied to banks in the USA. Following the 1973–74 and 1979 oil price rises **OPEC** members too made substantial deposits in the eurodollar market. Indeed 'offshore' banking in order to escape domestic monetary regulation became established for many 'key' currencies and spread to other European centres, such as Paris and Frankfurt, and to financial centres in other parts of the world. In the early 1990s the size of the eurocurrency market was estimated to be of the order of $6 *trillion*. This is the pot from which speculative activity in the foreign exchange markets is financed. When we couple the rapid growth in unregulated offshore banking with the increasing technological sophistication of the financial markets, the basis of the new 'global' casino is clearly apparent.

With its obvious connotations of substantial risk – even recklessness – the word 'casino' is often used pejoratively in the literature. But is this the appropriate way in which to characterize currency speculation? The noted champion of flexible exchange rates, Milton Friedman, thinks not. In his view speculation is actually a source of *stability* – rather than instability – in the foreign exchange markets. Friedman argues that because speculators are well informed they will be aware of the long-term exchange rates generally appropriate to the economic performances of countries. Accordingly they may reasonably be expected to sell a currency for which depreciation is economically warranted, but as it nears its sustainable level they will

OPEC: The Organization of Petroleum Exporting Countries, founded in 1960.

stop selling and perhaps even buy. This means that speculation actually serves to put a higher floor under the currency than would be present if the market was wholly trade centred. For a currency that is liable to appreciate, the same kind of analysis puts a lower ceiling in place.

Against this argument for speculators as economic social workers, helping currencies to find their appropriate place in the world, there is the view that because currency turbulence is inimical to trade, and as speculation fosters turbulence, speculation is of itself an economic 'bad'. From this perspective it is far better to manage exchange rate movements so that they both conform to the secular drift of long-term trade performance and retain the kind of short-term stability conducive to trade development and wider economic growth. Whether this is best done through managed flexibility or a fixed but adjustable exchange rate system is an open question.

"How's the wobble doing against the jitter?"

16.8 European Monetary Union

We conclude this chapter with a brief overview of the issue of European Monetary Union (EMU). What kind of context does the preceding discussion provide for the notion of a single currency in Europe? With the advent of a single currency, there would in fact be no exchange rate fluctuations inside the region formed by participant countries, and moreover the balance of payments relationships that currently exist between these countries would appear in a wholly different form. Why are such developments thought desirable, and what are the possible costs of a single currency in Europe?

The first thing to say is that we have been part way down this road before. In 1970 the *Werner Plan* anticipated that monetary union for the six original members of the European Economic Community (EEC) would be completed by 1980. (The original members of the EEC were West Germany, France, Italy, the Netherlands, Belgium, and Luxembourg.) However, the resurgence of worldwide inflation over the course of the 1970s prompted differing policy responses amongst the six, and this prevented the kind of monetary policy convergence and gradual tightening of exchange rates that was to presage full monetary union. Present European ambitions for monetary union were revived in the EU's Single European Act (SEA) in 1986. As discussed in Chapter 2, Section 2.5, this was the legislation that provided for the European single market. Recognizing that a fully integrated market requires as high a degree of monetary coherence as possible, the SEA committed member states to the principle of a single currency. Recall the *integration argument* for fixed exchange rates discussed in Section 16.5. This states that a market will operate most efficiently and competitively when it is served by one currency. In Section 16.5 we used the hypothetical example of Italy to show that the presence of different regional currencies inside the Italian economy would be likely to prompt the fragmentation of markets, reducing efficiency and competition to levels below those prevailing when the single national currency – the lira – is employed. The SEA simply applied the same principle to Europe as a whole: that the evolution of a *single market* in Europe should be mirrored by the emergence of a *single currency* in Europe.

The details of EMU have since been clarified by the *Delors Report* (1989) and the *Maastricht Treaty* (1991). The Delors Report set the tone for the general form and evolution of monetary union, while the Maastricht Treaty formally endorsed Delors in its key respects, and established the timetable and criteria for the introduction of the single currency.

The Delors Report laid down three important and interconnected principles. The first concerned the nature of the new European central bank (ECB), which would oversee EU monetary policy upon the advent of the single currency. This institution would replace the various national central banks that had hitherto been responsible for the conduct of policy in each EU country. Thus it would set the one European interest rate and manage the exchange rate of the new single currency against others outside the EU.

What we might term the 'general disposition' of the ECB would therefore be of crucial importance. The Delors Report left no room for doubt as to what this should be. The ECB would be modelled on German Bundesbank: it would in other words be committed to *price stability*, and would operate *independently*, free of political control as exercised by either national governments or EU authorities. Because the ambition is for the single currency to exhibit a tendency towards low inflation, rectitude in monetary policy (on the part of the ECB) would have to be matched by similar parsimony in the conduct of fiscal policy, which is to remain in the hands of national governments. The second principle of the Delors Report was therefore that national budget deficits in the EU should be reduced, and that national fiscal policies should be set on a path of convergence.

Finally, the Report recognized that setting an austere tone for the conduct of macroeconomic policy at the European level would have negative implications for employment prospects, particularly in the less economically advanced regions of the EU, such as parts of Portugal, Greece, southern Italy and some northern areas of the British Isles. The third and final principle of Delors was therefore that EU structural intervention funds be doubled in size. The purpose of these funds is to assist the economic development of EU regions in chronic decline.

Building upon the Delors Report, the Maastricht Treaty agreed that full monetary union would begin on 1 January 1999 for those EU nations able to meet a series of economic convergence criteria. Full EMU would involve the irrevocable fixing of national exchange rates with a view to their replacement by the single currency – the 'euro' – by 2002. The convergence criteria established at Maastricht were:

- that the inflation rate in each national economy should not exceed that of the average of the best three EU national performances by more than 1.5 per cent

- that long-term interest rates in each national economy should not exceed the average of the lowest three rates in the EU by more than 2 per cent

- that the indebtedness of national governments should be limited, expressed as either a 3 per cent ceiling on annual budget deficits or a ceiling on accumulated debt equivalent to 60 per cent of GDP

- that national currencies must be maintained in the narrow (that is, 2.25 per cent) band of the ERM for two years, without undue tensions arising.

The position established at Maastricht was that for a country to be entitled to participate in monetary union all four criteria would have to be met. However, developments since 1991, not least the successive crises of the ERM, have prompted the emergence of more flexible interpretations. Thus the exchange rate criterion was ultimately based on the post-1993 version of the ERM, with its much wider margins of fluctuation, and there was tacit acceptance of 'creative accounting' on the part of some governments in order to allow them to clear the indebtedness hurdles. It is not unreasonable to conclude on the basis of these manoeuvres that the wider economic and political will that favours monetary union in Europe came to override what were perceived as narrower technical objections to this process.

On 1 May 1998, of those countries deemed to have met the Maastricht criteria, 11 elected to proceed to EMU. These are: Austria, Belgium, Finland, France, Germany, Ireland, Italy, Luxembourg, Netherlands, Portugal, and Spain. Of the remaining EU member states, the UK, Sweden and Denmark decided against joining in this 'first wave', and Greece failed to meet the convergence criteria. The UK government's position is that a successful single currency in Europe would be of benefit to those who subscribe to it. Thus in principle the UK is committed to the EMU project. However, despite the fact that the UK economy satisfied the Maastricht convergence criteria (except for participation in the ERM), the government considers that the business cycles in the UK and Europe are, for the moment, too far apart to allow UK participation at the inception of the euro. Relatively high interest rates in the UK are at present necessary to curb inflationary pressures there, while elsewhere in Europe interest rates are generally lower. Thus participation in EMU in the first wave could saddle the UK economy with an interest rate regime inappropriate to prevailing UK economic conditions. Eventually, the government expects that the UK economic cycle will become more closely matched with that generally evident in Europe. Participation in EMU – following a referendum – will then be the right thing to do. However, in the government's view the UK is some years away from this position.

What then are the great advantages of a single currency in Europe: the bigger prize that has allowed some of the 'technicalities' of Maastricht to be swept aside? We saw in Chapter 2, Section 2.5, how the European single market was conceived as the EU's response to the fragmentation of the customs union created by the 1957 Treaty of Rome. Recall that the poorer collective performance of the EU economy, relative to the USA and Japan in particular, had prompted concerns in the EU that it had lost something of its competitive edge. This was to be restored by raising the level of economic integration in the EU: substituting the customs union for a single market. The addition of the single currency will entail even further integration and, its proponents claim, will confer specific benefits on Europe as a whole. The most important of these include, at the 'macro' level, a stronger presence in the global monetary system provided for by the euro than is currently enjoyed by most national EU currencies. If it begins to eclipse the dollar as the world's key currency, the financial markets may accept lower interest rate premiums as the price of holding the euro; this of course means a lower EU interest rate than would otherwise prevail and consequent stimuli to investment and consumption in Europe. In micro terms, the single currency will necessarily eliminate the transaction costs associated with exchanging the many different currencies that currently circulate in Europe. Similarly it will end the information uncertainties that arise from the denomination of prices in many different currencies in the European market. Because all prices will be expressed in euros, producers and consumers will be working with clearer price signals, and this will strengthen competitive processes in Europe.

The single currency has two main types of cost associated with it. First, there are the obvious once and for all costs of redenomination. At present, the financial and wider economic systems of each EU country are tailored to national currencies. When the euro is introduced all these systems will have to be recalibrated to accommodate it. The second 'cost' is associated with the loss of the option to devalue the national currency. Following the introduction of the single currency, devaluation for any one country will clearly not be possible as there will be no national currency to devalue. For countries that have traditionally resorted to this device as a means of restoring some degree of international price competitiveness – arguably, the UK falls into this category – the loss of the option to devalue may be regrettable.

There is a further issue here. This concerns the balance of payments positions that currently exist between the EU countries. What happens to these surpluses and deficits upon the advent of the single currency? The simple answer is that they will be transformed into *inequalities between regions*. In the same way that regions in (say) the British economy grow at different rates, enjoy different levels of income, and endure different levels of unemployment, so will different parts of a fully integrated Europe. The anticipation is that the greater competitiveness prompted by integration will serve to ameliorate these inequalities, as will the improved EU structural intervention funds referred to earlier.

■ Summary

◆ An economy's balance of payments and its exchange rate are inextricably linked. In theory, a floating exchange rate will automatically produce a balance of payments balance; policy may then be concentrated on other objectives free of any concern for the external account. However, where exchange rates are fixed or managed, the emergence of balance of payments disequilibria requires active forms of policy correction. Expenditure reduction involves internal deflation, and invokes movement out of deficit by virtue of lower domestic aggregate demand and a reduced demand for imports. In the face of a deficit, the second form of policy, expenditure switching, usually involves currency depreciation, which improves the price competitiveness of exports and import substitutes.

◆ Since 1945 the world economy has relied upon both fixed exchange rates (under the Bretton Woods system) and flexible rates (under the 'non-system'). The non-system has, however, not been characterized by freely floating exchange rates. Indeed at times during the 1980s exchange rates have been collectively managed by the major industrialized nations. Moreover, inside the non-system regional fixed exchange rate regimes such as the ERM have been developed. Although the ERM has been damaged by the activities of currency speculators, it is to be succeeded in 1999 by monetary union in Europe.

■ Key terms

◆ Current account
◆ Capital account
◆ Autonomous transactions
◆ Accommodating transactions
◆ Balance of payments disequilibria
◆ Exchange rate

◆ Depreciation

◆ Appreciation

◆ Flexible exchange rates

◆ Fixed exchange rates

◆ Expenditure reduction policy

◆ Expenditure switching policy

◆ Currency speculation

◆ Monetary union

Self-test questions

True (t) or false (f)

1. Foreign direct investment is recorded in the current account of the balance of payments.

2. Accommodating transactions are those undertaken for their own sake.

3. If a country runs a surplus on autonomous transactions, it has a net monetary claim on foreign residents.

4. Balance of payments disequilibria are usually only a problem when they become persistent.

5. When the dollar falls in value, USA exports become more expensive.

6. When the pound sterling increases in value against the French franc, holidays in France become cheaper for UK residents.

7. A dirty float occurs when the value of a currency moves wildly up and down.

8. The Bretton Woods system was centred on the US dollar.

9. Some economists think that currency speculators exert a stabilizing influence on foreign currency markets.

10. One 'cost' of EMU will be the loss of the option for individual countries to engage in unilateral devaluation.

Complete the following sentences by inserting the missing word(s)

1. Balance of payments disequilibria are a problem only when they become ____.

2. An exchange rate is the ____ of one currency expressed in terms of another.

3. Balance of payments deficits on current account can be tackled by either ____ or ____.

4. For a devaluation to prompt an improvement in the current account, the ____ condition must be observed.

5. Exchange rates are determined by the laws of ____ and ____.

6. Short-term movements in exchange rates may be caused by the activities of ____ and the interest rate policies of ____.

7. The two main arguments for fixed exchange rates are the ____ and the ____.

8. The Bretton Woods system was undermined by the manifestation of the ____.

9. The emergence of worldwide ____ in the early 1970s necessitated a more flexible exchange rate environment.

10. The 1985 Plaza Agreement achieved a managed ____ of the dollar.

■ Questions for discussion

◆ Outline the structure of the balance of payments accounts.

◆ Explain the significance of autonomous and accommodating transactions in the balance of payments.

◆ What is meant by balance of payments surplus and deficit, and which general forms of policy are appropriate to each?

◆ How are exchange rates determined?

◆ Explain the differences between fixed and flexible exchange rate systems and the advantages and disadvantages of each.

◆ Outline the basis upon which the evolution of the single European currency has so far proceeded.

■ Further reading

Jepma, C.J., H. Jager and E. Kamphuis *Introduction to International Economics* (Harlow: Longman, 1996). Chapter 2 provides a complementary introduction to balance of payments theory.

Scammell, W.M. *The Stability of the International Monetary System* (Macmillan: Basingstoke, 1987). Chapters 3 and 5 offer a good historically based guide to the development of exchange rate systems and issues.

Stubbs, R. and G.R.D. Underhill (eds) *Political Economy and the Changing Global Order* (Basingstoke: Macmillan). Provides a very wide-ranging overview of contemporary change in the world economy.

■ Internet links

The *European Monetary Institute*, the forerunner of the European Central Bank, has a Web site that will keep you up to date with the development of the euro. The site can be found at: **http://www.ecb.int/**

The International Monetary Fund offers news releases and a number of online publications including the World Economic Outlook. The IMF's Web site is at: **http://www.imf.org/external/index.htm**

CHAPTER 17

Issues in the International Economy

Key issues

▶ Is there a global economy?

▶ What are the economic prospects of the less developed countries?

▶ What is the appropriate role for the state in the promotion of development?

Contents

17.1 Introduction

In Chapters 15 and 16 we introduced the 'open economy' concepts of the balance of payments and exchange rates. Our discussion in part concentrated on the problems and issues that such concepts posed for *national* economies. For example, we saw that, because a country cannot ignore a persistent balance of payments imbalance, it may choose to confront potential balance of payments problems by (say) allowing its currency's exchange rate to float freely against other currencies. Alternative measures to promote balance of payments adjustment are of course also possible. In this final chapter we move beyond national economic concerns of this nature to further explore two key *international* economic issues. We have previously reviewed the development of international trade policy under the auspices of the General Agreement on Tariffs and Trade (GATT) and the World Trade Organization (WTO), together with the evolution of key aspects of the international monetary system since 1945. In this concluding chapter we consider, first, the issue of *globalization* and the supposed recent emergence of a new 'global' economy. This concept is often invoked, but what exactly does it mean and what is its basis in reality? Second, we consider the problem of *economic development in less developed countries*. Despite the evident material progress of the established industrial economies, together with a few newly industrialized countries and oil producers, the majority of the world's nations and population remain relatively poor. We review the dimensions of such 'underdevelopment', reflect upon some explanations for its apparent persistence, and finally, using the 'market versus state' framework that has been at the core of this book, consider the policy options for assisting economic development in poor countries.

We begin by justifying our use of the term 'international' in the title for this chapter.

As noted, this may be contrasted with the alternative and increasingly popular conceptualization of the 'global economy' and the purported 'globalization' of economic processes. It is important that we undertake this discussion and defend our preference for the 'international', as any issue-based analysis posed at the level of the international or global economy inevitably tends to be conditioned by the choice of general context. Our major concern about the invocation of the 'global' is that it is often too glibly done, with insufficient thought for what the term actually means, or what the implications of its use might be.

For example, in our view too many discussions of *transnational firms* as a dimension of the 'globalization process' find a neat correspondence between on the one hand their immense financial, industrial and geographical scales and on the other their (asserted) 'globalized' immunity from *national* concerns. A recognition that some firms are big and powerful is transformed into an assessment that collectively these same firms are now free to, literally, roam the globe without so much as a passing interest in the aspirations of sovereign nations or even supranational bodies such as the European Union.

There are two major problems with this kind of approach. The first is that at the outset it prescribes clear limits to the competence and authority of policymakers. It does not matter what you, I or the President of France think about the activities of the transnationals – they are apparently so powerful and globally unconstrained that we cannot deal or reach accommodations with them. The second problem is that the very presence of transnationals appears sufficient to 'prove' the globalization thesis. Against this, in our view, it is important to begin by thinking carefully about how, in several important respects, the international economy has evolved in the last 30 or so years. As we shall demonstrate, as far as transnationals are concerned there have been changes, but their development also betrays some significant continuities, and it is by no means certain either that transnationals are now beyond sovereign influence or that their presence validates notions of the 'global'.

17.2 The international or the 'global' economy?

Let us develop this theme by posing an apparently simple question. What is an economy?

- Economies can be local, operating at say the level of a city, as in 'Berlin's economy has been transformed by the removal of the Berlin wall.'
- They can be regional: 'The economic prospects for the North-West of England have been improved by the decision to extend Manchester Airport.'
- They can be national: 'The French economy grew by 3 per cent last year.'
- They can encompass groups of nations: 'The European economy will become much more closely integrated after the introduction of the euro.'
- Finally, there is the international or 'global' economy.

This list suggests that in one sense an economy is really a conceptual device: a way to parcel up and think about economic processes, which in capitalism, as we know, are articulated by markets. But as well as a means of analysis, economies are also very real structures, which decide the central economic questions introduced in Chapter 1:

what is produced, how is it produced, and for whom. Economies therefore can be interpreted both as vehicles for understanding and as concrete frameworks of production. In both cases, however, note that our interest is in the levels at which markets are articulated and cohere (from the local through to the international/global).

Now, which is the more helpful as an aid to understanding and accurate as a representation of actual market processes: an international or a global economy? To resolve this issue we need to reflect a little more carefully on the precise meanings of the terms 'international' and 'global'. 'International' means *between nations*. The international economy is therefore one in which markets have become generalized beyond the national level but, crucially, the relevance of individual nation states is retained in important ways. In contrast, 'global' means *worldwide*. A strong definition of a global economy might then refer to a situation in which markets have transcended national boundaries to the extent that individual nation states lose much of their economic and even cultural significance (see Box 17.1). This view is clearly radical: it implies that the most important economic decisions are now taken not by sovereign governments or their agents but by rootless transnational corporations, currency speculators, those who operate in stateless markets in finance capital, and so on. There is, however, also a *softer* definition of globalization. This suggests that while markets have become increasingly global and do therefore threaten national sovereignty, it is still possible for states, in recognition of their resultant growing interdependence, to collectively work to solve common economic problems through institutions such as the World Trade Organization and the G7. Indeed, given the immense power of globalizing market forces, collective action is on this definition now deemed necessary if economic instability is to be avoided.

We have then three approaches to the international/global economy:

- an internationalist perspective, which recognizes that important changes have taken place in the international economy over recent years (we shall have more to say on the question of the timing of change in a moment), but which also argues that such changes have not rendered nation states irrelevant as economic actors or indeed as discrete economic spaces

Box 17.1

A global culture

Normally, globalization refers to the international flow of trade and capital. But the international spread of cultures has been at least as important as the spread of economic processes. Today a global culture is emerging. Through many media – from music to movies to books – international ideas and values are being mixed with, and superimposed on, national identities. The spread of ideas through television and video has seen revolutionary developments. There are now more than 1.2 billion TV sets around the world. The United States exports more than 120 000 hours of programming a year to Europe alone, and the global trade in programming is growing by more than 15 per cent a year.

Popular culture exerts more powerful pressure than ever before. From Manila to Managua, Beirut to Beijing, in the East, West, North and South, styles in dress (jeans, hair-dos, T-shirts), sports, music, eating habits and social and cultural attitudes have become global trends. Even crimes – whether relating to drugs, abuse of women, embezzlement or corruption – transcend frontiers and have become similar everywhere. In so many ways the world has shrunk.

Source: United Nations Development Programme, *Human Development Report 1997* (Oxford: Oxford University Press, 1997)

- a strong globalization thesis, which argues that the worldwide – to all intents borderless – articulation of market forces *has* undermined the economic sovereignty of states

- a softer globalization position, which contends that while markets have become much more generalized and beyond the meaningful influence of many individual states, it is both possible and necessary for states to collectively influence the new global economic forces.

As noted, our preference is for the first approach. We shall now explain the reasons for this choice in more detail. *The crucial issue in our view remains market coherence*: can we really say that markets are now organized on a global basis, and if we can, has the course of globalization been consistent only with our softer definition or with the strong version? Alternatively, is the long-standing international coherence of these markets still prevalent? To explore such questions, let us think about the recent developments in:

- international trade

- foreign exchange markets

- foreign direct (transnational) investment.

17.3　International trade: a global process?

As discussed in previous chapters, during the postwar boom (1945–70) most advanced nations enjoyed a combination of sustained economic growth, low unemployment, and low inflation. In this period flourishing international trade, especially in manufactured goods, served to open up markets and stimulate demand (see Chapter 15, Section 15.4). However, it is true that during the boom most trade took place between the advanced countries. Although some less developed countries (LDCs) managed to gain a foothold in the markets for internationally traded manufactured goods and thereafter successfully industrialized – especially the Asian 'tiger' economies such as South Korea – most LDCs remained on the periphery of the trade boom. According to GATT estimates, in 1963 the developed country (DC) share of world manufacturing exports was 82.3 per cent. In 1973 the DC share was virtually unchanged at 83.1 per cent. Over the same period the LDC share of world manufacturing exports increased from 4.3 to 6.9 per cent. These figures indicate that, while the LDCs were competing more successfully in world manufacturing trade, they were doing so on a relatively small scale and *not* at the expense of the developed countries (in fact the LDCs were displacing the then centrally planned economies of, for example, eastern Europe). The implication here is that in trade terms the postwar boom was largely confined to the developed countries: therefore at this time the world economy was segmented between different country groupings. This, clearly then, was not a globalized trading environment.

Now, the key question: have things changed significantly since 1970? One might expect the hypothesized process of globalization to have embraced the formerly peripheral parts of the world, unevenly and hesitantly at first perhaps, but there should be some evidence that trade is now less dominated by the DCs and, as a corollary, that it is increasingly articulated at a global level. In fact little appears to have changed: *trade in the international economy remains segmented largely along old lines*. Referring back to Table 15.5, recall that in 1970 the OECD's share of world merchandise trade was 68.1 per cent; in 1992 it was 68 per cent. In other words, since 1970 the DCs have continued to enjoy remarkable stability in their trade share. Over the same period the Asian tigers maintained their steady progress but again not at the expense of the established industrial countries (Japan and those in North America and the EU). In fact, from the table, those countries that have performed worst in international trade are in Africa and Central and South America. Indeed, according to a recent United Nations' estimate the world's least developed nations, with 10 per cent of the world's population, now have only a 0.3 per cent share in world trade – and this is half their share two decades ago. On this evidence then globalization has simply not happened; rather, there appears to be a decisive continuity in general patterns of international trade.

Of course there remains the *expectation* of change. Box 17.2 summarizes a recent World Bank report, which anticipates that a new 'big five' group of countries (Brazil, China, India, Indonesia, and Russia) will 'become a dominant force in global trade' at the expense of the established industrial countries by 2020. We would make two comments on forecasts of this kind. First, they are clearly not evidence of change now, and therefore cannot be used to *currently* validate the globalization thesis. Second, recent developments in trade policy suggest that change will be fiercely resisted by the advanced nations. As noted in Chapter 15, Section 15.5, the DCs have typically responded to shifting comparative advantage and the exposure of certain industries to LDC competition by introducing protectionist trade policy in an attempt to hold on to market share. This indicates that any nascent globalization imperatives will not unfold unchallenged.

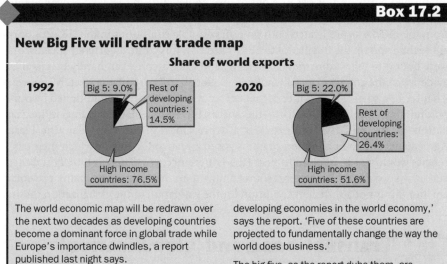

Box 17.2

New Big Five will redraw trade map

Share of world exports

The world economic map will be redrawn over the next two decades as developing countries become a dominant force in global trade while Europe's importance dwindles, a report published last night says.

The World Bank report says that the biggest five developing nations' share of world trade, currently barely a third of the EU's, will surge to 50 per cent more than Europe's by 2020.

'The next 25 years will see an unprecedented boost in the prominence of developing economies in the world economy,' says the report. 'Five of these countries are projected to fundamentally change the way the world does business.'

The big five, as the report dubs them, are Brazil, China, India, Indonesia and Russia. Between them they hold half the world's workforce, but currently account for less than a tenth of world output and trade.

Source: *The Guardian* 10 September 1997. © *The Guardian* 1997.

17.4 A 'globalized' foreign exchange market?

On the face of it, here the evidence for globalization appears more compelling. In Chapter 16, Sections 16.6 and 16.7, we discussed the growing importance of currency speculation as a source of exchange rate instability, and noted in this context the ERM crises of 1992 and 1993. Recall that in 1992 speculative pressures on sterling forced the suspension of UK participation in the ERM. In 1993 speculation, primarily against the French franc, resulted in a significant widening of the ERM target zones for most participant currencies. Crises such as these are taken as indicative of the *new* powers of currency speculators to 'take on' and defeat the collective will of sovereign governments to set exchange rates for their own currencies. Remember that the ERM is a system jointly sponsored by several of the world's most advanced industrial economies (four of the G7). If nations such as these are rendered impotent then – the argument runs – this is clear evidence of the power of agents in new global markets.

But again what exactly is new here? Sterling and destabilizing speculation are hardly strangers. In 1931 speculation forced the pound off the Gold Standard (an earlier fixed exchange rate regime). In 1949 and 1967 UK governments reluctantly conceded devaluations inside the Bretton Woods system. Indeed, in 1971 the Bretton Woods system itself collapsed as a result of a loss of market confidence in the US dollar. Speculation has been an established feature of the international economy for most of this century! Moreover, in each of the cases to which we refer, adverse market sentiment towards a currency arose not because omnipotent speculators 'fancied having a go' but because of *legitimate* underlying doubts about the sustainability of the established parity and/or because of unredeemable faults in the fixed exchange rate system at issue. As we explained in Chapter 16 (Section 16.6), sterling's suspension from the ERM was predicated both on unfavourable conditions in the UK economy at the time and on the fragility of the ERM itself. In this context currency speculators were bound to take a dim view of sterling, and the outcome can hardly be taken as evidence of the emergence of a wholly new 'globalized' currency market. Moreover, Chapter 16 also provided evidence that currency markets can be conditioned by purposeful state intervention. Recall the successful efforts of the leading industrial nations in the mid-1980s to engineer a depreciation of the US dollar (the Plaza Agreement) and their adoption of undisclosed target zones outside which their currencies would not be allowed to float (the Louvre Accord). There is little doubt that currency speculators are better resourced now than they have been in any previous era, but this is not a sufficient condition for the validation of the globalization thesis.

17.5 Transnationals and 'globalization'

For transnationals, the globalization thesis implies a new openness in the world economy: they should be free to use the planet as a borderless space in which to organize production. Traditional affinities to countries of origin or particular markets will disappear as transnational firms adjust to the new locational discretion they enjoy. However, when we look for evidence of such change, little is readily apparent, and one is again struck by the continuities that can be observed instead.

Table 17.1 describes the distribution of accumulated foreign direct investment

Table 17.1 Distribution of accumulated FDI by area (%)

	1938	1960	1973	1983
Developed countries	34.3	67.3	72.9	75.5
LDCs	65.7	32.3	27.1	24.5

Source: Dunning, J.H. *Explaining International Production* (London: Unwin Hyman, 1988)

(FDI) in the world economy for selected years since 1938. Accumulated FDI is representative of transnational activity. Notice that in 1938 approximately two-thirds of FDI was accounted for by less developed countries, with the remaining third concentrated in the developed part of the world. This distribution is reflective of the general form of transnational activity prior to the Second World War. At that time transnational investment was driven primarily by *commodity production*: that is, the production of food and raw materials. The natural resource endowments of LDCs encouraged them to specialize in commodity production, but without foreign investment they often lacked sufficient capital to do so competitively. Many LDCs were also locked into subservient relationships with colonial powers. For these reasons transnationals from the developed and colonial countries were ideally placed to invest in and organize commodity production in less developed parts of the world.

However, in the postwar period, the table shows that the distribution of FDI in the world economy has been radically altered, with the dominant share now going to the developed countries instead of the LDCs. The reason for the shift is a change in the form of transnational activity. From the 1950s onwards transnational investment in the production of *manufactured goods* increased sharply, and most of this activity was retained in the more developed parts of the world. Moreover, in what we might term the new 'era' of hypothesized globalization – the 1980s and 1990s – it is clear from the table that transnational preferences for the developed world are actually *strengthening*. In 1960 the accumulated FDI split between the DCs and LDCs

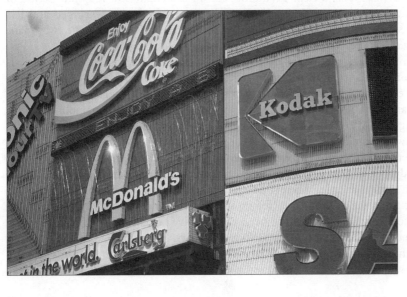

Globalized brand names?

was roughly two-thirds/one-third in favour of the former; by 1983 the split was three-quarters/one-quarter in the DCs' favour. The United Nations (UN) estimates that currently North America, Europe and Japan – together with the coastal provinces of China – receive 90 per cent of the world's FDI. Thus the rest of the world (comprising 70 per cent of its population) gets only 10 per cent. Moreover, again according to the UN, a third of all LDCs have seen their levels of FDI fall in relation to GDP over the last ten years.

These trends run completely against one of the most popular implications of globalization: that transnationals are forsaking developed areas of the world in order to take advantage of cheap labour or lax environmental controls, or whatever, else-where. Of course we do not deny that the less developed countries do indeed hold such 'attractions' for transnationals. Indeed, Box 15.1 provides a specific example of the link between shifting comparative advantage in the clothing industry and relatively low wages in Morocco. But what is clearly in dispute is that this is part of any new and decisive trend in globalization.

17.6　The origins of the globalization thesis

The question then arises: if the notion of globalization is really so contentious, how can we account for its popularity? A recent study by Hirst and Thompson (1996) – see guide to further reading at the end of this chapter – links the ascent of the global-ization thesis to the uncertanties of the international economy since the end of the postwar boom. Their argument is that a number of widely experienced economic problems, together with important forms of structural economic change, have fostered the perception that individual nations are increasingly at the mercy of de-stabilizing 'globalized' market forces. Hirst and Thompson suggest that the collapse of the Bretton Woods system, the OPEC oil price shocks, and the emergence of worldwide inflation in the early 1970s caused a crisis of confidence in what had been long-standing policy regimes of the advanced countries. As economic growth slowed and unemployment re-emerged as a significant problem in many nations for the first time since the 1930s, a clear need arose for an explanation of this new period of turbulence. At the same time structural changes in both the developed and less developed parts of the world, and indeed in the relations between the two, made 'globalization' a convenient way to conceptualize what was going on.

One of the key structural changes cited by Hirst and Thompson is the industrial-ization of some less developed countries. They note the coincidence of this process and the emergence of *deindustrialization* in several of the advanced nations such as the UK and the USA. Deindustrialization refers to the absolute loss of jobs in manu-facturing industry. In the UK, deindustrialization has accelerated since the end of the postwar boom as UK industry has cut jobs in an attempt to improve its domestic and international competitiveness. The temptation is of course to explicitly link LDC industrialization and DC deindustrialization: the former 'causing' the latter. While in some industries this might be a valid connection to make (see Box 15.1), as we have seen, the general case (for most industries and most countries) is much harder to sustain. There has not been any decisive reshaping of the international division of labour in manufacturing in recent years. Hirst and Thompson's point is that such limited forms of structural economic change, coincident with the end of the postwar boom, have been improperly elevated to the status of a global process.

Finally, Hirst and Thompson argue that the popularity of the globalization thesis reflects the current difficulties of international economic policy. Over the last quarter of the twentieth century it has clearly not been possible to re-establish the conditions for sustained expansion in the international economy. Governments, acting alone or collectively, appear less convinced than previously that they can positively affect the long-term course of economic change. Why? Part of the answer, in Hirst and Thompson's view, is that policymakers have effectively become preoccupied with 'globalization'. The assumed presence of global market forces invalidates the underlying assumption of the Bretton Woods institutions and the GATT that there can be a managed capitalism 'without losers'. Thus the notion that the international economy can be made to function for the collective good of many nations has partly given way to a *laissez-faire* perspective that countries must engage in a process of febrile 'global' competition if they are in any way to prosper. Hirst and Thompson call this 'the pathology of over-diminished expectations'; or, to put it another way, policymakers are effectively saying, 'globalization makes it impossible for us to make the kinds of commitments in world economic affairs that we used to, so we won't try.'

17.7 Justifying the internationalist perspective

Earlier in this section we offered three approaches to the conceptualization of the international/global economy. Our preference was for the *internationalist* perspective. The intervening discussion should make the reasons for this choice apparent. In international trade, the markets in foreign exchange and in foreign direct investment flows, while there is some evidence of change it is of insufficient magnitude to validate the notion of a new and wholly different global economy. This would at least seem to undermine the stronger globalization approach. But in essence it also negates the softer version too. The key aspect of 'soft globalization' is its recognition of the collective potency of states as regulators of new global markets. But if there are no global markets, the entire premise may be readily dismissed. This does not mean that the internationalist perspective is ambivalent about collective action by states – far from it. The postwar boom was predicated on cooperation between the major industrial nations. In our view, the further such cooperation extends amongst the developed *and* less developed countries, the better the chances of achieving widespread and sustainable economic development and the greater the possibility of suppressing the 'diminished expectations' of the globalization thesis. We shall now examine the implications of the internationalist perspective in respect of the second issue to be discussed in this chapter: the economic prospects of the less developed countries.

17.8 The economic prospects of the less developed countries

The orthodox view of development

Given that there are developed and less developed countries, the problem for those in the latter group appears a simple one: how best to become developed. Yet the

Table 17.2 Average annual growth of real GNP per capita 1965–1990

	%
Asian NICs	7.0
Japan	4.2
OECD	2.4
South Asia	1.9
Latin America and Caribbean	1.8
Sub-Saharan Africa	0.3

Source: Adapted from *OECD Economic Survey Korea 1993/1994.* © OECD 1994. Reproduced by permission of the OECD

notion of *development* is itself not necessarily straightforward. The traditionally accepted interpretation of the term has centred on the achievement of relative improvements in real per capita income. As we know, the Asian newly industrialized countries are the world's success story in this respect. Table 17.2 compares their average rate of per capita income growth with other groups of countries over a 25-year period. Notice from the table that while the Asian NICs comfortably outstrip income growth in the developed world (represented by the OECD), the LDCs of Latin America, the Caribbean and – especially – sub-Saharan Africa all languish behind the developed countries. This means that the gap between the rich countries and the majority of poor ones has widened over the period in question. Now the acknowledged success of the newly industrialized countries implicitly sets down a standard for the remaining LDCs to follow. If, like the NICs, they too can shake off old dependencies on the production of food and raw materials and reallocate resources into manufacturing, where international trade has grown fastest over the postwar period, then industrialized status will be within their grasp. The big question of course is how this is to be done. Later we shall see that, as for many other questions in economics, the development issues centre on a debate over the free market and its ability to generate desired ends. However, for the moment we need to reflect a little further on the meaning of development.

In Chapter 10, Section 10.3, we suggested that real GDP per capita figures provide only a crude measure of national economic welfare. This implies that, where real GDP is used as a measure of a country's development, some important questions are put to one side. For example, GDP data do not take account of many forms of pollution and environmental despoliation that economic activity generates. In the specific context of development, the United Nations has since 1990 published a *Human Development Index*, which ranks countries by per capita income together with measures of life expectancy and adult literacy. Table 17.3 reproduces part of the Human Development Index for 1994. According to the UN the intention behind the index is to 'indicate human capabilities in three fundamental dimensions – a long and healthy life, knowledge and a decent standard of living.' The Human Development Index suggests that, in the wider terms that it defines, several of the world's more affluent nations such as oil-rich Bahrain and the United Arab Emirates (with real GDP per capita incomes of $15 321 and $16 000 respectively) are relatively modestly placed despite their evident wealth. At the same time, other relatively poor countries – Costa Rica and Poland, for example (with respective real GDP per capita incomes of $5919 and $5002) – still manage to achieve a relatively high Human Development Index ranking.

Is development inevitable?

While wider conceptualizations of development such as that provided by the Human Development Index are an advance on the blunt per capita income approach, the United Nations still insists that GDP growth is fundamental to the achievement of human objectives. This means that for most LDCs development continues to be primarily about trying to emulate those countries that have successfully industrialized over the last 30 or 40 years. Some commentators detect a problem here. For example, Raymond Williams – see guide to further reading at the end of this chapter – has argued that this interpretation of development, with the industrialized and newly industrialized countries as its 'model of mandate', tends to take

Table 17.3 Human Development Index 1994 (selected countries)

HDI rank (ex 175 countries)	Country	Life expectancy at birth (years)	Adult literacy rate (%)	Real GDP per capita (ppp$)[a]	Real GDP per capita rank minus HDI rank [b]
1	Canada	79.0	99.0	21 459	7
2	France	78.7	99.0	20 510	13
3	Norway	77.5	99.0	21 346	6
4	USA	76.2	99.0	26 397	−1
5	Iceland	79.1	99.0	20 566	9
6	Netherlands	77.3	99.0	19 238	13
7	Japan	79.8	99.0	21 581	0
8	Finland	76.3	99.0	17 417	15
9	New Zealand	76.4	99.0	16 851	15
10	Sweden	78.3	99.0	18 540	11
11	Spain	77.6	97.1	14 324	19
12	Austria	76.6	99.0	20 667	1
13	Belgium	76.8	99.0	20 985	−1
14	Australia	78.1	99.0	19 285	4
15	United Kingdom	76.7	99.0	18 620	5
33	Costa Rica	76.6	94.7	5 919	27
43	Bahrain	72.0	84.4	15 321	−14
44	United Arab Emirates	74.2	78.6	16 000	−17
58	Poland	71.2	99.0	5 002	14
171	Mali	46.6	29.3	543	1
172	Burkina Faso	46.4	18.7	796	−9
173	Niger	47.1	13.1	787	−8
174	Rwanda	22.6	59.2	352	1
175	Sierra Leone	33.6	30.3	643	−4
	All LDCs	61.8	69.7	2 904	
	Sub-Saharan Africa	50.0	55.9	965	
	All DCs	74.1	98.5	15 986	

[a]Real GDP per capita expressed in US dollars ($) using purchasing power parities (ppp).
[b]A positive figure indicates that the HDI rank is better than the real GDP per capita rank, a negative the opposite.
Source: United Nations Development Programme *Human Development Report 1997* (Oxford: Oxford University Press, 1997)

on connotations of *inevitability*: that is, LDCs *will* in time achieve progress as they 'naturally' industrialize. Williams cites the Brandt Report, perhaps the most influential reflection on the relationship between rich and poor countries published in recent years:

The successive industrial revolutions of the past two hundred years in Europe and North America are now being followed by industrialization in Latin America, Asia and Africa, *a natural and indeed inevitable development* which is already beginning to change the pattern of comparative advantage in the world economy. (Emphasis added)

W. Brandt, *North South* (London: Pan, 1980)

Williams contrasts this rather benign perspective, which does indeed see LDC advancement as 'natural', with the much more sombre and stubborn realities of the international division of labour. Recall that this describes the patterns of

specialization in production in the world economy. The point here is that the anticipated and 'natural' development of the LDCs does not sit well with an international
division of labour which apparently *requires* large numbers of countries to continue
to engage in relatively poorly rewarded forms of economic activity. Given that
industrialization has been achieved by only a handful of countries in the last 30 or so
years, most LDCs appear locked into subordinate roles as producers of food, raw
materials, and certain limited kinds of basic manufactures. If development is indeed
'natural and inevitable' *when* will it happen for the majority of countries and the
majority of the world's population?

17.9 Promoting development: the state versus the market

The fact that wider development has not happened, despite the evident affluence of
the world economy as a whole, suggests that the present conduct of international
economic affairs is unsatisfactory. As the 1997 United Nations Human Development Report puts it:

> Although poverty has been dramatically reduced in many parts of the world, a quarter of the
> world's people remain in severe poverty. In a global economy of $25 trillion, this is a scandal –
> reflecting shameful inequalities and inexcusable failures of national and international policy.
> United Nations Development Programme, *Human Development Report 1997*
> (Oxford: Oxford University Press, 1997)

If there have indeed been policy failures, questions then arise as to the appropriate
forms of action that would ensure that widespread development does occur. In keeping with the 'state versus market' theme introduced in Chapter 1, we shall review
here two general approaches to development policy. One suggests that because
market processes have not proven effective in ensuring economic advance in LDCs,
new forms of national and international state intervention are required. The
second approach argues that the judicious use of the market is the best means of
development promotion.

17.10 Unequal exchange theory

The pro-intervention position we shall now describe rests on the theory of unequal
exchange, associated (independently) with Raul Prebisch and H.W. Singer. In its
original (1950) formulation, the work of Prebisch and Singer suggested that international trade tended to favour developed countries relative to less developed countries
because of certain characteristics of the traded goods that each group specialized in
producing. The DCs produced manufactured goods that tended to rise faster in
price relative to the prices of food and raw materials, which typically were produced
by the LDCs. This meant that the export earnings of the DCs would over time grow
more rapidly than the earnings of the LDCs, thus enhancing the wider growth
prospects of the DCs *vis-à-vis* the LDCs. Moreover, in considering the trading relationships between the two groups, it should be clear that in order to purchase a
given volume of manufactures from the industrial countries, the LDCs would have
to export a steadily increasing volume of commodity exports: hence the phrase

'unequal exchange' (one group of countries has to export more and more in order to maintain its desired level of imports from the other group). The ratio of export prices to import prices for a country is known as its *terms of trade*. In essence, then, the unequal exchange approach suggests that the terms of trade tended to move against the LDCs and in favour of the DCs.

Why then do the terms of trade tend to move against food and raw materials and the countries that specialize in their production? There are several explanations, but as space constraints prevent us describing them all, we shall concentrate on two of the most obvious. The first explanation concerns the *relative income elasticities of demand for food and manufactures*. Income elasticity of demand expresses the relationship between changes in income and demand (see Chapter 3, Section 3.10). Now, because the demand for food in the advanced nations in particular is adequately met, increases in income in these nations tends to be spent not on more food but on tradable manufactures. Moreover, as the advanced nations account for most of the world's income, the world demand for manufactures tends to be relatively stronger than the world demand for food, and this explains why the prices of manufactures tend to rise relative to food prices. The second explanation of adverse movements in the terms of trade for primary commodities *vis-à-vis* manufactures has its basis in *technological change*. Given the development of a range of synthetics and their adaptation for industrial use, the demand for many raw materials has stagnated. Once again then, demand constraints help to explain the relative sluggishness of commodity prices. Although the original empirical work for unequal exchange theory was based on the period 1873–1938, the secular movement in the terms of trade against food and raw materials has not yet abated. Thus the UN estimates that since the early 1970s the least developed countries have suffered a 50 per cent decline in their terms of trade. It also notes that in 1990 real commodity prices were 45 per cent lower than in 1980 and 10 per cent lower than the lowest prices experienced during the Great Depression of the 1930s.

One initial implication arising from unequal exchange was the need for LDCs to uncouple themselves from what amounted to an overdependence on a set of exports that were possessed of structural weakness in international trade. Accordingly, a key policy recommendation of unequal exchange theorists was *LDC industrialization* and the adoption of strategies conducive to manufacturing export-led growth. Via a process of *export substitution* (manufactured goods for food and raw materials) such strategies, it was argued, would permit the LDCs to begin to trade with the developed world on less unequal terms. Prebisch suggested that specific courses of action that LDCs could take could include the fiscal promotion of manufacturing industry and complementary currency devaluation. The first of these measures might involve, as an example, state subsidies to domestic firms for investment purposes, while currency devaluation would improve the price competitiveness of goods exported to foreign markets. Notice that the basic premise here is that industrialization will emerge from state intervention: the unequal exchange perspective holds that the market cannot be relied upon to produce the same desired outcome.

However, more recent work by unequal exchange theorists, particularly Singer, has cast some doubt on the export substitution policy prescription. Despite the acknowledged achievements of the small number of newly industrialized countries, Singer has argued that the problem of unequal exchange is now characterized not by structural differences between primary commodities and manufactured goods but by *differences between types of country*. On this reckoning most LDCs are subordinated in exchange with the developed world, regardless of whether they export primary commodities or manufactures. Singer argues that most instances of LDC industrialization tend to be limited to low-skill, labour-intensive forms of production (clothing, footwear, toys, and so on).

The problem here is the relatively low claims on world demand that the resulting output can make compared with the technologically more sophisticated output of the DCs. Partly this is again an income elasticities issue: rising incomes in the richest parts of the world tend to produce sharper increases in demand for manufactures with a high technology content. But it also reflects an innate capacity of the DCs to outmanoeuvre or offset threatening shifts in comparative advantage. Thus Singer notes that the contours of DC protectionism are precisely shaped to make access to the world's richest markets difficult for the limited range of manufactured goods produced by LDCs. The Multi-Fibre Arrangement (MFA) – which restricts DC imports of clothing and textiles from the LDCs – is the most infamous example of this kind of action (see Chapter 15, Section 15.5). Finally, even where the LDCs have managed to overcome the constraints of unequal exchange – for instance through the monopoly power of the OPEC oil producers' cartel, which imposed significant oil price increases in 1973–74 and 1979 – the effect has been short-lived. The technological capabilities of the oil-importing industrial nations – not least in developing more fuel-efficient car engines – has since reduced the rate of increase in the demand for oil and as a consequence has pegged back oil prices.

The central feature of Singer's revised version of unequal exchange is the apparent *technology gap* between the industrial countries and the rest of the world. This explains the deterioration in the terms of trade for (low technology) manufactured goods produced by the LDCs (which fell by 35 per cent between 1970 and 1991, according to the UN). It is the technology gap that allows the rich countries to grow richer relative to most of the rest of the world as their technologically enhanced output consistently secures a disproportionate share of rising world incomes. Moreover, in turn, it is the very affluence of the industrial nations that then permits them to dominate the formation of international economic policy. In international trade, for example, the MFA has effectively been imposed on LDCs by the advanced countries. This has been possible because it is access to the huge markets of the advanced countries that is at issue. Hence, in Singer's view, technology breeds affluence, which in turn breeds power, influence and a vested interest in the *status quo* in the international economy. Breaking into this 'virtuous circle' is no easy matter, and this may help to explain why so few LDCs have managed to attain developed status, and why so many continue to lose ground on the established industrial nations (see Table 17.2). It also partly explains why the transition to a more open 'globalized' economy has not happened: simply, the rich and powerful interests of a relatively small number of countries demand that it should not. For an alternative view of the nature of the 'economic gap' between the rich and poor nations, which concentrates on differences in *human skills*, see Box 17.3.

We are now left with the question of development policy in the light of this revised and, on the face of it, more depressing version of unequal exchange. One initial conclusion is that market processes are insufficient to instigate 'natural' or 'inevitable' forms of development. Most LDCs appear consigned to relatively low levels of growth because they have no ready means of access to the sophisticated forms of industrial production (whether based on technology or skill) that have favourable terms of trade. The inference that most unequal exchange theorists – and

Box 17.3

Skill differences between the industrial and less developed countries

Adrian Wood has recently argued that differences in skill – rather than technology or capital – are central to understanding the trade between the industrial countries and the less developed countries in manufactured goods. Because the 'North' (the industrial countries) has a relatively large supply of skilled labour and the 'South' (the less developed countries) a relatively large supply of unskilled labour, it is appropriate for the North to specialize in producing skill-intensive goods and the South to specialize in producing goods that require low-level skill inputs. As Wood notes, this version of the international division of labour follows the Heckscher–Ohlin interpretation of the theory of comparative advantage (see Chapter 15, Section 15.3).

In rejecting the view that technology retained in the North is responsible for that region's continued economic superiority over the South, Wood points out that the (Northern) firms that control production technologies could, in principle, establish factories

anywhere. Given the very low relative wage levels there, the South would surely be a most attractive industrial location, if other problems did not get in the way. Chief amongst these is skill. Modern manufacturing workers need basic literacy or primary education, but in many countries literacy rates are low (the adult literacy rate in sub-Saharan Africa is 55.9 per cent – see Table 17.3). Thus it is a skills gap rather than a technology gap that explains the development problem in large parts of the South.

The main policy implication for development that Wood draws from this analysis is clear: less developed countries need to raise their average skill levels. This is the necessary condition for the emergence of manufacturing activity, and therefore for wider development.

Source: Adapted from Wood, A. *North South Trade, Employment and Inequality* (Oxford: Clarendon Press, 1994)

those who have some sympathy with the general approach – draw from this is that intervention is necessary to achieve a greater degree of equity of opportunity in international economic affairs. The most obvious requirement is that the rich nations should concede that they enjoy a privileged position in the world economy, and that this demands of them some concessions towards other poorer nations. The exact form of such concessions varies according to authorship.

- Keynes (in the 1930s), for example, proposed the creation of an *International Clearing Union*, which would serve to stabilize primary commodity markets and prices. When prices were falling, the Clearing Union would buy and store surplus output. This additional demand would have a price support effect. Conversely, when prices were rising, stocks could be sold.

- Prebisch, in his later work, favoured non-economic (charitable) action by the rich countries to directly compensate LDCs for adverse movements in the terms of trade. He suggested that the emergent gap between manufacturing and primary product prices should be tracked as a guide to the appropriate level of income redistribution from the developed to the less developed parts of the world.

- In 1974, the UN General Assembly adopted the proposal for a *New International Economic Order*. This had originated with the United Nations Conference on Trade and Development (UNCTAD), a collective of developing countries concerned that they were being increasingly marginalized in the international economy. Amongst the major proposals of the anticipated New International Economic Order there was to be improved access to industrial markets for LDC output. This resulted in the *Generalized System of Preferences*, which gives low-tariff access to LDCs for selected goods: not, however, textiles, clothing and other 'sensitive' items, the trade in which is arguably most in need of liberalization. There was also a second mechanism – the *Common Fund* – intended to stabilize primary product prices along the lines suggested by Keynes. However, hesitantly implemented, this too has failed to address the fundamental terms of trade problem for commodities.

- The 1997 UN Human Development Report proposes *inter alia* 'a fairer institutional environment for global trade', such that the products of less developed countries are treated in the same way as those of the richer nations in world markets. This would inevitably mean trade concessions by the richer nations. The Development Report also argues for 'selective support for global technology priorities'. Here the suggestion is that the current revolution in information technology and, in particular, the development of 'information superhighways' is bypassing many poorer countries, which do not have the skills or the hardware to participate. The answer again is resource commitments from the richer countries. Finally, in this selective list, the Report suggests the implementation of a programme of international debt relief. It notes that 'providing effective relief to the 20 worst affected countries would cost between $5.5 billion and $7.7 billion – less than the cost of one stealth bomber and roughly equivalent to the cost of building the Euro-Disney theme park in France.'

All these proposals have two common features: they involve both resource obligations on the part of the industrial countries and a working assumption that development cannot be orchestrated through the market. Admittedly, calls for trade liberalization do suggest some faith in market processes, but generally liberalization is seen as a necessary but not a·sufficient condition for LDC advancement. Thus, in the view of unequal exchange theorists and their sympathizers, for development to touch many poor countries rather than just the few it has so far, more systematic forms of intervention are required.

17.11 A critique of 'development economics'

But from another perspective this is (possibly dangerous) nonsense. In Chapters 2–5 we saw how markets can be used to resolve the by now familiar economic questions of 'what, how, and for whom'. Indeed, as we are also aware, some economists are convinced that market-based resource allocation is generally preferable to the alternative of allocation determined by the state. This view does not change as we move from the national to the international level. We saw in Chapter 15, for example, that the orthodox approach to international trade, with its Ricardian foundations, supposes that *free* trade is superior to any form of protected or managed trade because it offers mutual benefits to all participants, and encourages them to allocate resources to their most productive uses. Similarly, in Chapter 16, we reviewed Friedman's argument for flexible – that is, market driven – exchange rate determination. This suggests that the free movement of exchange rates is preferable to their management by government because it promotes openness and clarity in international trade, and it facilitates domestic policy freedoms. Now, consider the range of proposals for the promotion of development described at the end of the previous section. How would market economics assess these? It would surely judge them inadequate because most substitute resource allocation led by the market for some form or other of state intervention. However, this is only a first approximation. In fact the market critique of what it pejoratively terms 'development economics' is more refined than a simple 'market good, state bad' approach might suggest.

By 'development economics' market economists such as Lal – see guide to further reading at the end of this chapter – mean the kind of *strategic* intervention, envisaged by the likes of UNCTAD and the UN, intended to effect early and fundamental shifts in the material prospects of poor countries. Adopting a line of argument similar to that of the liberal school (see Chapter 6, Section 6.6), Lal suggests that strategic intervention may in fact be *inimical* to development – it may make the positions of poorer countries worse rather than better. This is because it appears to rest on the assumption that in the development sphere, as markets do not work perfectly, they must require substantial modification by the state or international agencies. In Lal's view such reasoning is flawed. Market economists *do* accept that markets can fail, but they argue that this sets up a contest between an imperfect market and unproven forms of state intervention: a contest, in other words, between two inferior options. It is the error of 'development economics' to suppose that one must proceed from an acknowledgement of market failure to the 'logic' of strategic intervention.

Indeed, in Lal's view the imperfect market *is* usually better than strategic intervention. Why? We know that orthodox microeconomic theory permits *precise* forms of intervention in order to address identified shortcomings of the market. For example, if the market cannot recognize a negative externality, such as atmospheric pollution, then the state may reasonably take action to suppress it. But, Lal argues, where intervention is intended to promote development, instead of focusing on the *particular* shortcomings of the market that are preventing resources being used in their most appropriate uses, 'it turns by a process of normative manipulation into a Pandora's box of incremental *ad hocery.*'

As an example, Lal considers the measures that might be taken to encourage an emergent industry in a less developed country. Given that the goods produced by the new industry may formerly have been obtained solely as imports, in Lal's view the 'development economics' approach would suggest a policy of import substitution based on the imposition of a tariff. This would protect the new industry from established sources of foreign competition. But this is a general measure, which fails to specify the precise nature of the problem that the industry faces. Moreover, as it is one that may provoke retaliatory action by other countries, further forms of intervention may be required as a result. This is one aspect of what Lal means by 'incremental *ad hocery*'. The alternative market approach would seek first to identify the particular burdens under which the emergent industry labours. Lal suggests that these might include high wage costs, compared with the wages earned from agricultural activity – an obvious source of alternative employment in less developed countries. Typically, agricultural wages are relatively low because they contain an implicit rent element from the ownership of land. When labour leaves agriculture this rent element is lost, and therefore people transferring to industry demand higher wages in compensation. Using this analysis, Lal identifies the problem for the emergent industry as arising in the peculiarities of the LDC labour market. But, as we have seen, the 'development economics' response is protection in the *goods* market. A much more appropriate form of intervention therefore would be the payment of a wage subsidy to industrial employers. This would allow them to recruit workers at competitive wage levels, and the immediate obstacle to development would be overcome at source. If, however, it is not possible for the state to intervene in the labour market in this way, it may be best to *do nothing*, as the status quo may be preferable to the uncertain chain of events that an indulgence in protectionism would unleash.

In summary, then, the tenor of the market approach to development is to permit *limited* forms of intervention where these address specific problems that the market itself appears unable to solve. It strongly counsels against the grander and more ambitious forms of intervention favoured by 'development economics'.

■ Summary

◆ While there is some evidence of change in the international economy, the case for 'globalization' has been overstated. Globalization implies the widest possible articulation of market forces, to the extent that the economic interests and capabilities of individual nation states become irrelevant.

◆ Against the globalization thesis, there appears to be a sometimes remarkable degree of continuity in the international patterns of trade and foreign direct investment. Foreign exchange markets too are by no means beyond sovereign influence.

◆ The origins of the globalization thesis appear to lie in the period of economic uncertainty that followed the end of the postwar boom. A particular focus has been change in the international division of labour and the appearance of limited forms of industrialization in less developed parts of the world. This, coupled with pronounced deindustrialization in some developed countries, has given rise to claims of the existence of new generalized 'global' market forces.

◆ The conventional approach to economic development envisages that less developed countries can and will industrialize. However, this sanguine view sits uneasily with the reality of the present international division of labour. The majority of the world's nations appear locked into relatively poorly rewarded forms of economic activity.

◆ Unequal exchange theory explains the difficulties faced by less developed countries by highlighting the relatively poor terms of trade characteristics of the kinds of goods they produce. It posits the existence of a 'technology gap' between rich and poor countries. This keeps the rich countries rich and allows them to dominate international economic policymaking: a duality that makes economic development for the majority of the less developed world an unlikely prospect. Another explanation of the persistence of general international economic inequality and the particular 'tiger economy' exceptions to this rule concerns differences in human skill.

◆ Unequal exchange theory has interventionist policy implication, which at least in part involve concessions or resource commitments on the part of the industrialized countries intended to assist less developed countries.

◆ However, a market approach would be highly critical of what it terms 'development economics'. The concern here is that intervention does not usually address the specific shortcomings of the market that might be hindering the economic aspirations of less developed countries. Instead, intervention tends to involve grandiose strategies, which have the potential to actually interfere with market processes and worsen the prospects of poor countries.

Key terms

◆ Globalization
◆ Global economy
◆ International economy
◆ International division of labour
◆ Industrialization
◆ Deindustrialization
◆ Development
◆ Human development
◆ Unequal exchange
◆ Technology gap
◆ Skills gap
◆ Intervention
◆ 'Development economics'
◆ The market

Questions for discussion

◆ What would be the main characteristics of a 'global' economy?
◆ What evidence is there against the existence of a global economy?
◆ Why has the globalization thesis proven so popular?
◆ What do you understand by the term 'development'?
◆ Reflecting both on the critique of 'development economics' in this chapter and on the theory of comparative advantage outlined in Chapter 15 (Section 15.2) explain why, in the view of some economists, free markets are the best way to secure development.
◆ What would be the unequal exchange critique of the answer to the previous question?

Further reading

Hirst, P. and G. Thompson *Globalization in Question* (Cambridge: Polity Press, 1996). Offers a jaundiced view of the globalization thesis.

Daniels, P.W. and W.F. Lever (eds) *The Global Economy in Transition* (Harlow: Addison Wesley Longman, 1996). Part 3 of this book sketches out the major contemporary trends in the 'globalization' of production.

Williams, R. *Towards 2000* (Harmondsworth: Penguin Books, 1985). Provides a non-orthodox approach to development.

United Nations Development Programme *Human Development Report 1997* (Oxford: Oxford University Press, 1997). Offers a concise and empirically informed overview of current development issues.

Lal, D. *The Poverty of Development Economics* (London: Institute of Economic Affairs Hobart Paperback 16, 1983). Summarizes a market perspective on development.

▮ Internet links

As noted in the Internet links for Chapter 15, the *United Nations Conference on Trade and Development* (UNCTAD) is the United Nations body that deals with trade and development issues. Its Web site is at: **http://unicc.org/unctad/en/enhome.htm** The joint *World Bank* and *United Nations Development Programme* initiative sponsors missions to less developed countries in order to analyse country-specific trade policy issues and help to reform trade regimes. Details of work in particular countries can be found at: **http://www.worldbank.org/html/iecit/tep.html**

Answers to Self-Test Questions

Chapter 1

True (t) or false (f)
1. f 2. t 3. f 4. t 5. t 6. f 7. t 8. f 9. t 10. t
Missing word(s)
1. positive 2. consumer sovereignty 3. wants
4. opportunity cost 5. *laissez-faire* 6. invisible hand
7. division; labour 8. entrepreneur 9. postwar boom
10. planned

Chapter 2

True (t) or false (f)
1. t 2. f 3. f 4. f 5. f 6. t 7. t 8. f 9. f 10. t
Missing word(s)
1. the quantity demanded 2. extension; contraction
3. complement 4. equilibrium 5. clear
6. intervention 7. substitutes 8. disequilibrium

Chapter 3

True (t) or false (f)
1. f 2. t 3. t 4. f 5. f 6. t 7. t 8. t 9. t
10. f
Missing word(s)
1. satisfaction 2. marginal social cost 3. disbenefit
4. segmentation 5. responsiveness; price
6. unit elastic 7. close substitutes 8. income
9. inferior 10. one

Chapter 5

True (t) or false (f)
1. t 2. t 3. f 4. t 5. f 6. t 7. f 8. f 9. t 10. t
Missing word(s)
1. perfectly elastic 2. homogeneous 3. exceed
4. minimum 5. barriers to entry 6. MC = MR
7. makers 8. kinked 9. planning sector
10. revised sequence

Chapter 7

True (t) or false (f)
1. t 2. f 3. t 4. f 5. t 6. f 7. t 8. t 9. f 10. t
Missing word(s)
1. derived 2. marginal physical product 3. wage
4. substitution; income 5. reservation wage
6. wage rate 7. human capital 8. normative
9. transfer earnings 10. demand

Chapter 8

True (t) or false (f)
1. f 2. t 3. f 4. f 5. f 6. f 7. t 8. t
Missing word(s)
1. normative 2. Lorenz curve 3. line of complete
equality 4. Lorenz curve; line of complete equality
5. Gini coefficient 6. zero; one

Chapter 9

True (t) or false (f)
1. t 2. f 3. t 4. t 5. f 6. f 7. t 8. f 9. t 10. t
Missing word(s)
1. real 2. G7 3. actively 4. perfectly anticipated
5. helps; penalizes 6. hyperinflation 7. international
transactions 8. surplus 9. John Maynard Keynes
10. Keynesianism; monetarism

Chapter 10

True (t) or false (f)
1. t 2. t 3. t 4. f 5. f 6. f 7. t 8. t 9. t
Missing word(s)
1. private-sector investment; government expenditure;
exports 2. savings; taxes; imports 3. real GDP per
capita 4. leisure; externalities 5. diminishing returns
6. steady state 7. exogenous 8. Paul Romer; Robert
Lucas Jr. 9. human capital

Chapter 11

True (t) or false (f)
1. t 2. t 3. f 4. f 5. t 6. t 7. f 8. t 9. f
10. t 11. f 12. t
Missing word(s)
1. real wage 2. frictional; structural; demand-deficient
3. autonomous 4. frictional; structural 5. aggregate
demand 6. Milton Friedman 7. microeconomic
8. labour turnover; adverse selection; shirking; fairness
9. NAIRU 10. hysteresis

Chapter 12

True (t) or false (f)
1. t 2. t 3. t 4. f 5. t 6. f 7. f 8. f 9. t 10. t
11. t 12. f 13. t 14. f
Missing word(s)
1. monetary 2. stable; predictable 3. Phillips curve

4. excess demand for labour 5. demand-pull inflation
6. expected rate of inflation 7. vertical; natural
8. independently 9. cost-push; sociological 10. prices
and incomes policy 11. outside 12. sustained

Chapter 13

True (t) or false (f)
1. t 2. t 3. f 4. f 5. f 6. t 7. f 8. t 9. f 10. f
11. t
Missing word(s)
1. long-term trend path 2. expansionary phase;
contractionary phase 3. multiplier process; accelerator
4. multiplier 5. monetary shocks 6. fixed 7. Robert
Lucas Jr 8. unanticipated 9. supply-side shocks 10.
Finn Kydland; Edward Prescott 11. boom; slump

Chapter 14

True (t) or false (f)
1. t 2. t 3. t 4. t 5. f 6. t 7. t 8. f 9. t 10. f
Missing word(s)
1. fine tuning 2. passive 3. unstable 4. aggregate
demand 5. inside 6. outside 7. stable
8. unanticipated; short run 9. rational expectations
10. Lucas critique

Chapter 15

True (t) or false (f)
1. t 2. t 3. f 4. t 5. t 6. t 7. f 8. f 9. t 10. f
Missing word(s)
1. mercantilism 2. free 3. labour productivity
4. factor endowments 5. Leontief paradox
6. infant-industry 7. inter-industry
8. Multi-Fibre Arrangement

Chapter 16

True (t) or false (f)
1. f 2. f 3. t 4. t 5. t 6. t 7. f 8. t 9. t 10. t
Missing word(s)
1. persistent 2. price 3. expenditure reduction policy;
expenditure-switching policy 4. Marshall–Lerner
5. demand; supply 6. speculators; governments
7. integration argument; anchor argument
8. Triffin/dollar dilemma 9. inflation
10. depreciation

Glossary

Absolute advantage The ability of a country to produce more of a particular commodity than another country, using an equal quantity of factor inputs.

Accelerator principle The theory that the level of net investment depends on the change in output.

Accommodating transaction One undertaken for balance of payments purposes.

Activist policy rule A prespecified rule for the conduct of policy that is linked to the state of the economy; also known as a feedback rule.

Adaptive expectations An approach that assumes that people's expectations of the future value of a variable are based solely on recently observed values of that variable.

Aggregate demand (AD) The total planned expenditures of all buyers of final goods and services; composed of consumer expenditure, investment expenditure, government expenditure, and net exports.

Aggregate demand management The use of fiscal and monetary policies to influence the level of aggregate demand.

Aggregate production function A functional relationship between the quantity of aggregate output produced and the quantities of inputs used in production.

Aggregate supply (AS) The total planned output in the economy.

Appreciation The appreciation of a currency involves an increase in its value in terms of other currencies when the currency in question is not part of a formal exchange rate system.

Autonomous expenditure Expenditure that does not depend on the level of national income.

Autonomous transaction One undertaken for its own sake.

Average cost The total cost of producing any given output divided by the number of units produced. Average cost can be divided into average fixed costs and average variable costs.

Average revenue Total revenue divided by the number of units sold; it also equals price.

Balance of payments A record of a country's international transactions.

Barriers to entry Barriers or restrictions that prevent the entry of new firms into an industry.

Bretton Woods system A fixed exchange rate system established at the end of the Second World War. The system broke down in the early 1970s.

Business cycle Fluctuations in aggregate economic activity; in particular movements in output around its trend.

Cairns Group Comprises Argentina, Australia, Brazil, Canada, Chile, Columbia, Fiji, Hungary, Indonesia, Malaysia, Philippines, New Zealand, Thailand, and Uruguay.

Capital goods Goods, such as plant, machinery and buildings, that are used (and eventually wear out) in making other goods and services.

Capital–labour ratio The amount of capital per worker; the ratio of the quantity of capital inputs to the number of workers.

Capital–output ratio The ratio of the amount of capital to the amount of output produced by it.

Cartel A group of firms or producers that agree to act as if they were a single firm or producer, for example, with regard to pricing or output decisions.

Centrally planned economy One in which resource allocation is predominantly organized by the state.

Ceteris paribus All other things being equal or remaining constant.

Classical economics A pre-Keynesian approach based on the assumption that wages and prices adjust to clear markets, and that monetary policy does not influence real variables such as output and employment.

Clear A market is said to clear when all goods or services supplied in it are sold.

Cold turkey A rapid and permanent reduction in the rate of monetary growth, aimed at reducing the rate of inflation.

Collective bargaining Involves negotiations between a trade union and one or more employers over pay or workplace conditions.

Collective provision The provision of goods and services by the state. Also called social provision.

Comparative advantage The ability of a country to produce a commodity at a lower opportunity cost, in terms of other commodities forgone, than another country.

Complement A good that complements another good.

Constant returns to scale The proposition that a proportionate increase in all factor inputs will lead to the same proportionate increase in output.

Consumer surplus The difference between what a consumer would have been willing to pay and what the consumer actually pays.

Consumers' expenditure The aggregate purchases of goods and services by households for their own use.

Consumption function The relationship between aggregate consumer expenditure and aggregate income.

Convergence The tendency for output per worker in different countries to converge over time.

Cost-push inflation Inflation caused by cost increases even though there are no shortages of goods and services and the economy is below full employment.

Credibility The degree to which people believe the authorities' announcements about future policy.

Crowding out The reduction in private sector expenditure that results following an increase in government expenditure.

Cyclical unemployment See *demand-deficient unemployment*.

Demand The quantity of a good or service that consumers wish to purchase at each conceivable price, other things being equal.

Demand-deficient unemployment Unemployment that results because aggregate demand is insufficient to provide employment for everyone who wants to work at the prevailing real wage; also known as cyclical unemployment.

Demand-pull inflation Inflation caused by an excess demand for goods and services when the economy is at or above full employment.

Depreciation The depreciation of a currency involves the lowering of its value in terms of other currencies when the currency in question is not part of some formal exchange rate system.

Depression A very severe and prolonged recession.

Derived demand Arises for a factor of production because of the demand for the output the factor helps to produce. The factor in itself does not generate demand.

Devaluation The devaluation of a currency involves the lowering of its value in terms of other currencies when the currency in question is part of some formal exchange rate system.

Diminishing marginal utility The decline in marginal utility that occurs as more and more of a good or service is consumed.

Diminishing returns A situation in which successive increases in the use of a factor input, holding other factor inputs constant, eventually result in a fall in the additional output derived from a unit increase in that factor input.

Dirty flexible/floating exchange rate See *managed exchange rate*.

Discretionary policy A situation in which the authorities are free to vary the strength of fiscal and/or monetary policy in any way they see fit, in order to achieve their desired objectives.

Disinflation A decrease in the rate of inflation.

Disposable income Income that households have at their disposal after the payment of tax.

Eclectic approach One that combines themes and policies from different schools of thought.

Economic growth An increase in real GDP over time.

Economic rent Payment to a factor of production above that necessary to retain it in its present use.

Economically active Describes individuals who are people of working age that are either in work or actively seeking it.

Economies of scale Arise when a larger output is produced without a proportionately equal increase in the costs of production.

Efficiency wage A real wage paid by firms above the market-clearing real wage rate because it is both profitable and rational for them to do so.

Elasticity of labour supply Measures the responsiveness of the quantity of labour supplied to changes in the wage rate.

Endogenous variable A variable that is explained within a particular model.

Entrepreneur The risk-taking individual producer who perceives a demand in the market and organizes resources to meet that demand in the anticipation of profit.

Equilibrium price The price at which the quantity demanded equals the quantity supplied.

Equilibrium quantity The amount of a good that is bought and sold at the equilibrium price.

European Free Trade Association (EFTA) Created in 1960; was a free trade area formed under British leadership to rival the EEC. It has more recently been absorbed by the EU single market.

Eurosclerosis A term used to describe the belief that Europe suffers from excessive labour market rigidities.

Excess demand Occurs when the quantity demanded exceeds the quantity supplied at some given price.

Excess supply Occurs when the quantity supplied exceeds the quantity demanded at some given price.

Exchange rate The price of one currency expressed in terms of another.

Exchange rate mechanism (ERM) The fixed but adjustable exchange rate element of the European Monetary System (EMS).

Exogenous variable A variable that is not explained within a particular model; its value is taken as given.

Expenditure reduction policy Involves a reduction in the level of aggregate demand in the domestic economy in order to improve the balance of payments position on the current account.

Expenditure-switching policy Switches domestic and foreign demand away from foreign goods and towards home-produced goods.

Externalities The costs incurred by, or benefits received by, other members of society not taken into account by consumers or producers. Externalities are also known as third-party effects.

Factor inputs Any goods and services used in the process of production.

Factor intensity Refers to the emphasis in production towards the use of one particular factor of production above others.

Factor markets Markets in which factors of production – land, labour and capital – are bought and sold.

Feedback rule See *activist policy rule*.

Final output Goods and services that are sold to their ultimate users.

Fiscal policy Measures that alter the level and composition of government expenditure and taxation.

Fixed costs Costs that do not change with the output level; also referred to as overhead costs and unavoidable costs.

Fixed exchange rate An exchange rate that is fixed at a predetermined level by intervention by the country's central bank in the foreign exchange market.

Flexible exchange rate An exchange rate that is determined in the foreign exchange market by the forces of demand and supply; also known as a floating exchange rate.

Floating exchange rate See *flexible exchange rate*.

Foreign exchange reserves Stocks of foreign currencies held by central banks.

Free market economy One in which resource allocation is predominantly market based.

Frictional unemployment Unemployment that results because it takes time for workers to search for suitable jobs; also known as search unemployment.

Full employment A situation in which all unemployment is frictional and structural and cannot be reduced by increasing aggregate demand.

Full employment output See *potential output*.

G5 The world's five leading industrial nations: the USA, Japan, Germany, France, and the UK.

G7 The seven main industrial economies in the world: the USA, Japan, Germany, France, Italy, the UK, and Canada.

GDP in current prices See *nominal GDP*.

GDP in real prices See *real GDP*.

Gini coefficient A measure of the overall degree of inequality in the income distribution. Found by dividing the area between the Lorenz curve and the line of complete equality by the total area below the line of complete equality.

Goods Tangible products.

Goods markets Markets in which goods and services are bought and sold.

Gradualism An approach to disinflation that involves a slow and gradual reduction in the rate of monetary growth.

Gross domestic product (GDP) The total value of goods and services produced in a country by the factors of production located in that country regardless of who owns them.

Gross national product (GNP) The value of final goods and services produced by domestically owned factors of production; GDP plus net property income from abroad.

Human capital The knowledge and skills of workers in an economy.

Hyperinflation A situation in which the rate of inflation is extremely high for over a year or more.

Hysteresis The proposition that the equilibrium value of a variable depends on the history of that variable. For example, if the actual rate of unemployment remains above the natural rate for a prolonged period the natural rate will tend to increase, and *vice versa*.

Imperfect competition A market structure in which there are a large number of firms selling similar but differentiated products; also known as monopolistic competition.

Imperfectly anticipated inflation A situation in which the actual rate of inflation differs from the anticipated or expected rate of inflation.

Income elasticity of demand The proportionate change in the quantity of a good demanded divided by the proportionate change in consumers' incomes.

Inferior good One for which demand decreases when income increases.

Inflation A situation in which the overall or general level of prices rises over time.

Inflation rate The rate at which the general level of prices increases; expressed as a percentage on an annual basis.

International Monetary Fund (IMF) An international agency, located in Washington, which promotes stability of member countries' exchange rates and assists them in correcting balance of payments disequilibria.

Investment expenditure Purchases of capital goods, such as plant, machinery and buildings.

Keynesian economics An approach based on the belief that capitalist economies are inherently unstable and can come to rest at less than full employment for prolonged periods. Keynesian economists favour the use of discretionary aggregate demand policies to stabilize the economy at, or near, full employment.

Labour market segmentation Situation that arises when labour faces barriers to entry to a particular labour market.

Laissez-faire A situation in which there is little or no state interference in the market economy.

Law of diminishing returns States that if more of a variable input is employed, while the quantity of other inputs is held constant, the marginal product of the variable input will eventually decrease.

Legal monopoly As defined in the UK, a legal monopoly arises when a firm enjoys a market share of 25 per cent or more.

Long run A period of time in which all inputs may be varied.

Lorenz curve A graph of the cumulative percentage of total income received against the cumulative percentage of the population, beginning with the bottom group.

Lucas critique The argument that traditional policy evaluation may be misleading as it fails to take into account that people may change their expectations and behaviour when policy changes.

Macroeconomic policy Policies that governments use to try to influence overall economic performance.

Macroeconomics The study of the economy as a whole.

Managed exchange rate An exchange rate that is influenced by intervention of the country's central bank in the foreign exchange market; also known as a dirty flexible, or dirty floating, exchange rate.

Marginal cost The change in total cost resulting from increasing production by one unit.

Marginal physical product The change in total output resulting from a unit change in the variable factor.

Marginal propensity to consume The change in consumption expenditure resulting from an additional unit of income.

Marginal propensity to import The change in import expenditure resulting from an additional unit of income.

Marginal propensity to withdraw The fraction of an additional unit of income that is withdrawn from the circular flow of income.

Marginal revenue The change in total revenue resulting from a one-unit change in output sold.

Marginal revenue product The change in a firm's total revenue resulting from the sale of output produced by one more unit of the variable factor.

Marginal social benefit The money value of the benefit from one additional unit of consumption.

Marginal social cost The cost of producing one additional unit of output. It includes both the marginal cost incurred by the producer and any marginal costs incurred by other members of society in the form of externalities.

Marginal utility The change in total satisfaction resulting from a one-unit change in the consumption of a good or service.

Market A framework that brings buyers and sellers together.

Market failure Arises where the market either fails to provide certain goods, or fails to provide them at their optimal or most desirable level.

Market segmentation Involves the division of a market by the producer into a number of discrete parts between which consumers cannot easily move.

Market structure Characterizes a market according to the degree of competition in it.

Microeconomics The study of the behaviour of individual households and firms, and the determination of the relative prices of particular goods and services.

Mismatch unemployment See *structural unemployment*.

Mixed economy One that combines market and state forms of resource allocation.

Monetarism An approach based on the belief that capitalist economies are inherently stable, unless disturbed by erratic monetary growth, and will return fairly rapidly to the neighbourhood of the natural level of output and employment after being subjected to some disturbance.

Monetary policy   Measures that alter the money supply and/or interest rates.

Monopolistic competition   See *imperfect competition*.

Monopoly   A market structure in which there is a sole supplier of a good or service that has no close substitutes and for which there are barriers to entry into the industry.

Monopoly power   Arises where potential competitiors can be excluded from a market.

Multiplier   The ratio of the change in income to a change in autonomous expenditure.

National income   The income that originates in the production of goods and services supplied by residents of a nation.

Natural monopoly   Arises where a single firm is the most efficient structure for the production of a particular good or service.

Natural rate of unemployment   The rate of unemployment that exists when the labour market is in equilibrium; composed of frictional and structural unemployment.

Net exports   Exports minus imports.

New classical economics   An approach based on the three assumptions of continuous market clearing, incomplete information, and rational expectations.

New Keynesian economics   An approach that explores a variety of reasons for wage and price stickiness that prevent market clearing.

Nominal GDP   The value of gross domestic product measured in terms of the prices prevailing at the time; also known as GDP in current prices.

Non-accelerating inflation rate of unemployment (NAIRU)   The rate of unemployment at which inflation is stable.

Non-system   The broad system of flexible exchange rates prevailing in the world economy since 1973.

Normal good   One for which demand increases when income increases.

Normal profit   The minimum amount of profit that a firm must earn to induce it to remain in the industry.

Normative issues   Those that are a matter of opinion.

North American Free Trade Agreement (NAFTA)   Free trade area that covers the US, Canadian and Mexican economies.

Oligopoly   A market structure in which there are a small number of firms.

OPEC   The Organization of Petroleum Exporting Countries, founded in 1960.

Opportunity cost   The cost of an action measured in terms of the best forgone alternative action.

Organization for Economic Cooperation and Development (OECD)   An intergovernmental organization, based in Paris, which provides a policy forum for the major industrialized countries for the promotion of economic growth, expansion of multilateral trade, and provision of foreign aid to developing countries.

Overhead costs   See *fixed costs*.

Pareto efficiency   A situation in which it is impossible to make someone better off without making someone else worse off; also known as Pareto optimality.

Passive policy rule   A prespecified rule for the conduct of policy not linked to prevailing economic circumstances.

Pay differentials   Exist where there are wage rate premiums attached to particular kinds of work.

Perfect competition   A market structure characterized most notably by a situation in which all firms in the industry are price-takers and there is freedom of entry into and exit from the industry.

Perfectly anticipated inflation   A situation in which the actual rate of inflation is equal to the anticipated or expected rate of inflation.

Perfectly elastic demand   Arises where the response of quantity demanded to a price change is infinitely large; price elasticity of demand is ∞ (infinity).

Perfectly inelastic demand   Arises where the quantity demanded does not respond to a change in price; price elasticity of demand is 0.

Permanent income   The average income that people expect to receive over a period of years in the future; also known as normal income and average expected income.

Phillips curve   The relationship between the inflation rate and the unemployment rate.

Policy ineffectiveness proposition   The proposition that anticipated changes in monetary policy will have no effect on output and employment.

Political business cycle   Fluctuations in the level of output and employment caused by the manipulation of the economy for electoral gains or due to partisan differences.

Positive issues   Those that are factually based.

Potential output   The maximum output that can be produced in an economy, given its factor endowments, without generating accelerating inflation; also known as full employment output.

Price elastic   Describes a situation where the proportionate change in quantity demanded is greater than the proportionate change in price; elasticity is greater than 1.

Price elasticity of demand The proportionate change in the quantity demanded of a good divided by the proportionate change in its price that brought it about.

Price elasticity of supply The proportionate change in quantity supplied of a good divided by the proportionate change in its price that brought it about.

Price inelastic Describes a situation where the proportionate change in quantity demanded is less than the proportionate change in price; elasticity is less than 1.

Price index A measure of the average level of prices of a set of goods and services relative to the prices of the same goods and services in a particular base year.

Price-taker A firm that takes the market price of its product as given.

Prices and incomes policy Measures that establish guidelines or controls for wage and/or price increases.

Private good One that is wholly consumed by an individual.

Producer surplus The difference between the price at which a producer would have been willing to supply a good and the price the producer actually receives.

Profit The difference between total revenue and total cost.

Progressive tax One that takes a larger percentage of income from people as their incomes rise.

Public good One that, once produced, can be consumed by everyone.

Public sector borrowing requirement (PSBR) The amount by which the expenditure of the public sector exceeds its revenue.

Pure monopoly A market structure in which there is a sole supplier of a good or service that has no close substitutes, and for which there are barriers to entry into the industry.

Quantity demanded The amount of a good or service that consumers wish to purchase at a particular price, other things being equal.

Quantity supplied The amount that producers wish to sell at a particular price, other things being equal.

Random walk The path of a variable whose changes over time are unpredictable.

Rational expectations An approach that assumes that people make the best use of all available information to forecast the future.

Real business cycle approach An approach in which fluctuations in aggregate output and employment are driven by persistent supply-side shocks to the economy, most notably random fluctuations in the rate of technological progress.

Real GDP The value of gross domestic product measured in terms of the prices that prevailed in some particular base year; also known as GDP in constant prices.

Real wage The money wage divided (or deflated) by a price index; the amount of goods and services that a money wage can buy.

Recession A decline in real GDP that lasts for at least two consecutive quarters of a year.

Relative price The ratio of the price of one good to the price of another good; expressed as the number of units of one good that one unit of another good will buy.

Reservation wage The minimum rate required to induce an individual to accept a job.

Revaluation An increase in the value of a currency in terms of other currencies when the currency in question is part of some formal exchange rate system.

Rules Prespecified guidelines that determine the conduct of policy.

Say's law States that supply creates its own demand.

Search unemployment See *frictional unemployment*.

Services Intangible products.

Short run A period of time in which some inputs such as capital are fixed, while others such as labour may be varied.

Short-run Phillips curve The relationship between inflation and unemployment that exists for a given expected rate of inflation.

Social provision See *collective provision*.

Stabilization policy Policies aimed at stabilizing output and employment at or near their full employment or natural levels by influencing the level of aggregate demand.

Stagflation A situation in which high unemployment and high inflation occur simultaneously; a combination of stagnation and inflation.

Steady state A situation in which output per worker and capital input per worker are no longer changing.

Structural unemployment Unemployment that results from a mismatch between the skills or location of existing job vacancies and the present skills or location of the unemployed; also known as mismatch unemployment.

Substitute A good that can be substituted in place of another good.

Supernormal profits Profits that exceed the minimum amount that a firm must earn to induce it to remain in the industry.

Supply The quantity of a good or service that producers wish to sell at each conceivable price, other things being equal.

Time inconsistency The tendency of policymakers to deviate from a previously announced policy once private decision-makers have adjusted their behaviour to the announced policy.

Total cost The sum of the costs of all inputs used in producing a firm's output; can be divided into fixed costs and variable costs.

Total revenue The amount of money that a firm receives from the sale of its output; equals the price of output multiplied by the number of units sold.

Transfer earnings Payments to a factor that are necessary to retain it in its present use.

Transnational A firm that owns and controls assets in more than one country.

Unemployed People who are available for work and are actively seeking jobs but cannot find them.

Unemployment rate The percentage of the labour force who are unemployed.

Unit elasticity Situation in which the proportionate change in quantity demanded is equal to the proportionate change in price; elasticity is 1.

Unlimited liability Places the entire personal wealth of the owner of a firm at risk in respect of losses that the firm may incur.

Utility The satisfaction that a consumer receives from the consumption of a good or service.

Variable costs Costs that vary with the output level; also referred to as direct costs and avoidable costs.

Bibliography

Alt, J.E and K.A. Chrystal (1983) *Political Economics* (Brighton: Wheatsheaf Books).

Artis, M.J. (ed.) (1996) *The UK Economy* (14th ed.) (Oxford: Oxford University Press).

Atkinson, B., F. Livesey and B. Milward (1998) *Applied Economics* (Basingstoke: Macmillan).

Barr, N. and D. Whynes (1993) *Current Issues in the Economics of Welfare* (Basingstoke: Macmillan).

Barrell, R. (1994) *The UK Labour Market* (Cambridge: Cambridge University Press).

Begg, D., S. Fischer and R. Dornbusch (1997) *Economics* (5th ed.) (London: McGraw-Hill).

Blanchard, O. (1997) *Macroeconomics* (London: Prentice-Hall).

Chrystal, K.A. and S. Price (1994) *Controversies in Macroeconomics* (3rd ed.) (Hemel Hempstead: Harvester Wheatsheaf).

Crafts, N. and G. Toniolo (eds) (1996) *Economic Growth in Europe Since 1945* (Cambridge: Cambridge University Press).

Daniels, P.W. and W.F. Lever (eds) (1996) *The Global Economy in Transition* (Harlow: Addison Wesley Longman).

Dawson, G. (1992) *Inflation and Unemployment: Causes, Consequences and Cures* (Aldershot: Edward Elgar).

Denison, E.F. (1985) *Trends in American Economic Growth* (Washington, DC: Brookings Institution).

Dunnett, A. (1992) *Understanding the Market* (2nd ed.) (Harlow: Longman).

Dunning, J.H. (1993) *Multinational Enterprises and the Global Economy* (Harlow: Addison-Wesley).

Dunning, J.H. (1988) *Explaining International Production* (London: Unwin Hyman).

Eatwell, J., M. Milgate and P. Newman (eds) (1987) *The Invisible Hand – The New Palgrave* (Basingstoke: Macmillan).

Foot, M. (1975) *Aneurin Bevan 1945–1960* (London: Paladin).

Friedman, M. (1962) *Capitalism and Freedom* (Chicago: University of Chicago Press).

Friedman, M. (1968) 'The role of monetary policy', *American Economic Review*, March, pp. 1–17.

Friedman, M. (1970) *The Counter-Revolution in Monetary Theory* (London: Institute of Economic Affairs).

Friedman, M. (1975) *Unemployment Versus Inflation?* (London: Institute of Economic Affairs).

Friedman, M. and A.J. Schwartz (1963) *A Monetary History of the United States, 1867–1960* (Princeton, NJ: Princeton University Press).

Galbraith, J.K. (1973) *Economics and the Public Purpose* (Harmondsworth: Penguin).

Galbraith, J.K. (1987) *A History of Economics* (London: Hamish Hamilton).

George, K.D., C. Joll and E.L. Lynk (1991) *Industrial Organization* (4th ed.) (London: Routledge).

Gordon, R.J. (1997) *Macroeconomics* (7th ed.) (New York: Addison-Wesley).

Griffiths, A. and S. Wall (eds) (1995) *Applied Economics* (6th ed.) (London: Longman).

Hayek, F.A. (1944) *The Road to Serfdom* (London: Routledge).

Heidensohn, K. (1995) *Europe and World Trade* (London: Pinter).

Hills, J. (ed.) (1996) *New Inequalities* (Cambridge: Cambridge University Press).

Hirst, P. and G. Thompson (1996) *Globalization in Question* (Cambridge: Polity Press).

Hoekman, B. and M. Kostecki (1995) *The Political Economy of the World Trading System* (Oxford: Oxford University Press).

Jackson, P.M. and C.M. Price (eds) (1994) *Privatization and Regulation* (Harlow: Longman).

Jepma, C.J., H. Jager and E. Kamphuis (1996) *Introduction to International Economics* (Harlow: Longman).

Johnson, C. and S. Briscoe (1995) *Measuring the Economy* (Harmondsworth: Penguin).

Jowsey, E. (1998) *100 Essay Plans for Economics* (Oxford: Oxford University Press).

Keegan, W. (1984) *Mrs Thatcher's Economic Experiment* (Harmondsworth: Penguin).

Keynes, J.M. (1936) *The General Theory of Employment, Interest and Money* (London: Macmillan).

Kitson, M. and J. Michie (1995) 'Trade and growth: a historical perspective', in J. Michie and J. Grieve Smith (eds) *Managing the Global Economy* (Oxford: Oxford University Press).

Kirzner, I. (1992) *The Meaning of Market Process* (London: Routledge).

Lal, D. (1983) *The Poverty of Development Economics* (London: Institute of Economic Affairs).

Layard, R., S. Nickell and R. Jackman (1994) *The Unemployment Crisis* (Oxford: Oxford University Press).

Le Grand, J., J. Propper and R. Robinson (1992) *The Economics of Social Problems* (3rd ed.) (Basingstoke: Macmillan).

Levacic, R. (1993) 'Markets as coordinating devices', in R. Maidment and G. Thompson (eds) *Managing the United Kingdom* (London: Sage Publications).

Lipsey, R.G. (1960) 'The relationship between unemployment and the rate of change of money wage rates in the UK 1862–1957: a further analysis', *Economica*, February, pp. 1–31.

Lipsey, R.G. and K.A. Chrystal (1995) *An Introduction to Positive Economics* (8th ed.) (Oxford: Oxford University Press).

McDonald, F. and S. Dearden (eds) (1998) *European Economic Integration* (3rd ed.) (London: Longman).

Mankiw, N.G. (1997) *Macroeconomics* (3rd ed.) (New York: Worth).

Marin, A. (1992) *Macroeconomic Policy* (London: Routledge).

Martin, S. and D. Parker (1997) *The Impact of Privatization* (London: Routledge).

Michie, J. and J. Grieve Smith (eds) (1994) *Unemployment in Europe* (London: Academic Press).

Moon, B.E. (1996) *Dilemmas of International Trade* (Boulder: Westview Press).

Morgan, B. and J.R. Shackleton (1990) 'The ups and downs of business cycle theory' in Shackleton, J.R. (ed.) *New Thinking in Economics* (Aldershot: Edward Elgar).

OECD (1995) *Main Developments in Trade* (Paris: OECD).

Ormerod, P. (1994) *The Death of Economics* (London: Faber and Faber).

Parkin, M., M. Powell and K. Matthews (1997) *Economics* (3rd ed.) (Harlow: Addison Wesley Longman).

Paterson, I. and L. Simpson (1993) 'The economics of trade union power', in N.M. Healey (ed.) *Britain's Economic Miracle, Myth or Reality?* (London: Routledge).

Penn, R., M. Rose and J. Rubery (eds) (1994) *Skill and Occupational Change* (Oxford: Oxford University Press).

Peston, M.H. (1984) *The British Economy: An Elementary Macroeconomic Perspective* (2nd ed.) (Oxford: Philip Allan).

Phillips, A.W. (1958) 'The relation between unemployment and the rate of change of money wage rates in the United Kingdom, 1861–1957', *Economica*, November, pp. 283–99.

Putterman, L. and R.S. Kroszner (eds) (1996) *The Economic Nature of the Firm* (Cambridge: Cambridge University Press).

Rees, T. (1992) *Women and the Labour Market* (London: Routledge).

Ricardo, D. (1817) *The Principles of Political Economy and Taxation* (1948 reprint) (London: J.M. Dent and Sons).

Scammell, W.M. (1987) *The Stability of the International Monetary System* (Macmillan: Basingstoke).

Seabrook, J. (1990) *The Myth of the Market* (Bideford: Green Books).

Shaw, G.K. (1984) *Rational Expectations* (Brighton: Wheatsheaf Books).

Shepherd, W.G. (1990) *The Economics of Industrial Organization* (Englewood Cliffs, NJ: Prentice-Hall).

Sloman, J. (1998) *Economics* (3rd ed.) (Hemel Hempstead: Prentice-Hall).

Smith, A. (1776) *An Inquiry into the Nature and Causes of the Wealth of Nations* (1930 reprint) (London: Methuen).

Smith, D. (1987) *The Rise and Fall of Monetarism* (Harmondsworth: Penguin).

Snowdon, B. and H.R. Vane (eds) (1997) *Reflections on the Development of Modern Macroeconomics* (Cheltenham: Edward Elgar).

Snowdon, B., H.R. Vane and P. Wynarczyk (1994) *A Modern Guide to Macroeconomics: An Introduction to Competing Schools of Thought* (Aldershot: Edward Elgar).

Stewart, M. (1986) *Keynes and After* (3rd ed.) (Harmondsworth: Penguin).

Stubbs, R. and G.R.D. Underhill (eds) (1994) *Political Economy and the Changing Global Order* (Basingstoke: Macmillan).

United Nations Development Programme (1997) *Human Development Report 1997* (Oxford: Oxford University Press).

Vane, H.R. and J.L. Thompson (1993) *An Introduction to Macroeconomic Policy* (4th ed.) (Hemel Hempstead: Harvester Wheatsheaf).

Waller, P.J. (1981) *Democracy and Sectarianism: A Political and Social History of Liverpool 1868–1939* (Liverpool: Liverpool University Press).

Williams, R. (1985) *Towards 2000* (Harmondsworth: Penguin Books).

Wood, A. (1994) *North South Trade, Employment and Inequality* (Oxford: Clarendon Press).

Index